GENDER AND PARTY POLITICS

GENDER
AND PARTY POLITICS

edited by

Joni Lovenduski and Pippa Norris

SAGE Publications
London • Thousand Oaks • New Delhi

Barnard
HQ
1236
.G455
1993g

First published 1993

Sage Publications Ltd
6 Bonhill Street
London EC2A 4PU

Sage Publications Ltd
2455 Teller Road
Thousand Oaks, California 91320

Sage Publications India Pvt Ltd
32, M-Block Market
Greater Kailash – I
New Delhi 110 048

British Library Cataloguing in Publication Data

Gender and Party Politics
  I. Lovenduski, Joni II. Norris, Pippa
  324.2082

  ISBN 0–8039–8659–9
  ISBN 0–8039–8660–2 (pbk)

Library of Congress catalog card number 93–085415

Typeset by Mayhew Typesetting, Rhayader, Powys
Printed in Great Britain by Biddles Ltd, Guildford, Surrey

Contents

npb 199ใ.5.26

Acknowledgements

The ideas for this book grew out of different meetings of researchers who are interested in the area of women and politics. Many of these meetings took place at the ECPR Joint Sessions of Workshops, and three of the chapters were originally given as papers at the Essex Joint Sessions in 1991.

We are grateful therefore to the ECPR for providing a forum in which political scientists can meet and discuss their work. We also want to thank our editor David Hill for his patience and encouragement and particularly for his calm flexibility at the moments when this whole project seemed set to fall apart. Similar thanks are due to Denise McKnight who chased up different chapters of the book, maintained communications and did most of the work of assembling the final manuscript.

Contributors

Andrew Appleton is Assistant Professor of political science at Canisius College, Buffalo, New York, where he teaches courses in comparative and European politics. He has authored works on developments in French party politics in *Comparative Politics, French Politics and Society* and in edited volumes.

Barbara Burrell is Honorary Fellow in the Women's Studies Research Center and Researcher in the Survey Research Laboratory at the University of Wisconsin at Madison. She is author of a number of scholarly studies of women candidates in the USA, notably *A Woman's Place is in the House: Campaigning for Congress* (University of Michigan Press, forthcoming).

Lynda Erickson is Associate Professor of political science at Simon Fraser University, Burnaby, British Columbia, Canada where she specialized in Canadian politics and women and politics. She has recently co-authored a book on British Columbia party activists and published work on the nomination process in Canadian political parties.

Yvonne Galligan lectures in Irish politics at the Institute of Public Administration, Dublin and is a co-ordinator of the Women and Politics in Ireland network. Her research interests include public policy analysis, with specific reference to gender issues, and comparative politics. Among her recent publications are 'Women's interest representation in the Republic of Ireland: the Council for the Status of Women' in John Coakley and Nicholas Rees (eds), *Irish Political Studies Yearbook*, vol. 6 (1991) and 'Women in Irish politics' in John Coakley and Michael Gallagher (eds), *Politics in the Republic of Ireland* (Galway: PSAI Press, 1992).

Marila Guadagnini teaches the Italian Political System at the University of Turin. She has written articles on parties and the party system including 'Partiti' in *Il Mondo contemporaneo* (La Nuova Italia, 1981), and the introduction to the volume *Sistemi di partito* (Franco Angeli, 1986). Her major field of research on women has focused on women's presence in Italian decision-making arenas at the national and local level since 1948. She has published articles in such journals as the *Revista Italiana di Scienza Politica* and the *Quaderni di Sociologia*. She frequently conducts research projects for the Committee for Equal Opportunity for

Women and Men of the Regional Council of Piedmont and is author of a book on the legislation on equality between men and women at work promulgated by international organizations such as the EC, the Council of Europe, the UN and the ILO.

Eva Kolinsky is Professor of Modern German Studies and Director of the Centre for Modern German Studies at Keele University, UK. She has published extensively on aspects of contemporary German politics, political culture and the situation of women. Her books include *Parties, Opposition and Society in West Germany* (1984), *Opposition in Western Europe* (editor, 1987), *The Greens in West Germany* (editor, 1989), *Women in West Germany – Life, Work and Politics* (1989), *Political Culture in France and Germany* (co-editor with John Gaffney), *The Federal Republic of Germany – End of an Era* (editor, 1991), *Women in Contemporary Germany* (1992). She is co-editor of the journal *German Politics* and editor of the *German Studies* series with Berg.

Monique Leijenaar is Associate Professor of political science at the University of Nijmegen, Netherlands. She specializes in local politics, elections studies and women and politics and has published several articles and books on these topics. She is editor of *Gender and Power* (Sage Publications, 1991, with K. Davis and J. Oldersma) and co-author of *Equality in Participation and Decision Making* (Martinus Nijhoff Publishers, 1991, with B. Niemoller). She is a member of the editorial board of the journal *Women and Politics*. Currently she is chairing the Research Committee on Sex Roles and the Politics of the International Political Science Association.

Joni Lovenduski is Professor of Comparative Politics in the Department of European Studies at Loughborough University. She is author of *Women in European Politics* (1986), co-author of *Contemporary Feminist Politics* (1993), *Politics and Society in Eastern Europe* (1987), co-editor of *Different Voices, Different Lives* (1993), *The New Politics of Abortion* (1986), *The Politics of the Second Electorate* (1981) and various scholarly publications on the women's movement, sex equality policy and comparative politics. She is co-director of the British Candidate Study and a former convenor and active member of the Standing Group on Women and Politics of the European Consortium for Political Research and the Women and Politics Group of the Political Studies Association of the UK.

Amy Mazur is Assistant Professor of political science at Indiana University–Purdue University at Indianapolis. She is author of

Gender Bias and the State: Women's Rights at Work in France (forthcoming). She has also published articles in various scholarly publications on equal employment policy for women and sexual harassment policy in France.

Pippa Norris is Associate Director of the Joan Shorenstein Barone Center on the Press, Politics and Public Policy at the Kennedy School of Government, Harvard University and Senior Lecturer in Politics at Edinburgh University. She is author of *British By-elections* (1990), *Politics and Sexual Equality* (1987), co-editor of *Different Voices, Different Lives* (1993) and *British Election Yearbook* (1991, 1992, 1993), as well as scholarly articles and chapters on British elections and political parties, US elections and women and politics. She is the British representative on the executive of the International Political Science Association and co-director of the British Candidate Study and the American Candidate Study.

Diane Sainsbury is Associate Professor of Political Science at the University of Stockholm. She is editor of *Democracy, State and Justice* (1988) and a special issue of the *European Journal of Political Research* on 'Party strategies and party-voter linkages'. Her most recent publications include 'Programmatic renewal of the Swedish Social Democrats and the Legacy of continuous reform', *West European Politics* (1993) and 'Dual welfare and sex segregation of access to social benefits', *Journal of Social Policy* (1993).

Hege Skjeie holds a doctorate in political science from the University of Oslo and works as a researcher at the Institute for Social Research, Oslo. Her current research is on national political leadership, focusing in particular on cabinet government. She has published on Nordic equal opportunity legislation and policies; trade union politics and women's participation in national political elites. Her most recent articles in English are 'The rhetoric of difference: on women's inclusion into political elites' in *Politics and Society* (1991) and 'The uneven advance of Norwegian women' in *New Left Review* (1991).

Marian Simms is Senior Lecturer in Political Studies at the Australia National University. She has published widely on women and politics and Australian politics. Her latest book is the second edition of *A Woman's Place: Women in Politics in Australia* (1992, with Marian Sawer).

1
Introduction: the Dynamics of Gender and Party

Joni Lovenduski

The issue of the political representation of women has changed substantially since women first secured the franchise. When nineteenth century feminists sought the right to vote they also wanted the right to stand in elections because they were convinced that changes in women's condition would come about only when women themselves became members of elected legislatures. In contrast, during the 1960s and 1970s many second wave feminists were cynical about political institutions and electoral politics, preferring the political autonomy they found in new social movement organizations. By the early 1980s, however, there had been a reconsideration of the importance of mainstream politics and feminists became active members of political parties. Meanwhile some of the women who were already established in their parties began to claim parity of political representation. The struggle for equal pay was a watershed. Once parties became committed to the policy of equality at work it was only a matter of time before more substantial demands for equal political representation than 'one person, one vote' were made. During the 1980s support for getting more women into politics grew in each of the countries discussed in this book. There was a shift in the agendas of both the parties and their women members.

Over the same period political parties were a major site of women's activity. There was a clear challenge to parties by women who claimed a voice in decision-making and pressed for changes in the political agenda. Women demanded and secured party reforms with varying degrees of success. In some countries this led to the appearance of new issues in party programmes, new systems of candidate selection, new means of policy-making, and the establishment of new structures of government such as ministries for women, equal opportunities ombudspersons and publicly funded women's committees. In response to pressure from women activists, members and voters, gender became an explicit issue for many political parties. This took place in contexts affected by different kinds of party politics. The extent and the manner of party accommodation of gender has been influenced by increased party competition via the entry of new parties and/or the decline of established parties, the erosion of established coalitions, modernization strategies devised to replace or renew declining constituencies, system level constitutional change and altered party–state relationships.

Demands for women's representation have had the most dramatic success in Scandinavia. Norwegian feminists were early in advocating the integration of women into the existing party structure as a strategy of empowerment. It has now been more than twenty years since the 'women's coup' overturned agreed party preferences on candidates lists for local authority elections and returned three local councils with a majority of women. The implications of this initial display of women's solidarity were understood rapidly by parties and the progress that Norwegian women have made since then is remarkable. As Hege Skjeie recounts in Chapter 10, the representation of women grew from below 10 per cent of elected representatives in the 1960s to about 25 per cent in local and national assemblies by the end of the 1970s, and 35 per cent in the early 1980s. At least 40 per cent of the members of every Norwegian government since 1986 have been women. Moreover, much of the women's agenda that has emerged in other countries is complete or well advanced in Norway where a new and wider-ranging equality agenda has developed.

Near the other end of the scale is Britain, where demands for equality in women's representation came later, gathering force in the opposition parties only in the early 1980s and becoming a feature of the ruling Conservatives' strategies of representation as late as the early 1990s. By then women comprised fewer than 10 per cent of members of the House of Commons. Of course, the timing of demands for representation is only part of the story. The Norwegian and British political systems present different possibilities for women. In general the rules of the game in Norway favour the representation of women while in Britain they do not.

This raises the question of what we mean by political representation. In democratic societies, the representation of a group's interests has two dimensions: the presence of its members in decision-making arenas and the consideration of its interests in the decision-making process. An implication of the first dimension is that, to be democratic, the composition of the elected assemblies should mirror the composition of the society it serves. But the second dimension implies that it is enough that an assembly takes into account the interests of all its electors. There have been intense theoretical arguments about which of the two formulations should prevail and these arguments have been reflected in debates amongst feminists who have disagreed sharply about the nature of women's interests and the political strategies required to press them. In practice the demands women have made to be represented in party politics reflect both programmatic and organizational concerns. Thus parties have been under pressure to promote policies to attract women voters, to undertake campaigns to recruit women members, to promote women into key positions in the party organization and to nominate women candidates. Party programmes have been expanded to include policies on equal opportunities and reproductive rights, as well as to revise traditional party positions on family policy to take into account new understandings of gender and power.

Our objectives in compiling this volume are to explain how gender has affected party politics and how the imperatives of party politics influence the patterns of women's political representation. We argue that liberal democracies offer women the means to claim equality of representation by utilizing the political opportunities offered by the party system. Party systems have responded to women's demands, but to varying degrees. Women's share of parliamentary seats ranges from 5.7 per cent in France to 38 per cent in Sweden, of party candidacy from 9 per cent in the USA to over 40 per cent in Sweden, of government from 6 per cent in Italy to over 45 per cent in Norway. These contrasts have both general and particular explanations. They indicate changes in party politics to accommodate women's demands for political representation but they also reflect different social, cultural and historical circumstances. And there are common patterns here as well. Women's demands for political representation inevitably affect party politics, party politics inevitably affects the strategies that women employ to press their claims. A continuous process of adjustment and accommodation takes place on both sides. We need to look beyond the particular and specific cultures in which that adjustment takes place if we are to gain a good overview of women in contemporary party politics. To do this we have, as far as possible, separated the two sides of the process. In this introductory chapter, I discuss the development of the demands that women have made on political parties. In the concluding chapter, Pippa Norris assesses the factors that condition party responses. In the intervening substantive chapters, the interplay between gender and party politics is examined in detail in eleven countries. The central focus of each chapter is the political representation of women in programmatic and organizational terms. The contributing authors describe a variety of party systems and a range of strategies to represent women. They include multi-party, one party dominant, two and two-and-a-half party systems, centralized and decentralized party organizations and the full panoply of political ideologies. In each of the eleven countries demands have emerged from within the political parties to increase the political representation of women. An important purpose of this book is to account for those demands in their particular political context. In order to offer such an account we asked each of the contributors to describe the particularities of the country about which they were writing and to explain the roles and status of women in its political parties. For each country our authors describe unique elements of the way women have struggled for representation and parties have responded.

The development of women's claims

Women have made demands on political parties since the issue of female suffrage was first raised. In this discussion I consider three aspects of their development:

1   How women have made their claims.
2   How they intervened in party politics.
3   The mutual accommodation between parties and women claiming increased political rights.

The development of party gender politics in recent years is an effect both of the infiltration of feminist ideas and the attention women influenced by those ideas have paid to the imperatives of party politics. There are four identifiable components to the strategies such women devised. First, women's issues were brought to the political agenda. Prominent party women, supported by women's organizations and networks raised issues of sex equality in the parties. Often they began with demands for policies to secure sex equality in employment, but the implications of equality for childcare, reproductive rights and family policies were also issues. Secondly, seeking to avoid accusations of sectionalism, they sought to transform women's issues into universal issues. Thirdly, women used a dual strategy of working within women's networks and in male-dominated areas of the party. Finally, women paid close attention to the rules of the game. They sought to transform gender relations in politics from within, hence they were careful to affirm their commitment to their parties.

The gains made during the 1970s and 1980s must be considered in the light of a large mobilization of women. This background gave credence to efforts to get women's issues on the political agenda. The emergence of the second wave of feminism after the end of the 1960s had important effects. Even in countries in which a widespread and radical women's liberation movement did not appear, ideas about sex equality were in the air and women began to seek inclusion in a variety of areas of social life. Gradually campaigns for equality gained support and parties began to respond. But the momentum built up by wide-ranging movements in support of equal rights would not have been enough to secure changes in party policies. Political parties moved on women's issues when they were pressed to do so. What Diane Sainsbury terms 'women's agency' is of great importance. Sweden, for example, has a widespread egalitarian ethos and the several features of its electoral system favour women but these cannot account by themselves for the increase in women's representation at all levels of the system since the 1960s. There, it was women who changed, who made new claims on the party system.

Once a party committed itself formally to the principle of gender equality in one sphere, then party women were able to use this commitment in their arguments for increased representation. In Ireland awareness of the gender dimension in politics came with the appearance of equality in employment on the political agenda. In Norway a similar process occurred until, by the beginning of the 1990s, high levels of women's representation had been achieved and all but one of its political parties offered a comprehensive sex equality strategy that encompassed the range of public policy concerns.

An implicit goal of feminist infiltration of parties is to secure changes in attitudes about gender, mainly by increases in understanding and awareness of gender differences and their implications for power relations. Women in the Italian parties, especially the Democratic Left (the largest successor party to the Communists) were not only active in forcing the implementation of party initiatives favouring women's concerns, but also developed a debate (called the *rappresentanza sessuata*) about the necessity of a gender-based viewpoint in politics. A similar strategy was employed by feminists who entered the British Labour party and by women in the German Social Democratic party during the 1980s. In Norway the challenge to attitudes was particularly successful, apparent in the recognition that has been given by policy-makers to women's various roles. In the early 1970s Norwegian party feminists led a political recognition of women's search for paid employment. Later, women politicians were regarded as responsible for bringing the politics of women's care and career roles to the political agenda.

In almost all of the parties that are considered here, women kept to the rules of the political game. Party divisions outweighed gender divisions. Cross-party alliances are exceptional within and outside legislatures. Party women have primarily sought change from within the parties except in the United States where party loyalties are exceptionally weak and the rules of the game allow greater flexibility in making coalitions.

Attention to party imperatives presents a dilemma for feminists who seek to transform parties into more women-friendly entities, but risk incorporation as they adapt to the rules of the game. A great dilemma for second wave feminism has been whether women will change institutions before institutions change women. Originally, some feminists were dismissive of party structures with their hierarchies and rituals, preferring separate autonomous organizations that sought political change from outside the established political structures and institutions. However, the cost of such separatism was low effectiveness. Understanding this, many feminists acknowledged the necessity of party politics, implicitly by their activism and explicitly in their publications and debates.

Party change

The justification for such a strategy is that parties will adapt to accommodate the new demands, and in so doing will become carriers of feminist ideas. This raises a number of questions, the most obvious of which is whether parties do adapt. To answer we need to look at the main sites of women's interventions in the parties. This requires us to examine the ways that parties differ in their policies to represent women. Here we must consider both the programmatic and the organizational dimensions of representation: how parties differ in their treatment of women's issues and in their strategies to promote women's representation.

Programmatic change

Parties devised gender policies to respond to the claims of women voters, members and activists. Over the past twenty years the sort of sex equality policies women demand has developed from a set of fairly straightforward employment laws to a wide-ranging programme affecting the whole of society. Most political parties have accommodated these demands in ways that are congruent with their ideologies. There was a tendency for parties to converge in the sense that, eventually, they all adopted particular policies to satisfy women voters and members, for example by making laws about equal pay or childcare, but the policies themselves reflect the ideology of the party.

Norway is a good example of this syndrome. Hege Skjeie's analysis of the priorities of the Norwegian political parties shows how gender issues are filtered through the ideological preferences of the parties. So, parties of the right prefer policies that are more supportive of the 'caring mother' while parties of the left prefer to strengthen the position of the 'woman worker'. The new policies brought to the political agenda by women have been subjected to established political cleavages, in this case, the left–right ideological division. In Canada too we have further evidence of the relationship between the kind of changes the parties have made to represent women and the ideological position of the parties. The right of centre party, the Progressive Conservatives, was slower to adopt new reforms and more voluntaristic in its approach to increasing women's representation. Liberals were more responsive to the feminist movement and to demands for gender parity. On the centre left the NDP (New Democratic party) was more responsive still, offering a comprehensive programme of affirmative action to promote women in the party hierarchy. These differences were congruent with the attitudes of party activists except over the issue of abortion where the religious dimension confused the left–right polarities.

The activity of party women is vital if such changes are to be secured. There is considerable evidence now that, within political life, women take an active part in creating definitions of reality that support efforts to make new policies. In Norway there were two differences that women made to party politics: first, they got parties to address gender issues which then became arenas of political competition; secondly, as the initial policies were implemented and debates were developed shifts in attitude about the types of solution that were possible and the costs that might be paid took place. Parallel to women's integration into party politics, new agendas were established including strategies to get more women into political office.

Organizational change
Parties have developed strategies to promote women internally into decision-making positions in the party organization and externally into elected assemblies and public appointments. Generally they have been more radical, determined and imaginative in devising

policies to bring women into internal positions than to nominate women as candidates for elected office. There appear to be three party strategies for increasing the proportion of women in decision-making positions. These are:

1   *Rhetorical* strategies whereby women's claims are accepted in campaign platforms and party spokespersons make frequent reference to the importance of getting more women into office.

2   Strategies of *positive* or *affirmative action* in which special training is offered to aspirant women, targets are set for the inclusion of women and considerable encouragement, including, sometimes financial assistance, is given to enable women to put themselves forward to be considered.

3   Strategies of *positive discrimination* in which places are reserved for women on decision-making bodies, on candidate slates, on shortlists. In addition, special women's committees with significant powers may be set up parallel to or within existing party decision-making structures and institutions. All three strategies may be controversial, but most parties now have rhetorical strategies to promote women and many have adopted strategies of positive action. Positive discrimination, however, is much less common and tends to be restricted to women's access to internal party structures.

Rhetorical strategies

Rhetorical strategies often begin as a pious set of public statements that women are necessary to party politics by leaders who have little intention of devising and implementing policies to include them. Political parties in France, for example, have wholeheartedly accepted French women's claims in their campaign rhetoric, and they actively compete for women's votes, but they are considerably less enthusiastic about strategies to promote the participation of women in party affairs. Often announcements of party interest in sex equality are accompanied by assertions that women are not interested in political office and that, anyway, they are satisfied with what the party offers. Sometimes party leaders claim, with some degree of truth that they do not have the power to influence the choice of officials, delegates or candidates. But this does not mean that such strategies are invariably insincere or doomed to failure. A commitment to women's representation in party rhetoric may be the beginning of a process that will lead to more substantial policies of inclusion. Once the public commitment to equality is made, women then start to expect effective action. Such a process is apparent in the British Conservative party where pressure from women for a greater share of candidacies during the 1980s has led to several informal, but significant attempts by Central Office to encourage women to seek nominations, and to encourage constituencies to nominate women. The result so far is a small increase in the proportion of women nominated, combined with slightly greater attention by the party to the presentation of its women activists, leaders and MPs.

Positive action

In many parties rhetorical strategies have been the first step towards the introduction of strategies of positive action. Programmes have been implemented to encourage women, provide special training, and aid searches for women to fill vacant positions. But the adoption of targets has been more difficult. Initially targets were introduced for internal party boards and executives and later extended to party candidacies.

Most political parties have long had some kind of internal or associated women's organization. These have been a site of women's campaigns for political equality and, often, debates about women's roles in the party turn on the issue of the status of the women's organization. Such strategies are important, but they are most effective when accompanied by women's activity in the main party decision-making bodies, that is, a *dual* strategy is required. Otherwise opponents may claim that women's organization leaders are not representative of the party, and, in some cases, of its women. During the 1970s and 1980s women struggled to obtain places in delegations to party conferences, on executive committees and councils, regional boards and local management committees. The responses varied, often by the political fortunes of the party, but also by party ideology. For example, the Australian Labor party adopted affirmative action at its special national conference in 1981. Their poor performance in the 1977 elections gave women the opportunity to push for better representation. The party constitution was altered to call for a minimum of 25 per cent women in each state delegation and to declare that women should be represented on decision-taking bodies in proportion to their membership. The new rules stopped short of requiring parties to undertake positive discrimination to implement them – they were targets rather than quotas. But they had some effect. As a result the proportion of women delegates rose from 4 per cent (two of forty-nine women) in 1979, to at least 25 per cent of the total in 1982 and 40 per cent by the end of the 1980s.

In many countries by the 1980s internal party debates about targets and quotas were widespread as parties sought to feminize their image in response to perceptions of the demands of their women voters and to the explicit demands of their women members and activists. These debates often took place in the context of struggles to modernize the party. In the British Labour party, decisions to introduce quotas for women in the various ruling committees at different levels of the party structure, to be implemented by the mid-1990s, were taken in the context of an overhaul of party structures designed to reduce the power of the Trade Unions and control its left wing. These objectives were incorporated in a modernization and democratization strategy that offered opportunities for women to press claims for representation.

Party change also offered opportunities for German women. Eva Kolinsky notes shifts in the nature of membership in German political parties in the post-war years. Party membership became more individual, more clearly linked to political interest and to a motivation of shaping the course of politics, contributing to the policies of a given party and holding political office. For men activists, she writes, these changes simply intensified business as usual, but for women the meaning of membership was transformed and one result was that the women's track of membership started to become integrated into the party mainstream, leading inevitably to demands for inclusion that spread across the party spectrum from the left to the right, a process that was accelerated by the rise of the Greens and the subsequent increase of political competition during the 1980s. As a result the German parties adopted positive discrimination strategies in the form of quotas for women at different levels of the party structure. These were soon followed with requirements for quotas of women on the candidates' lists.

Positive discrimination
The form of positive discrimination that has been most controversial in political parties is mandatory quotas for women. These are regarded as reverse discrimination and are often opposed on ideological grounds. The more important the office or position in question, the more opposition the policy meets, and parties are particularly reluctant to introduce positive discrimination into their candidate selection procedures. Indeed it would be impossible for some parties to do so. In the USA for example, the widespread use of primaries means there is virtually no conventional selectorate in the sense of a group of party gate-

keepers who make decisions about candidacy. The problems to be overcome by women candidates in the United States are the obstacles of a political marketplace in which many significant resources are controlled by political action committees (PACs), rather than party organizations. In Canada imposing gender requirements on individual constituency organizations is viewed as a limitation on local organizations. The situation is similar in the British Conservative party. But other systems are more flexible. In Germany during the 1980s all the parties except the CSU set targets of women legislators and the SPD adopted temporary quotas of women candidates. Their idea is that once the barrier is broken, once women have experience in political positions, quotas will no longer be necessary. Temporary quotas are likely to be easier to justify than permanent ones. Another idea is the 'negotiable quota'. In the Netherlands a form of negotiable quotas has been implemented in which the localities and the party centre agree the quotas they will meet. This 'thin end of the wedge' approach has the merit that local selectors agree in principle to accept quotas and they have a responsibility to nominate women.

In this sensitive area of party activity, virtually all of the obstacles to women's representation come into play as do most of the strategies party women have devised to improve their representation. The fortunes of women's demands for representation as candidates and in legislatures have varied significantly in the countries we consider here. But there is a common dynamic to the claims and responses which suggests a logic to the process itself. Once a party accepts a demand for sex equality it is vulnerable to arguments that the political under-representation of women is unjust. The first step is to secure agreement that more women should be nominated. Then strategies must be devised to overcome obstacles to such an increase. Many of the obstacles are specific to a party or party system. Sometimes rules have to be changed to allow women access. Often resources must be reallocated to facilitate access. Demands for the selection of more women candidates for good seats tend to begin with pressure to get more women with 'standard' qualifications nominated. In the course of getting an increase in women's nominations accepted and implemented, questions about the appropriateness of the standard qualifications get raised and debates about the desired composition of the legislature begin. At the same time selection procedures are scrutinized and strategies of elite insulation whereby male party members protect their monopolies of power are identified and criticized.

The rules of the game: ideology, organization, political careers and gender

The claims that women make and the strategies they employ are considerably affected by the kind of party they seek to influence. All political parties have decision-making procedures consisting of formal rules, informal practices and customs. These reflect the party's political environment and patterns of internal conflict as well as expressing its ideology and goals. They also structure the party's organization. When women become political claimants, when they seek political representation, they must take the rules into account and pay attention to the ideology and organization of their party. All their claims will be contested in the party, but the most intense opposition will occur when the inevitable claim for an increased women's presence in the national legislature is made. Seats in the legislature are the political prize towards which much of party politics is directed, hence access to them is usually carefully guarded.

The pattern of the political careers of party parliamentarians tells us a great deal about the rules of the game. In the past, in many systems, women's political careers have differed from those of men, and in many systems women have not been nominated because they do not have appropriate 'qualifications'. Inhibitions about the appropriateness of their qualifications may stop women from seeking candidacy. The qualifications a party requires of its candidates are, of course, a function both of ideology and organization. This is an area of some variation. Different countries and parties have developed different political apprenticeships and it is clear that some are more accessible to women than others. In Ireland the traditional route for women to elected office was (and in Fianna Fail continues to be) kinship with the previous incumbent. This used to be termed the 'widow factor' in the USA and Australia. In the Netherlands and in the Italian PCI and its successors, the long party career is the main qualification for candidacy to the legislature. Requirements for continuous and lengthy apprenticeships in firms are thought by equal opportunities experts to favour men as employees. In politics the effect appears to be similar.

But requirements for *local* experience need not have a negative effect on women. It has long been argued that women's political concerns tend to be centred on the locality and the community, hence an emphasis on local experience should benefit them. In Sweden, which has the highest proportion of women legislators in the liberal democratic world, this is borne out. The political qualification for the Riksdag is local elected office. This is the case across the political parties and men's and women's career paths do not diverge. A similar tendency is becoming apparent in the British Labour party. In Italy, where pre-parliamentary careers are important, candidates in good positions tend to have held local or party elected office simultaneously. Italian women's political careers are coming to resemble men's. By contrast, in France, the absence of women in elected office may in part be explained by their exclusion from local politics. Local political bases are essential to the careers of French politicians and there is great competition amongst men for likely offices. Women have been largely excluded from these competitions and have not therefore been able to make the first steps of a standard French political career.

When party rules alter to facilitate women's candidacy they may well upset normal career paths. Eva Kolinsky notes that the adoption of quotas of candidates in the German SDP has changed the nature of the political apprenticeship there. It has sharply reduced the *Oschentour* (slaving like an ox), the long haul necessary to become qualified as a candidate. The backlog of 'qualified' women who sought careers was very quickly cleared after which novices became candidates. Quotas broadened access routes and increased the pool of women who were 'eligible'.

Parties of the left have traditionally been more willing than parties of the centre and the right to make agreements to nominate women and they also appear to be more able to deliver on such agreements. But ideology is a less reliable indicator of party support for women's representation than it once was. Today the trend is for parties across the ideological spectrum to seek ways of promoting women.

Party organization is another variable that we must take into account. As we have seen, weak or decentralized party organization means that party centres are less able to implement policies to promote women because they have low levels of control over their local branches and constituency organizations. Federal party organizations embracing affiliates of various kinds are similarly impeded. In the British Labour party, it is difficult to exercise effective control over the way that affiliated trade unions exercise their considerable selection powers. Marila Guadagnini makes use of Panebianco's work on party organization in her chapter on Italy to argue that the way a party is structured has considerable impact on the capacity of its leadership to influence the composition of the candidates list. This is both because of the power that the centre has over the localities and because centralized parties with relatively large bureaucracies are able to recruit, develop and support officials who constitute a corps of professional politicians. The bureaucracy also offers the security of paid employment for politicians who lose their seats. But she also remarks that in Italy's factionalized parties with weak bargaining structures (notably the Christian Democrats), it is still the core elite who are in control, the difference between the two types is that the elite is fragmented rather than cohesive. In practice the localities in almost all parties have some bargaining power in the candidate selection process, but the amount of local power will vary considerably by the type of electoral system and by the strength of the party. The level of competition for candidacy also varies considerably by party and is closely associated with party fortunes. But other factors are also important. In Italy, high levels of political competition for candidacy impede women's chances of securing nominations. In Canada, where levels of turnover are high and there are comparatively few safe seats, women have relatively high rates of entry. In most countries minor parties with lower chances of electoral success are more likely to nominate women, but this is not a reliable indicator that they wish to see more women in power. Such parties are generally more likely to nominate atypical candidates because they have a limited choice of applicants.

The disadvantages that women candidates may experience are sometimes transformed by political circumstances. In the USA in the 1990s women have the advantage of being perceived as outsiders by the public at a time when it is a 'plus' to be outsiders. Similarly in Italy, the contemporary crisis is essentially about political representation, hence the issue of women's representation is readily incorporated into the current debates about restructuring the party system.

There is no party in which efforts to nominate more women have occurred without an intervention by women making claims. In Sweden, organized women pressed their parties to nominate women candidates and place them in favourable positions on party lists by several means. At first, they simply put women's names forward, a tactic that was very important in the early stages. They also conducted campaigns to promote women candidates and made proposals to get women into better positions on party lists. Finally they acted as watchdogs and protested whenever reversals occurred. The task of securing substantial increases in women's electoral fortunes has been achieved without recourse to formal quotas. Recommendation, arguments and the threat to work for quotas achieved agreements to set targets of 40 per cent of nominations going to women. Once these targets were set, considerable progress was made.

The dynamic of gender and party politics

In conclusion, it is evident that there is a dynamic between women's claims and party responses whereby initiatives on women's representation lead to more radical such initiatives by both sides. When parties fail to respond or, as is the case when they adopt rhetorical strategies, they respond only minimally, women increase their demands. As a result rhetoric leads to positive action strategies which by the same dynamic become more comprehensive as time passes. When positive action strategies lead to good results women become more integrated into their parties and thus better positioned to secure and maintain adequate levels of representation. When insufficient change results from positive action, demands for positive discrimination are made and these have been adopted in many countries

In the rest of this volume examples of the claims that women have advanced and the responses parties have made in particular liberal democratic systems are explained in detail. They demonstrate clearly that the way a party responds to women's claims is a product both of the nature of those claims and the strategies used to press them. But it is also conditioned by the party's place in its political environment. Accordingly, in the concluding chapter, Pippa Norris discusses the party responses and considers the effect of systemic factors on party strategies to represent women.

2

Two Steps Forward, One Step Back: Women and the Australian Party System

Marian Simms

The mainstream debates about Australian political arrangements have paid little attention to the place of women. It was not until the revival of feminism as an organized political force in the late 1960s and early 1970s that the place of women in the 'working man's paradise' was extensively discussed. Miriam Dixson (1975), for example, argued that Australian women were the 'doormats' of the western world. She maintained that this had been 'caused' by the peculiar circumstances of the settlement of Australia. The Irish–Catholic legacy of the convict heritage had led to the exclusion of women from public life in a variation of the 'madonna–whore' theme. Anne Summers (1975) argued in a book of the same title, that Australian women had been treated as 'damned whores' or 'God's police'.

Australian political history, from a woman's perspective, has been characterized by the paradox of the early granting of political rights and the late achievement of even minimal levels of political power. The first women did not sit in the Commonwealth (that is, national) Parliament until during the Second World War in 1943. Women had been able to vote in federal elections since 1902, just after the six colonies had federated under the Commonwealth of Australia Constitution Act. In several of the colonies (later states) women had already achieved the right to vote prior to federation. Women were also elected to several of the state parliaments before 1943, when Dorothy Tangney (Labor) and Enid Lyons (United Australia Party, that is, conservative) were elected to the Senate and the House of Representatives, respectively.

This chapter constitutes part of a process of writing Australian women into the debate over the nature of Australian politics. Given the centrality of Australian parties to the political process it is appropriate to write women into the discussion of parties. In particular if we can understand why women have had a marginal role in the parties then we can begin to comprehend their limited role in politics and government more generally. Also, a discussion of the process by which Australian parties have been forced to examine the position of women (both as party activists and as voters) gives analysts and political actors alike insights into the ways in which change could be furthered or frustrated.

This discussion will be divided into four main sections; an overview of the party system and women; an analysis of two recent major empirical surveys of parliamentary candidates in Australia; a discussion of the position and views of women politicians in Australia; and, finally, an examination of the relations between women activists, party strategists, policies and voters under the heading of the attempt to introduce 'gender gap' strategies in Australia.

The two (or two-and-a-half) party system and women

Australian politics cannot be understood without reference to the importance of the federal system and the party system. The constitution established a federal compact in which residual powers stayed with the states. The Commonwealth was given a list of enumerated powers. Gradually the Commonwealth has gained pre-eminence of federal finances, but the administration of much policy remains with the states. Consequently the state governments have been important arenas for the development of women's policies, including those dealing with abortion, rape, domestic violence, equal opportunity and employment. Those governments, along with the Commonwealth, have been key arenas within which the different arms of the women's movement have operated.

The constitution established a bicameral Federal Parliament, at the national (that is, Commonwealth) level. Conventionally governments have been made in the lower house, the House of Representatives and in terms of much of their practice governments have operated on the British Westminster-style model. The upper house, the Senate was envisaged as a states house, and each state has the same number of parliamentarians, but the Senate has become divided along party lines. The adoption of proportional representation in 1949 has facilitated the presence of minor parties and women. (In February 1990 women comprised 22 per cent of Commonwealth Senators.)

The party system is also organized on a federal basis. Australia is seen as having either a 'two party' or a 'two-and-a-half party' system. There are (and have been since 1909) two major parties. After federation in 1901 the labour movement made its mark upon the institutional framework of Australian political economy. Labour and capital made a deal which involved the establishment of a centralized wage fixing system guaranteeing a 'living wage' and a tariff wall which sheltered a nascent manufacturing sector and the industrial working class. The deal was called 'new protection' and it had been set in place through a political arrangement between the Australian Labor Party (ALP) and the Protection group. In the first decade of this century there were two main anti-Labor groups in the Commonwealth Parliament, the Protectionists and the more *laissez-faire* Free Traders. In 1909 they merged and became the Liberal party, which was to change its name and focus several times. The party and its heirs have provided the main alternative to the ALP and have been in office nationally for much of this century. The ALP has been in government for short bursts, mainly during the two world wars and the Great Depression. Since 1983 the ALP has enjoyed its longest continuous period of office. The major parties grew out of the key economic sections or classes and the links in organizational, financial and voting terms have remained important, particularly when compared with other liberal democratic countries. Since 1920 there has been a third party, the Country party, which has never governed by itself but often governed in coalition with the much larger (conservative) Liberal party. In some accounts the Country party is treated as part of the conservative coalition team and in other accounts it is seen as an independent *albeit* relatively small party in its own right (see Jaensch, 1988).

The federal factor is reflected in the fact that the state branches of the political parties select candidates for both state *and* Commonwealth elections. National parties as such do not really exist. There has been an increasing centralization of power in the national office of one of the two major parties, the ALP. Its election in 1983 has been correlated with the trend for the party's national executive to intervene to protect sitting members of the Commonwealth Parliament from deselection or demotion.

The ALP is the oldest Australian party, having celebrated its centenary in 1991. The ALP is a trade union party and grew out of the aspirations of the labour movement to have direct political and parliamentary power. Its internal politics have always been dominated by the trade union element. Not all unions are affiliates and the majority are the traditional blue-collar ones which, in turn, have been largely male-dominated. Since the late 1970s, however, there have been successful moves to increase the influence of the 'rank and file' or branch element of the party. It has never been a mass-based party along the style of the Social Democratic parties of western Europe. One estimate was that the ALP's membership had dropped to around 42,000 in 1990 (see Ward, 1992: 8). According to Ward the ALP's own figures are higher, but even the party concedes that membership had dropped considerably from about 75,000 in the mid-1970s. Women have generally constituted about one-third of the total branch membership.

Labor women activists were able to make some inroads into the party's power base in the late 1970s. A special National Conference of the party in 1981 adopted a series of recommendations which were intended to democratize the party, to make it more electorally appealing and *inter alia* to adopt affirmative action for women. The ALP had performed disastrously in the 1977 elections and women activists were able to use this situation to push the case for women.

It is interesting to compare snapshots before and after the so-called modernization of the late 1970s/early 1980s. In 1979, of the forty-nine delegates to the ALP's supreme policy-making body, the National Conference, only two were women. The 1982 National Conference was an enlarged and somewhat feminized gathering of ninety-nine delegates:

> For the ALP there was for the first time a constitutional requirement that a minimum of one-quarter of each State's delegation be women. This was more than met: 40 per cent of delegates and one-third of Tasmanian and Western Australian delegates and proxies were also women. Only Victoria managed to hit exactly on the 25 per cent minimum; yet Victorian delegates Joan Coxsedge (MLC) and Jean McLean were among the more active Conference participants. (Hutchison, 1982: 9)

Under the affirmative action rules the state branches were also required to increase the representation of women on their decision-making and policy-making bodies proportionate with their membership, which as we have seen has been around one-third. These requirements, however, stopped short of forcing parties to apply affirmative action to the selection of parliamentary candidates.

The ALP has been opposed from the right by a number of different parties. Since 1909 there has been one party of 'town capital', the Liberal party, which has undergone several important transformations. In 1916 it became the National party (after the ALP split), and then in 1932 became the United Australia party after yet another schism in the Labor party. In the summer of 1944–5 the UAP became the Liberal Party of Australia (LPA).

Confusingly the Liberal party has been more like a conservative party than a liberal one. In its formative period the party founders had long debates over the name and decided that 'conservative' would be off-putting to Australian voters and toyed with the 'progressive' label. It was consciously set up to be a mass party and its membership has always been double that of the ALP. The women's presence has always been important for the Liberal party. The Australian Women's National League (AWNL) was strongest in Victoria and consequently the Victorian division (or branch) of the LPA incorporated the equal representation of women and men on executive bodies (see Simms, 1979).

For historical rather than ideological reasons the Liberal party does have party offices reserved for women. The doctrine of equal representation has stopped at a vice-presidential level (there are two female and two male vice-presidents, a metropolitan and a rural representative of each sex). Women state presidents and treasurers have been rare. In 1976 Joy Mein became the first woman state president in Victoria, and in the same year Yvonne McComb became the first woman state president of the Queensland division and Margaret Reid became president of the Australian Capital Territory Division. The proportion of women on the range of executive committees has been very small.

The AWNL's political presence and clout were also reflected in the establishment of Women's Sections. These are formed on a state electorate basis from amongst ordinary branch members. In Victoria the peak organization is a Central Committee composed of three delegates from each section – and *ex-officio* the two women state vice-presidents of the party, the immediate past chair of the section and any Victorian women parliamentarians. The committee has many and varied functions including traditional women's auxiliary functions – for example, the Women's Sections provided the refreshments at state council meetings for many years – but extending beyond that. Most significantly its elected chairwoman is a member of the state executive and a Victorian delegate to the Liberal party's national governing body, the Federal Council.

The situation is different in the five other states, lacking as they do the guarantee of equal representation. One partial exception is the New South Wales division where the constitution requires a minimum representation of women on the main deliberative body, the state Council, and also the state executive. Also, in New South Wales, two of the four vice-presidents must be women. Partly as a result of this requirement, about one-third of state councillors and one-fifth of state executive members had been women as at 1973 (see Encel et al., 1974: 255). In all the state divisions women, although comprising at least half the branch members (and in South Australia a clear majority of members in the metropolitan areas), and with a presence in the state councils, are almost non-existent in the higher ranks.

The party of 'country capital', now called the National party, has been the junior partner of the Liberal party since its formation at the national level in 1920. A coalition of those parties was in government for much of the post-war period (1949–72, 1975–83). This partnership has been facilitated by the operation of the preferential voting system (the 'alternative vote'). In most states (bar Queensland) clear arrangements for the exchange of preferences have operated in a fairly disciplined fashion and senior Members of Parliament (MPs) of both parties have also been 'protected' from competition from the other side.

The National party (NSW) has reacted against criticisms to the effect that 'little need be said except that women are free to join it' (Encel et al., 1974: 256). It has responded by attacking the harshness of the judgement, and by taking action to correct the imbalance of the sexes. One of the party's historians (Aitkin, 1972: 126) has discussed the subordinate role of women: 'While this situation reflects the patriarchal society in which the Country Party operates, and applies to some extent to all Australian political parties, it is a source of weakness in the Party's organisation.' The party itself has admitted that the work of feminist groups forced it to examine its own house. In particular, impetus came at a grassroots level from women who called for the establishment of a 'Committee which includes women to formulate policy on current issues and issues that arise with reference to women and that this Committee has direct access to our Parliamentary Leaders' (quoted in Briggs, 1977: 37).

The party of country capital gained its first woman national president, Shirley McKerrow, in 1981. She had been the president of the Victorian branch of the party from 1976 to 1980. She was keen to press the merits of equal opportunity and to condemn affirmative action, maintaining that women should and can succeed on their own merits and arguing that singling them out for special measures can lead to their ghettoization.

The Women's Section had been part of the Victorian (then) Country party since its formation in 1916. It had had its own annual conference. By the late 1960s, however, numbers involved in Women's Section branches had been 'dwindling' (McKerrow, 1982). In 1978 it was disbanded for a trial period of two years. Then in 1980 a special conference of Victorian women decided to abolish it. In its stead, five positions were reserved for women on the party's Victorian Central Council. McKerrow (1982) saw this disbanding and the movement by women into mainstream branches as signs of maturity. In South Australia and Queensland, by contrast, the separate women's branches and conferences have not been disbanded. In New South Wales the party has been seen by one of its members (O'Brien, 1982) as a most 'liberated organization' with little need for affirmative action.

In 1977 the Australian Democrats (ADs) were formed. They have had a small number of Members of Parliament and have often held the balance of power in the upper house, the Senate. They have so far been unable to win a seat in the House of Representatives. The ADs have become a significant source of political influence for many women. They have proved more accessible to women candidates than the other three parties where battles over selection have been more problematic for women than men. Within the ADs, candidates are selected and policies are developed on the basis of postal ballots.

The Australian Democrats have run a relatively high percentage of women candidates since their formation in 1977. Heather Southcott, the Democrats' national president, has said this is because of the party's relative newness (see Macgregor, 1989). It lacks the entrenched vested interests and hierarchies of the other parliamentary parties; consequently, the Democrat women 'didn't have to get into an existing system dominated by men. We had the opportunity to start things on an equal basis. That made things much easier' (Heather Southcott, quoted in Macgregor, 1989). The Democrats have not only elected a woman president of the extra-parliamentary wing of their party, but they have also had two women leaders of their parliamentary party in their short history. Senator Janine Haines was the first woman leader of the Democrats. In fact she was the first woman leader of any Australian political party at the national level.

Senator Janet Powell, who replaced Janine Haines as leader from 1990–1, argued that her party positively encouraged women's participation:

> There I was in 1977, a woman in a small country town. I had four children – two of them in nappies. And this new party was saying: 'You can become a functioning member. You need never attend a meeting.' All our voting, then and now, is done by post. (Quoted in Macmillan, 1989)

Women candidates were rarely fielded by the major political parties before the late 1970s. Since the 1970s Australian women

Table 2.1　*Party affiliation of women candidates, House of*
Representatives 1969–90

Year	ALP	Lib	NP	DLP	LM/AP	AD	Ind and others	Total
1969	3	1		8	3		14	29
1972	4	3		7	14		10	38
1974	3	5	1	4	27		7	47
1975	6	3	1	3	8		10	31
1977	15	2	1			22	9	49
1980	23	5	1	1		30	15	75
1983	20	10	1	1		25	29	86
1984	18	14	9	11		36	19	107
1987	26	12	4			44	21	107
1990	19	18	6			39	57	139

Source: Sawer, 1993

Table 2.2　*Women candidates for the federal*
parliament, 1901–90

Decade	Number of women	Number of candidates
1901–09	4	743
1910–19	10	1047
1920–29	2	840
1930–39	9	898
1940–49	62	1598
1950–59	63	1672
1960–69	94	2022
1970–79	283	2840
1980–89	593	3242
1990–	206	1005

Source: Hughes, 1990

have been rewriting the history of campaigning in Australian
federal politics (see Table 2.1). The image of the Australian
woman candidate as a political oddity running as an independent
or for a fringe party has been changed. The majority of women
candidates, like the majority of men candidates, still campaign as
Independents or for the minor parties, but the three major parties
in the House of Representatives and the four major parties in the
Senate have been pressured to run an increased percentage of
women candidates (see Table 2.2).

The general picture, however, is not one of unmitigated success.
Some Liberal women have said there are a lot of 'discouraged'
women within the party, which is not 'attuned to the value of
women candidates'. Others have said that women simply need to
learn 'ambition' in order to counter any residual bias in the party.

The candidate surveys

In the 1970s at various forums on women and political parties in Australia (and probably elsewhere) it was often asserted that women were not presenting themselves as potential candidates and consequently could not hope to be selected let alone elected. Little empirical work had been done on the subject of candidate selection (known as 'pre-selection' in Australia). For the 1987 federal election, a group of us in Canberra undertook a survey of parliamentary candidates.[1]

The questionnaire included questions on candidate selection. We thought that by asking successful candidates about their 'pre-selection' experience (for example the numbers who contested and whether they were male or female) we could get some kind of snapshot of the process. Clearly, for example, if all the candidates had defeated male contestants during their pre-selection contests then there might have been some truth in the assertion that women did not come forward. Conversely if the candidates had defeated female contestants then it would tell us that it was highly likely that massive discrimination was occurring within the Australian party system.

We discovered that the picture was somewhat different for the two major parties. Data from the 1987 candidate study were interpreted to mean that women were not coming forward in great numbers at the pre-selection stages of the Labor party. For the Liberal party the fields were larger and there were more women coming forward in comparison with the ALP and in terms of the final numbers actually selected by the party. Women constituted around 13 per cent of the Liberal candidates but they were closer to 20 per cent of Liberal nominees. Hence there is a bias of some kind in the selection process for the Liberal party which discriminated against women for the 1987 federal elections.

In March 1990 there was another federal election and a slightly different group of us in Canberra organized a second candidate study. We asked the same two questions about candidate selection as in 1987. We also added some new questions *inter alia* about candidates' political styles and political networking, and these will be discussed below.

In the 1990 case the apparent 'bias' against Liberal women in the selection process was present but was not as great as in 1987. For the Labor party there were also differences between the 1987 and 1990 federal elections. More women sought nomination in 1990 and in percentage terms greater numbers of Labor women were unsuccessful in becoming endorsed candidates for the 1990 elections than had been the case in 1987. In 1987 and in 1990, however, women nominees were clustered in selection contests in which women were successfully selected. In the election itself there were a number of 'woman against woman' contests. Very few Labor or Liberal women were selected for safe seats.

The candidate studies provided us with further information about male and female candidates. The question about the political history of candidates can throw light upon the competing supply (few women came forward) and demand (women are not wanted) models for the under-representation of women. If, for example, we were to discover that women candidates had undergone longer political apprenticeships than men, it would imply *inter alia* that women were being treated differently by the political parties than were men.

Instead the data suggest that the male and female parliamentary candidates from the major parties have remarkably similar political histories. In examining the information about the apprenticeships of candidates one observes that both sexes had similar mean scores on features such as the age of first interest in politics, the year of joining the relevant political party, the year of first federal contest, the history of involvement in local government and the amount of work with voluntary service organizations. The mean score for ages for women and men was identical if we take the parties separately. Both men and women from the ALP registered a mean score of 44 and for the Liberal party it was 42.

This evidence suggests that women were not being forced to jump through extra hurdles before being selected. This proposition, however, ignores the extent to which women might be discriminated against by being over-represented amongst the so-called 'flagwavers' running in hopeless seats.

Moving to the 1990 candidate study, some interesting patterns emerged based on a somewhat different list of questions. Low percentages of men and women had used local or state government experience as 'pathways to Parliament'. Taking the Labor and Liberal parties separately the men and women showed similar scores in their responses regarding the length of party membership. A high percentage of Labor women (as compared with other candidates) had used employment in an MPs office as a springboard to their campaigns. It could be seen as one of the perks of having one's party in government at the Commonwealth level and in the majority of states. A similarly high percentage of Liberal women registered active involvement in business organizations. Traditionally Liberal women had seen their lack of access to business networks as a significant factor in their lack of progress within the party. In other words, minor but potentially significant changes had occurred between the 1987 and the 1990 snapshots.

Women politicians

The most important background feature of women parliamentarians in Australia is their political party. Other factors such as, for Labor party women, their membership of a faction, are also significant. To these features can be added the fact that many of the women were elected as parts of more general swings at key elections. For some this has meant the consequent achievement of ministerial office. Many of these women have achieved 'firsts'. The 1980s saw the 'first' Labor woman federal cabinet minister, the 'first' woman Speaker of the Federal House of Representatives, the 'first' woman leader of a political party, the 'first' woman state premiers and the 'first' woman chief minister of a Federal Territory.

It is interesting to note that most of the women Parliamentarians elected in the early 1980s have reported both obstacles and a high level of media attention. Women elected in a slightly later period claimed that things were easier for them because of the efforts of the earlier trailblazers. Many of the ALP women, state and Commonwealth parliamentarians, for example, who in turn comprised the majority of those elected, mentioned Senator Susan Ryan and Senator Pat Giles both as role models and women who have given assistance.

In 1989, with the assistance of Diane Stone, I undertook a study of state and Commonwealth women politicians for a UNESCO project on women and politics in the Asian region. Over 90 per cent of those women interviewed agreed that women were under-represented in Australian politics. The cross-partisan agreement stopped there. Labor women tended to blame the existing structures and to criticize the pre-selection processes and the ALP internal factions. The overwhelming sentiment was summed up in the words of one woman who referred to the 'very organized men who won't give up roles of power'. Liberal women tended to blame women themselves and called for measures such as speaking to girls in school to encourage the women of the future to join the parties and 'to bite the bullet' by seeking endorsement as parliamentary candidates.

Several Liberal women broke ranks to admire the ALP's policy of affirmative action, suggesting that their party should borrow the policy. Most of the Liberal and the National party women, however, opposed affirmative action or indeed any kind of positive action, referring to it as 'not helpful' or counter-productive. The concept, which treats men and women as separate groups, was apparently anathema to their idea of individualism. Several of the Liberal women (at the state parliament level) even opposed affirmative action despite the fact that they themselves have gained rapid endorsement because their party saw an urgent need for more women candidates. (This has been the case, for example, in the state elections in New South Wales in 1988.) Several Liberal women could list examples of discrimination against them but did not view sex discrimination as a barrier to women's entry into politics. One Liberal woman politician interviewed for the study had been very critical of the discriminatory behaviour of a leading department store but was unwilling to accept that the same kind of behaviour was present in contemporary political institutions such as political parties. She proceeded to criticize the concept of separate and identifiable women's issues, referring to them as 'vestiges of the early days' of the women's movement.

A number of the women Senators interviewed were optimistic about the prospects for women politicians. Yet the view from the House of Representatives was not as sanguine. There was much talk among ALP women (the ALP has been the party with the most women in the House) of 'tokenism' and male power structures.

These expressions of frustration are perhaps understandable if we examine the data on the position of Labor women in the 1980s and into the 1990s. The number of federal ALP MPs has remained static (see Table 2.3) and the number and percentage of ALP women candidates has actually declined! It is ironic that while the position has been slightly worse for the Senate than for the House, the strongest expressions of frustration have emerged from the House. The high points for ALP women were the 1980 and 1983 federal elections. In 1980 the ALP became the first major party to field a group of women candidates in winnable seats in a House of Representatives election. For the 1983 federal election the ALP increased its number of women candidates (see Simms, 1984). (The ALP's internal affirmative action campaign was undoubtedly one factor in this improvement.)

The 1983 and 1984 federal elections were to see a significant increase in the numbers of women candidates fielded by the Liberal party, and a consequent increase in the number of Liberal women in the Federal Parliament. This development complicated the simplicity of the model for the late 1970s and early 1980s which saw the ALP dominating the field in sheer numbers of

Table 2.3 *Women members of federal parliament, 1980–90*

Party	House	Numbers after election in				
		1980	1983	1984	1987	1990
Labor	Senate	4	7	6	5	4
	House of Reps	3	6	7	8	7
	Total	7	13	13	13	11
Liberal	Senate	4	4	5	7	7
	House of Reps	0	0	1	1	3
	Total	4	4	6	8	10
National	Senate	1	1	1	1	1
	House of reps	0	0	0	0	0
	Total	1	1	1	1	1
Democrats	Senate	1	1	1	3	4
	House of Reps	0	0	0	0	0
	Total	1	1	1	3	4
NDP[1]/Vallentine	Senate	n.a.	n.a.	1	2[2]	1
Group	House of Reps	n.a.	n.a.	0	0	0
	Total	n.a.	n.a.	1	2	1
Total	Senate	10	13	14	18	17
	House of Reps	3	6	8	9	10
	Total	13	19	22	27	27

[1] NDP = Nuclear Disarmament Party.
[2] This figure includes Irina Dunn who was not elected in 1987 but replaced the NDP's Robert Wood soon after.

women candidates and MPs. The views of some of these Liberal women belied the notion that women politicians will necessarily share a feminist or even a female consciousness. Many of the Liberal party's women candidates in 1984 disagreed with the idea that there were separate and identifiable 'women's' issues (see Simms, 1985). At the eve of the 1990 federal election, for example, the Liberal women senators outnumbered the Labor women by seven to four. These Liberal women have been called the 'shoulder-pad brigade':

> Apart from making the Opposition look more like a gridiron team than a political party, this group of women has shaken awake the Senate, which, unlike the bear-pit that has always been the House of Representatives, is traditionally known for its sedative effects rather than its action. (Lynch, 1989: 17).

It is clearly not the case that the election of more women to Australian legislative assemblies will necessarily lead to an increase in expenditure by governments on services to women and children.

Furthermore, some ALP women MPs as well as many anti-Labor women MPs have proved to be wary of the feminist label.

The factors militating against cross-party cooperation are greater in Australia than in comparable countries such as Britain. To institutional factors such as the regularized opportunity for private members' bills and the greater number of free votes in Britain could be added the absence of formal intra-party factions. The ALP's factions have in some cases provided opportunities for individual women to become candidates and MPs, but at the same time they have allowed a macho-politics to dominate which has redefined and limited the kind of interaction and debate which can occur between ALP women members, candidates and politicians. Formal national factions within the ALP have developed since the election of the Hawke government in 1983 (see Lloyd and Swan, 1987). There are three national factions, the right, the centre–left and the socialist left. Between them they manage the process of the 'election' of cabinet ministers and have a major even if informal role in the selection of parliamentary candidates.

The Liberal and National parties have lacked such formal factions but do have tendencies, which are looser groupings of individuals who share similar ideas. The most significant are the 'wets' and the 'dries'. The latter have adopted a free-market approach to economic and social policies. These have also had notable women politicians amongst their ranks including the high-profile Senator Bronwyn Bishop, the Liberal party's first woman senator from New South Wales. In contrast, Queensland's Kathy Sullivan (Liberal MHR for Moncrieff) has been identified with more progressive, namely 'wet', views on social and economic issues. Feminist voices have been, at best, muted within the Liberal party where particularly since the mid-1980s the rhetoric of individualism and self-help has been dominant.

Gender gap politics in Australia?

Feminists in the Labor party have tried to replicate American-style gender gap politics in Australia. In 1980 Senator Susan Ryan, ALP Spokeswoman on Women's Affairs, produced an important discussion paper which was redrafted to become *The ALP and Women Towards Equality* (1982). (Ryan became the first Labor woman cabinet minister when the Hawke government was elected in March 1983.) She emphasized gender-based economic inequality which required a gender-based electoral strategy. The ALP also conducted research which demonstrated that good women candidates could be electoral drawcards.

Table 2.4 *Women and men's support for Labor in 1984, 1986, 1987 and 1990*[1]

Year	Party identification		Voting identification	
	Women	Men	Women	Men
1984 (n = 2972)	46	46	52	56
1986 (n = 1479)	46	48	41	46
1987 (n = 1610)	45	49	44	46
1990 (n = 2318)	42	46	39	41

[1] Figures are expressed in rounded percentages.

Source: National Social Sciences Survey.

Throughout the 1970s women voters had been more likely to support the non-Labor (that is, conservative parties) and Senator Ryan was able to convince the party that developing policies for modern women and increasing the numbers of women candidates could increase the ALP's share of the female vote and consequently allow it to be elected to the national government. Labor strategists pushed women's issues at the 1983 elections but this emphasis had practically disappeared by the next elections in 1984. (Australia does not have fixed parliamentary terms at the national level and prime ministers are able to call elections before the conclusion of the three-year maximum term.)

In the meantime the Labor government had pursued hard-line economic rationalist policies of financial deregulation and budget-cuttings and had flirted with the idea of introducing a consumption tax. The ALP's support amongst women declined over this period (see Table 2.4). One could speculate that the Labor government's hardline economic policies and its rejection of social democracy and feminism meant that Australian women treated it as their American counterparts had treated the Reaganite Republicans. Certainly the demotion and subsequent resignation of the high-profile feminist Senator Ryan from both the government and the Parliament in late 1987 angered many women.

The ALP's own research demonstrated the need to seek support from women in the 1987 election campaign. The research conducted by both major parties had discovered that young women between the ages of 25 and 35 were a key group of swinging voters (see Simms, 1988). The ALP, on the basis of this research, conducted an aggressive advertising campaign based upon Wendy Woods (an employee of John Singleton whose advertising agency was doing the Labor campaign for the first time). Labor's 'Wendy' television advertisements received a lot of prominence. Wendy herself took up one of the major themes of Labor's women's policies, namely that the Liberal party's policies would seriously disadvantage women economically.

Labor's declining popularity with women showed up in ANU survey research from 1986 onwards (see Table 2.4). After initial successes it was not able to capitalize on the women's vote after the 1984 election. This broad picture was also borne out in the Morgan Gallup Polls. It was noted in a press release on the eve of the 1990 election that:

> In the 1983 and 1984 ALP-won elections, the women's vote favoured the ALP. In the extremely close 1987 election the women's vote favoured the L–NP, but only by 2 per cent. Analysis of the most recent Gallup Poll conducted March 3–4 [1990] shows that the crucial women's vote is favouring the ALP over the L–NP, 42 per cent over 39 per cent. (Morgan Gallup Poll, 7 March 1990).

Consequently in Australia we never had a gender gap in the northern hemisphere sense, namely, a tendency for a greater percentage of women than men to support the 'nominally' left of centre party. There are several possible explanations. In the first instance the Labor government under Prime Ministers Hawke (1983–91) and Keating (1991–) has adopted conservative economic policies similar to those of the new right Labor government of Prime Minister Lange in New Zealand. It would be possible to argue that there has been no 'left' party in Australia in the 1980s except, perhaps, for the Australian Democrats. Secondly and consequently women in greater numbers than men have supported the Australian Democrats, which started life as a centre party but has come to be perceived by its members and by others as more left than the ALP. Thirdly the Liberal party began to court modern women by the mid-1980s, moving away from its traditional emphasis upon women's role within the family (Simms, 1988). To be sure some within the party still looked back to the 1950s model of women in the family but for the most part 'family values' were increasingly the province of its more socially conservative-minded partner, the National party.

The 1987 election was important not only because some women deserted the ALP but also because women's issues were seen by both sides of politics as 'important in deciding the outcome of [the] polls' (Liberal leader John Howard quoted in the *Canberra Times*, 10 July 1987). This was very much an afterthought as during the 1987 campaign the 'family' had been a prominent Liberal party issue. It was not the first time that the Liberal party had discovered the power of the female voter. The significance of the 1987 elections was that the Liberal party had discovered the modern woman.

> The majority of women under 35 are either in paid work or planning to be in paid work. The dual role of homemakers, and outside paid work, can present special problems to women.
>
> In recent time many women have achieved success in their chosen work. But often success has been achieved because of unusual talent or determination. Good social and political policies should not require that all successful women be heroines or pathfinders. (Eggleton, 1987: 5,1)

The topics covered in this party document included 'equal opportunities', 'taxation', 'childcare and children', 'education, training and re-training', 'dual role', 'older women' and 'women's representation'. On some topics there were echoes of the party's traditional family orientation. For example under 'taxation' it referred to the need to 'positively acknowledge in our tax system the contribution of women at home'. (Eggleton, 1987: 3). In Australia for many years all taxpayers (included married women) have been taxes as individuals but heads of households have been able to claim 'a dependent spouse rebate'. Conventionally this has meant that husbands have gained taxation benefits from having the services of a wife. Feminist groups have long campaigned against this. Some groups have also called for the tax-deductibility of childcare expenses. Anti-feminist groups (and some individuals within the Liberal and National parties) have called for the introduction of income-splitting between couples to lessen the husband's tax burden and to encourage women to stay at home.

By 1987 the need for federally funded childcare was accepted by all but the extreme right. The Liberal party in the 1987 and the 1990 elections attempted to 'outbid' the Labor government on childcare. In 1987 it promised to 'maintain Commonwealth funding for childcare services' and to 'encourage the growth of private sector childcare' (Eggleton, 1987: 3). Liberals also promised to reform the tax system to encourage 'the provision of work-based child care' (Eggleton, 1987: 4).

Tax reform was to become an even bigger item of the Liberals' reform agenda. In 1991 it produced an enormous and fully documented package of reforms called 'Fightback' which had as its centrepiece the commitment to a broadly based consumption tax, known as the Goods and Services Tax (GST). As we have already noted, Australian women have demonstrated a high level of scepticism about a consumption tax.

Conspicuous by its absence from the women's policy was the issue of reproductive rights. There are two main reasons for this absence. Firstly, and most importantly, under the federal structure abortion and indeed health and social policies more generally are state, not Commonwealth matters. Secondly, Australian parties because of their own internal reasons have been coy about sexual and social matters. Amongst the most disciplined parties in the world, they have allowed free or conscience votes on the matter. All parties are divided on abortion. The Liberals and the Nationals are divided between traditionalists and progressives and include in their parliamentary and extra-parliamentary ranks women who are opposed to the ready availability of abortion. The ALP has even greater problems. The Catholic right at both state and Commonwealth levels tends to be 'pro-life'. Its left faction, by contrast, includes the right to choose as one of its planks. Consequently in the Australian Capital Territory (one the two Federal Territories), under a Labor government dominated by the left faction, an abortion clinic was established as a priority at a time in 1992 when the health budget overall was being cut.

In general, however, since the middle of the 1970s, state and Commonwealth governments have been more aware of women's needs and have enacted changes to improve the situation of women. At a state level this has included increased funding for women's health, refuge and counselling centres. At the federal level, there were the reforms initiated by the Whitlam Labor government (1972–5), such as equal pay, and the Hawke Labor government's equal opportunity legislation. This includes the Sex Discrimination Act 1984, the Public Service Reform Act 1984, the Affirmative Action (Equal Opportunity for Women) Act 1986 and the Equal Employment Opportunity (Commonwealth Authorities) Act 1987, which have improved women's opportunities in job advertising, recruitment, training and service conditions. At both levels, bureaucratic machinery exists to undertake research into women's affairs, advising cabinet and informing the population of policy developments. However, the legislation enacted and machinery established has related more to the economic position of women as workers than to their political rights.

The ALP's policy of affirmative action and the strength of its socialist left faction have been the major factors in explaining the preponderance of Labor women over non-Labor women. The point about the salience of Labor's internal factions is highlighted by the case of the state of New South Wales. The dominant Labor faction there is the right wing, which had never seen a female member of its faction elected to the House of Representatives from New South Wales, until the Federal elections of March 1990 when Janice Crosio was elected. Prior to that the only woman MHR from New South Wales, Jeanette McHugh (elected in 1983), was from the socialist left faction. Women were never a presence in the right-dominated state Labor cabinets (Labor was in office from 1976 until 1988). The New South Wales right-wing faction is identified strongly with the Irish–Catholic based machine politics of the old-style Labor party. State and federal parliamentary members of this faction have generally opposed the availability of abortion and have expressed traditional views on the role of women.[2]

The feminist voice in Australian politics has probably not been as strong as it was in the first half of the 1980s owing to two major factors. First has been the growth in the significance of the ALP's internal factions, which do not appear to have been feminized and which have become a target for criticism by a number of the ALP's women parliamentarians. Secondly, the increase in the number of women in the two non-Labor parties has coincided with the emergence of pro-family rather than pro-feminist ideology. Most of those women have come from independent professional careers to the parliamentary arena but even in the face of examples of discrimination in their own lives prefer to emphasize the opportunities available to women rather than to acknowledge sexist barriers or male structures which might need to be eradicated.

Notes

I am grateful to Jacky McKimmie who prepared this chapter and helped in various other ways, to my colleague Christine Jennett who, as always, read an earlier draft, and to my friend Joni Lovenduski who exercised a keen editorial eye.

1 The 1987 team was Alvaro Ascui, Roger Jones, Ian McAllister, Tony Mughan and Marian Simms. Vance Merrill and Susan Fraser also helped out at crucial stages. The 1990 team was David Gow, Roger Jones, Ian McAllister and Marian Simms. Clive Bean and Susan Fraser were also involved.

2 Prime Minister Paul Keating is from this faction.

3

Gender and Party Politics in Britain

Pippa Norris and Joni Lovenduski

In Britain, attempts to gain political representation have been shaped by the influence of changing feminist ideas about politics. Political equality only recently became a goal for party women who for many years were ambivalent and divided. Many felt that seeking elected office was incompatible with feminism, others thought that prioritizing gender was inappropriate in their party. Second wave feminism in Britain was characterized by a desire for autonomy and offered a wide-ranging critique of party politics which was seen as sexist, hierarchical, old fashioned and irrelevant to issues important to women. In the Labour party, although women's organizations were energized by the resurgence of feminism, it was only during the 1980s that the aim of increasing the number of women in political office inside and outside the party became a mobilizing issue. In the Conservative party the influence of feminist ideas was much more muted and it took until the late 1980s for demands for a more equitable representation of women to be heard. The contemporary movement to increase the presence of women in the political elite is therefore a fairly recent phenomenon.

The responses of the political parties have reflected their politics and cultures. Labour women's organizations have used the broader process of party modernization to press for affirmative action programmes, with some success. Change in the Conservative party has been slower and more low-key, but equal opportunity policies have been implemented. During the 1980s women were brought into more visible leadership positions within internal party organizations, and as prospective Parliamentary candidates. The total number of women in Parliament nearly tripled in the past decade – from twenty-three in 1983, to forty-one in 1987 and sixty in 1992 – although the proportion of women in Parliament (9.2 per cent) remains relatively low compared with most European countries.

To understand these developments we first set out the general pattern of party competition in Britain. Secondly, we summarize trends over time in women's political participation within British parties – as voters, members, local councillors, Parliamentary candidates and MPs. Thirdly, we explore why there are so few women in the political elite, assessing the impact of the reforms to the Parliamentary selection process within the Labour and Conservative parties.[1] In this context we also consider the impact of organization to achieve equality by women within the major parties and the attitudes of candidates and members towards sex equality strategies. Finally, we consider the prospects for improving women's position within parties.

The British party system

The British political system is dominated by strong 'mass–branch' parties. Since the 1960s party loyalty has weakened in the electorate, and membership has declined. Nevertheless parties continue to serve three vital functions in government: they structure electoral choice; they determine the selection of Parliamentary candidates, members of the government and the prime minister; and they provide a legislative programme and the discipline to get it passed in Parliament. The House of Commons, the main legislative chamber, includes 651 members elected by simple plurality (first past the post) in single-member constituencies for a maximum period of five years. In 1992 Labour and the Conservatives held 607 seats. The remainder were distributed among the middle-of-the-road Liberal Democrats (20), and the regional parties – the Scottish Nationalists (3), Plaid Cymru (the Welsh nationalist party) (4), and those of Northern Ireland (17). The leader of the largest party in the Commons is normally appointed prime minister, and in turn he or she appoints the cabinet from Members of Parliament. In the post-war period, with the exception of a short period during the 1970s, governments have been majoritarian not coalition.

The history of the modern party system in Britain may be divided into three distinct periods. From 1945 to 1966 Britain was a stable, consistent, two party system. The Labour and Conservative parties shared 98 per cent of all Parliamentary seats: the 'in' party assumed all responsibility for government, through a united cabinet with a stable and disciplined Parliamentary majority, while the 'out' party provided responsible opposition, critical scrutiny of government actions and an alternative electoral choice. In general elections during this period the two major parties contested 98 per cent of seats, nominated 77 per cent of candidates, and won 92 per cent of the vote.

In the second period, from 1966 to 1979, minor parties became more competitive. The Labour and Conservative duopoly of Parliamentary seats, and single party monopoly of the executive government, remained almost unaltered, but their electoral base was seriously weakened. The two party share of Parliamentary candidates plummeted to 55 per cent, and their share of votes fell to 82 per cent. Party fragmentation increased when the major parties withdrew from competition in Northern Ireland in the early 1970s, allowing the entry of twelve to seventeen MPs from parties in the Province.

In the third period, from 1979 to 1992, the 'two party' pendulum appeared to 'stick'. The Conservatives won four successive elections, something no other party had managed in the ear of the mass franchise. By the next general election the Tories will have been in office for seventeen or eighteen years, the longest period of continuous government since the 1820s. The Liberals, in alliance with the new Social Democrat party, peaked in 1983, with one-quarter of the vote. The two merged to become the Liberal Democrats in 1988. The fortunes of the Scottish Nationalists have fluctuated in polls, but failed to produce new seats. Meanwhile Labour overhauled the party but failed to rise above 40 per cent of the vote for six consecutive elections. If these trends continue Britain may develop into a 'dominant party system', in which the Conservatives are unassailable in government, Labour remains the natural party of opposition, while the Liberal Democrats and Nationalists remain the minor parties of protest (Crewe et al., 1992).

Women's participation in parties

This is the context for developments in women's participation in British parties.

Voters

When suffrage was first granted to women over thirty years of age, with passage of the Representation of the People's Act on 6 February 1918, it was commonly assumed that many women would vote as a bloc, with significant implications for party fortunes. All parties courted the new 'women's vote'. As Strachey noted: 'The Representation of the People's Act had not been on the Statute Book a fortnight before the House of Commons discovered that every Bill which came before it had a "women's side", and the Party Whips began eagerly to ask "what the women thought?"' (Strachey, 1979: 367). In the next decade the Liberals and Conservatives produced a series of policy initiatives designed, in part, to attract the new female voter. These included the registration of midwives, making women eligible to stand for the Commons, admitting Peeresses to the Lords, opening the legal service to women, making women liable for jury duty, admitting women to the Civil Service and police force, equalizing the grounds for divorce, giving women equal custody over their children, granting widows equal pension rights, and making wives legally responsible for their criminal activity. Finally in the Equal Franchise Act (May 1928) the Conservative government extended the female franchise to all women over twenty-one years. As Baldwin said in the debate over the Bill: 'The subjection of women, if there be such a thing, will not now depend on any creation of the law, nor can it be remedied by any action of the law. It will never again be possible to blame the Sovereign State for any position of inequality. Women will have, with us, the fullest rights. The ground for the old agitation is gone, and gone forever' (Strachey, 1979). After 1929 women formed over half (53 per cent) of the registered electorate. There is no reliable evidence of women's voting patterns before 1945. Many observers thought women tended to favour the Conservatives, whose traditional emphasis on church and family was expected to prove popular among women. Others thought women did not vote as a bloc, since they were divided by class, region, age, and hence by party.

From 1945 onward systematic evidence of gender differences in party support became available, in the series of Gallup polls, and from 1964 in the British Election Surveys.[2] This confirms that from 1945 to 1979 women were consistently more likely to favour the Conservatives (Table 3.1). The gender gap reached its peak in the 1951 and 1955 general elections, with an 8 percentage point difference in Conservative support between women and men. Indeed, if Britain had continued with an exclusively male franchise, all other things being equal, there could have been an unbroken period of Labour governments from 1945 to 1979. The gender gap gradually diminished over the years; in the 1983 and 1987 general elections there were no significant gender differences in voting support (Norris, 1985b; Rose and McAllister, 1990; Welch and Thomas, 1988). Yet in 1992 the gender gap returned; men's votes were evenly divided between the major parties (41:40) while middle-aged and older women favoured the Conservatives by a decisive margin (45:36).[3] In their post-election inquest, the official Labour report pin-pointed this as one reason for their defeat, and stressed the need to target the older 'women's vote' (Table 3.1). Structural reasons are the most important explanation

Table 3.1   *Conservative vote by gender, 1963–92*

	Men		Women	
	Con. %	Other %	Con. %	Other %
1945	35	65	43	57
1950	41	59	45	55
1951	46	54	54	46
1955	47	53	55	45
1959	45	55	51	49
1964	40	60	43	57
1966	36	64	41	59
1970	43	57	48	52
1974	37	63	39	61
1974	35	65	37	63
1979	45	55	48	52
1983	45	55	45	55
1987	44	56	44	56
1992	39	61	43	57

Sources: 1945–1964 The Gallup Polls quoted in Durant (1969). 1964–1987 Crewe et al. (1991); Harris/ITN Exit Poll 9 April 1992

Table 3.2   *Voter participation by gender, 1964–1987*

	Men %	Women %
1964	92	90
1966	85	83
1970	87	83
1974	85	85
1979	84	85
1983	82	84
1987	85	87

Source: British Election Studies, 1964–1987

of gender differentiation amongst younger and older women (Norris, 1993).

It was assumed in the years after 1928 that women were less likely to vote than men. While this may be true, there is little systematic evidence to support this assumption before opinion poll results became widely available in Britain (Norris, 1991). Evidence from successive British election studies (Table 3.2), indicates that from 1964 to 1970 about 2–4 per cent fewer women voted. By the October 1974 general election, there was no gender difference in turnout, and in subsequent elections women's voting participation has been slightly higher than men's. This means in 1987 there were about 1.8 million more women voters than men.

Party members

The Conservative party A long-standing stereotype of British politics is that middle-aged housewives are the backbone of the Conservative party, acting as loyal volunteers for all the essential constituency work: canvassing, fund-raising, organizing social functions, inviting speakers, addressing envelopes, taking voters to the polls, delivering newsletters, as well as being well represented among the party faithful at annual party conferences. Party activity is often seen as a natural extension of women's social networks and voluntary labour in the community. Estimates about the number of women as party activists used to be fairly unreliable, because individual membership records were kept somewhat erratically at constituency level. What information there is tends to confirm the traditional image. Jill Hills found that during the 1970s women constituted 51 per cent of Conservative party members (Hills, 1981). More recently, the 1992 BCS survey found that about half of Conservative party members are women.

Traditionally, Conservative women were thought to be far more active at the grassroots than in higher-level policy-making bodies, and BCS data confirm this impression. Women are well represented as branch officers (in local wards, the smallest units which make up the constituency), and members of the constituency executive councils (Figure 3.1). Fewer women held regional party office, while at the higher level there are fifty women members of the National Union (20 per cent), and twenty women MPs in the Parliamentary party (6 per cent). Part of the explanation for this pattern is that the party's women members appear to be less politically confident and assertive than the men. For example, when members were asked whether they would be likely to carry out a series of activities, and whether they had done so, if a law was unjust, Conservative women were less likely to say that they would than men, an indicator that is conventionally taken by political scientists to demonstrate a slightly lower sense of political efficacy and potential activism. But the gender difference was modest, and not always consistent across all items (Table 3.3). The story is likely to be more complicated than traditional gender stereotypes allow.

The Labour party Labour's traditional cloth-cap image was based on a male-dominated membership, rooted firmly in the heavy industries like mining and the railways. This was most visible at the annual party conference: a survey in the 1970s estimated that

Percentage men   Percentage wom

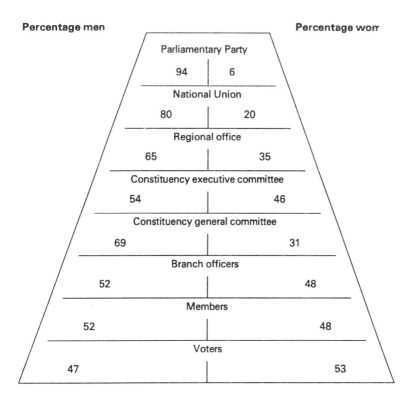

	Parliamentary Party	
94		6
	National Union	
80		20
	Regional office	
65		35
	Constituency executive committee	
54		46
	Constituency general committee	
69		31
	Branch officers	
52		48
	Members	
52		48
	Voters	
47		53

Figure 3.1   *Conservative party organization (British Candidate Study, 1992)*

86 per cent of Labour delegates were men. But in the years that followed, decline in British manufacturing, coupled with the rise of white-collar service-sector union members, gradually altered the basis of women's participation in the organized labour movement. During the 1980s, under Neil Kinnock's leadership, Labour made a great effort to change its public image, to attract more women into the party, and to adopt some radical affirmative action programmes (see below). Some of this was simply glossy packaging, for example the publicity material surrounding Labour's policy review presented strong images of women on its well-designed covers, but the review process had almost no input from party women's organizations. Other changes were more substantive: Labour women worked hard to enhance the role of women in the

Table 3.3   *Political efficacy and activism of party members by gender*

	Con. men	Con. women	Lab. men	Lab. women
Percentage 'would very likely'				
Sign petition	54	62	91	93
Contact MP	70	63	61	57
Contact media	30	21	34	31
Contact government department	28	26	23	26
Go on march	3	4	50	56
Join pressure group	15	11	37	43
Propose party motion	20	27	37	28
Percentage 'have often or sometimes'				
Sign petition	53	47	96	97
Contact MP	60	49	64	58
Contact media	30	30	51	46
Contact government department	30	25	32	25
Go on march	4	11	77	75
Join pressure group	17	15	58	64
Propose party motion	9	14	39	23
Political efficacy score[1]	6	5	10	10
Political activism score[2]	4	3	9	8

[1] The political efficacy score is computed by summing the top seven items scored on a four-point scale (very likely, quite likely, not likely, not at all likely).
[2] The political activism score is computed by summing the bottom seven items scored on a four-point scale (have often, sometimes, rarely, or never).

Source: British Candidate Study, 1992

party and tried to use the broader process of party modernization to achieve gender equality in the party organization and to get sex equality policies into the party programme (Lovenduski and Randall, 1993).

Yet surveys of Labour members suggest these steps, so far, have borne little fruit: women are generally less involved than men in most forms of party activities. During the 1970s Jill Hills estimated that women made up 40 per cent of individual members in the Labour party, and more recent surveys confirm that this remains unchanged (Hills, 1981).[4] The male dominance of the party is due, in part, to the party's long-standing ties with organized labour; almost one-fifth of male members (19 per cent) joined as a result of trade union work, compared with only 6 per cent of women members.[5]

But this is not the complete explanation since, among members, men were more active in party work across most indicators: men

Table 3.4 *Activism among Labour party members*

'Frequently'[1]	Men %	Women %	Diff. %
Displayed election poster	62	65	−3
Signed petition	56	59	−3
Leafletted during election	55	54	1
Donated money to Labour	32	30	2
Stood for party office	16	11	5
Stood for elected office	10	5	5
Attended party meeting	43	37	6
Canvassed voters	37	28	9

[1] Q. 'How often have you . . .?'

Source: Labour Party Survey 1989 [Seyd and Whiteley, 1992]

were more likely to see themselves as 'very strong' supporters, to represent Labour on official external bodies, to attend party meetings, to canvass during elections, and to be involved with party groups such as the Fabian Society, Campaign for Labour Party Democracy and Tribune (Table 3.4). More women than men were passive members, spending no time on party work (55–46 per cent respectively).[6] As in the Conservative party, there were modest gender differences in political efficacy and activism. But such disparities provide only a partial explanation for the gender gap in participation. And the reason does not appear to lie in the nature of party activity. In the membership survey people were asked to agree or disagree with a series of statements about party work, such as: 'Attending party meetings can be pretty tiring after a hard day's work', 'Many people find party meetings rather boring', and 'Party activity often takes time away from one's family'.[7] Across the range of items, women members were slightly more negative than men.

There is a gender gap evident at most levels of party office (Figure 3.2): men constitute 60 per cent of members but three-quarters of branch chairs, two-thirds of constituency general committee members, and two-thirds of constituency executive council members. At the highest levels in the Labour party, the National Executive Committee, five of the twenty-nine seats (17 per cent) are reserved for women.[8] In the Parliamentary party thirty-seven women Labour MPs were elected in 1992, or 14 per cent, up from 10 per cent in 1987.

The minor parties The Liberal Democrats do not record the sex of their members but women are 17 per cent of its Federal Policy

Percentage men   **Percentage women**

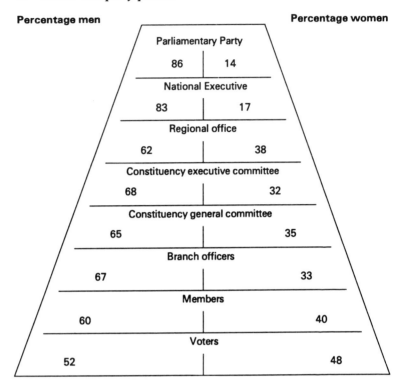

Figure 3.2   *Labour party organization (British Candidate Study, 1992)*

Committee, and 25 per cent of its Federal Executive. In the Scottish National party 35 per cent of members are women (Brand, 1992). Women are relatively well represented in the Green party, as party members (47 per cent), activists at party meetings, delegates at national conference, and candidates for local elected office (36 per cent), although there are relatively fewer women in regional and national party office (Rudig et al., 1991),

Local councillors
Information about women as local councillors is surprisingly scarce. The most recent published study, by the Widdicombe Committee in 1986, found that 19 per cent of local councillors were women in 1985. A study currently being conducted by Andrew Geddes suggests that in 1992 the figure was 25 per cent.[9]

Table 3.5   *Women candidates in British general elections, 1945–1992*

	Con.	Lab.	LDem.	PC/SNP	Total women	Total cand.	% women
1945	14	41	20	1	76	1542	4.9
1950	29	42	45	0	116	1721	6.7
1951	25	41	11	0	77	1349	5.7
1955	33	43	14	1	91	1367	6.6
1959	28	36	16	0	82	1487	5.5
1964	24	33	24	1	81	1661	4.9
1966	21	30	20	0	71	1605	4.4
1970	26	29	23	10	88	1686	5.2
1974 (Feb.)	33	40	40	10	123	1971	6.2
1974 (Oct.)	30	50	49	9	138	1971	7.0
1979	31	52	52	7	142	1929	7.4
1983	40	78	76	16	210	2009	10.4
1987	46	92	105	15	258	2004	12.9
1992	63	138	143	22	366	2003	18.3

Con., Conservative; Lab., Labour; LDem., Liberal Democrats; PC/SNP, Plaid Cymru/Scottish National Party.

Sources: Craig, 1989; *The Times Guide to the House of Commons,* 1983, 1987

Prospective Parliamentary candidates

From 1945 to 1970 the number of women selected by local constituencies as candidates for Parliament remained fairly stable; women accounted for about one in twenty candidates for the major parties. The number of Labour and Liberal women gradually started to increase from 1974 (Table 3.5), with a significant rise in all parties from 1979 onwards. In the 1992 general election about one in five candidates were women, a record number. Women were most successful in the opposition parties, in part because they normally include fewer incumbent MPs.

Members of Parliament

Trends in Parliament have lagged behind the rise in women's candidacies. Between 1945 and 1983 women were about 4 per cent of MPs. This was far lower than in most European countries, and indeed than in most developed democracies. The first signs of a break in this pattern came in 1987, when the number of women MPs jumped to 41, before rising to 60 in 1992 (Table 3.6). Women worked hard to achieve that improvement. Over time more women have been entering the campaign, but a lower proportion of female candidates have been successful.

During the post-war decade about one in three women candidates were returned to Parliament. In the early 1970s this

Table 3.6   *Women elected in British general elections,
1945–1992*

	Con.	Lab.	LDem.	PC/SNP	Others	Total women	% total MPs
1945	1	21	1	0	1	23	3.8
1950	6	14	1	0	0	21	3.4
1951	6	11	0	0	0	17	2.7
1955	10	14	0	0	0	24	3.8
1959	12	13	0	0	0	25	4.0
1964	11	18	0	0	0	29	4.6
1966	7	19	0	0	0	26	4.1
1970	15	10	0	0	1	26	4.1
1974 (Feb.)	9	13	0	1	0	23	3.6
1974 (Oct.)	7	18	0	2	0	27	4.3
1979	8	11	0	0	0	19	3.0
1983	13	10	0	0	0	23	3.5
1987	17	21	2	1	0	41	6.3
1992	20	37	2	1	0	60	9.2

Minor parties with no Parliamentary representation and parties from Northern Ireland are excluded. Abbreviations as Table 3.5.

Sources: Craig, 1989; The Times, 1992

ratio dropped to one in five women, and in the 1992 election it fell to one in six. This apparent paradox can be explained by three factors: the electoral weakness of the opposition parties, especially the Liberals who had the highest number of women candidates; low levels of incumbency turnover, which meant that there were few open seats; and the fact that where there were open party seats, few women were adopted. In short, women have had great difficulty getting selected for safe seats by major parties. As a result the successful reform party selection has come to be regarded as vital to the entry of women into the House of Commons.

In the major British political parties the process of candidate selection can be seen as a ladder of recruitment. At the base of the ladder are party voters, followed by party members, the national pool of eligibles, the constituency pool of applicants, the interviewees, prospective Parliamentary candidates and Members of Parliament (Figure 3.3). In Britain the critical stage is getting adopted by the Labour or the Conservative party for a good seat. Incumbency levels are high which means that relatively few 'safe' seats come up in a given election, competition is therefore fierce. The adoption of its parliamentary candidate is largely the prerogative of the local constituency party. National party bodies intervene to a limited extent: the Conservatives have a list of

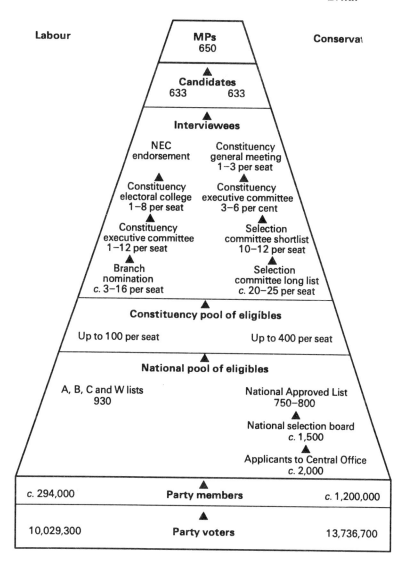

Labour **Conservai**

MPs
650

Candidates
633   633

Interviewees

NEC
endorsement

Constituency
general meeting
1–3 per seat

Constituency
electoral college
1–8 per seat

Constituency
executive committee
3–6 per cent

Constituency
executive committee
1–12 per seat

Selection
committee shortlist
10–12 per seat

Branch
nomination
c. 3–16 per seat

Selection
committee long list
c. 20–25 per seat

Constituency pool of eligibles

Up to 100 per seat

Up to 400 per seat

National pool of eligibles

A, B, C and W lists
930

National Approved List
750–800

National selection board
c. 1,500

Applicants to Central Office
c. 2,000

c. 294,000   **Party members**   c. 1,200,000

10,029,300   **Party voters**   13,736,700

Figure 3.3   *The Labour and Conservative ladder of selection.*
This diagram outlines the selection process for non-incumbents,
not the re-selection process for MPs. The figures represent the
approximate numbers involved at each state of the process in the
1987 general election (British Candidate Study, NEC Report
1990)

centrally approved candidates who can apply for seats, while Labour candidates must be endorsed at the end of the process by the NEC. Both parties have also established a set of national procedures governing the process: model rules in the Conservative party and a rather more lengthy, and more frequently revised, set of rules in the Labour party. Nevertheless, the importance of the local dimension means that there is limited scope in either party for initiatives from the centre to promote the candidacy of women.

Labour selection procedures   The Labour applicant faces a series of hurdles. The present procedures for the selection of Labour candidates came into effect in January 1989. The new rules replaced selection by the general committee of the constituency with a system involving the whole membership of the constituency party, via an electoral college which preserves a role for affiliated organizations, particularly the trade unions. Further reforms of Labour's candidate selection system await the results of a wide-ranging review of the nature of party membership which will focus on the relationship between the party and the trade unions. The rules had also been modified prior to the 1987 general election. Indeed, debate about candidate selection has been a feature of party politics for most of its time in opposition. At the time of writing it is difficult to predict the outcome of these debates. At the 1992 party conference it was clear that the trade unions were unwilling to give up their influence over candidate selection. But over time the direction of change has been towards democratizing the rules to increase the opportunity for individual members to influence the result. Thus we suggest (cautiously) that the current system is probably a staging post on the road to a 'one member, one vote' system of candidate selection.

Labour aspirants apply to be placed on the party's lists of candidates. There are four lists: the 'A' list of union sponsored candidates; the 'B' list nominated from constituencies; the 'C' list of Co-operative Party sponsored candidates; and the 'W' list of women candidates, drawn from the others. Being on these lists does not imply official Labour party approval. Labour lists are a fair indicator of the pool of candidates, but being on them is only a very preliminary, and unnecessary step in securing a nomination. Although the lists are distributed amongst selecting constituencies, often they are not consulted. Instead applicants must identify vacancies, then pursue nomination by a section of the constituency. The constituency branches and the affiliated organizations, such as union branches and the women's section, are empowered to put names forward to the constituency executive committee for shortlisting. Each branch and affiliate in a constituency may put forward one name. The shortlist is then drawn up according to detailed rules which are monitored by a representative of the NEC and by regional party agents. Once shortlisted, applicants address a constituency meeting. Under the present system voting takes place within an electoral college in which at least 60 per cent of the votes are cast by individual members and up to 40 per cent by affiliates. The recommended shortlist, in the absence of a sitting MP, is five names, although some may have more. The single transferable vote system is used: the individual with the lowest number of votes is eliminated until a candidate with an overall majority emerges. Once selected by the constituency, candidates need to be endorsed by the National Executive Committee, but this is usually a formality.

In the first stage of the process applicants circulate their curricula vitae amongst constituency branches and affiliates, to get invitations to address their meetings. Although branches normally determine their 'nominee' by election, affiliates may use other means and this has been the subject of considerable controversy. There are frequent accusations of trade union sharp practice at this stage of the process. Our observations of Labour selections for the BCS indicate that Labour selections for good seats are rarely 'open'. Most applicants go into the process believing there is a 'favourite' to beat. Although canvassing for nomination is explicitly banned, it is important to be known in the constituency. The successful applicant will normally have spent some time cultivating a constituency, a process that benefits local candidates who are also favoured by the rules governing the selection process. Securing the nomination can be a time-consuming and expensive business – the cost of travel and accommodation may deter some people. Moreover the extension of the selection decision to individual party members has given an advantage to well-known local activists, for example councillors or local trade union officials. Further democratization of the process would probably accelerate this trend.

Incumbent Labour MPs are currently subject to mandatory reselection within the lifetime of each Parliament. Although 'deselections' sometimes occur, it is not uncommon, where there is a sitting MP, for a shortlist of one (i.e. the sitting member), to be placed before the local association. Many MPs have received 100 per cent of the votes cast, thereby placing doubt on the merits of this expensive and time-consuming business. Further reform will replace mandatory reselection with a trigger mechanism where local parties can initiate new selection procedures when they are unhappy with their sitting MP.

Conservative selection procedures   The most significant difference in the Conservative party selection process is the role of Central Office in establishing the Approved List of candidates, an identifiable pool of talent into which local associations cast their nets. First, individuals are assessed by a regional officer of the party and the vice chair responsible for candidates. If successful, applicants are invited to attend a residential selection board where their political skills are assessed by leading party figures, officers of the National Union, and MPs. About half of those who attend are added to the list of approved candidates. Once on the list individuals are informed of impending selections. As in the Labour party, Conservative applicants must apply to selecting constituencies. To apply for a vacant seat applicants send their curricula vitae to Central Office which then forwards details to the constituency.

Local Conservative Associations establish a selection committee of fifteen to twenty, who sift the curricula vitae. This can be an onerous job in safe Tory seats, which may attract 200–300 applicants. The selection committee conducts interviews with selected applicants, and generally recommend four to six candidates to the executive committee – the governing body of the local association, which in safe seats could comprise about one hundred members. The executive interviews candidates, usually accompanied by their spouse, since many Conservative associations see themselves as selecting a team. Typically the executive recommends one to three candidates, who appear before the special general meeting which, in safe Conservative seats, may be attended by around 300 people. After interviews the winning candidate requires an overall majority, so there may be more than one round of voting.

The impact of the selection process   What do the selection processes mean for women aspirants? Is there discrimination against women by the party selectors? Or do women party members fail to come forward as applicants? And, equally important, how might we set about answering such questions? Discrimination is normally difficult to prove and is a complex matter to measure. There are a number of indicators which can be used to investigate this question (Lovenduski and Norris, 1989, 1991; Norris and Lovenduski, 1992; Norris et al., 1990). Within the space of this chapter, we will confine ourselves to one simple measure, the success rate of the women who come forward. In our study of candidacy in the 1992 general election all prospective Parliamentary candidates and a selection of unsuccessful list applicants were asked three questions about their experience:

1 For how many seats had they applied?
2 For how many were they interviewed?
3 For how many were they on the final shortlist?

Their replies detail the number of women and men at different rungs on the ladder of recruitment – as voters, party members, the national pool of eligibles, constituency interviewees, the shortlisted, prospective Parliamentary candidates and MPs.

For this analysis candidates can be divided into three categories. 'Incumbents' are all MPs elected in the previous general election who are re-standing in the same seat, and for the same party, in the subsequent general election. 'Inheritors' are candidates who have been selected for an open seat previously held by their own party, where the previous MP has retired. 'Challengers' are candidates fighting a seat held by another party.

In the Conservative party very few women take the first step of seeking a Parliamentary career, of applying to be on the Approved List. As a result there are few women at all the later stages – as constituency applicants, interviewees, and adopted candidates (Table 3.7). There is no evidence from these figures that Conservative women face any discrimination in this process, except possibly at the stage of inheriting a good seat.

For Labour the pattern is slightly more complex. Although 48 per cent of Labour voters are women they constitute only 40 per cent of party members, 37 per cent of aspirants on the party lists and 25 per cent of applicants to constituencies. After they apply, however, the proportion of women slightly increases in terms of those interviewed and shortlisted, decreasing again amongst those finally selected and decreasing more amongst 'inheritors'. This pattern can probably be explained in part by the Labour rule which stipulates that if a woman is nominated by any branch, then at least one woman must be shortlisted for interview.

We cannot conclude that either party operates direct discrimination against women applicants for winnable seats. In the 1992 general election women were only five of the fifty-seven Conservative inheritors, and three of the twenty-four Labour inheritors (Norris et al., 1992) But the numbers involved at this level are very small and we cannot be certain how many women applied for these seats. What is certain is that these are the crucial seats. Unless

Table 3.7   *Gender and the ladder of recruitment, 1992*

| | Conservative | | Labour | |
	Men %	Women %	Men %	Women %
Incumbents[1]	95	5	89	11
Inheritors[1]	89	11	88	12
Challengers[1]	86	14	72	28
Final shortlist	84	16	68	32
Interviewees	83	17	69	31
Seat applicants	87	13	75	25
List eligibles	83	17	63	37
Apply National Board	85	15	No equivalent	
Party members	52	48	60	40
Party voters	47	53	52	48

[1] See text for details.

Sources: British Candidate Study, 1992; Harris/ITN Exit Poll 9 April 1992

women get opportunities to inherit party seats and to be challengers in good target marginals, the masculine dominance of the Commons will continue.

Party strategies to promote women   Both Labour and the Conservatives have considered the use of positive discrimination for women candidates. For the Tories, so far, such consideration has been largely rhetorical. Party leaders have raised the issue in order to dismiss it as unjust in a party that promotes on the basis of merit. The Conservatives affirm that, while it is important for the party to have more women MPs, they are not prepared to consider the use of mandatory quotas for any stage of parliamentary selection. The implication is that the use of positive discrimination would result in the selection of women who are less qualified than the men that they would displace. Labour, on the other hand, has become more receptive to radical strategies of sex equality during the last decade. There are now rules to require that women are shortlisted, there are widespread debates about all-women shortlists and the party is in the process of implementing gender quotas on all of its internal councils and deliberative bodies. But, despite strong pressure, Labour has not adopted a quota of women MPs and instead has approved the weaker target of 40 per cent women's presence in the Parliamentary Labour party by the year 2000.[10] At the time of writing there is widespread concern amongst party feminists that it has no way of ensuring the target will achieved.

What else could be done? When we asked party members and candidates about the representation of women, they expressed clear dissatisfaction with the present situation. When asked – 'Do you think there should be more women in Parliament, about the same as now, or fewer women in Parliament' – there was overwhelming support for increasing female representation (Table 3.8). The problem is evaluating which reform measures would be most effective, within the context of the British political system. British parties often claim they would like to improve the number of women in Parliament, yet if the final selection is left in the hands of the local selectorate it can be argued there is little that the national organizations can do to change matters. Accordingly we asked party members, candidates and MPs whether they approved or disapproved of a series of measures proposed to remedy the under-representation of women (Table 3.9)

The results suggest there was almost unanimous support within the Labour party for three proposals: party training programmes for women, better childcare facilities within Parliament, and changing the hours of Parliamentary sittings. These measures were also supported by a majority of Conservatives. These can be seen as largely 'facilitating' steps, which may make it easier for women to embark on a Parliamentary career. As such, they might encourage more women to come forward, if they feel that they are trained in the appropriate skills for political life, and if Parliament was reformed to make an MP's workload more compatible with normal family life. In contrast there was less bipartisan support for affirmative action and financial aid for women candidates. A majority of Labour party members and candidates favoured the use of positive quotas and financial support designed to help women candidates but these options found little or no support among Conservatives. Programmes designed to compensate for discrimination against certain groups within the selection process are therefore more controversial ideologically.

Accordingly, if parties want to increase the number of women in Parliament, facilitating measures including party training programmes and the reform of Parliament command general support but there are differences over the use of quotas. So far neither party has implemented quotas of women for its Parliamentary wing. But this similarity should not obscure important party differences in sex equality strategies. Although effectively more decentralized and less feminine, Labour has been much more

Table 3.8   *Attitudes towards women in Parliament*[1]

	Conservative			Labour		
	Members	PPCs	MPs	Members	PPCs	MPs
More women	72	78	79	94	94	97
Same as now	26	10	8	5	0	2
Fewer women	1	1	4	1	0	0

[1] Q. 'Do you feel that there should be many more women in Parliament, a few more, about the same as now, or fewer women in Parliament?'

Source: British Candidate Study, 1992

Table 3.9   *Approval of policy proposals*[1]

	Conservative			Labour		
	Members	PPCs	MPs	Members	PPCs	MPs
Party training for women	79	73	70	92	98	93
Better childcare facilities in Parliament	58	63	52	93	100	97
Changing the hours of Parliament	58	56	47	90	95	76
Financial support for women PPCs	24	9	2	59	62	37
Positive quotas	26	4	4	64	79	62

[1] Q. 'Do you approve or disapprove of the following proposals for increasing the number of women in Parliament?' Combined percentage for 'strongly approve' or 'approve'.

Source: British Candidate Study, 1992

successful in promoting women. Women accounted for 14 per cent of the Parliamentary Labour party in 1992 but only 6 per cent of Conservative MPs. During the 1980s Labour adopted a series of measures explicitly designed to promote women in the party. These measures included the adoption of targets and quotas at most levels of the party that have become part of the party rulebook (Atkinson and Spear, 1992; Lovenduski and Randall 1993). During the same period the Conservatives have stepped up their informal encouragement of women in their party, but have made no explicit commitments to securing gender equality or parity in positions of influence. This striking difference between the two parties is partly the result of the different ways that they do politics. Differences in their treatment of issues of sex equality in political representation parallel different understandings of the meaning of equal opportunities and of political representation. However, the obvious differences in the *priority* that equality of representation is given results from differences in the ways that women in the two parties have organized and worked to achieve it.

Party women and equality strategy

During the 1960s and 1970s both parties supported the legislation of equal pay and equal opportunities for men and women at work. That support had been won by long campaigns by women in each party, campaigns that were often led by women MPs, and supported by women's party organizations and women's trade union branches. The campaigns also brought new women's organizations and alliances into existence within the parties and strengthened those that already existed. By the end of the 1970s Labour women, reinforced by an influx of feminists from the Women's Liberation Movement, were looking for ways to increase women's representation in the party.

Although some Labour party women continued to regard feminist politics as an unacceptable diversion from the class struggle, their influence and number declined during the 1980s. At the beginning of the 1980s Labour party women's organizations lacked power and were not easily used to press issues of interest to women. The Labour party women's organization is a structure of sections, councils and conferences that parallel key party organizations and which depends upon the National Executive Committee for its influence. In the early 1980s, a strong internal feminist campaign, led by the Labour Women's Action Committee (LWAC), pressed the party to empower its women's organization and to increase the number of its women MPs. At first the campaign appeared to be unsuccessful, but, gradually, many of its objectives gained support. By the end of the decade the Labour leadership was in the process of implementing a wide-ranging programme to enhance the status of party women, including quotas for women at all levels of the party organization although, as stated above, this stopped short at the point of designating a mandatory quota of women candidates.

Throughout the 1980s Labour was engaged in a programme of internal reform and modernization designed to increase its electoral appeal. Although the LWAC was too closely associated with the left of the party to influence policy, many of its arguments were taken up by women better placed to get their proposals accepted. They were able to persuade the party leadership to seek to expand its electoral constituency of women (Lovenduski and Randall, 1993: ch. 5) All this made it more receptive to internal feminist pressure to address issues of sex equality in its organization and on its programme. Women organized within the party were a driving force in this process (Lovenduski and Randall, 1993; Perrigo, 1991).

In the Conservative party a different philosophy has developed. Women are the mainstay of the party organization, the majority of its members and the bulk of its electoral support. But it is difficult to identify a rising feminist tendency in the party itself. The Conservative tradition of unity and loyalty normally obscures its internal divisions. During most of the 1980s the Conservatives, led by Mrs Thatcher, appeared to take their capacity to represent women for granted. Some Conservative women with political ambitions complained about the lack of opportunity for women (Campbell, 1987). Many were active in the 300 Group, an all-party group established to get at least 300 women into Parliament. But, within the party, sustained and visible organizational efforts on behalf of women were focused on policy issues such as equal taxation and childcare provision rather than on organizational matters or the equitable representation of women and men (Lovenduski et al., 1993). Nevertheless, at the beginning of the 1990s there were some signs that the Conservatives were becoming more sensitive to the need to promote women's representation. When John Major failed to include any women in his first cabinet there was an uproar in the party. His second cabinet included two women. After the 1992 election the new party chairman, Norman Fowler, said he wanted at least 100 women candidates by the time of the next general election. Party managers announced their efforts to recruit more women candidates and a number of conspicuous public appointments of women to prominent positions were made (Lovenduski and Randall, 1993: ch. 5). Some young women candidates were given prominent roles in key debates at the 1992 party conference.

The way that the Conservatives address the issue of sex equality is typical of the party's recruitment practices. These techniques will, more and more, be mobilized in support of party women. A 'tap on the shoulder' in the form of a special invitation to apply might be offered to a likely candidate and party managers will highlight the need to have more women candidates in their discussions with constituency leaders. This is the way that things are done in the party and often it works. But resistance to affirmative action is strong and much, ultimately, depends on what Conservative women do to claim their place. At present the party has two constituencies of women to satisfy within its membership: the modern working women who are juggling their political ambitions with a variety of domestic and employment roles, and the traditional, older local women members who are not in paid employment and who exercise considerable influence in constituency organizations. A strategy to 'encourage' qualified women to stand is perhaps the only way of satisfying both constituencies.

Conclusions

Although most British political parties profess official support for an increased political role for women, our analysis of the two major parties shows that the imperatives of internal party politics are a major factor in the success women have had in securing party and parliamentary positions. There are significant differences in the way that women have organized in the two parties and the degrees of success that they have had. Labour women organized to increase women's representation over a decade ago, and their repeated calls for positive action are now official party policy. Conservative women have raised the issue on an individual basis, and their organizations have not made demands for positive action for women candidates. There are two ways of interpreting the results. On the one hand it may be argued that Labour women have done better. Despite having a smaller membership and voting base than the Conservatives, Labour women have succeeded in persuading their party to take up issues of women's representation and to adopt a number of far-reaching policies to enhance it. One result is that Labour has fielded more women candidates and elected more women MPs. On the other hand, it may be argued that women are the backbone of the Conservative party and play a major role as voters, members and local leaders. Although there are fewer Conservative women candidates and MPs, this is because fewer women apply. Those who do are relatively more successful. Thus a strategy to encourage women informally is appropriate to the circumstances of the party and women have no need to press for more radical methods.

It is easier to agree about the impact of the political environment on the parties. A party's receptivity to women is influenced by its political fortunes, and Labour has looked hard for ways to attract women to the new coalition of support that it must form if it is to govern. The Conservatives, too, became more interested in promoting women towards the end of the 1980s, when voting patterns indicated that it could no longer take the support of British women for granted.

Notes

The authors gratefully acknowledge the financial support of the ESRC, Research Grant R-000-23-1991, which has funded the British Candidate Study.

1 The data for this chapter are derived from the British Candidate Study, 1992 (BCS), a two-part survey of party members and potential candidates. The BCS survey of party members is based on a sample of 1634 Labour and Conservative activists attending selection meetings in twenty-six constituencies throughout Britain. The constituencies to which we had access were chosen to be broadly representative in terms of party, major census region and marginality. Fieldwork was conducted between January 1990 and October 1991. The main questionnaire was distributed to members at meetings with a more detailed follow-up postal questionnaire for self-completion. Because the survey was distributed at selection meetings, it may well over-represent the more active party members. Accordingly supplementary information about Labour was derived from the Labour Party Membership Survey 1989, a random sample of members with 5065 respondents, directed by Paul Whitely and Pat Seyd. The authors are most grateful to them for releasing this dataset. For further details see Seyd and Whitely (1992) *Labour's Grassroots: the Politics of Labour Party Membership*. Differences between comparable items in this survey and the BCS were found to be very minor.

Lastly we used the BCS candidate survey, distributed to all MPs and prospective Parliamentary candidates in Britain for the Conservative, Labour, Liberal Democrat, Scottish Nationalist, Plaid Cymru and Green parties. Fieldwork was conducted in two main waves from April 1990 to October 1991. Out of 1913 names we received completed replies from 1320, a response rate of 69 per cent. The candidate questionnaires were followed up in the summer and autumn of 1992 with forty in-depth interviews of a balanced sample of the pool of candidates. In addition all parts of the study were supplemented by in-depth interviews with party agents and officials.

2 The Gallup surveys are reprinted in Durant (1969). The British Election surveys (BES) are in Crewe et al. (1991). For the traditional literature see Lipset (1960), Pulzer (1967), Almond and Verba (1963). For a critique of the traditional literature see Goot and Reid (1984) and Randall (1987).

3 Harris/ITN Exit Poll 9 April 1992, N.4, 701.

4 The Labour Party Membership Survey 1989 found that women were 40 per cent of party members and this figure was confirmed by the BCS in 1992.

5 The Labour Party Membership Survey 1989 question was 'Did you become a party member as a result of voluntary work in your trade union or staff association?'

6 The question was 'How much time do you devote to party activities in the average month?' Labour Party Membership Survey 1989.

7 The figures were as follows. 'Attending party meetings can be pretty tiring after a hard day's work': strongly agree – 25 per cent of women and 14 per cent of men. 'Many people find party meetings rather boring': strongly agree – 16 per cent of women and 17 per cent of men. 'Party meetings often take time away from one's

family': strongly agree – 18 per cent of women and 20 per cent of men. Labour Party Membership Survey, 1989.

8 This is due to be replaced by a 40 per cent quota in the mid 1990s.

9 We are grateful to Andrew Geddes for supplying us his interim results.

10 We use the term quota when the policy is mandatory, and target when the figure refers to goal or guideline proportion of women that party leaders wish to encourage selectors to achieve.

4

Making Her Way In: Women, Parties and Candidacies in Canada

Lynda Erickson

During the 1980s, national party politics in Canada began to take on a new face as women mobilized in increasing numbers to address the gender inequities that pervaded politics. Yet while parties responded to women's activism in a variety of ways, one touchstone of women's success, the election of a substantial number of women to the House of Commons, remained an elusive goal. Evidence from aggregate voting patterns suggests the Canadian electorate does not discriminate against women at the polls (Hunter and Denton, 1984), but it is also clear that selection as a major party candidate has been virtually essential for election to Parliament.[1] Not surprisingly then, the issue of women candidacies has become a central aspect of gender politics for the parties. In exploring ways in which the three major Canadian parties have responded to women's demands for greater equity in national politics,[2] this chapter focuses on responses of the parties to demands for greater representation of women among their candidates, especially in candidacies with a chance of success. Special attention is given to two factors that are important for the issue of women candidacies. The first is the highly localized nature of candidate selection in Canadian parties, something that complicates attempts to increase the number of women candidates. The second is party ideologies that vary in terms of their interventionist versus voluntarist approaches to equity issues such as the under-representation of women.

The Canadian national party system

The current Canadian party system is in flux. Three parties, the Progressive Conservatives, the Liberals and the New Democrats (NDP), now dominate the House of Commons, but they face strong regional pressures in the form of a Quebec separatist party, the Bloc Québecois,[3] and a right-wing western Canadian party, the Reform party.[4] The expanded political agenda represented in these two new parties has especially undermined support for the governing Conservative party and may ultimately reshape the national party system.

While the future of the current party system may be in doubt, the three parties that now monopolize the legislature have, in the past, shown remarkable survival capacities. The Conservative and Liberal parties, the only ones to have formed national governments in Canada, have their roots in politics that predated the creation of the country in 1867 (Thorburn, 1991). The NDP had its beginnings in the Great Depression as a socialist alternative that called itself the Cooperative Commonwealth Federation (CCF). In 1962, in an attempt to extend its ties with labour and expand its electoral support, the party reorganized and took on its present name. Although it has usually held fewer than half the number of Commons seats of either the Conservatives or Liberals,[5] the NDP has been an important factor in national politics because of its potential to take seats from the two larger parties.

The political spectrum represented by the three major parties is fairly narrow. For much of the post-war period, the Conservative and Liberal parties behaved in a highly brokerage manner, hugging the centre of the political spectrum and appealing to the electorate more in terms of competence and leadership than on grounds of policy differences. But in the mid-1970s, the Conservative party adopted a more neo-conservative approach to policy issues and it now stands to the right of the Liberals, albeit retaining much of its centrist cast (Brodie, 1991). On the other side of the spectrum, the NDP is a moderate, social democratic party. Early in its history as the CCF, the party began modifying its socialist platform and rhetoric (Young, 1968; Zakuta, 1964), putting more emphasis on the notion of a mixed economy. It now advocates a substantial welfare state presence in society, but no fundamental restructuring of the economy.

The single member plurality electoral system used in elections for the House of Commons tends to favour the two larger parties, but the regionalism of Canadian politics has supported both the persistence of the NDP and the sporadic appearance of other regional parties. As a result, although there has been only one exception to single party government, on a number of occasions the party in power has not had an absolute majority of seats in the House of Commons.

Women's organizational participation in Canadian parties

The three major parties have experienced different pressures from and have responded in different ways to the political activism of women that began with the second wave women's movement in the late 1960s.[6] As will be seen below, different responses were apparent in the organizational accommodations made to women and in the parties' approach to the problem of increasing their number of female candidates. To an important degree these differences reflect the ideologies of the parties and the women who participate in them.

In the late 1960s the role of women in Canadian parties paralleled the story well known elsewhere in the western world. Women's electoral work was an important mainstay of the parties, particularly the local associations, but except for the job of local party secretary, women seldom occupied major executive positions at either the local or national party level (Royal Commission on the Status of Women in Canda, 1970). Even more unusual was the selection of women as party candidates in national elections. In the 1968 federal general election only 3 per cent of the candidates for the three major parties were women and more than three-quarters of these ran for the NDP, the least electorally successful.

The Conservatives and Liberals had separate women's auxiliaries in their local branches and parallel women's organizations at the national level. Although women from these organizations were given occasional *ex officio* positions in the parties' decision-making structures, the auxiliaries were typically outside the mainstream of party politics, performing many service tasks but lacking any essential influence in party policy-making (Bashevkin, 1985). Few auxiliaries saw their role as one of supporting women for important positions within the parties, or for party candidacies.

Perhaps the most influential function performed by the national organizations of the extra-parliamentary parties in Canada is choosing the party leader. Thus, the specially convened national conventions that assumed this task have been important as forums of representation, with delegates from many sectors of the parties, including the local constituency associations. In 1967 and 1968 the Conservatives and Liberals, respectively, held national leadership conventions that, for the first time, had delegate selection rules requiring at least one delegate from each local constituency association be a woman (Royal Commission on the Status of Women in Canada, 1970).

In contrast to the other major parties, the NDP never had

separate women's organizations nor any other system of special membership for women. Local and national women's committees were created to address the special needs and problems of women, but through most of the 1960s these committees tended to focus on more traditional fund-raising and social activities, and did not function as organizations which promoted women within the party hierarchy (Bashevkin, 1985). Furthermore, at their leadership conventions the NDP kept with their philosophy that neither women nor men should have special membership status, and made no provision in their delegate selection rules for guaranteed representation of women.

For the growing feminist movement of the time, the position of women in the parties was an object of considerable criticism. Women's auxiliaries in particular were characterized as an institutionalization of the second-class (and service) role of women. Demands for organizational reform that included the abolition of women's auxiliaries as well as the inclusion of more women in national party elites became more frequent and were given semi-official sanction in 1970 by the report of a royal commission on the status of women. This commission characterized women's roles in the parties as primarily 'supportive' and recommended the women's associations in the parties be 'amalgamated with the main bodies of [the] parties' (Royal Commission on the Status of Women in Canada, 1970: 384).

Pressures on the parties to reform and accommodate more women into their power structures came from the women's movement generally, and from women within party ranks. Pressure from within was especially apparent in the New Democratic and the Liberal parties, as feminists were more attracted to them compared to the Conservative party (Bashevkin, 1985). An early NDP response to women's demands was the creation of a committee on the Participation of Women (POW) in 1969 and the establishment of a position of women's organizer in 1971. Although various factional splits in the party in the 1970s complicated the experience of POW and the women's organizers, their impact was felt by the end of the decade. In 1981 the party adopted an internal (voluntary) affirmative action programme to seek out and train women for party office. Then, in 1983, the party passed a resolution that required gender parity on the two governing bodies of the national party: the Federal Council and the Federal Executive. Since that time four of the five national party presidents have been women.

For national party conventions, the NDP continued its policy on delegate selection, having no provisions guaranteeing representation for women. The requirements for gender parity in the governing councils of the party do, indirectly, guarantee some female representation, since such officers are given positions as *ex officio* delegates, but these *ex officio* delegates compose only a small proportion of each convention (Wearing, 1988). Another route to delegate status is as a representative for the trade union affiliates of the party, but these trade union delegations have few women members, a reflection of the gender structure of the trade union movement. As a result, women typically come to the conventions as constituency representatives. The number of women attending national party conventions are not officially recorded, however, surveys of the conventions suggest women are outnumbered two to one (Whitehorn, 1989). Yet, notwithstanding this representational structure, the NDP was the first major party in Canada to elect a woman as national leader. Audrey McLaughlin was selected leader of the party in December 1989.

In the Liberal party, organizational reform began with the abolition of the national women's auxiliary in 1973 and its replacement by the Women's Liberal Commission (National Women's Liberal Commission, 1990), later renamed the National Women's Liberal Commission (NLWC). Unlike its predecessor, the Commission is part of the larger party organization, not a separate affiliate, and membership is open to all women members who belong to Liberal Party of Canada organizations (Bashevkin, 1985).[7] Its mandate has been to 'represent and promote the interests of women within the Party', (Liberal Party of Canada, 1986) a different focus than the service ethic that tended to pervade the earlier organization. But in 1973 this change was not without its critics among women party members (Myers, 1989; Wearing, 1981), who were more divided in their support for feminist objectives than were NDP women.

Other programmes to move women into the organizational hierarchy of the Liberal party were later in coming and tended to be less interventionist than those of the NDP. With the exception of provisions for delegates to national conventions, affirmative action efforts were largely limited to data collection, and the guarantee of a woman's position on various national party committees and commissions. By 1983, however, 43 per cent of the national executive were women (Bashevkin, 1985) and the party elected its first woman president. In 1986 the party's constitution was revised to include the provision that the party shall 'respect the principle of equal division between men and women in the structure and operations of the Liberal Party to the greatest extent possible' (Liberal Party of Canada, 1986). The

Women's Commission used this provision to pressure the national executive to add women members to various national party committees whenever appointments to such committees were made. The current policy is for gender parity in appointments to committees, but elected positions in the party are not subject to gender regulations. On the national executive the proportion of women representatives has declined since 1986 and currently stands at 35 per cent.

Provisions for women delegates at national Liberal party conventions were in contrast to the more voluntarist approach of most of the other party efforts with respect to women. From 1968, the party increased its gender requirements so that for the last leadership convention in 1990, women were guaranteed half the delegate positions from local constituency associations and half the delegates from youth clubs. Women were under-represented among the *ex officio* delegates but they were assured of a number of other delegate positions by virtue of the women's Liberal clubs that were allocated representation (Liberal Party of Canada, 1986).[8] According to the final tally at the 1990 convention, 47 per cent of the delegates were women (Bashevkin, 1991).

The Conservatives' responses to the demands of women came more slowly. The party retained its separate national women's association until 1980, and then, the following year, created a new organization (Bashevkin, 1985). Originally titled the National PC Women's Caucus and now called the National Progressive Conservative Women's Federation (NPCWF), this association provides a 'formal executive structure for the representation of women' in the party (National Progressive Conservative Women's Federation, 1989: 2). In 1981 the party also established a national Women's Bureau, the goal of which is to 'encourage and assist women to become involved' in the party (*Network*, 1990: 4).[9] Part of the agenda of this bureau has been to organize local or regional women's caucuses that function at a more intimate level, recruiting and training women for participation in the mainstream of the party organization. (By 1991 twelve caucuses had been formed.) Like the Liberals, the Conservatives reserved some of the positions on the party's national executive for representatives of their women's federation, but still, in 1983 the proportion of women on the Conservative national executive was only 24 per cent. By 1990, however, this had increased to 43 per cent.

With respect to guarantees for women's representation at leadership conventions, the Conservatives have increased their requirements for local constituency delegations although they have not matched those of the Liberal party. According to the

Conservative party constitution, only two of the six regular delegates sent from local associations must be women and there are no gender quotas for the additional three youth delegates to which each association is entitled. Unlike the Liberals the party does not have gender requirements for the delegates from its youth clubs, although it does allocate representation for its affiliated women's associations. At its most recent leadership convention, in June 1993, the proportion of female delegates was lower than that at the Liberal convention of 1990 – 34 per cent of registered Conservative delegates were women[10] – however the party did become the second major national party to select a woman leader. Kim Campbell was elected to replace the retiring leader and as a result she became Canada's first woman prime minister.

Not surprisingly, the kind of changes the parties have made to accommodate women within their organizations reflect the way in which the parties are arrayed on the ideological spectrum. The right-of-centre party, the Conservatives, has been both slower to adopt new reforms and more voluntarist in its approach to increasing female representation. By comparison, the Liberals responded more quickly to the feminist movement and although their affirmative action provisions primarily focused on delegate selection for national conventions, their regulations on delegate representation came closer to demanding gender parity. But the NDP adopted the first organizational reforms in response to women's demands and the NDP has been more interventionist, developing the most comprehensive programme of affirmative action to promote women within their party hierarchy.

These party differences appear to reflect differences in attitudes on women's issues generally among party activists. Thus, surveys of delegates attending the Liberal and Conservative conventions in 1983 and 1984 found significant inter-party differences on two of the three survey questions that could be identified as women's issues, with the Liberals more likely to choose the feminist response (Brodie, 1989). On the third question, on abortion, the left–right ideological dimension was confounded by a religious dimension: the more left-wing Liberal party had proportionally more Catholics among its delegates than the Conservative party did. A survey was also done of the 1983 NDP biennial national party convention (which was not a leadership convention) but the only comparable question included in the survey protocol was one on abortion. On this issue the NDP delegates were clearly pro-choice (85 per cent chose the pro-choice option) and substantially more so that either the Liberal or Conservative delegates.

Women and party candidacies

While the struggle to improve women's position within the party organizations has not been a particularly easy one, it pales in comparison to the problem faced by those attempting to increase substantially the number of women selected as national party candidates, especially in ridings they can hope to win. Some of the difficulties in achieving this objective can be attributed to a variety of social factors similar to those encountered by women in other western countries. But in addition, in Canada the system of candidate selection is extraordinarily localized and this has further confounded the task.

Party selection

The process of selecting major party candidates has been dominated by the local party constituency associations that form the basic organizational units of the parties. These associations, which each choose a single party nominee, have determined most of their own rules and practices for choosing their candidate and they have done so with little supervision from the wider party establishment (Carty and Erickson, 1991). The procedure usually consists of a special meeting of the constituency association at which any number of individuals may be nominated for the candidacy. Those local members who are present at the selection meeting vote to decide who will receive the party endorsement.

The local members, virtually all of whom are eligible to participate in the selection process, typically have not wanted direction from outside party officials as to how, or whom, to choose as their local candidate. For most members, their right to select the local party candidate is one of the few ways in which they can exercise any influence within the national party. Thus local independence in the performance of this important party function has been supported by norms of party democracy and grassroots participation.

This has left the national party organizations with little voice in the selection process. The mechanisms by which national parties could intervene have been limited, and party leaders have been reluctant to use the most draconian means available to affect local choice: the use of the leader's veto over those who are allowed to register officially under the party's label. (Since 1972, when it first became part of the electoral law, the leader's veto has been used only twice by the major parties.) Party officials from outside an association could perhaps have played an informal role in the outcome of local selection, if, for example, they assisted local organizations in finding prospective candidates. But even this was not done very often (Carty and Erickson, 1991). With such a decentralized system it was difficult for a party, or women within a party, to coordinate the efforts necessary to effect gender quotas or a gender strategy.

The selection of women candidates: 1968–1984

Women have not been very well served by this local selection system. From 1968 until the 1980 election, the proportion of major party candidates who were women increased from 4 to only 8 per cent. In 1980 the proportion of women among those who won was only 6 per cent. Given this context of glacial change, the 1984 election was a remarkable event. The percentage of women candidates in the three parties virtually doubled and 10 per cent of the candidates who won seats were women. The political circumstances of the time influenced this progress. In particular, the strength of the women's movement and the perceived importance of a 'women's vote' prompted the parties to focus more attention on women's issues and to consider nominating more women as part of their overall gender strategy (Brodie, 1985; Erickson, 1991).

The increased strength and visibility of the women's movement was partly a result of the effective struggle it had waged in the intense constitutional politics of the early 1980s. With the prospect of a Charter of Rights being placed in the Canadian Constitution, women's groups had mobilized in order to ensure that women's rights would be protected as effectively as possible. In the process, they gained media attention and popular exposure. But the experience of those directly involved in this exercise had also taught them that for many politicians, women's interests were expendable (Hosek, 1983). The result was a more focused and vigilant women's constituency. Its success in demanding attention from politicians was evident in the 1984 election campaign when a nationally televised leaders' debate on women's issues was held in response to demands by the National Action Committee on the Status of Women, an umbrella organization that includes a substantial proportion of Canada's women's groups in its membership. For an hour the leaders were questioned about their parties' policies on issues of particular concern to women.

The perceived importance of a 'women's vote' had grown in response to an increased awareness of gender differences in party preferences. Public opinion polls documenting these differences had become an issue of media comment (Kome, 1985) in which the gender gap was being linked to the parties' sensitivities to women's issues. The Conservatives became concerned because their popularity among women voters lagged behind that of men (Terry, 1984),[11] while the Liberals, who appeared to be the major beneficiaries of this, had a clear interest in reinforcing their support among women voters. The NDP had always seen itself as the pioneer on women's issues and, for the first time in its electoral history, appeared poised to benefit from this position.[12]

But the parties' efforts varied when it came to women candidates for the 1984 election. All three party leaders proclaimed their goal was to increase the number of women from their party elected to the House of Commons. And having heard from their women party members that fighting elections was financially onerous for women, both the Liberal and New Democratic parties established special funds to assist their women candidates in the election. The Conservatives followed, establishing a similar fund after the election. There were also various party workshops for women, including some on becoming a candidate. Activities that specifically targeted women were more extensive, systematic and centrally directed in the NDP while among the Liberals and Conservatives such programmes were largely left to local initiatives.

Notwithstanding these party differences, the reality of localized candidate selection was apparent in all three organizations. It was difficult for the national parties to play a major part in local nominations and their role in the selection of women was primarily one of encouragement as opposed to direct intervention. The results of this localized selection reflected the pattern in other organizational reforms: the NDP ran the largest number of women (23 per cent of their candidates), the Liberals were second (16 per cent) and the Conservatives ran the fewest of the three (8 per cent).

While the 1984 election marked a shift in the pace of change, as these figures indicate, it did not herald anything approaching gender parity. The total number of women running for Parliament was still small and many of them had been selected for constituency battles they had little hope of winning. Among major party candidates, only 21 per cent of the women won their seats compared with 36 per cent of the men. Moreover, among these successful women were a number of Conservative MPs who had won unexpected victories in Quebec. In that province the Conservative party had traditionally been a very weak competitor – during the previous decade fewer than 2 per cent of Conservative MPs were from Quebec – but a disproportionate number of its women candidates ran there in 1984. Almost half (48 per cent) of the Conservative party's women candidates ran in Quebec ridings whereas only 27 per cent of the seats the party contested were in that province.

Women and candidate selection in the 1988 election

The context and party activities
Candidate selection for the November 1988 election took place in the context of a highly competitive three-way race for public popularity. The timing of selection was, in most instances, the choice of the local party and from January to October there was a continuous series of local meetings. During most of this period, all three parties had reason to be optimistic about their chances in the election. For the first time the NDP could seriously consider itself as much a contender for government office as the other two parties, given it had topped the opinion polls for a few months in 1987. For their part, the Liberals struggled with a continuing leadership crisis, but by November of 1987 they had edged above the NDP in the polls. The Conservatives were also beginning to retrieve some of their popularity, which had plummeted only a couple of years after they had won the 1984 election with an unprecedented number of seats in the House of Commons. Moreover, as the governing party they enjoyed a number of advantages available to those in power, including the choice of the election date.

Prior to, and during the selection period, women's organizations voiced their demands for more women candidates. A new non-partisan organization, Canadian Women for Political Representation, was formed and held conferences across the country publicizing the importance of having women in public office and encouraging women to run for Parliament. The Canadian Advisory Council on the Status of Women, a national government research and advocacy agency for women, published a background paper which focused on the issue of women candidates (Canadian Advisory Council on the Status of Women, 1987). This was distributed in late 1987 before most local constituencies selected their candidates.

As in the 1984 election, the parties continued to be sensitive to the 'women's vote'. The governing Conservative party had announced a childcare policy late in 1987 and pointed to this as evidence of their commitment to women's concerns. They also argued their record of appointing women to senior positions via patronage and other appointment procedures was a substantial improvement on the record of previous (Liberal) governments. The opposition parties unveiled their own, more extensive childcare policies and continued to criticize the government's record on women.

The leaders of all three parties made it clear they remained committed to the goal of increasing the number of women who ran for their parties. But again, in terms of party activity directed to achieving this goal, the NDP led the others. It had a national party committee that identified ridings where there were women who might consider contesting the party candidacy and the national party president or an NDP member of parliament then contacted those women and encouraged them to run. The party continued its regional workshops for women, including ones on contesting a candidacy, and there was a national party conference for women who were actual or potential contestants. Finally, the party put a freeze on candidate selection until January 1988. It was thought that this would assist women because later selection gives people without a high profile in the party a better chance of being competitive for a candidacy and because the nature of women's employment may make it difficult for many of them to commit to an electoral race far in advance of an election.

In the Liberal party, targeting and encouraging women for candidacies was a more informal and decentralized enterprise. The NLWC published brochures on how to contest local candidacies and sent them to local constituency associations, not directly to individual Liberal women. Training programmes for women, when they occurred, were again undertaken on local initiative.

Among the Conservatives, workshops directed to women were also locally orchestrated. In May of 1988, there was a national conference sponsored by the NPCWF and the Women's Bureau but its primary concern was the overall involvement of women in the party. It did not specifically target the issue of how women could become candidates. The problem of increasing the number of Conservative women candidates was exacerbated by the few candidacies that would likely be available. The party had a very large number of incumbents intending to seek reselection and systemic norms almost guarantee incumbents will be reselected.[13]

The selection of women
The data used for the following analysis of candidate selection in the 1988 election include both aggregate statistics from the Office of the Chief Electoral Officer[14] and the results of a local selection survey conducted immediately following the 1988 general election.[15] These data indicate there was an improvement in the overall percentage of women running as candidates for the major parties but the pace of change was modest compared with that recorded in the previous election. According to the aggregate statistics, 20 per cent of those contesting the election for the three parties were women, a one-third increase from the 1984 election. If

we look only at candidates who were not incumbent members of parliament, the picture improves, but only modestly: 23 per cent of all non-incumbent candidates were women.

The partisan distribution of female candidates reflected the previously established pattern: the NDP selected the largest number (28 per cent of their candidates were women), the Liberals were second (with 18 per cent), while only 13 per cent of the candidates for the winning Conservative party were women. The Conservative numbers improve when we look at non-incumbent candidates, but even here they still trail the Liberals and especially the NDP (Table 4.1). Sixteen per cent of non-incumbent Conservative candidates were women compared with 19 per cent of non-incumbent Liberal candidates and 30 per cent of non-incumbent NDP candidates.

The record on the placement of women candidates was also similar to previous patterns. Women were under-represented in those candidacies with the best chances of electoral success. This was evident in the aggregate and survey data. Using the former, a measure of local party competitiveness was constructed from the local parties' electoral showing in the previous general election.[16] According to this measure, only 12 per cent of the female candidates, compared with 25 per cent of the male candidates, contested in their parties' safe seats (Table 4.2). The proportions of women and men in safe candidacies become more similar among non-incumbent candidates, 4 and 7 per cent respectively, but as these numbers suggest, there were few such safe candidacies available outside of those occupied by incumbents.

The survey findings reflect the aggregate figures. Respondents to the survey had been asked if their local party association considered its electoral chances in the local riding to be 'safe', 'good chance', 'unlikely' or 'hopeless' *at the time the party was nominating its candidate.* This measure is a useful complement to one based on local party performance in the previous election because it assessed party perceptions of local competitiveness in the context of highly fluid party preferences among the public. According to these survey data, 11 per cent of women candidates compared with 20 per cent of men, ran in safe seats (Table 4.3). Given both the aggregate and survey findings, it is not surprising that women won proportionately fewer seats than did men. Only 23 per cent of the female candidates from the three major parties won seats in this election compared with 36 per cent of their male counterparts.

The allocation of competitive seats within the parties tended to follow the familiar pattern. According to the aggregate data, the

Table 4.1 *Women candidates by party (non-incumbents only),*
1988

	Women candidates %	Men candidates %	N
Progressive Conservative party	16	84	128
Liberal party	19	81	264
New Democratic party	30	70	264

Source: Office of the Chief Electoral Officer

Table 4.2 *Women and men candidates by*
competitiveness of local party, 1988

	Female candidates %	Male candidates %
Competitiveness of local party:		
Safe seat	12	25
Good chance	18	26
Unlikely	14	12
Hopeless	56	38
N	171	706

Source: Calculated from Election Statistics, Office of the Chief
Electoral Officer

Table 4.3 *Women and men candidates by perceived*
competitiveness of local party

	Female candidates %	Male candidates %
Competitiveness of local party:		
Safe seat	10	22
Good chance	52	47
Unlikely	32	24
Hopeless	6	7
N	69	275

Source: Local Selection Survey, 1988

NDP ran proportionately more women in each competitive
category, except in seats in which the NDP was characterized as
having a good chance (Table 4.4). This is an important exception,
given the NDP was a third-place party and had fewer safe seats

Table 4.4   *Sex of candidates by competitiveness of local association by party, 1988*

	Conservative candidates %	Liberal candidates %	NDP candidates %
Safe seat:			
Women	8	16	20
Men	92	84	80
N	147	25	20
Good chance:			
Women	18	13	10
Men	82	87	90
N	93	79	41
Unlikely:	17	17	46
Women	83	83	55
Men			
N	35	49	22
Hopeless:			
Women	7	21	31
Men	93	79	69
N	14	141	209

Source: Calculated from Election Statistics, Office of the Chief Electoral Officer

than the other two. The Liberals' better record compared with the Conservatives was also reversed in this category.[17] This too is an important exception, given the much smaller number of safe seats available for Liberals compared with Conservatives.

If we look at the distribution of seats from the perspective of local party associations' judgements of their competitiveness, the partisan pattern is more consistent. In every competitive category the proportion of women candidates who ran for the NDP is greater than the proportion for the Liberals, which is in turn greater than that for Conservatives (Table 4.5). The difference between these figures and those from the aggregate data is primarily attributable to optimism among the opposition parties when they assessed their chances of electoral success. The opposition were more likely to judge their electoral prospects as 'good' while the performance-based measure categorized them as less competitive.[18] Given the highly fluid nature of partisan support among the public over the months before the election was called, such optimism is understandable.

Table 4.5 *Sex of candidates by perceived*
competitiveness of local association by party

	Conservative candidates %	Liberal candidates %	NDP candidates %
Safe seat:			
Women	7	17	18
Men	93	83	82
N	45	12	11
Good chance:			
Women	11	19	32
Men	89	81	68
N	46	57	63
Unlikely:			
Women	17	17	46
Men	83	83	55
N	13	34	40
Hopeless:			
Women		21	31
Men		79	69
N	1	11	11

Source: Local Selection Survey, 1988

Party effects

The partisan pattern in these data is clear: in the selection arena
women have been most successful in the NDP, less so in the
Liberal party and least successful with the Conservatives. But how
do such party differences occur? Do local constituency associations' preferences and practices encourage or discriminate against
women and if so, are these effects variable by party? And what is
the role of national party activists? Have national party efforts
contributed to the party effects we have observed?

Local level preferences and practices
According to the survey data, when at least one woman's name
was officially placed in nomination for a local party candidacy, a
female candidate was selected 73 per cent of the time. Part of the
reason for this high success rate was that candidacies – for both
men and women – were often awarded by acclamation. But even
when local party members had a choice of a male or female for

their candidate, women won 54 per cent of the races. Since the total number of men (95) seeking candidacies in these contests involving both sexes was greater than the total number of women (60), the success rate of the women is especially notable. It appears local party members who participate in choosing candidates do not discriminate against women, and indeed may favour them.

Although the sample numbers are small, the survey results do suggest a party effect. When aspiring women candidates faced male counterparts in selection ballots, 62 per cent of NDP associations selected a woman candidate compared with 50 per cent of Liberal party associations and 40 per cent of Conservative party associations.

Since women were effective competitors in so many selection races, and given that the success ratio (69 per cent) for women aspirants, contested or otherwise, was greater than the success ratio for men (59 per cent), it seems part of the problem of female candidacies is that few women formally seek the position. But our data also indicate the number of women seeking candidacies can be modified by party practices. For example, local candidate search committees can encourage women to place their names on selection ballots. Among associations in which incumbent members were not seeking reselection, 43 per cent of those with candidate search committees had at least one woman competing for the local candidacy. By comparison, among associations without search committees, only 27 per cent had women on their selection ballots. Associations with search committees were also more likely to choose women candidates: 30 per cent did so in comparison with 16 per cent of associations with no such committees.

Party differences were also evident in search committee activities. The NDP was more likely to have local search committees, and such committees were more likely to produce women aspirants and women candidates (Table 4.6). For the Liberals, the differences produced by search committees are not statistically significant although the direction of the numbers is consistent with the pattern among the NDP. On the other hand, among Conservative associations no such pattern is evident. While it seems that search committees can encourage women aspirants and they can contribute to women candidacies, they are not a sufficient condition for either of these effects.

Another measure suggesting the effects of local party activities comes from a survey question in which the respondents were asked if their party candidate was 'talked into running' by the local association. Twenty-nine per cent of the women compared with 19 per cent of the male candidates had been 'talked into running'.

Table 4.6 *Local search committees and female aspirants and*
candidates (non-incumbent associations only)

| | Search committee | | |
| | Yes | No | |
Party	%	%	N
New Democrats			
Woman aspirant(s)[1]	52	28	107
Woman candidate	42	18	112
Liberals			
Woman aspirant(s)	37	24	99
Woman candidate	20	14	105
Conservatives			
Woman aspirant(s)	26	30	39
Woman candidate	10	19	42

[1] Cell entries are percentages of local associations in which at least one woman ran for the nomination.

Source: Local Selection Survey, 1988

And women were not just convinced to run for 'hopeless' causes, as used to be the case. A majority of the female candidates who were talked into running did so for local associations that judged their chances of local success were good. On the other hand, a majority of the men talked into running did so in candidacies where chances for election were considered unlikely or hopeless.

The practice of convincing women to run appears to be another means by which party effects were created: in none of our Conservative associations were their women candidates talked into running, while 15 per cent of the women who ran for the Liberal party and fully 36 per cent of those who ran for the NDP were talked into running.

The role of the national party organizations
Since party selection is so localized and local control is protected by the norms of party democracy, national party organizations were limited in the influence they could exert over candidate selection, whatever the objectives they may have wished to achieve in the candidate arena. However, our data suggest that the activities of the national organizations had some effect on the number of women selected and that this was another means by which party differences in female candidacies occurred.

National party officials can attempt to influence local selection most directly by assisting riding associations in their search for

Table 4.7   *Women candidates by outside party assistance (non-incumbent associations only)*

| | Outside party officials assisted local party candidate search | |
	Yes %	No %
Sex of candidate		
Female	36	22
Male	64	785
N	61	195

Source: Local Selection Survey, 1988

prospective candidates. In parties with a gender strategy in mind, officials could focus some of their efforts on finding prospective women candidates. In our survey, a woman candidate was selected in 35 per cent of those associations that reported they had received assistance from party officials outside of the local constituency. By comparison, only 17 per cent of those reporting no such assistance selected a woman. When constituencies that had an incumbent seeking reselection are excluded from the calculations the figures are 36 and 22 per cent respectively (Table 4.7). In NDP associations that reported assistance from outside party officials, 45 per cent nominated a woman candidate; in the Liberals, 36 per cent nominated a woman while only 11 per cent of the Conservative ones did.[19] But even among the NDP, where the incidence of national party assistance was greatest, fewer than one-quarter of the local associations said they sought (or accepted) help from party officials. It seems national parties had to rely, to an important degree, on more indirect methods to effect greater gender parity.

One of the ways national parties could attempt to influence selection indirectly was by encouraging local associations to nominate women. Since the national leadership of all three parties had said they wanted to increase the number of women among their party candidates, it was anticipated many of the local associations would tell us they had been encouraged by their parties to choose a woman. But this was not the case. Less than a fifth of our respondents said their local party had received such encouragement and most of those were from NDP associations. Even where no incumbents were seeking reselection, only 21 per cent of the local parties reported their national or regional party encouraged them to run a female candidate and 83 per cent of

Table 4.8   *NDP organizational effort to increase female
participation (non-incumbent associations only)*

Local association encouraged by party to choose woman candidate	Woman contested candidacy %
Yes	56
No	37
N	100
	Woman candidate selected
Yes	53
No	21
N	105

Source: Local Selection Survey, 1988

these were NDP associations. The latter were almost half the non-incumbent NDP associations in our sample.

Encouragement from the party organization may have been a factor in the selection of more NDP women candidates: among the non-incumbent NDP associations reporting such encouragement, 56 per cent had at least one woman who sought the local candidacy and 52 per cent selected a female candidate. By comparison, of those that said they were not encouraged, only 34 per cent had a woman seek their candidacy and 21 per cent chose a woman candidate (Table 4.8)

Although their party was the most active in promoting female candidacies and the most responsive to issues of gender within their organization, for NDP women the results of the 1988 election were especially discouraging. Only five of the forty-three seats the party took were won by women, and it elected proportionately fewer women than did the Liberals or Conservatives. Only 11 per cent of NDP MPs were women compared with 15 per cent of the Liberals and 12 per cent of the Conservatives.

Subsequent developments

Since the 1988 elections, many women in the parties have continued to work on behalf of gender issues within their organizations. Among New Democrats, the focus has been on the candidate question and the effects on party policy on this subject have been substantial.

As part of their election preparatory work, the NDP Strategy and Election Planning Committee (SEPC) developed, in 1991, a set of affirmative action proposals on selecting and electing women in the next general election.[20] These proposals were prepared for the Federal Council, the party's national decision-making body,[21] and contained target guidelines, implementation strategies and support programmes, including subsidies for women seeking candidacies. The guidelines prescribed that 50 per cent of all ridings should have women candidates and in a designated group of 'winnable' or 'priority' ridings, 60 per cent of the candidates should be women. Incumbent ridings where the member was seeking re-election would be exempt from the latter designation.

For the Participation of Women (POW) committee of the party, target guidelines were insufficient: a mandatory policy was, they argued, the only way to ensure that women were actually selected as party candidates, not just given the opportunity to seek a candidacy. In response to the demands by POW, the Federal Council returned the policy to the SEPC, who were to 'find a way to make [the guidelines] mandatory' (Edney, 1991: 14). Further, a constitutional amendment was passed at the 1991 national party convention that gives the Federal Council the 'authority to establish rules for nomination [i.e., the selection procedure for candidacies] to achieve affirmative action goals' (New Democratic Party, 1991a: 10). The national party was now supplied with more formal power and some legitimacy to intervene at the local level.

But the problem of devising a mandatory policy which preserves an element of democracy at the local riding level was not inconsequential, and was complicated by some internal resistance and by party concern about the negative press response to a policy which was seen as *requiring* that half the party's candidates be women.[22] The solution was one that stipulates a mandatory process, not mandatory outcomes. This process requires that regional clusters of riding associations create their own plans for achieving the affirmative action goals and devolves to riding associations the responsibility to implement these plans.[23] Incumbent ridings are, however, to be treated differently. Where incumbents are seeking reselection, their constituency association does not have to participate in the affirmative action plan. Where incumbents are not seeking reselection, the national party will take direct responsibility for the affirmative action plan for that constituency association.

The rest of the policy involves financial and other support mechanisms for women who are or wish to become party candidates. Financially, subsidies will be available for some women seeking candidacies and spending limits will be set for all NDP selection races.[24] Other support mechanisms for women include workshops, information packages and regional training opportunities.

While the NDP have struggled with the problem of implementing an affirmative action strategy, the Liberal party has been engaged in a party-wide exercise of reform. Faced with chronic deficits and an organization that was deeply divided by a leadership race in 1990, the party began to reassess some of its procedures. At a constitutional convention held in February of 1992, delegates ratified a number of changes to the party constitution, some of which have implications for gender issues. First, women are guaranteed co-chair positions on the party's National Platform Committee, the National Election Readiness Committee and the Permanent Appeals Committee that has responsibility for appeals arising from candidate nominations, leadership selection and delegate selection for national conventions. Second, the National Campaign Committee now has the power to establish rules on the selection of party candidates, including rules that cover gender equity and minority representation.

The day before the constitutional convention that made these changes, the party leader announced the formation of a Special Task Force on Women in the party. The mandate of this task force is to find means to attract more women to the party and to increase their participation in it. For its part, the NWLC has begun planning a programme for the next election that anticipates a more centralized approach to the identification of potential women candidates. A NWLC search committee will be used to identify and to encourage women in each province to seek selection in local associations, and a brochure designed to solicit potential women candidates is planned.

In the Conservative party, which was unsuccessful in its attempts to bridge the gender gap in the 1988 election (Wearing and Wearing, 1991), the executive of the NPCWF has addressed the issue of women in the party with a new strategic plan. This plan, adopted in September 1989, consists of ten proposed initiatives and clearly reflects the party's concern over the softness of their support among women voters. In both the presentation of the overall plan, and the stated objectives of the specific programmes, this concern is made clear. Quoting from a party report on its Women's Bureau, the NPCWF places its initiatives in the following context.

The expansion of the voter base by attracting 'the women's vote' should be a critical focus during this mandate. In reviewing election data on women ... there is strong evidence that the 'gender gap' exists. This [sic.] data indicates that in elections women make up a large percentage of the swing vote and that their support for the PC Party tends to soften dramatically between elections. Given that women represent 52% of the voting population, with this trend moving upward, the 'women's vote' in future elections will be crucial for a majority government. (National Progressive Conservative Women's Federation, 1989: 1)

Of the ten initiatives outlined by the NPCWF executive, six were directed towards improving communications among women within the party, or expanding the party's contacts with women outside the organization, and two were a continuation of previous activities. Two new proposals that addressed the issue of women candidacies were the creation of a NPCWF talent bank of names and resumés of women suitable for the position of party candidate,[25] and the development of a training programme for prospective women candidates. But these programmes were subsequently deferred, for reasons which appear to be both financial and organizational. It seems that for the next election, like the last one, the encouragement of prospective female candidates within the PC party will remain an informal and decentralized enterprise, although one which may be facilitated by the party's recent selection of a female leader.

Conclusions

The Canadian data on candidacies point to a number of conclusions concerning women's access to seats in national legislatures. First, the number of desirable candidacies available for women is severely constrained when norms protect incumbents from challenges in the selection process. Incumbents can tie up most of the parties' safe seats so that when pressures emerge to alter existing representational patterns, as they have from the women's movement, the response by the parties is slowed. The fact that there are relatively few safe seats in Canada (Blake, 1991) helps explain how the proportion of women climbed more quickly in the Canadian House of Commons in the 1980s than it did in the legislatures of Britain and the USA.

Secondly, the single member plurality system presents a special challenge to those attempting to redress gender inequalities in representation. It is, simply, easier to balance lists of candidates in multi-member systems than to designate single candidacies as reserved for women. Moreover, balancing lists accords more readily with popular notions of equality. As the NDP has found, imposing gender requirements on individual constituency associations is often viewed as a limitation on local choice and individual access. The Canadian data suggest that even when local selectors do not discriminate against women, decentralized selection is a problem for those concerned with increasing the representation of women. It is more difficult to coordinate activities directed to multiple centres of decision-making as must be done in a highly localized system and the programmes necessary to increase the number of women candidates require effort at both local and national levels.

The Canadian data also suggest that the supply and demand issue of female candidates is a complex one. Fewer women than men do formally allow their names to stand for selection ballots, but party activities and practices can make an important difference to the number of women who come forward.

Finally, the Canadian example confirms the role of party ideology in the recruitment of women, even in the context of a culture in which the leaders of all the major parties pronounce their concern about gender inequalities and their desire to increase the representation of women in their party candidacies. Given the parties' recent activities on candidacies, it appears likely the existing party differences in recruitment will continue.

Notes

The author would like to thank Cynthia Cusinatto, Johanna den Hertog, Mary Meldrum, Abby Pollonetsky, Linda Scales and Marry-Anne Viet for the assistance they provided me in learning about their parties. I am grateful also to R.K. Carty for his role as co-investigator in the candidate selection project.

1 Independents are rarely elected to the Canadian House of Commons and in the 1980s no minor party candidates were successful in general elections.

2 In Canada, national and provincial party politics are comparatively independent of one another, organizationally as well as in terms of political strategies (Dyck, 1989). Since a full picture of party responses provincially would require analyses of ten different political systems, this chapter will discuss only the national parties.

3 The Bloc Québecois was formed when seven Quebec members, from both the Progressive Conservative and Liberal parties, left their respective caucuses to form a separatist party after the failure of a major constitutional proposal, the Meech Lake Accord. This Accord would have met a number of constitutional demands made by the Quebec government.

4 The Reform party was formed in 1987 to redress what it sees as regional inequalities which discriminate against Western Canada. It has one seat in the House of Commons, won in a by-election held in March 1989 (McCormick, 1991). Although the original party constitution restricted party activities to the West, a change in those provisions has allowed the party to move into other parts of the

country. Yet, while it claims Reform membership has flourished in Ontario, the popularity of the party is greatest in the West in general and the province of Alberta in particular.

5 The last two elections were exceptions to this. In 1984 the NDP won 30 seats compared with the Liberals' 40 and the 211 won by the Conservatives. In the 1988 election the NDP won 43 seats compared with 83 won by the Liberals. The governing Conservatives won 169 seats.

6 On the beginnings of this movement in Canada see Black (1988) and Adamson et al. (1988).

7 Membership in the NWLC now requires membership in a local Liberal constituency association (National Women's Liberal Commission, 1990).

8 Women's clubs are under the jurisdiction of the NWLC, which sets the rules under which they are established.

9 The Women's Bureau consists of a small paid staff headed by a Director.

10 The information on women delegates at this convention is from party records made available to the author.

11 The Conservative party's concern with its image among women voters was reflected in the campaign schools held for Conservative candidates prior to the election. A session on sensitivity to women voters was developed by the party leader's adviser on women's issues and included in these schools (Kome, 1985).

12 Ironically, although the NDP was historically the most progressive party on women's issues, until the late 1970s it attracted more male than female voters (Wearing and Wearing, 1991).

13 Virtually all sitting members must face a selection meeting if they wish to run again, but their reselection is seldom challenged by other prospective candidates and challenges that are mounted are seldom successful (Carty and Erickson, 1991).

14 The invaluable assistance provided to this project by the Office of the Chief Electoral Officer is gratefully acknowledged. That Office provided the author with much of the aggregate data used in this chapter and supplied a list of the party agents to whom the survey questionnaires were sent.

15 The survey consisted of a mail questionnaire sent to a representative of every local association of the major parties. The questionnaires, which addressed issues concerning all phases of local selection activities, produced a return rate of 42 per cent. The returns were equally distributed among the parties and were well representative of the ten provinces and two languages groups in Canada. For further description of this survey see Carty and Erickson (1991).

16 For details on the composition of this measure, see Carty and Erickson (1991). The measure incorporated the changes in constituency boundaries made just before the election and took into account the atypical nature of the 1984 election, when the Conservatives won in such an unusual landslide. Thus, for example, a candidacy was designated as 'safe' if it was a Conservative one in a riding in which the Conservative Party won the seat by a margin of more than 15 per cent of the votes. A safe Liberal or NDP candidacy was one in which the seat was won by a margin of more than 5 per cent in the last election.

17 This pattern is the same when we look only at non-incumbent candidates.

18 It should be noted that these two sets of figures are also based on different populations: Table 4.4 is based on the universe of major party associations whereas Table 4.5 is based on those constituency associations that responded to our questionnaire. However, Table 4.4 looks very similar if we use the performance measure with only our sample constituencies. In other words, the differences

between the two sets of figures do not appear to be attributable to an unrepresentative sample.

19 Since the sample size of Conservative associations without incumbents has so few numbers, conclusions concerning the Conservatives must be tentative.

20 The proposals were for a general affirmative action programme which encompassed not just women, but also other minority group members, including natives, other visible minorities and the disabled.

21 In the NDP, national conventions, held bienially, are the official governing body of the Party. However, the Federal Council, which meets at least twice a year, assumes this role between conventions.

22 For an example of the press response to the NDP policy on gender equality see Sheppard (1991).

23 The policy retains the provision that at least 60 per cent of ridings in which the party has a 'reasonable chance of winning' shall have women candidates. SPEC will supervise the mandatory process by lifting the freeze on selection imposed by the national party when it is 'satisfied that the cluster has presented a coherent plan to achieve the affirmative action policy goals' (New Democratic Party, 1991b: 2).

24 Subsidies (of $500) will only be available to women if they seek a candidacy in a riding where the NDP incumbent is retiring, or in a rural riding. There will also be a $500 subsidy for childcare expenses incurred by women as a result of seeking selection.

25 The Talent Bank was proposed as a source of names for consideration for a variety of party and government positions, not just for candidacies.

5

Transformation or Modernization: the Rhetoric and Reality of Gender and Party Politics in France

Andrew Appleton and Amy G. Mazur

According to a Louis Harris–*Le Pèlerin* poll conducted in early 1990, 86 per cent of those asked declared that they would 'have confidence in a woman leading France' (*Libération*, 7 March 1990). On 15 May 1991, Edith Cresson (Parti Socialist (PS)) was appointed prime minister, the first time in French history that a woman has occupied this office. At the time, 86 per cent of women and 77 per cent of men surveyed indicated their approval of a woman as prime minister.[1] Although by the end of the year, with the unemployment rate nearing 10 per cent, Cresson's personal popularity had plummeted, the most popular political figure in France was another woman, Simone Veil (UDF).[2] Thus, the French have generally accepted women as national political leaders.

Despite these examples, however, recent studies have shown women to be under-represented in the French political elite (for example, Sineau, 1988; Stetson, 1987). Furthermore, studies of local political recruitment have demonstrated that the traditional pathways to political office have tended to exclude women (Abélès, 1989; Garraud, 1989; Sellier, 1983). There appears to be a gap between the rhetoric of the acceptance and the reality of the presence of women in French political life.

Yet, in the context of the comparative study of gender and party politics, this paradox is even more compelling when placed against the fundamental transformation of the French party system since 1958. Under the Fifth Republic, the number of significant parties has been reduced and those that remain have undergone profound organizational change (Wilson, 1982). This raises a series of interesting questions. Have these changes affected the political recruitment of women and their status in the political elite? To what extent has this transformation in France taken account of women's demands? Does looking at gender as an explicit issue facing political parties provide further insight into the internal life of party organizations?

In fact, we will argue that gender has had a significant impact upon the transformation of French political parties at the programmatic level, but less so at the organizational level. In other words, French parties have wholeheartedly embraced women's demands as campaign rhetoric, yet have been much more reluctant to incorporate these issues into the daily reality of party life. Our analysis will show that, whereas parties have actively competed for 'the women's vote' by broadening their platforms to cover certain salient gender issues, they have been less forthcoming regarding strategies to promote the participation of women in party affairs. The absence of positive action strategies calls into question the extent to which transformed French political parties can be seen as modernized.

This chapter will be divided into two sections. In the first we will examine the broader systemic context framing gender and party politics in France. In particular, we will describe the contours of the political system in contemporary France, the status of women in that system, and, lastly, gendered patterns of electoral behaviour. In the second section, we will shift the level of analysis to focus upon the organizational and programmatic changes within individual parties in recent years.

Systemic context

The political system

The political system established under the constitution of the Fifth Republic inaugurated in 1958 has been described as semi-presidential with a bicephalous executive (Wright, 1989). Since the referendum of 1962, the French president has been directly elected for a seven-year term. The president has the constitutional power to appoint the prime minister (Article 8) and, although not formally in the constitution, the ability to dismiss him or her (Ehrmann and Schain, 1992: 323). However, this effective power of dismissal may disappear under conditions of *cohabitation*, such as the period between 1986 and 1988 (Duhamel, 1989). France has never had a woman president.

According to the founders of the Fifth Republic, chief among them Charles de Gaulle and Michel Debré, the role of the president was to arbitrate the constitution leaving the day-to-day running of the government to the prime minister, although in practice successive presidents have constantly intervened in a policy-making capacity. As pointed out by Ehrmann and Schain, all four French presidents have taken on both the role of chief of state and chief of the executive (1992: 295). However, a significant limitation on the power of the president is that the prime minister and government require a parliamentary majority. Since the National Assembly is elected for five-year terms, the possibility exists for that majority to be hostile to the incumbent president, as happened in 1986. When a conservative majority was returned following the legislative elections, President Mitterand, a socialist, chose to appoint Jacques Chirac, a conservative, as prime minister. This period of *cohabitation* which lasted for two years, until 1988. showed the limits of presidential action under such conditions.

The prime minister is charged by the constitution with 'directing the operation of the government' (Article 21). In practice, the prime minister coordinates the government, which is composed of ministers responsible for particular policy areas, although portfolios are variable. Significantly, one area of presidential intervention has been in the selection of members of the government. One notable example was President Giscard d'Estaing's appointment of Françoise Giroud as the first State Secretary of Women's Status (*condition féminine*) over the objections of his prime minister, Jacques Chirac (Mazur, 1991).

Other than the large established ministries (*ministères de gestion*), such as finance, education and defence, the French government structure has increasingly included a flexible category of ministry (*ministères de mission*), which deal with topical policy areas, such as immigration, the environment and consumer affairs. It was in the context of the proliferation of this latter kind of ministry under President Giscard d'Estaing's initiative, that the first ministerial level bureau for women's affairs was established in 1974. Françoise Giroud, as head of this bureau, was allocated a position in the cabinet (*conseil des ministres*). In 1976 Giroud was replaced in a ministerial reshuffle, and the bureau was moved to Lyons, at the same time losing its cabinet status. The new head, Jacqueline Nonon, resigned after only three months in protest at its lack of status. Her successor, Nicole Pasquier, was eventually moved back to Paris in a reshuffle in 1978 to a new position as State Secretary for Women's Employment. At the same time, Monique Pelletier was appointed as Junior Minister for Women's Status and the Family (*la condition féminine et de la famille*). Following the election of François Mitterand in 1981 to the presidency, a new Ministry of the Rights of Woman was created, headed by Yvette Roudy. In 1985 this was upgraded to a full ministry, but in 1986, under the conservative government, it was once more downgraded to a non-ministerial status (*délégation*) under the tutelage of the Ministry of Social Affairs.

When the socialists returned to power in 1988, even this entity disappeared in the transitional government. After much criticism, however, Prime Minister Michel Rocard included a State Secretary of Women's Rights[3] under Michèle André. Finally the government named by Edith Cresson in 1991 included a State Secretary of Women's Rights and Daily Life (*la vie quotidienne*), Véronique Neiertz.

With regard to the treatment of gender issues by the French administrative apparatus, it is also important to mention the presence of various committees within other ministries. The most important of these was the Comité du Travail Féminin (CTF), which from 1965 to 1983 served as a pressure group within the French state for equal rights policy for women. Together with the coordinated actions of women in the personal staffs of ministers (*cabinets ministeriels*) and other parts of the administration pursuing policies that promote women's rights the activity of these state structures has been termed 'state feminism' (Mazur, 1992).

The French parliament is comprised of two houses, the National Assembly (*Assemblée Nationale*) and the Senate (*Sénat*). The lower house, the National Assembly, is elected for five-year terms by a constituency-based, two ballot, plurality vote electoral system. Under the constitution of the Fifth Republic, it lost much of its policy-making power compared with previous regimes, both by rules and by practice. The National Assembly does retain the power to censure the government by vote of no confidence, although it has been made clear by successive presidents that such a vote would automatically entail the dissolution of the Assembly, which the president has the power to do (no more than once per year – Article 12). In recent years, however, there has been a slight resurgence in the assertiveness of the National Assembly *vis-à-vis* the government. In particular, the material resources available to individual members of the assembly (*députés*) have increased, as a result of the better organized political parties.

> Better organized parties have both enhanced the role of the deputy as a part of a group and further diminished his role as an independent actor, capable of influencing the legislative process. (Ehrmann and Schain, 1992: 343)

The upper chamber of the French parliament, the Senate, is chosen by electoral colleges in each of the ninety-six departments (*départements*), made up of local, regional and national elected figures. One-third of its members are appointed every three years. Although in theory the Senate is an equal partner, in practice it has played a subordinate role in the policy-making process. Because of the composition of the electoral colleges and the apportionment of seats by department, Senators tend to represent the least-developed and more conservative parts of the country, what is often referred to as 'deep France' (*la France profonde*).

There are three major tiers of government in France at the sub-national level. The first of those tiers is made up of the twenty-two regional councils (*conseils régionaux*) which have been directly elected since 1986 by proportional representation. Each of these regions groups together a variable number of departments, of which there are ninety-six in metropolitan France. The departments also have councils (*conseils généraux*) which are elected under a similar constituency-based, two ballot, plurality vote system similar to that used in parliamentary elections. The lowest hierarchical element of government in France is composed of municipalities (*communes*) which have councils (*conseils municipaux*) that are elected according to a two ballot, list system whose specific rules depend upon the size of the municipality. There are currently some 36,547 such councils, although over 28,000 of the towns have less than 1,000 inhabitants (INSEE, 1991: 155). The chief executive of the municipal council is the mayor (*maire*), to which office most French feel the most positive attachment (Ehrmann and Schain, 1992: 72).

In 1982 the Socialist government proposed a law (which had actually been initiated by Monique Pelletier under the previous centre-right government: see *Le Monde* 23–24 November 1980) which would have imposed a limitation of no more than 75 per cent of candidates from one gender on any list in municipal elections. The law was voted by parliament in July 1982, but was annulled by decision of the Constitutional Council (*Conseil Constitutionnel*) on 18 November 1982 (*Le Monde*, 27 January 1983). This decision in effect equated positive action strategies with reverse discrimination in France, and has had an important influence on subsequent discussion of quotas in public policy by delegitimizing their extensive use.

There have been two important developments in recent years at the sub-national level. The first of these is the decentralization programme undertaken by the Socialist government beginning in 1981. Under this initiative, power at the sub-national level has, broadly speaking, tended to shift from the administrative to the political arm of the French state. The second recent development of note is the limitation placed on the practice of multiple office holding (*cumul des mandats*). The simultaneous retention of the offices of mayor, departmental councillor and deputy traditionally provided a channel of transmission that allowed a politician to negotiate with or by-pass the cumbersome administrative apparatus of the French state that was otherwise dominant and highly centralized (Worms, 1966). In 1986, a law was passed limiting the number of elective offices that can be held at the same time to two (Mény, 1987). The apparent impact of this law (which takes effect progressively) has been the movement away from the regional councils by established political figures, in favour of the combination of deputy and mayor. However, this in turn has opened up the political space at the regional level to other aspirants (including women) and new political formations (Ehrmann and Schain, 1992: 391).

Developments under the Fifth Republic illustrate how institutional changes can shape the universe of party competition and contribute to the emergence of a transformed party system (Bartolini, 1984). However, the new bipolar, four party system that emerged by the end of the 1970s experienced a further transformation in the 1980s. Disagreement exists as to the interpretation of these systemic developments. Wilson (1989) sees the two-bloc model, although 'under siege', as still being essentially dominant, while Machin (1991) portrays the stable party system of the 1970s as fragile and illusory. Irrespective of which view of the party system is adopted, five political formations deserve mention here: the Parti Communiste Français (PCF), the Parti Socialiste (PS), the Union pour la Démocratie Française (UDF), the Rassemblement Pour la République (RPR), and the Front National (FN). All of these parties are structured in federations at the departmental level, coordinated by strong national organizations.

The PCF is a traditional communist party that is organized according to the principle of democratic centralism. Until the emergence of the PS in the 1970s, it was the largest party of the left, averaging 25 per cent of the vote during the Fourth Republic. Today, with only 11 per cent of the vote and twenty-six deputies in 1988, it has lost much of its influence. In contrast, the PS, which emerged out of the moribund SFIO (Section Française de l'Internationale Ouvrière) between 1969 and 1971, has regrouped the non-communist left into an effective electoral force. Under the leadership of François Mitterand, the PS has become the dominant party of the left, shedding much of its Marxist dogma on the way. In 1981, Mitterand gained the presidency and the PS won an absolute majority in the National Assembly, the first time the left had controlled both the legislature and the executive since 1936.

The UDF is, of the four larger parties, the most disparate and weakly organized. Formed in haste in 1978 before the legislative elections out of various centre-right parties that supported the presidency of Valéry Giscard d'Estaing, the UDF remains a somewhat fluid umbrella formation, marked by internal disputes between its composite parties. The RPR, heir to the legacy of Gaullism, under the leadership of Jacques Chirac, has attempted to become a more traditional conservative party. Drastically reorganized in 1976–7, the party has developed stronger internal structures and a true activist base. Together, the UDF and RPR, largely in coalition, received 41 per cent of the vote in the 1988 legislative elections. Finally, the extreme-right FN, with a racist and anti-immigrant platform, has emerged since 1983 as a major electoral force at the local level.

Women in French politics
To what extent have women succeeded in penetrating the French political elite in recent years? As far as the executive branch is concerned, there has been little change over the past two decades in the number of women of ministerial rank.[4] These figures are presented in Table 5.1. While in 1983, women occupied 14 per cent of all ministerial positions, this proportion increased to 16.2 per cent in the first Rocard government of 1988 (although it is interesting to note that under the conservative cohabitation government of Jacques Chirac between 1986 and 1988 there was only one woman minister). However, this marginal increase was negated in the second Rocard government of 1988, in which women occupied just 14 per cent of these posts. In the new government named by Edith Cresson in May 1991, 13.3 per cent of ministerial positions were allocated to women.

Table 5.1   *Number of women of ministerial rank in France, 1974–1991*

Year	No. of women
1974	4
1977	5
1983	6
1986	1
1988	6
1988	6
1991	6

Sources: Lecocq and Fabre, 1988; *Le Monde*, 22 May 1991

Table 5.2 *Percentage of women in positions in* cabinets ministeriels

Post	1981	1985
Staff director (*Directeur de cabinet*)	4.0	9.1
Chief of staff (*Chef de cabinet*)	20.0	16.1
Technical adviser (*Conseiller technique*)	14.0	16.5
Parliamentary aides (*Attachés parlementaires*)	46.0	53.3
Others	–	35.1

Sources: INSEE, 1986: 88 and Ministère des Droits de la Femme

On the other hand, there has been a significant increase in the number of women in the personal staffs of ministers (*cabinets ministeriels*). In 1981, 15 per cent of these staffs were women, a figure that had risen to 24 per cent by 1989. Within each cabinet, however, there were fewer women in positions of leadership, while they tended to occupy lower posts in the hierarchy, a trend which is shown in Table 5.2. It is interesting to note that, in 1991, President Mitterand's personal staff had a much higher proportion of women, 38 per cent, than this average (Michel Rocard, the Prime Minister, had 19 per cent women in his *cabinet*). Furthermore, two of the most important positions on Mitterand's staff were held by women – Anne Lauvergeon (*Secrétaire Générale Adjointe du Gouvernment*) and Béatrice Marre (*Chef de Cabinet*) (Evin, 1991: 102). As noted by the SEDF at the 1990 Montreal conference on women and political power, 'Thus there has without doubt been an improvement in the last 10 years, albeit insufficient, but this improvement involves *appointed* and not *elected* offices' (SEDF, 1990: 62).[5]

Turning now to the legislative branch of government, the percentages of women in both houses of the French parliament are shown in Figure 5.1. The percentage of women in the National Assembly has never exceeded the 6.9 per cent attained in 1945 at the end of the Second World War (when women had just gained the right to vote), while there are currently only 3.4 per cent women members of the Senate. The low numbers of women in the French parliament is indicative of the problems women have in gaining elected, as opposed to appointed, office. Table 5.3 shows the breakdown by party affiliation of women in both houses in 1990: it can be seen that there is little significant variation between parties of the left and right.

What factors account for this absence of women in elected offices? Sineau (1988) argues that women lack the necessary resources to gain office, that in France their status is inferior to

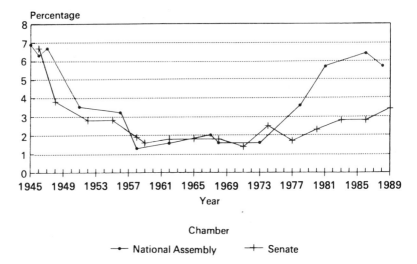

Figure 5.1   *Women legislators in France, 1945–1989*
(InterParliamentary Union, 1991: 85)

that of men in general, and that political parties have failed to advance women as members and candidates. Beyond the obstacles to women posed by the parties themselves, which will be treated below, it has also been argued that the type of electoral system plays a determinant role in the number of women elected (Beckwith, 1984; Thiébault, 1988). Support for this hypothesis can

Table 5.3   *Party affiliation of women legislators in France, 1990*

	Total	No. women	% women
National Assembly	577	33	5.7
PS	272	17	6.3
PCF	26	1	3.8
RPR	129	9	6.9
UDF	91	1	1.1
UDC	40	3	7.5
Non-party	19	2	10.5
Senate	321	11	3.4
PS	70	1	1.4
PCF	16	5	31.2
RPR	91	5	5.5

Source: INSEE, 1991: 155

be found in the French case. First, the proportion of women elected to the National Assembly has only exceeded the 6 per cent mark when proportional representation was in use as the electoral system. Secondly, the number of women elected to the European Parliament, using a proportional list system, has been significantly greater than for elections to the French parliament. In 1984, 19.8 per cent (16 out of 81) of French MEPs were women, and in 1989 this figure had reached 22.2 per cent (18 out of 81).

Additionally, the lack of women in national elected offices can be explained by the exclusion of women from local politics. It has long been established in France that,

> a career in local government has served as the selection process and the jumping-off point for the politically ambitious ... Traditionally, the combining of the functions of a deputy or senator with those of a mayor, a member of a departmental council, or often both (*cumul des mandats*) has been one of the goals of a political career. (Ehrmann and Schain, 1992: 133)

Studies have shown that the pathways to local office have tended to emphasize the accumulation of resources to which women do not traditionally have access (Garraud, 1989; Sellier, 1983).

From the literature, five factors emerge which explain the overall under-representation of women in the National Assembly:

1 Women's inferior socio-economic status.
2 Women's lack of social and educational capital.
3 The type of electoral system.
4 The paucity of women in local office.
5 The small number of women candidates presented by the political parties.

The manner in which these five factors interact can be best depicted by a series of concentric circles. The outer circle is the social and economic environment which determines the inferior status of women as compared to men, as well as the former's lack of economic and educational resources. The second circle is the political environment, which includes the type of electoral system. The inner ring represents the behaviour of the male elite within the political parties which directly limits the selection of women candidates for elected office at the local and national level.

As Figure 5.2 illustrates, this inside ring is affected by the two outer rings and has the most direct impact on the lack of women in elected office. Therefore, the final two factors, low levels of women in local office and the reluctance of male party leaders to back women candidates, can be incorporated in this final ring. All

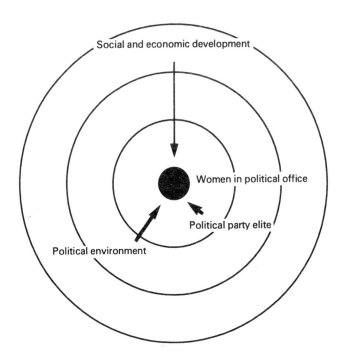

Figure 5.2   *Model showing proximity of political parties to the under-representation of women in political office*

three of these environmental influences combine cumulatively to prevent women from attaining elected public office in France. Clearly, however, the role of the political parties is central in this process of exclusion reflected in the statistics analysed below.

In 1986, the first year that direct elections were held to regional councils, 143 women succeeded in gaining office in the 1,682 places available, a rate of 8.5 per cent (INSEE, 1991: 155). These elections, held at the same time as the legislative elections on 16 March, operated under a system of proportional representation, Women are also under-represented in the ninety-six councils; in 1977, there were just ninety-five women out of 3,529 (or 2.7 per cent) (Lecocq and Fabre, 1988). This low figure none the less represented an increase under the Fifth Republic, as just 0.8 per cent of departmental councillors in 1958 and 2.3 per cent in 1967 were women (INSEE, 1991: 154). By 1986, there were 154 women out of a total of 3,694 holding this particular mandate, or 4.2 per

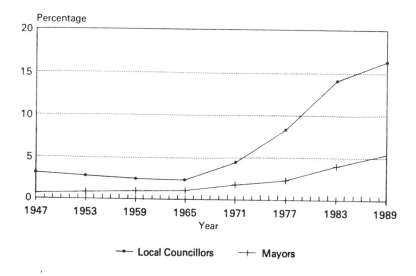

Figure 5.3   *Women in municipal councils in France, 1947–1989*
(Lecocq and Fabre, 1988; SEDF, 1990)

cent (Lecocq and Fabre, 1988). The PCF has tended to be more
open to electing women to departmental councils than other
parties: following the 1989 elections, 11.7 per cent of this party's
representatives in these assemblies were women, as opposed to 4.7
per cent for the PS, 4.9 per cent for the RPR, and 3.9 per cent for
the UDF (INSEE, 1991: 155).

Figure 5.3 shows the limited increase in the number of women
in municipal councils (*conseils municipaux*) since the Second
World War. The most progress has been made at the level of
municipal councillor (*conseiller municipal*), where women comprised 16.3 per cent of the 505,248 elected to this office in 1989
(SEDF, 1990: 60). Fewer women accede to the executive position
of mayor, with just 1,996 (5.4 per cent) of the 36,340 mayors in
France being women in 1989 (SEDF, 1990: 62). However, it is
interesting to note that there has been a significant change in the
rate of increase of women elected to these positions since the
beginning of the 1970s, the period that coincides with the major
era of party reform.

Yet the breakdown of the figures for the number of women in
municipal councils following the 1989 elections shows an equally
interesting trend. These figures are given in Table 5.4. While it

Table 5.4   *Women in municipal councils in France (1989)*

Size of town	Total	No. women	% women
Municipal councillors:			
less than 3,500	432,450	70,403	16.3
3,500–9,000	40,051	8,571	21.4
9,000–30,000	22,260	5,120	23.0
+ 30,000	10,402	2,455	23.6
Mayors:			
less than 1,000	28,612	1,653	5.7
1,000–5,000	6,275	281	4.4
5,000–9,000	759	23	3.0
9,000–30,000	676	36	5.3
30,000–120,000	199	7	3.5
+ 120,000	26	1	3.8

Source: INSEE, 1991: 155

appears that there is a positive correlation between the proportion of ·women elected as municipal councillors and the size of the town, the inverse is true for women as mayors: that is, the larger the size of the town, the less likely it is for a woman to be mayor. This is particularly important since the decentralization programme of 1981–2, in the context of patterns of political recruitment, given that, 'The mayors of larger towns with considerable resources are able to do what they did informally before, perhaps somewhat more freely, while mayors of rural towns with fewer resources remain as dependent as they were before' (Ehrmann and Schain, 1992: 387).

Finally, the small number of women in elected office reflects the pattern of candidacies. In general, a larger proportion of women are presented by electorally insignificant political parties and formations such as the Greens (before 1989), the radical left ard various extreme right-wing groups, while the major parties are more reluctant to present women as candidates. Furthermore, the number of women's candidacies has been inflated by the phenomenon of women-only organizations and lists, such as Choisir in the 1978 legislative elections (with candidates in forty-three constituencies, with none elected), and three lists in the 1989 municipal elections (of which one was elected in Bizenueille, population 343). If such formations are excluded from the analysis, then women formed just 6.7 per cent of the total number of candidates in the legislative elections of 1978, 7.4 per cent in 1981 and 7.0 per cent in 1986 (Thiébault, 1988: 89).

In the latest legislative elections in 1988, of the total number of candidates (6,104), 1,705 were women, or 25 per cent (Lecocq and Fabre, 1988). This is equivalent to the proportion of women candidates in elections to the European parliament, with 25 per cent in 1979 and 23 per cent in 1984 (*Femmes d'Europe*, 15 May–15 August 1984). In 1989, Lutte Ouvrière (LO) had forty-one women and forty men on their list, the Green party had thirty-four women and forty-seven men, while the RPR–UDF list had only sixteen out of eighty-one places for women, with only three in the top thirty positions (*La Croix*, 31 May 1989). The PCF list included twenty-three women, with six in the top twenty positions, while the PS had twenty-one women, of whom eight were in the top twenty (*Le Monde*, 26 May 1989). In the 1988 departmental council elections (*élections cantonales*), 8.9 per cent of PS candidates were women, 6.0 per cent for parties of the right, 14.0 per cent for the PCF, and 16.6 per cent for the extreme right FN (*Express*, 7 October 1988). Since 1973, the proportion of women candidates backed by the PS has never reached 10 per cent in legislative elections (Sineau, 1991: 77).

A gender gap in voting patterns?
Analysis of the closing of the gender gap in voting in France also suggests why the political parties have only recently been interested in placing women's rights issues on their party platforms as well as backing women candidates. It has often been argued that women have traditionally tended to vote for conservative candidates more often than men, a pattern often referred to as the gender gap. This gap was seen as very important in French politics in early studies of women's political participation (Dogan and Narbonne, 1955; Duverger, 1955). More recent studies have shown that this gap remained salient through the 1960s and 1970s (Mossuz-Lavau and Sineau, 1983); for example, in 1965, 61 per cent of women and only 49 per cent of men voted for General de Gaulle in the presidential elections (*La Croix*, 11 March 1988). Other studies have shown that, even taking into account other variables such as workforce participation, women have been more conservative in France than men in their voting behaviour (De Vaus and McAllister, 1989).

Data showing the evolution of the difference between the male and female vote for left-wing candidates in presidential and legislative elections since 1965 are shown in Figure 5.4. Studies of voting patterns by gender in France have shown that the gender gap narrowed in the 1970s, although there was still a four point difference in the legislative elections of 1981 (Sineau,

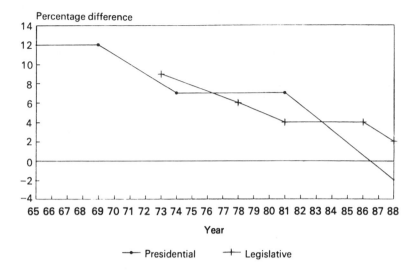

Figure 5.4   *Difference between male and female vote for left-wing candidates in France, 1965–1988 (difference = male minus female vote)* (Le Parisien, *17 March 1988; Sineau, 1991: 65)*

1991: 64). In the 1986 legislative elections, there was no discernible difference between men's and women's propensity to vote for left-wing candidates. While it has often been repeated that women were the decisive force in defeating Mitterand for the presidency in 1965 and 1974 (*Le Parisien*, 17 March 1988), by 1988 the female vote for Mitterand surpassed the male vote by 2 per cent.

Thus it would appear that, going into the 1990s, the conventional wisdom that women vote more conservatively than men no longer holds true. Indeed, the data suggest that if a 'women's vote' does exist, it would tend to favour left-wing candidates. This is most true for the higher socio-professional categories. The decline in this gap has been linked to the improvement in the socio-economic status of women, including workforce participation and changing social behaviour, such as the decline in church attendance (Mossuz-Lavau and Sineau, 1983). What also is shown by recent data is that women are less likely to vote for the extreme right-wing FN (Mossuz-Lavau and Sineau, 1988: 46–7).

Programmatic and organizational approaches to gender

Membership in French political parties has never attained the levels of those in other European nations (with the exception of the PCF). In consequence, they have not published reliable membership figures. Studies of French parties always contain a disclaimer regarding such statistics, and no accurate method has yet been found to estimate them.[6]

In 1978, the claimed proportion of women in the RPR was 41 per cent, 22 per cent in the PS (up from 16 per cent in 1973) and 33 per cent in the PCF. No figure was available for the UDF, created in 1978, but the PR, one of its major constituent formations, claimed 37 per cent of its members were women (Mossuz-Lavau and Sineau, 1981: 118). By 1985, these numbers, still according to the parties themselves, had evolved to 43 per cent for the RPR, 21 per cent for the PS and 36 per cent for the PCF (Sineau, 1988: 3). However, a 1986 Louis Harris poll (20 November) placed the proportion of women members in the RPR at just 37 per cent. The PS in 1989 claimed that 28 per cent of its members were women (*Le Monde*, 26 September 1989), a figure also reported in Philippe and Hubscher (1991: 45).[7] Table 5.5 compares the number of women within the RPR and the PS from 1978 to the present. These figures will be analysed in more detail below.

In the following section we will concentrate on four different areas of the treatment of gender issues by the PS and RPR in recent years.[8] First, we will analyse the penetration by women of party structures, including policy-making bodies, and party strategies to augment their presence in internal positions of responsibility. Secondly, linked to the above, we will examine the existence of gender-specific organizations both within and parallel to parties. Third, we will look at methods of candidate selection in each party, and discuss their impact upon women's candidacies. This section will conclude by presenting the evolution of party programmes concerning gendered political issues.

Parti Socialiste (PS)

In respect of women in the decision-making bodies of the PS, in 1990 the number of women in the executive organ (the *Bureau Exécutif*) was five out of twenty-seven places, or 18.5 per cent.[9] At the same time, twenty-eight women held positions in the party's 131-member legislative organ (the *Comité Directeur*), or 21.4 per cent. In addition, there was one woman holding the title of national secretary (*secrétaire nationale*), out of fourteen such posts allocated; her area of responsibility was for women's rights (*droits*

Table 5.5   *Women in the Parti Socialiste and the Rassemblement Pour la République, 1978–1990*

	PS			RPR		
	1978	1985	1990	1978	1985	1990
Members	22%	21%	28%	41%	43% 37%[1]	No change
Executive organ	19% (5/27)	22% (6/27)	18% (5/27)	14% (4/28)	7.1% (2/28)	n.a.[2]
Legislative organ	18% (23/131)	20% (26/131)	21% (28/131)	8% (14/170)	11% (19/170)	n.a.
National secretaries	n.a.	13% (2/16)	7% (1/14)	n.a.	5% (1/20)	24% (7/29)
Department secretaries	n.a.	n.a.	7% (7/96)	n.a.	n.a.	n.a.

[1] Lower numbers are from a Louis Harris poll conducted in November of 1986.
[2] n.a. = not available

de la femme). The most important post in the 100 local federations that make up the PS is that of First Secretary *(premier secrétaire)*; in 1990 there were just seven women in this position, or 7 per cent (Philippe and Hubscher, 1991: 228).

Comparison can be made with earlier periods in the party's history. In 1978, 19 per cent of the Executive Bureau were women, while the proportion for the legislative organ was 18 per cent (Mossuz-Lavau and Sineau, 1981: 118). Seven years later, in 1985, six out of twenty-seven members of the Executive Bureau were women (22.2 per cent), and they held twenty-six out of the 131 places on the legislative organ (19.8 per cent). In the same year, two out of the sixteen national secretaries of the party were women (Sineau, 1988: 3). Thus, although there has been a slow progression of women in the party legislature (3.4 per cent over twelve years), women have not entered this body in massive numbers. As far as the more powerful Executive Bureau is concerned, there was a lower proportion of women in 1990 than in 1978.

This singular lack of increase of the number of women in the decision-making structures of the PS is all the more striking when placed in the context of attempts to implement a positive action strategy within the party. In the 1970s, the agenda for such a strategy within the PS was defined by PS feminists, such as Marie-Thérèse Eyquem, Colette Audry and Yvette Roudy who had been in the Mouvement Démocratique et Féminin (MDF) and were close to François Mitterand. One of their core demands consisted of a quota for women in the party structures at all levels that would reflect the overall number of women within the party. In 1973 at the party congress in Grenoble, the party agreed to establish a quota of 10 per cent, which came into effect in 1974. Because a full 20 per cent of the 1973 party membership were women, this was seen by the PS feminists as only a half measure.

During the run-up to the party congress at Nantes in 1977, these same PS feminists wanted this quota raised to 20 per cent. The commission in charge of preparation of this congress, which was composed of leading figures in the party, refused this demand. However, at Nantes it was finally agreed that it would be raised to 15 per cent, the major argument for the limited increase being that small federations would have too much difficulty finding more than this proportion of women to fill these positions (Philippe and Hubscher, 1991: 226). At the highly charged congress in Metz in 1979 it was raised to 20 per cent, where it remained (despite much criticism from women within the PS feminist circles) until it was raised to 30 per cent in 1991.[10]

The debate over the level of this quota has, of course, been by-passed by the reality of party practice, as reflected in the figures presented above. Existing quotas have never been respected within the party, either at the national or the local level. Furthermore, the party has neither set up any oversight mechanism to enforce this positive action strategy, nor sanctioned non-respect. At the 1988 Convention on Women's Rights held at Chatellerault, women party members repeatedly expressed their frustration at this situation, to the point where, 'Quotas was the magic word of the convention, the "open-sesame" of all speeches' (*La Croix*, 16 March 1988).

The same PS feminists were in charge of a women's commission that had no budget or formal power. They considered that such a bureau should function to integrate women's demands into party discussions. Emphasizing the necessity of wielding power within the party structure, members of the women's commission pushed for a national secretariat, complete with budget and offices in the local federations, that would elaborate a coherent party pro-gramme in regard to women. By the Nantes congress of 1977, Yvette Roudy and her colleagues had secured a promise from the party leadership that the commission would be upgraded to a national secretariat. Since that time, the secretariat has functioned as a pressure group within the party leadership both at the national and the federal level.

Women from the Paris federation of the PS organized a group called MIFAS (Mouvement pour l'Integration des Femmes à L'Action Sociale). This short-lived group placed pressure on the PS from outside the party to change the party platform. According to MIFAS, the existing platform represented a superficial treatment of women's rights, arguing that it had incorporated few concrete measures. In particular MIFAS sought measures such as equal employment policy for women, the improvement of day care facilities, increased parental leave and legalized, state-funded abortion (*Libération*, 30 June 1977).

Another group of women within the party attempted to integrate certain strategies and ideas of the contemporary feminist movement into the PS. A collective of women disappointed with both the compromise outcome of the 1978 convention and the defeat of the left in the 1978 elections sought to organize a women's fraction (*courant*).[11] Those involved, chief among them Cécile Goldet, Edith Lhuillier and Françoise Gaspard, wanted to present a motion at the national party congress at Metz in 1979. The programme of the prospective fraction was unclear, but they argued that it would only be through constituting a separate women's current that gender issues could be properly studied (Gaspard, Goldet and Lhuillier, 1978). They asserted that the fraction would not compete in political rivalries within the party, but would be a place for women to contribute their specific and different cultural experiences as women (*féminism de la différence*).

PS feminists in the national secretariat opposed the women's current, which they called a 'ghettoization' of women in the party. The night before the congress, two of the co-founders, Goldet and Gaspard, abandoned the effort in the face of this opposition, and the motion (called the *courant* G) only received 0.3 per cent of the votes (Philippe and Hubscher, 1991: 227). The rest of the group remained together until 1983 and published a magazine called *Mignonnes Allons voir sous la Rose*. In the 1981 presidential elections this collective endorsed Huguette Bouchardeau's (Parti Socialist Unifié) candidacy for president. For many in the national secretariat, these activities were seen as undermining their own efforts on behalf of women in the PS.

Candidate selection in the PS is, in principle, highly decentralized, with the section or sections in any particular constituency choosing their own candidate by secret ballot. The departmental party organization ratifies these nominations, which are then transmitted to the national headquarters. However, as Thiébault (1988: 77) notes, the national party organization has very important supervisory powers that it can use to intervene and change nominations during the party mini-congress held to ratify candidacies. These powers have been used, as in the case of the 1978 and 1981 elections, to promote women as candidates; yet in 1981, they were also used to squeeze out some potential candidates who had supported Huguette Bouchardeau (Thiébault, 1988: 77)

The candidate selection process is marked by two major factors that have had an impact upon women. First, the party statutes state that the same quota by gender on the party's own decision-making bodies discussed above must be respected in the selection of candidates for elections using list systems.[12] Secondly, the PS decided in 1985, in the context of the new proportional representation method of election to the National Assembly, that candidate selection in future should respect the balance of forces between the internal fractions (*courants*) of the party.

In fact, the quota requirement of no more than 80 per cent of candidates to be of the same gender has not been respected by the party throughout the 1970s and 1980s, with the exception of the European elections of 1979, 1984 and 1989. Concerning elections to the national assembly, the party achieved a rate of 5.1 per cent women in 1978, 8.5 per cent in 1981, and 9.4 per cent in 1988. In the 1986 elections that were fought under proportional rules, the PS allocated 18.9 per cent of the places on its lists to women candidates, and 19.3 per cent of those on the lists for the regional elections held simultaneously. However only 9.8 per cent of those elected under the party banner to the National Assembly and 11.4 per cent of those elected to regional councils were women, as they tended to be placed in lower, non-electable, positions.

While the party was preparing its lists for the 1986 legislative elections at the national congress of Toulouse, a group of about 150 activists and leading women in the party interrupted a closed meeting of the national secretariat to protest the lack of women on the proposed candidate list (*La Vie*, 14–20 November 1985). According to Yvette Roudy, 'We have been treated like doormats, hardly gloriously. The party has thought of everyone except women' (*Libération*, 7 October 1985).[13] In 1989 the FNESR (*Fédération nationale des élus socialistes et républicains*) undertook a survey of women inside the PS who held elective office which revealed a lack of respect for this particular quota as a major concern of those interviewed (Saint-Criq, 1989: 35).

Out of all the political parties in France it has been the PS that has devoted the most attention to women's rights issues on its campaign platform. However, support for women's rights issues, such as day care, equal employment for women and state-funded abortion, was a result of the combination of the party's interest (and especially that of François Mitterand) in attracting the shifting women's vote, and the pressure from PS feminists (Mazur, 1991). As long as the party hierarchy felt that promoting gender-orientated issues in their party platform was electorally rewarding, certain demands of the PS feminists would be included on the party platform.

In the 1970s, Socialist themes of social and economic justice embraced a definition of women's rights which went beyond the guarantee of women's political rights to include formal equality. In 1977, the newly created new women's rights commission or Secrétariat des Droits de la Femme called for a mini-congress (*convention*) on women's rights to be held in January of 1978. Attended by party delegates from all federations, the convention was simultaneously a triumph for the PS feminists and a disappointment for the younger feminists in the PS who had hoped for a more pro-feminist movement line. This project would provide the basis of the Socialist government's policy on women in 1981, as expressed in Mitterand's campaign platform (*110 propositions pour la France*). The extent to which the PS chose to associate itself explicitly with feminist issues was illustrated in 1981 when the group Choisir invited all of the candidates for the 1981 presidential election to a forum on women's issues, *Quel Président pour les femmes?* (Choisir, 1981), and Mitterand was the only mainstream candidate to attend.

Even though the PS continued to articulate demands for gender issues throughout the 1980s, the influences of the PS feminists declined within the party. As a result, especially after 1986, women's rights issues received less attention in party discussions and were placed lower on the party agenda. This change was a result of the combined effects of the declining public interest in women's rights, the centrality of issues related to the economic crisis and the experiences of the Socialist party in government. For example, in the 1988 presidential elections Mitterand had replaced the specificity of his 1981 platform with a far more general pronouncement about equality between the sexes (*Le Monde*, 7 April 1988). In 1988, the second national convention on women's rights was held at Chatellerault. This convention, unlike the first convention in 1978, was attended mostly by the established PS feminists and not the mandarins of the party, which was indicative of the reduced interest in such issues among the party leadership.

Rassemblement Pour la République (RPR)
Currently, the RPR can count, in its new (1990) governing

structures, two women out of a total of eight assistant general secretaries (*secrétaires généraux adjoints*), or 25 per cent, and seven women out of twenty-nine secretaries (*secrétaires nationaux*), or 24.1 per cent. However, most of them have been placed in charge of sectors traditionally assigned to women, such as the family (*famille*), the elderly (*les personnes âgées*), women's activity (*action féminine*) and daily life (*la vie quotidienne*). It is also important to note that this higher proportion of women was appointed following the dramatic and public eviction of a leading woman in the party, Michèle Barzach, from the leadership.[14]

In previous periods, the number of women in top positions has not been so high. In 1985, there was one woman out of twenty on the national secretariat (5 per cent), and two out of twenty-eight on the Executive Bureau, or 7.1 per cent. The legislative body of the party had nineteen out of 170 women members, or 11.1 per cent (Sineau, 1988: 3). The same figures for 1978 are 14 per cent for the Executive Bureau and 8 per cent for the legislative organ (Mossuz-Lavau and Sineau, 1981: 118). The party has never had any formal quotas for internal offices for women. The party has taken the position that increased representation of women within the party structure would occur naturally as a function of the progress of women in society.

In 1965 the Centre Féminins d'Etudes et d'Information (CFEI) was created on the initiative of de Gaulle. He envisaged it as a civic organization, that would exist parallel to the political party, to help educate and mobilize women to become Gaullist voters. However, women active in the Gaullist movement saw it as a way of systematically marginalizing demands for change within the party from women and channelling their activities into a separate organization. They believed that the CFEI was established to remove internal threats from women members to force change in the party's platform on women. The CFEI still exists, claiming 30,000 members in 1988 (*Profession Politique*, 5 December 1988).

After the PS victory in 1981, the group, which by then had taken on the name *Femme Avenir*, became somewhat more active and politicized than before. Shifting its stance from that of a civic group to a more explicitly political agenda that promoted certain ideas about women's rights, it set up a new network at the local level to 'monitor strikes, discrimination in hiring practices according to union membership, and marxist text books' (Sigoda, 1984: 152). With a veneer of non-partisanship, *Femme Avenir* actively tries to support women candidates who have received the party nomination and it participated in the national congress of the RPR in October 1991 (*Femme Avenir*, December 1991).

Inside the party hierarchy, it is only recently that there has been an active women's section. The RPR did include a national delegation for women (*action féminine*) in the new structures that were inaugurated in 1976–7, but this had no voice in the national secretariat. In 1978, the then delegate Noëlle Dewavrin (now president of *Femme Avenir*), said that, 'My role is precisely to permit women to adapt by convincing them that they do not have specific complaints' (*Le Monde*, 26 June 1978). The delegation remained relatively moribund until 1988, when the RPR attempted to rejuvenate it. A new delegate was appointed, Danielle Refuveille, and the office today forms part of the national secretariat. Refuveille is much more sympathetic to the concept of equal rights for women, and in a recent interview was highly critical of her predecessors and the party's longstanding apathy towards gender issues. This secretariat within the party has delegates within each of the departmental federations.

Candidate selection in the RPR is rather centralized (Thiébault, 1988: 73), although the national party organization has always had to cope with the influence wielded by well-implanted local notables. The militant base, in practice, does not exert much control over the selection process, except in rare cases. The party does not have any positive action strategy to advance women as candidates: as the general secretary of the party in 1986, Jacques Toubon, said, 'The choice of a woman is not made because she is a woman, but because she is a good candidate. That is true democracy, anything else is sexism.' Yet Toubon was also quoted as recognizing that prospective women candidates do not generally have prior experience of holding office, and hence would not be considered as viable party candidates (Mangin and Martichoux, 1991: 227).

The lack of emphasis on promoting women as candidates was reflected in the party's candidate lists for the 1986 legislative elections. Out of the 388 candidates invested by the party on the joint lists (with the UDF), there were forty women, or 10.3 per cent of the total. However, only one of those women was at the head of a list, and another two in positions that could be considered electable (in fact, all three were elected). Thus the non-interventionist strategy of the party failed to advance women as candidates even under conditions of proportional representation.

One well-known example of the way women candidates have been treated by the RPR is that of Florence d'Harcourt, president of *Femme Avenir* before Noëlle Dewavrin. In 1977, d'Harcourt replaced Achille Peretti, appointed to the Constitutional Council, in the National Assembly.[15] She expected to receive the endorsement of the party in the 1978 elections, but was passed over for Robert Hersant, a wealthy press magnate. Peretti was quoted as having told the party that, 'She is well brought-up, she is a woman, she will step aside' (*Profession Politique*, 30 November 1989). D'Harcourt did not. Running as a dissident against Hersant, she was elected, and joined the UDF, being re-elected in 1981 and 1986. In 1988, Jacques Chirac asked her to make way for another man, Nicholas Sarkozy. D'Harcourt agreed, in exchange for a written guarantee of a seat in the European Parliament in the 1989 elections. However, in 1989, the RPR–UDF placed her in a completely non-electable position on their list. D'Harcourt is no longer a member of the RPR, having chosen to leave the party in protest (Mangin and Martichoux, 1991: 231–2).[16]

In general the approach of the Gaullist party to women's issues has been to support measures which encourage women to have children, yet allow them to work outside of the home. This was echoed in *Nation*, the publication of the Gaullist party, in a special electoral issue for the presidential elections in 1965. This article placed the improvement of women's rights within the context of the necessity of family roles. 'Women, even emancipated, must first take care of their families.'

On the right, although a few women expected their parties to redefine their programme for women's rights to reflect the changes in French society, the RPR did not significantly alter its agenda on women's issues in the 1980s. Concerns about the economic crisis overshadowed any pressure to express demands for gender equality in employment. An excerpt from a speech delivered by the General Secretary of the RPR in 1982 shows how the party's position on women's issues rejected any feminist claims, emphasizing women's familial role. 'No to feminism, yes to women and the family' (*Le Monde*, 26 January 1982).

In 1988, the revitalized women's section within the party attempted to force change in this long-held position. They organized a conference in November of that year, with the intention of redefining the party platform to cover three issues that they felt were central to French women's concerns: financial autonomy, the improvement of women's image and political participation. According to Danielle Refuveille, the party needed to 'present a new discourse on women' (*Politique Professionelle*, 5 December 1988). However, the reticence of the party to consider such a change was demonstrated by the fact that only three men from the party attended: Refuveille expressed her dissatisfaction at the lack of response from the party following this session.

Conclusions

Significant differences do exist between the formal approach to women exhibited by the two parties discussed, both in terms of their internal treatment and their external platforms. The PS has defined a positive action strategy to promote women within the party, while the RPR has always refused, on principle, to consider such a strategy. The PS has used women's rights issues as an important electoral carrot, whereas the RPR has always made their treatment of women's rights subservient to the promotion of women as mothers and family policy.

However, the data presented above show the limits to these differences. Despite the positive action strategy adopted by the PS, there is little significant difference between the parties in the numbers of women as members, leaders, candidates and elected officials. The criticisms often heard from women in both parties have a striking similarity. One PS woman activist was quoted as saying, 'If women want to move up the party hierarchy, if they want to get a post, they will not be able to do it, I would say, just as women' (Rey and Subileau, 1991: 82); similarly, Danielle Refuveille (RPR) stated that 'Parties are only concerned abut women before the elections, or afterwards when they have lost' (*Profession Politique*, 5 December 1988).

The dissatisfaction among women in the PS was clearly documented by Saint-Criq (1989). Of her sample of 484 women socialists in elected office, 53 per cent felt that the party 'does not promote women', 44 per cent felt that women 'are victims of speaking freely within the party', while 33 per cent even went so far as to say that 'the PS discourages women' (1991: 37). Regarding quotas, 59 per cent were in favour of their maintenance. Rey and Subileau note that their questionnaires elicited very little difference between the satisfaction level among male and female militants; however, the detailed interviews that they conducted showed a clear pattern of dissatisfaction among women (1991: 80–1).

Where women have advanced within both parties, it is often as much linked to what has been called *le fait du prince* (having a patron) as much as any positive action strategies. Within the PS, where the fractions are highly personalized, women's advancement often depends upon the personal desire of the leaders (all men) to include them. The dangers of this dynamic are shown by the fact that at least one fraction, the *courant C* (Rocard) has always had a reputation for failing to promote women, and only 15 per cent of its members are women. Rey and Subileau note 'the necessity of following a man by belonging to his fraction if women want to advance in the party's hierarchy and, even more importantly, gain access to elected office' (1991: 81). In the RPR, where the national leadership has tremendous power of appointment, this is equally pronounced; after Michèle Barzach was removed from the party leadership in 1990, Jacques Chirac claimed that, 'In any case, I made her . . . when I took her in hand, she was completely unknown' (Mangin and Martichoux, 1991: 252). It is true that men are also dependent upon patrons to advance within these French parties. However, these relationships escape the writ of formal party rules, and, as do similar informal practices in other organizations, on balance tend to discriminate against women.

Given these findings, we conclude that there are still significant internal barriers within French parties to the advancement of women. The rhetoric of gender equality, whatever the ideological nuances, that has become almost obligatory for leading party figures and party platforms, obscures the reality of the obstacles to women that permeate party hierarchies. From levels of activism to positions on decision-making bodies, from candidacies to elected office, women still lag behind their male counterparts. Rey and Subileau identify the 'gap that exists between the official discourse regarding women outside of the party [PS] and the unequal treatment that is reserved for them inside' (1991: 81). Although women have made great strides in other areas of modern French society, the political parties still present a formidable obstacle to their advancement in the political arena.

Notes

1 IFOP, *Le Journal de Dimanche* (19 May 1991), cited in Sineau (1991).

2 Of the 954 people polled by BVA-*Paris-Match* between 12 and 18 December, 47 per cent expressed confidence in Simone Veil (*Libération*, 31 December 1991).

3 While feminists pressed the ministry to use the term 'women's rights' (*droits des femmes*), the socialist government favoured 'rights of woman' (*droits de la femme*) after the French term for human rights – *droits de l'homme*. The feminists argued that whereas 'rights of woman' implied some distant vision of womanhood, 'women's rights' represented women as a collective. In the end, the socialists won this struggle over political meaning. Ironically, the title of the ministry changed to 'women's rights' in 1988 under the Rocard government after the office was demoted.

4 These include: full ministers (*ministres d'etat*), ministers (*ministres*), junior ministers (*ministres délégués*), and secretaries of state (*secrétaires d'etat*).

5 All translations are by the authors.

6 One interesting attempt to make such an estimate of the membership of the RPR was that of Bréchon et al. (1987b). They placed it at 331,000 in 1984, while the RPR claimed 850,000. However, their method depended upon an average of

estimates by delegates to the party's national convention, a method that is somewhat open to error.

7 Exhaustive research at the national offices of the PS and RPR failed to produce any more up-to-date figures of women's membership.

8 The PS and the RPR are currently the two most electorally important parties in France, both having a well organized national implantation. As pointed out above, the PCF has lost much of its electoral influence and membership, and the UDF is loosely organized with a negligible activist base.

9 See Table 5.5 for the comparative breakdown of the number of women PS structures.

10 The new quota was voted at the extraordinary party congress at Rennes in 1990, but did not come into effect until after the next regularly scheduled congress held in December 1991.

11 The PS allows for the existence of party fractions (*courants*) organized around motions presented and voted on at the bi-annual national party congress. The motion must receive at least 5 per cent of the congress vote in order for the fraction to receive official status, which then allows it proportional representation in the party's decision-making bodies.

12 This currently applies to regional and municipal elections. The 1986 legislative elections were fought under a proportional list system, although this has since been changed back to the old constituency-based method. The European elections also work by proportional list rules.

13 At the same conference, there was an impasse over the application of the quota for women on the *comité directeur*, as none of the incumbents wished to cede their place to a woman. The solution found was to increase the size of the CD . . .

14 Barzach, who had in the past been seen as one of Chirac's favourites within the party, was evicted for her sympathies with the opposition to Chirac (*les rénovateurs*) during 1989, although she claimed it was because she is a woman. However, on learning of the non-renewal of her mandate, she made a speech during which she burst into tears, an event that was carried as the lead story on the evening television news. Some have suggested that it was to efface this negative image for the RPR that seven new women were appointed to the national secretariat (*Libération*, 22 February 1990).

15 In France, each candidate for the legislative elections designates a replacement (*suppléant*) at the time of the election. In the case of resignation or death, that replacement automatically takes the seat until the next regular election. Women are often chosen in this position.

16 One of the more pithy sayings attributed to Chirac is that 'Promises only bind those who receive them'.

6

Party Change and Women's Representation in Unified Germany

Eva Kolinsky

Until the 1960s, women in Germany tended to prefer conservative political parties and took a relatively passive approach to politics, be it as voters, as party members or as activists competing for elite positions. The entry of the post-war generations of educated and qualified women into political life mobilized electoral choices while the interest in active political participation and in office-holding transformed party cultures. The introduction of quotas in the mid-1980s extended opportunities and recast the place of women in German politics. The new focus on women's equality in politics emanated from West Germany and reflected the political aspirations of West German women. In the East, the party practices and quota commitments of the West were, of course, instituted but women's orientations and preferences have tended to favour gender roles which had lost credibility in the West. We shall consider the impact of unification on women in German politics, and examine how participation and opportunities have widened in political parties and parliaments.

German unification and women in politics

Until 3 October 1990, the post-war history of Germany was one of contrasting political and social orders. Women seemed to fare better in the East and enjoy equality with men in the ubiquitous and prescribed role of *Werktätige*, working people. Marriage, motherhood and gender seemed to have lost their sting as obstructions to equal opportunities and socio-economic participation (Winkler, 1990). Yet, unification revealed that the presumed advantage of women in the East was in reality a disadvantage: an agenda of hidden inequalities and state-administered discrimination had short-changed East German women of their opportunities. A false sense of equality prevented the emergence of something which has stood women in the West in good stead – a keen sense of injustice paired with the confidence that improvements of opportunity and participation can be accomplished (Frevert, 1989).

In 1990 even the most optimistic forecasts spoke of years before social unification would take place, for the scars of unemployment and relative deprivation to heal and lifestyles to blend sufficiently between East and West to obliterate the former German–German border (Smith et al., 1992). Yet, the differences between the two societies are more superficial than the proclaimed contrast of social systems would suggest. In a country which regarded employment as a key dimension of citizenship, women had a duty to work, not merely a right to do so. The East German state had an elaborate web of incentives for childbearing, concessions at work and childcare facilities, but also of low pay and women's tracks in education and employment which amounted to a structural disadvantage for women. Moreover, in family lives, traditional role divisions remained virtually unchallenged and unquestioned. After unification, East German women were adamant that they wanted to continue in employment and avail themselves of institutional childcare as they had done during the lifetime of the GDR. Allowed to choose, eight out of ten women on either side of the former German–German border would choose part-time work and combine a variety of roles in their lives (Kolinsky, 1992a). East German socialism had produced little more than a thin layer of compliance. Underneath it, traditional values and orientations survived in the private niches, into which GDR citizens chose to retreat; and socialism itself was characterized by an essentially conservative sediment of assumptions and prescribed roles (Weidenfeld and Zimmermann, 1989)

The gender divide in German party politics

If the East–West gender divide can be regarded as transitional and likely to be smoothed out as the two German societies grow together, the gender divide of party politics in Germany has been more persistent. Long before women enjoyed the right to join political parties or attend public meetings – a right which was granted in 1908 – and long before they won the right to vote and stand for elections – a right offered in 1918 as a reward for women's contribution to the war effort – gender politics were embedded in the ideological and class divides of Imperial Germany. This divide remains visible to this day.

Until National Socialism banned all political parties and movements other than its own mass organizations, Germany had two rival women's movements: the socialist Women's Movement on the left, and the so-called Bürgerliche Frauenbewegung on the conservative right, the women's movement of the middle class (Thönessen, 1976). Both movements regarded women's education as a prime task. The socialist movement aimed to reduce the multiple disadvantages of working-class girls and increase their opportunities through education and training, while the bourgeois women's movement combined an emphasis on education and opportunities with imparting homemaking skills and espoused the values of motherhood and family life. The socialist women's movement were early champions of voting rights for women; by contrast, the bourgeois women's movement remained divided over voting rights until after they had been granted. Similarly, the Social Democratic party and the parties of the left which emerged in the wake of the First World War, professed to welcome the participation of women in politics, and the SPD even devised a special formula to increase the number of women delegates at party congresses in the days before women could legally take part in public and political meetings (Kolinsky, 1991b: 208ff). For the left, women's equality was a facet of equality for all. By contrast, the 'bourgeois' women's movement and parties interpreted equality in accordance with a given biological and social setting. For women, the roles of spouse, mother, carer were supposedly closer to their nature and thus better guarantors of equality than joining the man's world of politics, parties, parliaments (Wisniewski, 1984: 21–77).

Ironically, when voting rights were granted to women in 1918, conservative and bourgeois parties, which had been opposed to enfranchising women, attracted the bulk of female electoral support. This structural imbalance of the relationship between gender and party politics persisted throughout the Weimar Republic. The Catholic Centre party in particular appealed to women while the Social Democrats lost out. The uneven preferences of women can be linked to the relatively strong position of religion among women and the relatively weak position of trade unionism. Both these traits have carried over into the post-war era: women have been more inclined than men towards religious observance and more detached from trade unions. It has been suggested that in the 1920s the 'women's bonus' of the centre-right amounted to about 15 per cent (Hofmann-Göttig, 1986: 29). In the closing years of the Weimar Republic, women also shifted their preferences to the National Socialists after the liberal parties and much of the political centre collapsed.

The German party system was recast after National Socialism and the multi-partism of the Weimar years gave way to a pattern of two major and one or two minor parties strong enough to gain parliamentary representation (Oberreuter and Mintzel, 1990). The new party system avoided much of the ideological polarization of the 1920s and 1930s and encouraged a broad endorsement of democratic political processes and practices, but the left–right imbalance of gender and party politics continued to influence post-war German party politics.

Despite reorganization, party preferences after 1945 showed a high degree of continuity with the 1920s. Germans continued to vote according to their place in society. Social class, religious affiliation or affinity to trade unions were key factors in choosing a political party. In the Weimar Republic, the centre and the right had been more divided. In the Federal Republic, the Christian Democrats (CDU and CSU) succeeded in pooling the electoral support right of centre. Society, however, remained sharply divided between left and right and there was little movement between the two camps. In the mid-1960s, Rokkan and Lipset wrote of a 'frozen' party system (Rokkan and Lipset, 1967). In their view, party orientations had been frozen into rigidity since the 1920s. While the political system should have encouraged party pluralism and free electoral choices, there was little electoral mobility. German voters had yet to learn that party preferences could be changed, and that politics was not dominated by two hostile, class-based camps.

But the diagnosis of the 'frozen' state of German politics was made just as a 'thaw' set in. First, the political parties had changed to become *Volksparteien*, people's parties or catch-all parties without sharp-edged ideological divisions and with a broad commitment to the same political and economic system and similar policy goals (Smith, 1986). Parties had begun to represent cross-sections of society, not predominantly one group, milieu or class. The CDU/CSU established itself as the political force of the centre/right, while the SPD shed its commitment to socialism and emerged as the dominant political force left of centre which could appeal to a variety of orientations and political positions. Since both major political parties shared a substantial common ground of politics, changing from one to the other no longer meant changing sides but merely changing emphasis.

The second important development to unfreeze the German party system arose from the changing nature of German society. The rapid expansion of the economy transformed lifestyles, mellowed class divides, created new career path and expectations. For the new middle class, the fastest growing social strata in post-war society, political preferences were increasingly determined by personal preferences and the perceived competence of one political party against another (Smith, 1992). After the late 1960s, political behaviour in Germany became less predictable and more varied. As unprecedented social mobility and novel opportunities recast lifestyles in post-war Germany, inherited regional and class divides began to fade. Unfrozen compared with the founding years of the Federal Republic or the Weimar years, electoral choices and political orientations tended to reflect personal circumstances and interests.

The new diversity of political choices has been particularly evident among women. Electoral mobility reduced the dominant position of political conservatism in Germany and freed the SPD from the luckless 'women's deficit' which had plagued it since women won the vote. In 1949 the chairman of the SPD, Kurt Schumacher, blamed women for the election defeat of his party. Had women been interested in politics – he alleged – had they been able to withstand the temptations of misleading slogans from the other side, the better party would have won and bread prices would not be soaring sky high (Schumacher, 1949: 2). Two decades later the tide turned. When the 1972 elections returned the SPD as the largest party in the German parliament, party chairman and Federal Chancellor Willy Brandt made a point of explicitly thanking women for their support. From then on, no political party could take women's votes for granted (Table 6.1) although unification has brought a new gender gap whereby the right has an electoral advantage among women in the new Länder.

Participation in elections

In West Germany, women have long expressed less interest in politics than men and have been less inclined to discuss politics in their spare time. However, over the years, more women took politics seriously and wanted to influence events. As the post-war generations came of age, democratic socialization and values left their traces, as did better access to education and a broader range of accepted social behaviour (Schäfers, 1990: 196–200). In the late 1980s, 36 per cent of women declared they had no interest in politics, the remaining 44 per cent thought politics important. Half of those interested in politics believed they could also influence its course (Wohlfahrtssurvey, 1989: 545)

Turnout in elections is regarded as the most effective form of political participation by over 80 per cent of the German population. Except in the 1919 election, the first in which women

Table 6.1   *Party preferences of women and men (%) in Germany, 1953–1990*

Women

	CDU/CSU	SDP	FDP	Greens	B90	PDS	Others	+/–
1953	47	28	10				15	+19
1957	54	29	7				10	+25
1961	50	33	12		.		5	+17
1965	52	36	9				3	+16
1969	51	40	5				4	+11
1972	46	46	8				1	0
1976	49	43	8				1	+6
1980	44	44	11	1			.	0
1983	49	39	6	5			.	+10
1987	45	38	8	8			1	+7
1990a	45	34	11	4	1	.	3	+11
1990b	45	36	10	5	.	3	4	+9
1990c	43	24	13	–	6	11	15	+19

Men

	CDU/CSU	SPD	FDP	Greens	B90	PDS	Others	+/–
1953	39	33	12				17	+6
1957	45	35	9				12	+10
1961	40	40	14				6	0
1965	42	44	10				4	–2
1969	41	46	6				8	–5
1972	43	47	9				1	–4
1976	47	44	8				1	+3
1980	44	43	11	2			1	+1
1983	48	38	7	6			1	+10
1987	43	39	9	8			2	+4
1990a	43	34	11	4	1	1	5	+9
1990b	43	37	11	5	–	.	6	+6
1990c	39	25	13	–	5	12	5	+14

. denotes figures too small to give percentage; 1990a = unified Germany, i.e. territory since 3 October 1990; 1990b = territory of the FRG (West Germany, excluding Berlin) prior to unification; 1990c = territory of the former GDR only.

The +/– column is intended to show the imbalance of the party system as difference between CDU/CSU and SDP support.

CDU and CSU maintain a political alliance with the CSU based in Bavaria, the CDU elsewhere. In 1990, the Greens campaigned only in the old FRG, the B90/ Green Alliance only in the former GDR. These parties have since merged.

PDS is the successor party of the Socialist Unity party, but it did campaign throughout unified Germany in 1990.

Sources: Compiled from data in Kolinsky, 1992a: 201 and *Wirtschaft und Statistik 4*, 1991: 257

were permitted to vote, average turnout has been lower among women than among men (Metje, 1991: 358ff). Compared with other countries, turnout in Germany is high, and the lower turnout of German women may well have topped the participation charts in another electoral context.[1]

If we compare turnout at federal elections in West Germany, including the all-German election of December 1990, a more differentiated picture emerges (Table 6.2). Among the youngest voters, and among voters over the age of fifty, turnout among women has remained lower than among men. For voters over the age of seventy, the gender gap, which seemed to close after 1969, reopened, and stood at 10 percentage points in 1990. In 1969, women in the two youngest electoral groups, those aged between twenty-one and thirty were more ardent voters than their male peers. These age cohorts of women have continued to be active voters with a higher turnout than men in the same age groups.

The data on turnout suggest that women of this generation retained their interest in political participation throughout their adult lives. (Table 6.2). The lower turnout among older women than older men may reflect more traditional attitudes to political participation. This cannot explain the low turnout of young women, which declined throughout the 1970s and 1980s, reaching a low point in 1990.

In the West German regions of unified Germany, fewer than two out of three young women chose to vote; in the Eastern regions, participation was even lower and only one in two women under 25 voted. Within ten years, electoral participation among the youngest voters has dropped by 17 per cent (Mayer, 1991: 253). Several factors may contribute to non-voting. Scepticism about the usefulness of political parties has been widespread among young West Germans, including young women. Political parties tend to be regarded as too detached from their voters, and oblivious of people's needs. Studies of young women in West Germany found that they believed social movements could represent their interests better than any of the political parties of the day (Seidenspinner and Burger, 1982). Education may also have a role to play since educated young West Germans have been more detached from the established political system and its channels of conventional participation than those with less advanced education or the older generations. Among young women, the critical impact of education may contribute to recasting their electoral participation, with non-voting a deliberate gesture of detachment rather than a pointer to disinterest in politics or ignorance about it (Piel, 1989: 5–6).

Table 6.2   *Turnout at German federal elections by age and gender, 1969–1990*

Women

	Election turnout (% of votes cast)							
Age	1990a	1990b	1987	1983	1980	1976	1972	1969
Under 21	63	65	75	83	79	83	84	—[1]
21–25	60	62	72	81	78	83	85	**77**
25–30	**66**	67	75	84	**83**	87	89	**83**
30–35	**72**	**73**	**80**	**87**	**87**	**90**	91	86
35–40	**76**	**76**	**84**	**90**	**89** .	**92**	92	87
40–45	**80**	**80**	**86**	91	**90**	93	93	89
45–50	82	82	**88**	92	91	93	94	89
50–60	84	84	89	92	92	93	93	88
60–70	85	85	88	92	91	93	92	87
70 +	71	71	77	83	84	86	83	76
Total	76	76	82	88	87	90	90	85

Men

	Election turnout (% of votes cast)							
Age	1990a	1990b	1987	1983	1980	1976	1972	1969
Under 21	66	69	79	86	82	85	85	—[1]
21–25	63	65	74	82	80	83	84	76
25–30	66	68	77	84	82	86	88	80
30–35	71	72	80	87	86	89	90	86
35–40	75	76	84	89	88	91	92	86
40–45	79	80	86	91	90	93	93	90
45–50	82	83	88	92	92	94	95	91
50–60	85	85	90	93	93	95	95	92
60–70	88	88	92	94	94	95	95	91
70 +	81	81	85	89	90	91	90	86
Total	77	78	84	89	88	91	91	88

1990a, data relate to the FRG after unification; 1990b, data relate to West Germany (without Berlin) before unification.

Bold indicates turnout higher among women than among men.

[1] Voting age in 1969 was 21; then reduced to 18.

Source: Mayer, 1991: 252

It is too early to draw conclusions from the low electoral turnout in the former GDR. The federal election of December 1990 was the fourth election in one year, and the social impact of unification was not yet apparent. The low turnout may have been little more than election fatigue in a society not used to democratic elections. In the West, however, non-voting among women can be linked more directly to discontent with the existing parties and the choices they offer.

Party preferences

The pattern of party preferences among women changed significantly as the post-war generations moved into the German electorate. In the founding years of the Federal Republic, women voters were drawn to the governing Christian Democratic Party or its Bavarian sister party, the Christian Social Union. It was not unusual for party preferences to be determined by fathers or husbands and adopted by women. For the 1940s and 1950s, life stories and surveys of public opinion suggest that this was so. Gender differences were thus added to the social and economic cleavages based on class, denomination and trade union membership which have been emphasized as determinants of political behaviour in electoral analyses. Today, the 'women's deficit' experienced by the Social Democrats or the 'women's bonus' of the Christian Democrats are largely confined to the new Länder while politics in the old Länder and in the Federal Republic as a whole have become more balanced in terms of gender (Hofmann-Göttig, 1989: 11–28).

Since the early 1970s, the electoral margin between the two main political parties in the Federal Republic has narrowed to a few percentage points (Table 6.3). Women have played a major part in these developments. In 1972, the CDU/CSU and SPD ran neck and neck among female voters; in the 1980s, it was the emergence of the Green party and its capacity to win votes from the Social Democrats which altered the balance of the party system again and reinstated the advantage of the CDU/CSU. For 1990, the breakdown by regions reveals only a slightly stronger electoral performance of the CDU or CSU among women than men (Table 6.3). Indeed, in several regions – Berlin, Hesse, Lower Saxony, Schleswig-Holstein for instance – elections recently resulted in a change of government. By that time, the SPD performed as well among women as among men; in some regions, the SPD even had a women's bonus, although both the poor showing of the party in the new German Länder and the renewed shift towards the CDU/CSU have been larger among female than male voters.

Away from the two major parties, women's preferences have been no less important in narrowing electoral margins, and in challenging political parties to address the issues to which their potential voters attach priority. Initially, the Greens attracted

Table 6.3   *Preferences by regions and gender, 1990*

Women

Region	SPD	CDU	CSU	FDP	Greens	B90	PDS	REP	Others
S-H	39	44	–	11	4	–	.	1	1
HH	44	36	–	11	6	–	1	1	1
NS	39	46	–	9	4	–	.	1	1
BRE	42	32	–	13	8	–	1	1	3
NRW	42	40	–	11	4	–	.	1	1
HE	39	42	–	10	6	–	.	1	2
RH-PF	35	48	–	10	4	–	.	1	2
B-W	29	49	–	11	5	–	.	2	3
BY	27	–	54	8	5	–	.	4	3
Saar	52	39	–	5	2	–	.	1	1
B	31	40	–	9	4	–	10	2	4
M-V	26	40	–	10	–	7	15	1	2
BRA	31	38	–	10	–	7	12	1	2
S-AN	24	40	–	20	–	6	9	.	1
TH	22	47	–	15	–	6	8	1	2
S	18	51	–	12	–	6	9	1	3
FRG	34	38	7	11	4	1	3	1	2
FRG-old	36	36	9	10	5	–	.	2	2
FRG-new	24	43	–	13	.	6	11	1	3

Men

Region	SPD	CDU	CSU	FDP	Greens	B90	PDS	REP	Others
S-H	39	42	–	12	4	–	1	2	.
HH	40	34	–	12	8	–	2	3	1
NS	39	43	–	11	4	–	.	2	1
BRE	42	31	–	13	7	–	1	4	2
NRW	43	39	–	11	4	–	.	2	2
HE	38	40	–	11	5	–	.	3	5
RH-PF	37	45	–	11	4	–	.	3	2
B-W	30	45	–	12	5	–	.	5	3
BY	28	–	50	8	5	–	.	7	3
Saar	53	36	–	6	2	–	.	1	2
B	30	38	–	9	4	–	10	3	5
M-V	25	36	–	9	–	7	19	3	2
BRA	32	35	–	10	–	6	13	2	2
S-AN	26	37	–	19	–	5	10	2	1
TH	23	42	–	15	–	5	9	2	4
S	19	47	–	13	–	5	9	2	5
FRG	34	35	7	11	4	1	3	3	2
FRG-old	37	34	8	11	5	–	.	3	3
FRG-new	25	39	–	13	.	5	12	2	4

Source: Wirtschaft und Statistik 4, 1991: 257

more male voters (Kolinsky, 1988: 136). Since the late 1980s, however, the situation has been reversed and more women than men voted Green. As we shall see later, the Greens entered the 1987 elections with a commitment to quotas of women and more female than male candidates. Moreover, at the time women regarded the Greens as the most competent of all political parties in terms of equal opportunities (Kolinsky, 1989a). Men, by contrast, have been attracted more strongly to the right extremist Republican Party, and in the new German Länder more men than women supported the Party of Democratic Socialism,. i.e. the revamped Socialist Unity Party (the Communists) of the GDR.

Traditionally, women have been reluctant to support small or new political parties (Bürklin, 1987). The new electoral mobility of women has generated an interesting political distinction between preferred parties and parties which hold no interest for women. Whether a party is small or large, old or new has become less relevant than its perceived policy competence. Thus, parties of the extreme right have elicited more support from men than from women, and this gender difference has remained in place regardless of the lifespan of the party. For the Greens, the situation is different. Initially, the party campaigned on a policy blend of ecology and peace. Many of their leading politicians and party organizers originated from the splintered radicalism of the far left which succeeded the student movement (Fogt, 1989). As women's equality gained prominence as a key issue of the party, women began to turn towards the Greens and became the dominant force in the Green electorate.

In a broader perspective, the emergence of the SPD as a political party which could extend its support among women voters, and the decline of the CDU as the natural choice for women voters, follow the same logic. Parties have changed their policies towards women and offered new avenues to equality and political participation. They did so in response to a changing society and after their established approaches failed to produce the expected results, that of retaining or winning women as voters.

Generational perspectives on party choices

The divide of party preferences and the mode in which they are influenced is a generational effect: women born into the post-war period perceive the SPD as the party of innovation and opportunity while women of the older generation did not see the SPD in these terms. The post-war generation of women enjoyed improved access to education, qualifications and employment, expected different lifestyles, family sizes and social roles from those their mother knew and expected. Women of the post-war generation have become more politically mobile, choosing from a variety of parties where women of the older generation tended to focus on the CDU (Table 6.4). In most occupational groups, the SPD forged ahead of the CDU among younger women but trailed behind it among those born before 1945. The better educated in particular were prone to scatter their vote: for 39 per cent of the young women with advanced education the Greens constituted the preferred party; only 5 per cent of highly educated women of the older generation opted for it. In the lowest educational bracket, younger women were more likely to support the SPD, older women the CDU. In particular, the SPD gained ground in the key professions of the new middle class, in intermediate and managerial white-collar positions. Older women in these groups were closer to the CDU.

The generation gap in women's party preferences can be traced back to generational differences in orientations and values. Younger women are twice as likely as those of the pre-1945 generation to regard employment as a priority (55 per cent and 26 per cent) or demand abortion as a right (19 per cent and 7 per cent). Yet, across the generations women believe that women should have more influence in society (73 per cent and 64 per cent), a demand which is also made by over 50 per cent of men (Brinkmann, 1990: 66). Comparative studies of generations in Germany have shown that attitudes contrast sharply between different age cohorts. This is almost certainly an effect of the changes of political system during most lifetimes in Germany, and the rapid transition from the survival culture of the immediate post-war years to one of the most affluent societies in the world. Overall, lifestyles and attitudes changed faster in Germany than in other democracies. Thus young Germans in the 1940s could be regarded as authoritarian in outlook. While in the 1980s, critical attitudes to authority and an emphasis on self-realization prevailed. By comparison to young Americans whose views today are similar to those their peers held forty years ago, young West Germans have little in common with the youth after the Second World War (Lederer, 1983; Shell, 1985). Such change has been even greater for women whose opportunities in education, employment, social and political participation only began to emerge in the late 1950s.

Politically, the new expectations, attitudes and political preferences made themselves felt in the diversification of party

Table 6.4 *Party preferences by occupational group and generation (%)*

	Women voters born before 1945					
	CDU/CSU	SPD	FDP	Greens	NPD	Others
Occupational group						
All groups	52	39	6	3	0	0
Lower level white-collar/civil service	56	39	6	0	0	0
Intermed. level white-collar/civil service	55	33	6	6	0	0
Higher level white-collar/civil service	47	22	22	9	0	0
New middle class	51	23	19	7	0	0
Self-employed	70	21	7	3	0	0
Blue-collar workers	47	50	1	2	0	0
Education						
Lower	52	42	4	2	0	0
Intermediate	54	34	6	6	0	0
Advanced	46	18	32	5	0	0

	Women voters born after 1945					
	CDU/CSU	SPD	FDP	Greens	NPD	Others
Occupational group						
All groups	32	44	9	16	0	0
Lower level white-collar/civil service	33	46	6	15	0	0
Intermed. level white-collar/civil service	32	46	11	12	0	0
Higher level white-collar/civil service	29	35	6	29	0	0
New middle class	33	33	8	25	0	0
Self-employed	3	20	27	20	0	0
Blue-collar workers	30	52	5	14	0	0
Education						
Lower	31	52	7	10	0	0
Intermediate	39	32	7	22	0	0
Advanced	19	26	13	39	0	3

Source: Brinkmann, 1990: 60–1

preferences, and the demise of the CDU as the dominant electoral choice for women. The high electoral participation among women of the post-1945 generation, with their newly mobile preferences, modified the imbalance of the German party system. By boosting the SPD and later the Greens, women helped to consolidate a democratic political culture in Germany based on party competition, and on the ability of political parties to transpose salient issues into credible policies. Women's disinterest in the Republicans and similar parties has also bridled the forces of right extremism and curtailed their influence in the Federal Republic before and after unification.

Party membership

Party membership in Germany has been characterized by quantitative and qualitative change since the 1960s. Membership has grown and its meaning has changed. Since the early 1970s, parties have expanded their social base, party membership has increased from 2 per cent to 4 per cent of the electorate. At the beginning of the 1990s, nearly one in four party members are women, and women constitute about 40 per cent of new members in political parties.

At the end of the 1960s, overall party membership in West Germany was below one million (Table 6.5). Two-thirds belonged to the SPD; on average one in seven party members were women, somewhat more in the SPD, fewer in CDU, CSU or FDP. Ten years later, overall membership of political parties had doubled; the SPD briefly passed the one-million mark in 1976 and has since consolidated its position around 930,000. The CDU grew much faster and became a mass party with a membership close to 750,000. The CSU, the only party whose membership increased continuously since the 1950s, and reached 180,000 in 1992 while the FDP, troubled by changing coalition arrangements and political orientations, suffered losses and gains which kept its membership around 70,000 (Kaack and Roth, 1980: 8ff). The Greens, who seemed poised in the early 1980s to incorporate new social movements – ecologists, anti-nuclear or peace movements, the new women's movement – have remained relatively small with a membership of under 40,000.

Party membership itself has changed its meaning. In the 1950s, the most common reason for joining the SPD was to support the organization. SPD membership seemed a normal aspect of certain working and living environments – mostly working class, and cohesive enough to be called a **milieu** (Oberndörfer and Schmitt, 1991; Rohe, 1990). At that time, membership in the CDU was based on neighbourhoods.

The aspirations of party members also differed. While the majority of SPD members seemed contented with passive membership, joining the CDU was frequently linked to the intention of holding an office. In fact, the most common cause of

Table 6.5 *Women in political parties: membership developments 1962–1992 (%)*[1]

Year	SPD	CDU[2]	CSU	FDP	Greens[3]
1962	19	15	.	.	–
1965	17	13	5	7–8	–
1969	17	13	7	12	–
1972	19	15	10	14	–
1976	21	20	12	19	–
1980	23	21	13	23	30
1983	25	22	14	24	33
1987	25	22	14	23	33
1990	27	23	15	24	33
1991a	27	23	17	30	33
1991b	20	39	0	n.a.	40

1991a, average for FRG as a whole; 1991b, average for new Länder only.

[1] The span of thirty years was chosen since major changes of the membership composition commenced only in the 1970s, and since the data for party membership in the 1940s and 1950s are very patchy for all parties except the SPD. It had 15 per cent women members in 1946 and 18 per cent in 1962.

[2] The membership figure of 39 per cent for the CDU is quoted in the party's equal opportunities reports, but accounts from party managers in the new Länder suggest that the figure reflects the proportion of women members in the CDU when it was a bloc party, and that since unification at least it has allowed their membership to lapse. A survey of party members in Leipzig found membership had shrunk to one-fifth of the previous level, see Willy Koch et al. (1990) CDU Mitglieder in Leipzig, University of Leipzig, Discussion Paper.

[3] The Greens have not kept accurate membership records but claim that women constitute one-third of the overall party membership, and somewhat more in the new Länder.

Sources: Data obtained by the author from the federal party offices; also Fülles, 1969: 24ff; Hoecker, 1987: 42ff. and Kolinsky, 1989b: 210

disappointment with the CDU as a political party has been an inability to hold political office (Falke, 1982).

By the 1990s, party cultures appear to have moved away from conventional patterns of articulating political allegiance; for example, SPD members are now described as social risers (Becker et al., 1983) who are eager to contribute to the political process, and to influence events (Hoecker, 1987). Members of the CDU indicate that their main reason for joining the party is to be with like-minded people, although both the CDU and CSU are also perceived as offering members access to influence, networks of business contacts and other socio-economic advantages (*Der Spiegel*, 1992).

Less apparent but no less important is the key party function of recruiting the political elite of a country. Parties provide the lists of candidates for parliamentary representation, for political office and leadership positions at all levels of local, regional and national politics (see below). Party membership, therefore, has two key dimensions. First, it is a step towards holding an office in the party organization. The party also provides or obstructs access to administrative and government offices and electoral opportunities. Secondly, the party may function as a social network, a meeting place and institutional environment for like-minded people from activist to inactive members (at least 75 per cent),

As the post-war generations entered German politics in the 1960s, party membership has become more individual, more clearly linked to political interest and to a motivation of shaping the course of politics, contributing to the policies of a given party, and also holding political office (Greven, 1987). For men, these changes underpinned existing modes of activity. For women, the same changes of membership motivation transformed the meaning of membership. Traditionally, women's activities and organizational involvement was focused on women's associations and remained separate from that of the main party organization. These maintain their own parallel organizational structures, hold their own conferences, formulate their own programmes. Although representatives of the women's associations have been entitled to a specified number of positions in the mainstream party, the 'women's track' of politics has been essentially separate and with limited political impact on the main party organization or access to positions of political power.

The SPD started its post-war history with a women's section, a women's officer and a federal women's congress at the eve of the main party congress. *Frauenarbeit*, women's activity, in the SPD was geared to educating women in socialist ideas in order to assist them with bringing up their children in a suitable frame of mind. That women should wish for a share of the political power which parties make accessible was not seriously considered until the 1970s. In 1973, with the new generation of women determined to leave their mark on party and politics, the women's section was replaced by the Association for Social Democratic Women (Arbeitsgemeinschaft sozialdemokratischer Frauen, ASF), which turned itself into a vociferous and tenacious pressure group for women's equality in the SPD (Kolinsky, 1991a).

In the other parties the situation was similar. The women's association of the CDU, the Association for Christian Democratic Women (Frauenvereinigung) was designed to promote party views and to involve women who were not members of the party; it was not intended to be a training ground for female political leaders. Separate congresses for women, separate programmes, separate activities ensured that women's political participation occurred, but rarely led to positions of political influence. In the CSU, the Women's Union (Frauenunion), subscribed to similar aims.

The deficit of women's influence was even more pronounced in the Liberal party. The FDP never created a women's association – partly because its organizational base was too thin to sustain an additional tier, and partly because it has always claimed to offer equal opportunities to women whose participation at all levels would be assured if only enough women came forward to compete for it. Liberal women were less convinced of their opportunities. In 1990, Irmgard Schwaetzer founded an Association for Liberal Women outside the party organization in order to give a voice to the interests of liberal women and also to create a pressure group which could influence the party executive's position.

The influx of new members into all political parties in the 1970s changed both the organizational balance of the West German party system and the internal party cultures (Table 6.5). On both sides of the political spectrum the concept of a catch-all party or *Volkspartei* began to mean mass party organization and became a key dimension of party politics (Mintzel, 1989: 3ff, 1990). New members brought into the party of their choice expectations about the nature of political participation. The impact they wanted to make through party membership in politics had little in common with the milieu-approach of earlier days. Women in particular no longer regarded their membership of a political party as auxiliary activity, focused on women's associations, coffee mornings and talking to other women. Those who joined a party were more motivated than the average German woman at the time to play a political role in line with their abilities, and equal to that of men. The parties responded to their demands.

The implementation of quotas

The SPD

The pace of change was set by the SPD. Traditionally, the SPD combined an organizational segregation of women from the main business of holding party posts and parliaments with allocating a minimum number of seats at executive level to women – normally as additional advisers and without political muscle of their own. When the new generation of women entered the party, they insisted that both the segregation an the preferential treatment be discontinued, since they were confident that they could win political office on the strength of their political acumen. The ensuing lesson was a harsh one. At the first party congress without designated women's posts, two women instead of the usual five were elected to the party executive. The 1972 federal elections brought another shock result. The SPD had won an unprecedented level of electoral support from women and emerged as the largest party in parliament. The number of women members of the Bundestag for the SPD, however, hit an all-time low (see Table 6.9). Although the party was perceived in German society at the time as a harbinger of better opportunities and equality, it had failed to meet expectations about women's opportunities in political life inside the party organization.

SPD women responded with a concerted effort to get more women nominated to parliamentary seats, and elected to parliaments. In 1976, women organized an election campaign of their own, alongside the official SPD campaign. The main result of the low representation of women in the early 1970s was a drawn out and at times acrimonious internal debate about women's representation and the legality or effectiveness of obligatory women's quotas. A decade of conflict finally came to an end when the party voted at its 1988 congress in Münster to incorporate a women's quota into the party statutes (*Frauen in der SPD*, 1988) It was agreed that by 1994 women should hold no less than 40 per cent of all party offices. By 1998 the quota is to be applied to candidate lists and to parliamentary representation. Viewed as an emergency device to break conventional structures and attitudes about access to power for men and women, quotas are intended to apply for a 25-year period only, and are to be abolished in the year 2013. By then, the participation of women is expected to be a normal element of the SPD party culture.

To women in the SPD, the Greens were trailblazers of equality. Close competition between Social Democrats and Greens for the same cohort of younger generation women left the SPD with no choice but to introduce a quota to improve the opportunities for women members of the party organization and in German parliamentary politics (Frauenbeauftragte . . ., 1985). The annual reports on equal opportunities in the SPD confirm that access for women has been transformed through quotas, and women have begun to be represented at all levels of the party hierarchy (Table 6.6).

Table 6.6 *Women and party offices in the SPD (%)*

Level	1977	1979	1982	1984	1986	1988	1990
Party executive	6	17	15	18	25	35	36
	(2)	(7)	(6)	(7)	(10)	(14)	(18)
Presidium	8	8	9	9	27	37	38
	(1)	(1)	(1)	(1)	(3)	(4)	(5)
Party council	6	15	12	21	23	32	37
	(7)	(17)	(14)	(21)	(23)	(28)	(41)
Congress delegates	n.a.	14	13	19	27	37	42
		(59)	(55)	(83)	(118)	(159)	(214)

Absolute figures are given in brackets.

Sources: Gleichstellungsbericht . . ., 1991: 7; Frauen in der SPD, 1988

The Greens

The move of the SPD from internal discussions on women's equality to the institution of a quota system was intended to attract women to join the party; it also was an attempt to regain credibility in an area where others had forged ahead. From the left, the Greens entered German politics with an emphatic commitment to participatory politics and anti-hierarchical practices. This included a pledge to ensure equal access to party posts and parliamentary seats for men and women. In 1985, the pledge was hardened into a requirement when the Greens wrote a 50 per cent women's quota into their statutes. They have since proceeded to distribute posts, candidacies and parliamentary seats in such a way that women hold at least half of them. During their first term in the Bundestag, the Greens replaced their parliamentary leadership at the half-way point of the legislative period with a so-called 'women's council', a *Weiberrat*. This occurred at a time when women were still struggling in other parties to gain a voice at leadership level. In Hamburg, in 1986, the regional Greens fielded a team of women, a *Frauenliste*. No longer confined to traditional women's domains such as family, social issues, or health care, women in the Greens gained public visibility as experts on the economy, as spokesperson or chair of the party organization or business manager in parliament at regional or national level (Richardsen and Michalik, 1985). Although women in the Greens still complain that men continue to cling to notions of dominance and patriarchy in their social and political behaviour, the party offers equal opportunities. The only obstacle to this is that not enough women members join and come forward to take up the many available positions (Kolinsky, 1989a).

The CDU and the CSU

For the CDU, the focus on women took a different turn. The electoral losses prompted the business management of the party to modify the conservative focus on women as housewives and mothers and incorporate in CDU policy the new interest of women in combining employment and homemaking. In 1985, the party launched its updated image with a special party congress: in addition to the 700 or so regular delegates, 500 women from all walks of life were invited as special guests to discuss CDU policies on women (Geissler, 1986; *Leitsätze . . .*, 1985). Spurned by fears of losing electoral support among younger generation women who no longer endorsed conservative notions of women's roles and family commitments, and who increasingly felt that opportunities were unequal (*Frauen in der CDU*, 1985: 247), the CDU devised an imaginative package of policy blueprints on pensions rights for childrearing, parental leave for either parent with a right to return to employment within a year and similar benefits designed to encourage childbearing in an age of employment motivation among women. Internally, the CDU stopped short of instituting statutory quotas, but passed a recommendation that women should be represented throughout the party leadership and in parliaments in accordance with their share of the membership (*Frauenpolitik der CDU*, 1986).[2] Attempts by women of the post-war generations and from within the *Frauenvereinigung*,[3] to turn the recommendation into a requirement to ensure that women would occupy one in four party posts or parliamentary mandates met the disapproval of the party leadership, and also of the women's association establishment of dowagers who defended traditional values and organizational practices. Opportunities in the CDU have been more limited than in the SPD (Table 6.7). In the party organization, little has changed since the mid-1980s although CDU party congresses have taken to reiterating the commitment to equal opportunities of 1985, and have begun to compile regular reports on women's participation (Lang, 1989: 123–4).

The CDU has recruited prominent women into the political leadership, often over the heads of devoted party workers and from public or professional positions outside the party. Thus, with three women ministers at national level and a woman as President of the Bundestag, a record number of women occupy high office.[4] But no career track has been established. There is no women's through-road from party membership to political leadership in the CDU. The same is true for the CSU. Here, no demands were articulated by members of the Women's Union and the party leadership may have deflected such pressures by placing some

Table 6.7 *Women and party offices in the CDU (%)*

Level	1987	1989	1991[1]
Membership	22	23	23
Executive	21	21	21
	(7)	(7)	(8)
Presidium	15	15	18
	(2)	(2)	(3)
Congress delegates	18	18	17
	(143)	(141)	(177)
Delegates: party	20	20	19
committee	(30)	(29)	(32)

Absolute figures are given in brackets. Women members: 1987, 158,696; 1989, 152,411.

[1] Data relate to unified party, West and East.

Sources: Frauenbericht. Bericht des Generalsekretärs zur Umsetzung der Essener Leitsätze, des C-3 Beschlusses von Mainz und der Wiesbadener Richtlinien. Berichtszeitraum November 1987 to 15 July 1989: 37. Bunderparteitag Bremen, 10–13 September 1989: 15; Frauenbericht. 2. Parteitag der CDU, 14–17 December 1991, Dresden. Berichtszeitraum August 1989 to June 1991

women directly into top positions at ministerial level (Lang, 1989: 125ff.). Both the CDU and CSU have the capacity to utilize executive power to promote women. In this way opportunities have been broadened in both parties while neither has established an organizational culture of women's participation, entitlements or prospects comparable to those in the Greens and in the SPD.

The FDP

The Free Democrats also endorsed the need to promote women's opportunities but refused to consider 'inflexible' quotas (*fdk* 7.4., 1987). In 1987, however, the party adopted the practice of preparing regular reports on women's participation in party offices, and placed a new emphasis on including women at leadership level. Given the patchy organization underlying the FDP, the involvement of women depends more on local circumstance than in the larger parties or in the Greens, where women are specifically drafted in to hold posts earmarked by quotas. Free Democrats had been aware since the mid-1970s that women of the younger generation constituted an important political potential among members and voters which should not be ignored (Kolinsky, 1984).

Like the CDU and CSU, the FDP offered women political office without an extended period of service in the party organization. Despite its political function as a partner in government in

Table 6.8   *Women and party offices in the FDP (%)*

Level	1987	1988	1989	1990[1]	1991[1]
Membership	25	25	27	27	30
Executive	11	11	21	14	18
	(4)	(4)	(7)	(6)	(6)
Presidium	0	0	33	31	31
	–	–	(3)	(4)	(4)
Congress	n.a.	15	17	18	21
delegates	–	(61)	(67)	(118)	(141)
Party committee	n.a.	7	8	8	8
	–	(1)	(1)	(1)	(1)

[1] Data relate to unified party, West and East.

Sources: Compiled from the first four reports on equal opportunities: Bericht des Bundesvorstandes zur Umsetzung des Frauenförderplans der F.D.P. Beschlossen vom Bundesvorstand am 8 April 1987, Bonn 1988 (No. 1), 1989 (No. 2), 1990 (No. 3), 1991 (No. 4)

some regions and at the national level, the FDP party organization has always been small, and opportunities to hold an office or gain a seat in parliament may arise quickly. Women in the FDP have benefited from this situation, and many have risen faster to positions of influence than they might have done in larger parties. Women in the SPD and CDU tend to complain about a dearth of chances while the FDP purports to seek more women contenders for political office and complaints arise from active women that too few of their kind join the party. The annual reports on equal opportunities in the FDP indicate, however, that with the exception of the party presidium, women's representation at the key levels of organizational power has yet to reach the agreed target of women's share of the membership (Table 6.8).

Regional inequalities

The focus on women's quotas has considerably extended the chances for women to play an active role in political parties and to rise through office holding and candidacies to parliamentary seats and leadership positions. While Greens and Social Democrats adopted a prescriptive approach which remodelled their party elites (Table 6.6), Christian and Liberal Democrats were more cautious. In the CDU and CSU, established hierarchies were slow to admit women to positions at the top (Table 6.7); in the FDP, however, women increased their participation at leadership and management levels in the party (Table 6.8).

The strides of West German women in political parties are not matched in the East. One of the surprising legacies of forty years of socialism and political participation by decree is a women's deficit in participation. With the exception of the Party of Democratic Socialism, the political parties in the new Länder report fewer women members than those in the West. While the CDU in the East boast nearly 40 per cent women members, the statistics seem to reflect the prescribed women's quota of the state socialist era, not the contemporary, paid-up and active membership (see above). In reality, the CDU in the East does not appear to have more women members than the CDU in the West. In the SPD, the East–West divide is more clearly evident. In the East, women constitute 20 per cent or less of the party membership, yet 27 per cent in the West. However, even in the West, significant regional variations remain. For example, regions such as Rheinland Palatinate or Lower Bavaria offer fewer chances to women office holders than the new party organizations in the East (*Gleichstellungsbericht* . . ., 1991: 13).

Generally speaking, the pattern of opportunities for women in political parties has improved, and party membership can be translated more readily into active participation, party offices and political careers. Equal opportunities policies and the institution of quotas may in time recast the way in which parties operate internally. In Germany, the gender imbalance of political elites has been challenged and modified.

Women in parliament

The presence of women in parliaments has been the most visible indicator of access to political leadership positions. Until the mid-1980s, the representation of women in the Bundestag remained below the 10 per cent mark first reached at the very beginning of the Weimar Republic. In the East, one in three members of parliament were women, but their membership had been decreed from above and did not reflect a changing political culture as it did in the West. There, the number of women members in the Bundestag rose in the early 1950s, and then stagnated until the early 1980s (Table 6.9). The entry of the Green party boosted numbers in 1983 and 1987. But the major development was the increase in women members of parliament for the large parties. Between 1987 and 1990, numbers doubled for the SPD and FDP, and more than doubled from 18 to 44 in the CDU/CSU. While the increase of women members of parliament in the mid-1980s was largely a by-product of the Green quota commitment, the focus on

Table 6.9   *Women in the Bundestag, 1949–1990*

Year	All	CDU/CSU	SPD	FDP	Greens	Gr.B90	PDS	Others
Percentage of parliamentary party								
1949	7	8	10	0	–	–	–	5
1953	9	8	13	6	–	–	–	4
1957	9	8	12	7	–	–	–	6
1961	8	7	10	8	–	–	–	–
1965	7	6	9	7	–	–	–	–
1969	7	6	8	5	–	–	–	–
1972	6	6	5	5	–	–	–	–
1976	7	8	7	8	–	–	–	–
1980	8	8	8	13	–	–	–	–
1983	10	7	10	12	36	–	–	–
1987	15	8	16	13	57	–	–	–
1990	20	13	27	20	–	38	47	–
Absolute figures								
1949	28	11	13	0				4
1953	45	19	21	3				2
1957	48	22	22	3				1
1961	43	18	21	4				
1965	36	15	19	2				
1969	34	14	18	2				
1972	30	15	13	2				
1976	38	19	15	4				
1980	44	18	19	7				
1983	51	17	21	3	10			
1987	80	18	31	6	25			
1990	135	44	64	16	–	3	8	–

Source: Adapted from Kolinsky, 1992a: 222

women's opportunities in the other parties – be it the SPD quota or the less specific commitment of CDU, CSU and FDP – created new parliamentary access routes for women in the major political parties.

At the regional level, similar developments occurred. In the mid-1980s, the representation of women in regional parliaments (Landtage) amounted to 10.6 per cent on average compared with 7 per cent twenty years earlier (Fülles, 1969: 83; Hoecker, 1987: 62). Today, one in five regional members of parliament are women. Cross-party and regional variations are considerable. The Greens in the so-called old Länder developed the most predictable profile; normally half the members of parliament are women. In some of the regions which formerly were the GDR, notably Brandenburg and Thuringia, just 17 per cent of parliamentarians were women, and the quota commitment of the party had yet to be met.

Table 6.10   *Women in parliaments 1990–1992 (in order of SPD representation, %)*

Region	SPD	CDU	FDP	Greens	Others
Bremen	33	16	20	40	0
Berlin	33	19	29	51	40[2]
Schleswig Holstein	30	19	–	–	0
Hamburg	29	23	29	100[3]	–
Bundestag (2.12.90)	27	13	20	38	47
Saar region	27	17	33	–	–
Volkskammer (3.3.90)	24	15	0	17	46
Rhineland Palatinate	23	20	0	40	–
Lower Saxony	23	12	22	55	–
Sachsen–Anhalt	22	6	15	60	30
Saxony	22	7	22	40	27
Hesse	22	20	12	50	–
Mecklenburg Vorpommern	20	7	25	–	55
Thuringia	19	7	22	17	30
North Rhine–Westfalia	17	21	21	50	–
Bavaria[1]	16	8	29	60	–
Brandenburg	14	15	33	17	47
Baden–Württemberg	12	6	0	40	–

[1] In Bavaria, the CSU.
[2] Others for all the new Länder refers mainly to the PDS.
[3] In 1990 the Green Alternative List had turned itself into a Frauenliste.

Sources: Data compiled by the author from the parliamentary handbooks for the Land parliaments, and the Endgültiges Endergebnis for the Volkskammer (GDR) elections in March 1990, and the first all-German Bundestag elections in December 1990. Data for the regional parliaments refer to the situation in 1991 and tally with the representation reported in the *Gleichstellungsberichte* of SPD, CDU and FDP.

In 1991, similar East/West and cross-party discrepancies pertained elsewhere (Table 6.10). Only the PDS included at least one-third women among its members in regional parliaments. In the FDP, women's share of seats ranged from nought in Baden–Württemberg and Rhineland Palatinate to 33 per cent in the Saar region. In the CDU, the Eastern regions returned a dearth of women members while in most West German regions women held nearly one in five CDU seats. Bavaria also apparently offered very few opportunities for women. In the SPD, a gap of 21 percentage points separated Bremen and Baden–Württemberg. Table 6.10 suggests that Germany has a dual regional divide in addition to the party differences in gender politics. In the north chances for women tend to be better than in the south; in the western regions generally better than in the east. North Rhine–Westfalia, an SPD stronghold, does not fit this pattern. Here, women found it difficult to break established networks and oust sitting members of parliament, an experience which was repeated in the federal elections of 1990 and which prompted the ASF to voice public protests and call for a reinforcement of the quota by the party executive.

In the new Länder, quotas were instituted or were implied – mirroring the West – but neither the quota nor the organizational debates were prominent at the time of the 1990 elections in the newly founded regions, or the all-German parliament. The parties in the East were too new, too focused on unification and too rushed into electoral arrangements and into building a party organization to attend to women's participation. In the parliaments of the new German Länder, women held an average of 16 per cent of the seats in 1990. Apart from the PDS where nearly half the members of parliament were women, and the East German Greens where the share of women in parliaments showed considerable regional fluctuations, the highest proportion of women was elected for the FDP while the SPD trailed, and the CDU in the East returned fewer women in four of the five new parliaments than had been the case in the immediate post-war period.

Parliamentary candidacies and party cultures
In the political campaign to improve the representation of women in German parliaments, the national parliament – the Bundestag – provided the focal point to assess good or bad practice, and representation there functioned as a general yardstick for women's opportunities in German parliamentary politics. The emphasis on national politics overlooks the importance of the federal structure in Germany and the key role of regional parliaments as legislatures and important intermediate tiers in the policy process. Moreover, Germany has retained a strong tradition of local government and a network of assemblies at local and district level. Taking national and regional parliaments together, Germany had 2,414 elected members of parliament in the early 1990s, 662 in the Bundestag, the others in the eleven regional parliaments. These vary in size. The Bavarian Landtag for instance has at least 200 members, the Landtag in the Saar region just fifty. In addition, local government offers more than 10,000 seats in assemblies. Here, political parties have begun to matter. Until the mid-1970s, local government tended to be dominated by so-called electoral alliances, groupings of local people without a specific party affiliation. In the wake of administrative reforms in the early 1970s which removed the independent status from the smallest communities and created

larger administrative structures at local level, party organizations began to take root at local level and weaken the traditional non-party culture of local government. Today, local government has become a further important tier of party political activity, and involvement in local politics may constitute a stepping-stone to parliamentary or party positions at regional or national level.

When women in the German political parties began to question the gender bias in opportunities, they focused in the first instance on access to parliamentary positions, and – among these – to seats in the Bundestag. Although the agenda of equal opportunities has moved on since then and has been transformed by the implemen-tation of quotas, women's representation in the Bundestag continues to be regarded as a yardstick of opportunities and a potential access route to government posts at national level.[5]

The nomination of candidates for parliamentary elections at all levels of the political system rests with constituency parties and with the regional party organizations. This dual responsibility is closely linked to the electoral system and its two types of parliamentary candidacies: constituency candidates (for 'direct seats') and candidates on the party lists.

The territory of the Federal Republic is divided into 331 constituencies (248 before unification), and political parties may nominate a candidate to compete in a given constituency. A nomination as constituency candidate is open to party candidates and independents, provided they can secure 200 signatures in support of their application. In reality, only party candidates stand a chance of election. Between 1961 and 1990, only the two major parties, CDU/CSU and SPD, were able to win so-called 'direct seats'. In 1990, the FDP managed to win one such seat in the liberal stronghold of Halle, in the new Land of Sachsen-Anhalt.

The second type of candidate relates to the so-called second vote (*Zweitstimme*) contained on the ballot paper. This entitles the voter to opt for a political party, while the first ballot (*Erststimme*) is linked to an individual candidate in the voter's constituency, a choice which need not be determined by party affiliation or preferences. In terms of party representation in parliament and the share of seats gained by any one political party, the second ballot is the more important of the two. The share of the vote secured through the second ballot determines the overall number of seats a political party holds in a given parliament. In elections to the Bundestag, the share of the vote is calculated on the national level; in Land elections, for the region as a whole. In parliament, half the seats are distributed via constituency votes – votes for an individual candidate – and the other half via the party vote, the second ballot. This means that political parties which do not win constituency seats obtain their complement of seats on the basis of the second ballot. For political parties which have obtained constituency seats, the overall number of seats they hold is equally determined by the second ballot. The directly elected members of parliament are sure of a seat; additional members are added to the party contingent up to the percentage of seats to which a party is entitled by the second ballot. If a party wins more direct seats in a region than it would be entitled to hold on the basis of the second ballot, it may keep these seats. In German they are called '*Überhangmandate*' – additional mandates; the overall number of parliamentary members increases if such mandates have been won in a given parliament.

The two types of candidates are normally selected in two separate processes: the first round of nominations and selection concerns constituency members of parliament; the second round consists of establishing a so-called party list. Constituency candidates may also compete for a place on the party list to increase their electoral chances. The electoral law stipulates that the places on the list have to be clearly numbered, and the party list also serves as a reservoir of potential members of parliament to fill vacancies which arise for any one party during a legislative period. Germany does not have by-elections.

In theory, the selection of candidates is one of the main democratic functions of political parties, and in particular the main opportunity for the rank-and-file member to influence the political process. Any member has the right to nominate candidates, and the right to vote in the selection process for direct and list candidates. In reality, selection meetings in the constituencies attract fewer than 10 per cent of the membership, and it has been suggested that less than 0.1 per cent of the German electorate take an active part in the selection of the political elite which represents them in their parliaments.

In the selection process itself, party organizations at regional level, and a selection committee at constituency level have the major say. While local party organizations may submit names for nomination, the normal practice has been that lists of names for both types of candidacies are compiled at constituency and regional level and passed to the local parties for confirmation. Voting on the proposals takes place during party meetings. Only members in attendance are entitled to vote, and do so by secret ballot. The names of candidates should be known in advance, and candidates should normally be present at the selection meetings. However, irregularities have been the spice of the nomination process. A potential candidate from the new Länder for instance complained at the eve of the 1990 Bundestag elections that she had not been notified of the selection meeting, and that an absentee candidate was proposed and elected at the meeting in defiance of the recommended procedures (*JU Pressedienst*, 4 October 1990).[6]

Generally speaking, the electoral prospects of constituency candidates rest on the popularity of his or her party in that constituency. Nominations for direct seats, especially those with high electoral chances, are the most difficult hurdle in the selection stakes. Once secured, these nominations tend to remain unchanged until the candidates themselves opt out of politics; the emphasis on women's representation in parliament has created new pressures to discontinue the established practice of returning sitting members of parliament. The high premium placed on incumbency has made it very difficult for women to obtain nominations for direct and safe seats.

The party lists are compiled by the regional party executive and tend to reflect the interest structure of the party. As mentioned earlier, members vote on the list in the second stage of the nomination procedure. Through their electoral lists, political parties have the power to secure parliamentary representation for the interest groups to which they are aligned, and to bring various experts on whose services they wish to rely into parliament. Although the names of the candidates which are selected to compete on the party list are published, only the so-called top candidate may be known to a wider public; the other names on the list receive little publicity and the individuals in question may lack many of the political skills needed to appeal to the electorate and win a seat.

In the campaign to nominate and elect more women, the party lists have proved most adaptable. The quota regulations of the Greens and the SPD specifically target the composition of the party lists and stipulate separate ballots for men and women until the number of women required by the quota has been reached. Only then should men and women compete against one another. In the other parties, no such rule has been formulated, although the nomination process has recently been designed in such a way that a certain number of places at the top end of the list were earmarked for women. In the FDP, for example, one of the 1990 Land lists had men only compete for the first four places, and five women compete against one another for fifth place, which is their lowest normally elected position. In the CDU, CSU and FDP women tend to cluster at the bottom of the lists. By contrast the

Table 6.11   *Women in the Bundestag 1990 by candidacies and parties*

Party	Men and women			Women only		
	Seats	Cons.[1]	List[2]	Seats	Cons.	List
CDU	268	192	76	36	21	15
CSU	51	43	8	5	3	2
SPD	239	91	148	64	15	49
FDP	79	1	78	16	0	16
B90/Greens	8	0	8	3	0	3
PDS	17	1	16	8	0	8

[1] Constituency candidacy – member of parliament elected by majority vote in that constituency.
[2] Candidacy via party list – election depends on overall vote obtained by party and position (ranking) of candidate on party list.

Source: Author's calculations from electoral lists

SPD and Greens have linked the nomination of women to the order of places and enforced a more even gender distribution on their list. This approach has, of course, had the effect of reducing the chances of men of achieving secure nominations to parliamentary seats.

In the 1990 Bundestag elections quotas made a visible impact. More women than ever before were nominated in favourable positions, i.e. as direct candidates in safe seats or as list candidates in that section of the party list, which might translate into seats. There is some evidence that dislodging established constituency members is more difficult than gaining access to parliament via party lists (see Table 6.11). The important function of regional party organizations should be stressed here. In improving the representation of women in German political parties, the top levels of the party executive, i.e. regional and national party leaderships, have played a significant role in overcoming obstructions from below and in persuading local and district organizations to give women better chances.

Obstacles, however, remain. The SPD in North Rhine–Westfalia was castigated by the Association for Social Democratic Women (ASF) for its failure to meet the SPD quota (*Frankfurter Rundschau*, 24 September 1990). To meet the quota would have meant dislodging sitting members of parliament and this was resisted by the regional party. With 11 per cent women among its parliamentary contingent, the traditional slant of the SPD in North Rhine–Westfalia contrasts sharply with other regions, where women are one-third or more of the regional representatives. On the other hand, women headed the SPD Land lists 1990 in Hesse, Baden–Württemberg, Bavaria and Sachsen–Anhalt, and women were nominated to the second place on the lists of eight further regions. In 1987, no women had been at number one, and just four held the second position.

Table 6.11 shows the gender mobility among list candidates and direct candidates for the 1990 elections to the Bundestag: 331 members of parliament were directly elected; thirty-nine of them – 12 per cent – were women. Of the 331 members elected via party lists, ninety-three, that is 28 per cent, were women. The conservatives have traditionally found it easier to gain direct seats in their electoral strongholds, a trend which has been reinforced by unification with the CDU winning most of the new constituencies. In the Bundestag, the same number of women in the CDU and CSU were direct and list candidates. Although the CDU honoured its pledge of allocating 25 per cent of list places to women, many were at the lower end, and did not gain parliamentary seats. The SPD quota pledge transformed the composition of the party lists but had a limited effect on direct seats.

Membership duration and active involvement in the party organization have long been recognized as indispensable preconditions for a party member to be nominated to a winnable parliamentary seat (Handschuh et al., 1986: 149ff.). German party researchers and political practitioners coined a special term for the prolonged period of service which might be rewarded by a parliamentary mandate. The *Ochsentour*, slaving like an ox, suggests a party life of devotion to the cause, and also putting personal ideas and intentions behind the aims and purposes of the organization. This *Ochsentour* seems to have suffered a major blow in the age of women's quotas.

The changes worked by the new focus on women's participation have been most apparent in the SPD. Here the *Ochsentour* has long been regarded as a precondition for a political career. The political elite which would eventually lead the party or represent it in parliaments or governments had been fashioned by the organizations, moulded in its way of thinking, groomed to project its ethos. The elite was organizationally and intellectually the party's own product (Lohmar, 1968; Zeuner, 1969).

In the 1987 elections, when the new emphasis on women began to take shape, the majority of women members of parliament could boast ten years or more of party membership and organizational involvement (Kolinsky, 1991a: 69). Women who were then nominated as candidates or newly elected to hold parliamentary seats belonged to the generation of campaigners for women's opportunities who had been frustrated in their aspirations to make politics a career by the gender gap in German politics, and who were now the first to benefit from the new climate. The newcomers to parliamentary politics in the mid-1980s were themselves long-standing party members with their own extended history of organizational involvement in the women's association of their party as well as the other party for a level to which they could gain access.

By 1990, the *Ochsentour* syndrome had begun to wane. The effect of quotas was to recast the whole process of nomination, notably by altering the requirements of the political apprentice-ship. One in three women candidates for the SPD had been party members for less than two years. Only the East German Greens and the PDS recorded a similar influx of novice candidates. While the high proportion of newcomers in the East reflects the brief existence of its party organizations, the new prominence of organizationally inexperienced women in the SPD suggests that the backlog of would-be office holders who had forced the quota regulations into the party statutes had been cleared. In 1990 at least, the quota broadened access routes and offered new opportunities.[7]

The new SPD women politicians who do not come groomed into organizational conformity through the *Ochsentour* could infuse a spark of innovation into the SPD party culture where previous cohorts of party women may have been too absorbed for too long into the party business of the women's association and winning key offices in the mainstream party on their way into parliaments (Kolinsky, 1992b) The innovation may concern policy issues, but might also confront the hierarchical traditions of party politics, the unsocial hours required by party work and the failure of political parties to facilitate active political participation through childcare arrangements and women-friendly adjustments to the party culture.[8]

Outlook

The new emphasis on the political participation and representation of women in party organizations and parliaments has modified the overpowering influence of organizational involvement on political careers. In 1990, women succeeded in obtaining nominations and election to parliaments faster and with a less intensive history of party work than would have been possible in any party other than the Greens in the past. Even in the CDU where quotas are vilified as a slur on women's qualifications and competitive acumen, or in the FDP where they are suspected of impeding the constitutional right of equal opportunities, the existence of quotas and the explicit focus on access to political and parliamentary positions has generated a climate of improved opportunities. In all parties, debates are under way on measures to assist women to choose politics as a career. Suggestions range from childcare support to special programmes at local and national level for building women's political confidence and grooming them for leadership. The different parties will find different ways of revising their party cultures and of making political careers more accessible to women. Given the key position in Germany of women as an electorate and the widespread perception that opportunities for women and men have remained unequal, no political party can resist change. In the 1970s and 1980s, the test of party competence seemed to occur in the electoral arena. In the 1990s, it takes place inside the party organizations as elite recruitment has to stand the test of equal opportunities.

Notes

1 For our discussion of political participation East German elections before the collapse of state socialism are irrelevant since the official turnout of over 99 per cent did not reflect popular preferences.

2 The Resolution C3 of the CDU party congress in Mainz, 1986 was initiated by the women's association of the party, in order to ensure that the general assurances of equality which were issued at the congress in Essen in 1985 would be applied to the party organization as well: 'The CDU is duty bound to implement the principle of equal opportunities at all organizational levels in the party.' In 1988, a further resolution was passed which required the party to prepare an annual report on the representation of women in the party. For a summary, see Kolinsky (1989b: 293–6).

3 Until 1991, the women's association of the CDU was called *Frauenvereinigung*, that of the CSU was called *Frauenunion*. In 1991, the CDU adopted the name *Frauenunion* although the organizational activities have remained separate.

4 In 1992, a cabinet reshuffle reduced the number of women ministers to two: Gerda Hasselfeldt resigned in the wake of a phone-tapping scandal in her ministry. The attempt to replace the retiring foreign minister, Hans-Dietrich Genscher, with a woman, Irmgard Schwaetzer, was approved by the Chancellor but foiled by the FDP parliamentary party. Since April 1992, there have been two women ministers only.

5 For ministerial offices, membership of the Bundestag has not been an important prerequisite for women. Recent executive appointments included Gerda Hasselfeldt (CSU), Rita Süssmuth (CDU) and Ursula Lehr (CDU). They attained ministerial office via the 'executive route' and entered the Bundestag and electoral politics only after their appointment or not at all.

6 The case refers to Cordula Schubert, who was deputy chairman of the Young

Christian Democrats at the time: 'Of the 700 registered members, just 92 attended the meeting. Many, including Frau Schubert, had not been notified. Prior to the meeting she was regarded as the only candidate. Already, at the beginning of the meeting, two further candidates suddenly appeared; later on two more followed. After two ballots, a 56-year-old engineer was nominated. He had not been present. When asked why he wanted to stand as a candidate he replied: "I have the right age to enter the Bundestag".'

7 There is nothing in the new party statutes that access should generally be made more flexible. Thus, women who entered parliament in the age of quotas could hold on to their positions as inflexibly as men did in the past. Once implemented the quota will no longer favour mobility.

8 These points were raised in the survey on women's parliamentary careers in response to the question which adjustments women would wish to see in the political practices pertaining in their own political party (Kolinsky, 1992b).

7

Party Politics and Gender in the Republic of Ireland

Yvonne Galligan

The literature on party politics in the Republic of Ireland concentrates on providing historical and descriptive analyses of Irish parties (Gallagher, 1985; Garvin, 1981; Manning, 1972) and emphasizes the changing patterns of party competition in the system (Mair, 1987). The gender dimension to party politics does not receive attention in this body of literature. The process of candidate selection is an aspect of electoral politics which has received regular scholarly attention (Gallagher, 1980, 1984, 1988; Katz, 1981; Lijphart and Irwin, 1979; Marsh, 1981a, 1981b, 1989). With the exception of articles by Carty (1980), Darcy (1988), Manning (1978, 1987) and Randall and Smyth (1987), and analysis by Gallagher, gender has, to date, been given only a passing reference in research on candidate selection.

This chapter offers a contribution to the study of party politics in Ireland from the perspective of gender, tracing the development of party strategies to accommodate gender as an issue of both policy and representation in the context of electoral competition and intra-party practices over the past two decades. First, the salience of gender in terms of inter-party electoral competition is analysed through an examination of the patterns of candidate selection in Irish political parties and the stated commitments to gender in party election programmes. It will be suggested that party positions on issues of electoral importance converged during the 1980s. The level of identification with gender representation and policies became one method by which party differences could be defined, leading to a modest institutionalization of gender politics.

Second, the focus is placed on internal party responses to the issue of gender. While a renewed interest in gender as an electoral strategy has not significantly altered the representational balance in public life, it has had the unforseen consequence of opening up a debate at various times within the parties on the most effective methods of increasing women's representation in electoral and internal party structures.

In conclusion, it is suggested that the degree to which the parties have responded to the challenge of incorporating gender politics and the extent to which this opportunity has been exploited by party activists is greatly influenced by the persistence of traditional patterns of selection, the demands of electoral politics and the openness to change of the individual parties.

Party system, electoral system and government formation

Irish politics has been dominated by three parties since the establishment of the state in 1922. The two major parties, Fianna Fail and Fine Gael, owe their origins to a split in the radical nationalist party, Sinn Fein, after the signing of the Anglo-Irish Treaty with Britain in 1921 which resulted in the creation of the Irish Free State. Fine Gael, the smaller of the two parties, quickly became a party of the centre-right, while Fianna Fail developed a flexible centrist identity. The third party, the Labour party, has been the political vehicle for the expression of working-class and trade union interests. Between them, these three parties have accounted on average for 85 per cent of the vote at elections since 1922: Fianna Fail for 43 per cent, Fine Gail for 31 per cent and Labour for 11 per cent. Two smaller political parties offered a significant challenge in the 1980s, however: the Progressive Democrats, who have attracted an average vote of 7 per cent since 1987, and the Workers party which, prior to its split in 1992, drew 3 per cent support. The Green party have not to date won a significant level of voter support. (For a more complete analysis of the Irish party system, see Gallagher, 1985; Mair, 1987.)

The main divisions between parties in the Republic of Ireland do not arise from class or religion, as is common in other west European party systems (Marsh and Sinnott, 1990: 91–130). Nevertheless, as the nationalist cleavage which gave rise to the two major parties has been receding in importance, elements of the tensions between secular and traditional religious values have become evident in the party system, and this tension is important for the issue of women's representation. Thus newer parties such as the Democratic Left and the Progressive Democrats have placed themselves close to the Labour party at the secular pole of the spectrum, with Fianna Fail and Fine Gael remaining at the opposite end.

The electoral system – proportional representation by means of the single transferable vote (PR–STV) in multi-seat constituencies –

allows for a high degree of proportionality while permitting voters to exercise their franchise along a range of dimensions such as party, locality, ideology and candidate personality. However, the dimension of gender has not been available to the electorate to any significant degree until the 1980s. While the extent and the reasons for the dearth of women candidates in the Irish electoral process will be discussed more fully shortly, the electoral system is in itself a relatively fair one. Overall, though, women candidates do not fare as well as their male counterparts. A study of a number of general elections between 1948 and 1982 found that non-incumbent women candidates of Fianna Fail, Fine Gael and Labour received on average 595 fewer votes than men candidates with the same credentials (Marsh, 1987: 70). Further, Darcy (1988: 73) has noted that '[In 1987] women incumbents were almost 20 per cent less likely to return than men.' In the 1992 election, male candidates polled on average 1,200 more votes than female candidates. This suggests that when presented with a choice voters may appear to be more inclined to vote for male rather than female candidates.

Candidate selection and representation: gender differences

Routes of entry
Women's pathways to power have traditionally remained heavily dependent on family connections with former incumbents of political office. Analysing the significance of kinship in the nomination and electoral success of women candidates, Busteed observed that 'until recently this was the most usual route into the Dail for women' (1990: 151). Between 1957 and 1969, for instance, of the total of twenty-two individual women candidates chosen to contest the four elections and two by-elections in this period, nine were elected; all but one were widows of former members of the Dail (Commission on the Status of Women, 1972: 190). However, the extent to which women are 'inheriting' seats is decreasing. In the 1992 election, for instance, only five, or 25 per cent of the women deputies at some stage owed their seat to being a daughter, niece or granddaughter of a former parliamentarian. Yet, as Table 7.1 shows, the relationship between electoral success and family ties with previous political incumbents remains on average twice as significant a factor for women as for men.

The route of entry to political life has traditionally been less restrictive for men. In the three decades after 1922, involvement in the nationalist cause was a primary consideration in candidate

Table 7.1   *Relationship of parliamentarians to former legislators, 1981–1992 by gender*

	Male deputies			Female deputies		
	Total	Related[1]		Total	Related[1]	
		N	%		N	%
1981	155	35	22.5	11	6	54.5
1982 (Feb.)	158	35	22.1	8	5	62.5
1982 (Nov.)	152	35	23.0	14	7	50.0
1987	152	35	23.0	14	6	42.8
1989	153	41	26.7	13	5	38.4
1992	146	32	21.9	20	7	35.0
Mean	153	36	23.2	13	6	47.2

[1] A parliamentarian is described as 'related' to a former legislator if he or she is a brother/sister, son/daughter, husband/wife, niece/nephew or related in other ways through marriage to a person who has held a seat in parliament

Sources: Author's calculations based on information in Nealon, 1981, 1982, 1983, 1987 and 1989. The author is indebted to Michael Gallagher for providing the 1992 figures

selection and electoral preferences (Chubb, 1986: 186–7). By the end of the 1950s, this 'revolutionary generation' was giving way to a 'post-revolutionary elite' and with it there emerged a different set of criteria which were deemed appropriate for the selection of male political aspirants. Local government service, prowess in the national games of Gaelic football and hurling and the building of extensive networks at local level through business or professional interests were as significant for males as family connections in determining both selection and electoral success. In recent years, though, local government service has become the main route of entry into national politics for both women and men.

Candidate selection
Before taking a closer look at the extent to which each party manifests a gender bias in its candidate selection and electoral support patterns, it is necessary to provide a brief summary of the process of candidate selection in general in Irish political parties.

Candidates are, in the main, selected at constituency level by selection conferences or conventions attended by representatives from local branches. The size of the selection conferences varies from party to party, but on average about one-third of the membership of the parties is involved in the selection process (Gallagher, 1988: 246). Selection conferences, which up to the early 1980s, took place shortly before or after the calling of a

general election, are increasingly being held some time in advance
of an election in order to allow a candidate to build up or
consolidate a constituency profile. Prospective candidates in
Labour and the Workers party are generally required to have been
party members for a stated period of time, usually around one
year. This does not hold for the candidates of Fianna Fail, Fine
Gael and the Progressive Democrats. The system of election used
for choosing candidates also varies between parties, although some
form of proportional representation is adopted in the event of a
contest. While the selection process is heavily dominated by the
constituency party organization, each party has provided for the
imposition of additional candidates by the party leadership. This
power, while not widely exercised by the parties, is generally used
to balance party tickets through the addition of a further
candidate from the constituency rather than to 'parachute' outsiders as candidates into an electoral area. Local constituency
organizations are particularly resistant to the imposition of such
outsider candidates.

In terms of the overall priorities of selectors, the profile of
prospective candidates in constituency and party politics is a major
consideration. While incumbency is the strongest indicator of
success in the selection process, being an elected representative at
local level is a particular advantage. However, as Irish elections
are contested in multi-seat constituencies, parties generally select
more than one candidate. The lower placings are often used to
'balance' the ticket in terms of geographical distribution, age,
appeal to certain segments of the electorate, and, since the mid-
1970s, gender. These placings are often used to appease internal
party interests and to broaden the party's electoral appeal. In a
general analysis of candidate selection by Irish political parties,
Gallagher observed that:

> The prime determinant of electoral appeal is widely regarded as the
> candidate's reputation in the constituency. This, naturally, gives an
> advantage to incumbents (who rarely fail to be reselected), to holders
> of local elective office, to aspirants who have polled respectably on past
> candidacy, and to those, who have, by some other method, acquired a
> high local profile. (1988: 126)

These qualifications have applied more readily to male than to
female political aspirants. An examination of Irish politics reveals
that political representation was and has remained essentially a
male affair, as shown in Table 7.2. In the nineteen general elections
between 1922 and 1977, only 2.7 per cent of candidates and 2.5 per
cent of parliamentarians were women.

Table 7.2 *Women candidates and deputies, 1922–1992*

Election[1]	Candidates			Deputies		
	Total	Women		Total	Women	
		N	%		N	%
1922	176	6	3.4	128	2	1.6
1932	279	2	0.7	153	2	1.3
1943	354	10	2.8	138	3	2.2
1954	303	4	1.3	147	4	2.8
1969	373	11	3.5	141	3	2.1
1973	335	16	4.7	144	4	2.8
1977	376	25	6.6	148	6	4.1
1981	404	41	10.1	166	11	6.6
1982 (Feb.)	366	35	9.6	166	8	4.8
1982 (Nov.)	364	31	8.5	166	14	8.4
1987	466	48	10.3	166	14	8.4
1989	370	52	14.1	166	13	7.8
1992	481	89	18.5	166	20	12.0

[1] Figures relate to every fourth election from 1922 to 1969 and every election to date thereafter.

Sources: Browne, 1981; Gallagher, 1985: 161; Government Report, 1987: 51; *Irish Political Studies*, 1988: 129; *Irish Political Studies*, 1990: 139; *Irish Times*, 17 November 1992; *Sunday Tribune*, 29 November 1992; Tansey, 1985: 261

The record of the parties in selecting women candidates improved from 1977 onwards with a resultant increase in the representation of women in the Dail. However, progress could be said to amount to little other than tokenism, as there was not a serious attempt by political parties to redress the gender imbalance in candidate tickets. On closer examination, significant differences can be detected between the parties in terms of their criteria for candidate selection and their success in having their women candidates elected, as shown in Tables 7.3 and 7.4.

In the case of Fianna Fail, the percentage of both women candidates and successfully elected representatives has remained below 10 per cent since 1977, with the corresponding figure for male selection and election being above 90 per cent. Compared with Fine Gael, the numbers of successful women candidates conforming to the traditional pattern of being related to previous male incumbents is particularly high. In the November 1982 general election, for instance, three of the four or 75 per cent of the Fianna Fail women deputies were closely related to a former male incumbent while this applied to only three of the nine or 33 per cent successful women Fine Gael candidates. In the 1992 election, female kinship with former male incumbents was valid for

Table 7.3 *Women candidates by party, 1973–1992*

Year	Fianna Fail			Fine Gael			Labour		
	Total	Women	(%)	Total	Women	(%)	Total	Women	(%)
1973	119	2	(1.7)	111	4	(3.8)	55	2	(3.6)
1977	132	9	(6.8)	116	5	(4.3)	56	4	(7.1)
1981	138	10	(7.2)	126	15	(11.9)	60	9	(15.0)
1982 (Feb.)	131	9	(6.8)	113	12	(10.6)	41	5	(12.1)
1982 (Nov.)	132	7	(5.3)	115	12	(10.4)	40	5	(12.5)
1987	122	10	(8.2)	97	11	(11.3)	37	3	(8.1)
1989	115	9	(7.8)	86	11	(12.8)	33	3	(9.0)
1992	122	12	(9.8)	91	13	(14.2)	42	8	(19.0)
Mean	126	9	(6.7)	107	10	(9.9)	46	5	(11.3)

A total of 23 women (21.6 per cent) were selected by the Progressive Democrats to contest the three elections between 1987 and 1992. In the same period, the Workers party selected 13 women candidates (18.5 per cent) from 1987 to the present. The Green party have selected a total of 18 women candidates (39.1 per cent) since first contesting national elections in November 1982. Democratic Left ran 6 women (30.0 per cent) in the 1992 election.

Source: Farrell, 1992: 445

Table 7.4 *Women parliamentarians by party, 1973–1992*

Year	Fianna Fail			Fine Gael			Labour		
	Total	Women	(%)	Total	Women	(%)	Total	Women	(%)
1973	69	1	(1.4)	54	2	(3.7)	19	1	(5.3)
1977	84	4	(4.7)	43	1	(2.3)	17	1	(5.9)
1981	78	4	(5.1)	65	6	(9.2)	15	1	(6.7)
1982 (Feb.)	81	2	(2.4)	63	5	(7.9)	15	1	(6.7)
1982 (Nov.)	75	4	(5.3)	70	9	(12.8)	16	1	(6.3)
1987	81	5	(6.1)	51	5	(9.8)	12	0	0
1989	77	5	(6.5)	55	6	(10.9)	15	0	0
1992	68	5	(7.3)	45	5	(10.4)	33	5	(15.1)
Mean	77	9	(7.2)	107	11	(9.9)	46	5	(11.3)

The Workers party and Green party have failed to date to secure the election of a woman candidate. Democratic Left have one woman deputy (25.0 per cent). The Progressive Democrats have been quite successful, with an average of 3 women (30.0 per cent) returned to the Dail since 1987. Of the 10 parliamentarians elected for the PDs in 1992, 4 are women.

Sources: Farrell, 1992: 445; *Sunday Tribune*, 29 November 1992

four of the five (80 per cent) Fianna Fail women parliamentarians elected. Thus, the traditional route of entry into politics in the form of family relationship with a former incumbent is a significant factor in determining the electoral success of women with political ambitions in Fianna Fail.

Until the election of 1981, Fine Gael's record on the selection of women candidates was poor. However, a change of party leadership in 1979 brought a liberal emphasis to bear on party electoral strategy which included the positive promotion of women (Manning, 1987: 159). As Table 7.3 shows, sixteen women candidates were nominated by the party in 1981. However, the significance of these nominations rests not alone in the substantial number of women put forward relative to the numbers nominated by Fianna Fail, but in the type of candidate selected. Unlike Fianna Fail, the Fine Gael selectorates in Dublin middle-class constituencies were open to the candidacy of women with a background in the politics of the women's movement. This was a new departure from the traditional pathway to power for women, as most of these candidates had no family connections with politics. Gallagher noted the positive effect of party elite involvement in the selection and election of women candidates in Fine Gael in November 1982:

> Some of these Fine Gael women became candidates after encouragement from the leadership, sometimes coupled with pressure from the local organization. In contrast, the other parties which did not alter their selection processes between 1977 and 1982, had no more women TDs [a Teachta Dála is a member of the Irish parliament, the Dail] than in 1977. (1988: 141)

The electoral fortunes of Fine Gail women candidates without the traditional background in party politics were, however, mixed. Only one of the six winning women candidates in 1981 had a non-political background. That record improved in the November 1982 election with three women deputies with a history of involvement in feminist politics being returned to parliament. The level of the representation of women deputies from Fine Gael decreased to five after the 1992 election, with no increase in the overall representation of Fianna Fail women parliamentarians. However, kinship has not been as prominent a feature of female candidate selection in this party as it appears to be in Fianna Fail. In the 1992 election, only two of the thirteen candidates could claim a family relationship with a former legislator. Even then, the relationship was more distant than that applying in the Fianna Fail cases.

The majority of women from Fianna Fail and Fine Gael who

succeeded in being elected in the three elections held in 1981–2 consolidated their positions in later electoral contests. This breakthrough did not continue in subsequent elections. One possible reason for the success of women from these parties in the early 1980s is that during this time, party and electoral processes became slightly open to the incorporation of representatives of an 'outsider' group before reverting again to a status quo position. This openness coincided with a 10.8 per cent expansion of the number of seats in the Dail from 148 to 166 in 1981, offering electoral opportunities for women without having a negative impact on the electoral prospects of male incumbents. Women's representation almost doubled from six deputies in 1977 to eleven in 1981, constituting a 'take' of almost 28 per cent of the extra seats available. Overall, however, the percentage increase in women's representation was in the order of a modest 2.5 per cent.

The Labour party provides an interesting study in contrasting expectations and practices of candidate selection. It would be reasonable to expect that as a party with an orientation to left-wing politics and ideology, Labour would be sensitive to and accommodating of the need to ensure equitable gender participation in politics. Labour's minimal-risk strategy during the 1980s of fielding only one candidate in each constituency it contested in order to maximize its electoral support inhibited the selection of women candidates, as Table 7.3 shows.

In terms of the career paths of the candidates selected, the only successful woman candidate won the seat formerly held by her husband in the 1960s. Interestingly, for a party with strong trade union connections, none of the women candidates had a strong association with the trade union movement, although this was a distinctive feature of the male candidate profile.

The number of women candidates fielded by Labour decreased during the 1980s to minimal levels. None of the three women in 1987 and 1989 had direct family connections with politics, all were from constituencies in Dublin and two had established high profiles in local government politics during the 1980s. Their lack of electoral success, however, points to the important connection between overall electoral support for a party and the successful election of party candidates. Indeed, this point was clearly illustrated in the 1992 election, when these three candidates were elected without difficulty. Labour gained its highest ever share of the vote in 1992 and returned five women deputies in all from among the 33 candidates elected to the Dail.

The factors determining candidate selection in the Workers party prior to its split in 1992 appear to have been similar to those governing the choice of candidate in the Labour party. As with Labour, this party began to give serious consideration to the inclusion of women in the political and electoral process in the mid-1980s. Thus, in both the 1987 and 1989 elections, a modest proportion of Workers party candidates were women. The Workers party contested the 1992 election as a much smaller political organization. Although over one-quarter of their candidates were women, none were elected. In fact, the Workers party did not return a representative, male or female, to parliament after the 1992 election. This is in contrast to its offshoot, the Democratic Left Party, which returned four deputies, one of whom is a woman (see Table 7.4). While both the Workers party and Democratic Left accept the principle of providing electoral opportunities for women, the success or otherwise of their candidates, as with the candidates from the main parties, is largely bound up with the overall levels of electoral support obtained by the parties.

The Progressive Democrats and the Green party, both of which fielded over 40 per cent female candidates in the 1992 election, appear to be more permeable organizations in terms of gender representation. This may be in part due to their being relatively new parties without the institutionalization of interests and attitudes prevalent in the longer-established parties. The electoral success of women Progressive Democrat candidates, at 40 per cent of the total PD deputies in 1992, could be attributed to the fact that intra-party competition for selection in constituencies with a winnable seat for the party has not yet reached a maximum point.

As a party, the Progressive Democrats have attracted the candidacy of women with previous political experience and women with public profiles independent of party politics. Interestingly, their elected representatives do not have the same record of local government service as other party representatives, again suggesting that the PD party selection process was more open to newcomers, both male and female, then that of the more established parties.

Although the Green party has been established since 1981, it has only contested national elections since 1989. Both its ideology and its non-hierarchical format have encouraged a favourable predisposition to the selection of candidates in roughly equal gender proportions. Despite its strong internal affirmative action programme, the party has had only one male representative in the Dail since 1989, although almost 40 per cent of its councillors elected in 1991 are women (Galligan, 1992b: 17).

Thus, in terms of overall patterns of candidate selection and success, the traditional route of entry to politics for women, that of kinship with a previous incumbent, remains of overriding importance in Fianna Fail. This route does not have the same degree of significance in the case of the other parties, although it none the less remains a good predictor of electoral success across candidates, both male and female, in all the parties. Fine Gael is open to selecting women with a background in liberal feminist politics; the PDs are prepared to put forward women with 'national names' outside the sphere of politics. Labour, Democratic Left and the Workers party selectorate give preferential weight to prospective women candidates with records of local grassroots activism. A background in local politics is a strong advantage for prospective women parliamentary candidates across all parties. Yet some differences can be found in the priorities of the selectorate in Fianna Fail and left-wing parties on the one hand, Fine Gael and the Progressive Democrats on the other hand. The former group of parties have to date focused on the traditional criteria of 'bailiwick' politics, while Fine Gael and Progressive Democrat selectorates have been somewhat more flexible in their acceptance of women candidates who did not meet the customary criteria. Thus, there is evidence in the 1980s of atypical women candidates creating political careers. However, their hold on power is more tenuous than that of women with kinship connections or women in Fianna Fail, with Fianna Fail women incumbents retaining their seats more securely than other women incumbents.

Party politics and the institutionalization of gender

If one were to take a benign view of the discovery of gender by the three traditional parties from the 1977 general election onwards, one could analyse the slightly increased opportunities for the selection of women candidates for parliamentary contests as being the response of parties listening to the demands of the electorate. This may be to some extent true, given the fact that there was a strong campaign organized by the Women's Political Association directed at the parties and the public for the inclusion of women in parliament. But the altruistic promotion of women candidates is not a feature of Irish party politics. A more realistic explanation for the slow institutionalization of gender in terms of party and government policies can be attributed to the demands of interparty electoral competition. As the parties developed policies which sought to respond to the changing social and economic conditions of modern Ireland, the policy agendas of the parties began to differ in emphasis rather than in perspective. While this mattered little during the lifetime of a government, it became an important consideration during election periods. It was at these critical times that the parties sought to accentuate their distinctiveness in order to win the maximum level of support. An emphasis was placed on the 'women's vote' over this period and policies were designed to attract the support of an increasingly feminist-conscious and politicized female electorate. Thus, the strategies that focused on gender were governed by imperatives of electoral pragmatism as well as being a response to a perceived voter demand. Each party responded differently, with the response range being largely determined by the degree to which the party recognized and was willing to accommodate gender representation issues.

The election of 1977, which saw Fianna Fail wooing the 'women's vote' and fielding ten women candidates as opposed to two in the 1973 election, is generally seen as a watershed in gender politics in the Republic of Ireland. For the next three elections, the lessons learned by the parties about the perceived electoral value in mobilizing the support of women were put into effect. From 1977 to the November 1982 election, an appeal to women was a small but significant component of party election strategy. This was done in two ways – by the formulation of policies designed to attract women voters and by the selection of increased numbers of women candidates. The policies offered to women by Fianna Fail in 1977 were both minimal and aspirational in tone and content. Yet it was the only party to include even a passing reference to women in its election programme. By 1981, the three parties included specific references to women in their election manifestos. Fianna Fail and Fine Gael emphasized the role and status of women in the context of the family and employment. Fianna Fail also laid stress on its record of achieving equal rights for women while in government since 1977. Fine Gael sought to provide women in the home with a modest independent income through a system of tax credits. Labour issued a comprehensive analysis of discrimination against women and its plans to remove obstacles to gender equality. In the November 1982 election Fine Gael promised the establishment of a junior ministry for women's affairs and a parliamentary committee on women's rights. With the formation of a Fine Gael–Labour coalition government after this election, these specific promises were implemented.

The election manifestos of the parties in the 1987 election indicated a renewed commitment to eliminating gender-based discrimination in public policy, with the solutions proposed reflecting the ideological orientation of the respective parties. Interestingly, the new party, the Progressive Democrats, did not specifically address the issue of gender inequality. The only direct reference in the PD election programme occurred in the section entitled 'Protecting the Family', where joint ownership of the family home and family property was advocated.

The party manifestos of Fianna Fail and Fine Gael in 1989 indicated the most comprehensive treatment of gender issues, partly as a result of the political lobbying carried out by the largest women's representative organization, the Council for the Status of Women (Fitzsimons, 1991: 45). As in 1981, Fianna Fail placed an emphasis on its legislative record in advancing gender equality and redressing gender-specific discrimination with promise of further reforms. Fine Gael proposed a continuation and a broadening of structural and legislative initiatives to secure women's rights. Labour emphasized the need to reform existing employment equality legislation and proposed the introduction of broad anti-discrimination legislation incorporating gender. The Workers party presented the comprehensive interventionist programme on which it had campaigned in the 1987 election, with detailed specific proposals for ending gender inequality. The Progressive Democrats approached the issue in a gender-neutral fashion in the context of social welfare, civil liberties and family law reform.

Thus, as the 1980s progressed, the issue of gender received more attention from the parties as part of their respective electoral packages. The establishment of a junior ministry for women's affairs in 1982 and of the parliamentary committee on Women's Rights in 1983 complemented the work of the state-funded Employment Equality Agency, the Council for the Status of Women and voluntary women's interest groups. The politics of gender became institutionalized within the political processes. However, the extent of political recognition afforded to these parliamentary and executive innovations varied with the government in power. The Fine Gael–Labour coalition was predisposed to structural initiatives on the periphery of government decision-making. Fianna Fail, on taking office in 1987, abolished the ministry for women's affairs, and indicated a preference for dealing with the gender question through the expression of supportive sentiment, but with minimal structural change. In fact, it was some time before the women's affairs portfolio was allocated to a junior minister, and there was little progress on gender-based issues. The parliamentary committee on women's rights was re-appointed after both the 1987 and 1989 elections and continued its work of raising the awareness of politicians and the electorate of gender-related discriminations in public policies.

As a political initiative, the short-lived ministry for women's affairs proved to be a disappointment for many women. Public expectations had been raised during and subsequent to the November 1982 election that the ministry would be empowered to place gender issues on to the agenda of government. The appointment of a politician with a record as a feminist campaigner to the ministry served to fuel these expectations. In reality, many of the problems associated with the public perception of this ministry stemmed, not from a dearth of ministerial political will, but from other causes: lack of finances, its very broad brief involving a basic working cooperation from other ministries, its status as a junior ministry attached to two departments, and its lack of access to the cabinet table, all of which inhibited the development of a major legislative programme on women's rights. None the less, it had a solid record on legislative reform in the area of family law, particularly in relation to the rights of children.

Gender came into focus as a political issue after the election in 1990 of the feminist campaigner and constitutional lawyer Mary Robinson as state President. The Fianna Fail–Labour coalition government established after the 1992 general election has given definite commitments on legislating for the removal of gender inequalities in public policies. The task of introducing such reforms has been delegated to a Minister for Equality and Law Reform, pushing the institutionalization of gender politics a little more to the centre stage of political life. The gender equality agenda has been reinforced with the recent publication of the report of the Second Commission on the Status of Women. The report of this government commission details proposals for legislative change, including a suggestion for legislating for gender quotas in public life. It remains to be seen whether the increased institutionalization of gender will result in anything more than a minimal disruption to the political and legislative process.

Gender and internal party policies

The formulation of internal party strategies for redressing gender imbalances can be related to a number of factors, the principle one being the existence of a demand for change within the party. The scope and nature of the response to this demand was structured by party ideologies and by the sensitivity of party elites to gender representation.

On average, less than 10 per cent of the national executive positions were filled by women in Fianna Fail during the 1980s

Table 7.5 *Women's constituency office-holding by party, 1991 (%)*

	Fianna Fail	Fine Gael	Labour	Progressive Democrats
Chair	2.0	12.0	12.0	12.0
Secretary	15.0	63.0	32.0	51.0
Treasurer	33.0	56.0	11.0	37.0
Mean	16.6	43.6	18.3	33.3

Source: Political parties. The Workers party did not respond to requests for information. The Green party do not adopt this form of organization

and there were no internal mechanisms in place to assist in redressing the very striking gender imbalances in office holding at constituency level. In a reflection of the subordinate political role allocated to women, the majority of women filled the positions of secretary or treasurer, which in Irish political parties are supportive rather than executive posts. This situation has not altered, as Table 7.5 shows.

The continued pattern of women's absence from power within Fianna Fail can largely be attributed to the persistence of the view within the party that women provide the support services for the election of male candidates. With the domination of traditional attitudes on gender roles within the party from grassroots to leadership level, the only possible source of challenge could come from a women's group. Yet, the National Women's Committee has had a sporadic existence, being first established in 1981, revitalized in 1985 and given a further lease of life in 1990. Although a useful forum for women to have their views on policy issues heard through its annual conferences, women themselves have been slow to challenge male hegemony within Fianna Fail. Part of the problem lies in the fact that, by contrast to women members of other parties, women in Fianna Fail have until recently given the impression of accepting the dominant attitude on gender. The fact that the women who have made it to the top in Fianna Fail are a product of the traditional patterns of politics serves as a subtle reinforcement of the status quo. A second obstacle to the development of a 'feminist consciousness' in Fianna Fail is the continuation of the practice of the Women's Committee being accountable to the party leadership rather than to its own constituency. The composition of the Committee – at present it has twenty-two members – and the proposals for change emanating from it are subject to the approval of party elites.

While the Women's Committee has in recent years advocated the need for the implementation of positive action strategies to increase women's representation within the party, its demands have not as yet resulted in a positive outcome.

The sponsorship of women candidates by Fine Gael as part of its electoral strategy in the early 1980s had a beneficial effect on the balance of internal gender representation. Overall, the numbers of women holding positions as officers or as members of the national executive grew steadily during the decade. Although the opportunities for the holding of party office positions increased, however, the nature of the office-holding by women reflected the traditional patterns of role stratification. Thus, between 1980 and 1990, the proportion of constituency treasurer positions held by women increased threefold (from 17 per cent to 56 per cent) and the proportion of women holding constituency secretary positions grew to almost one-third (from 24 per cent to 63 per cent). The proportion of constituency chair positions held by women remained at a much more modest level, increasing only from 7 per cent in 1980 to 12 per cent by the end of the decade (Table 7.5). While the strategy of positive encouragement engaged in by the party leadership had beneficial effects in providing women members with opportunities to hold official positions within the party structures, the perceived office of power at constituency level – the chair – remained largely closed to women. Fine Gael has had an active Women's Group since 1985, funded by the party. Its purpose is to provide support, training and encouragement to women members through the organization of seminars and workshops, to encourage the development of a more woman-friendly image, to fund women's activities within the organization and to encourage women to seek selection as candidates for local and national elections. Yet, although women in Fine Gael are more conscious of the obstacles facing women in political structures, the acceptance of the positive encouragement strategy, facilitated by the dominance of a liberal *laissez-faire* social ideology, has militated against any real questioning of women's representation within the party.

The Progressive Democrat central leadership found that women became actively involved in the party even in the absence of a formal policy of favouring women's representation. The appeal of the party to a significant number of women rests largely on the fact that as a new political organization it has not yet institutionalized structural practices and attitudinal barriers militating against women's political advancement. Furthermore, the party's generally liberal position on social issues and the high political profile of its woman co-founder have been important factors in attracting women into its ranks. There are no plans at present for the introduction of gender-related positive action strategies within the party as it is expected that women's involvement in policy-making and in party decision-making will remain at the reasonably representative level of around 25 per cent. Unlike women in other political parties, PD women members do not yet feel the need to establish their own forum within the party or to demand equality of opportunity in terms of representation within the party structures.

Equality of class was a key concept in the ideology of the Labour party in the late 1960s until a combination of external and internal impulses led the party to recognize the gender dimension to equality. First, Labour's ideology became influenced by the radicalism of protest politics which was affecting changes in perspective in socialist parties in western democracies. Thus, between 1966 and 1969, the Labour party moved further leftwards and began to espouse a more radical political ethos. This period of flux and re-assessment of its political *raison d'être* facilitated a tolerance among party elites for women party members influenced by the emergence of the radical politics of feminism. Thus, in 1971, a small group of women activists established an ad hoc women's ancillary organization, the National Women's Committee (later to become the Labour Women's National Council) with the purpose of raising feminist consciousness within the political structures, contributing a feminist perspective to party policy-making, encouraging the adoption and public advancement of women's issues by Labour and increasing women's political representation. However, while the political climate within the party was conducive to a tolerance of feminist and radical ideologies, the structures were less yielding. The women's group was not formally recognized until 1979, and two years later the party agreed to reserve two seats on the national executive body, the Administrative Council, for the representatives of the women's section. Although party decision-makers indicated receptivity to a broad-ranging policy statement on equality in social and economic affairs as drafted by the women's organization in 1983, there was little change in the level of women's representation in positions of power in the party. While there was an effort to open up the selection process to women before the 1985 local elections with the setting of a quota of 25 per cent (raised after the elections to 33 per cent), the quota was not accompanied by specific guidelines or enforcing mechanisms. Furthermore, this quota was deemed to apply only to local elections. In the meantime, candidate selection strategy for general elections adopted by the party executive was changed to favour the selection of a single candidate in each constituency to consolidate the small Labour vote. Thus, while there was a recognition of the need to enact positive action strategies in order to redress gender imbalances in Labour's electoral politics, the priorities of vote-getting and vote-conserving assumed a greater significance than that of establishing a gender balance between the candidates.

The failure of the quota experiment to increase the numbers of women selected as candidates led to a build-up of pressure from within the women's organization for increased opportunities for women to hold positions of responsibility within the party structures. In 1989, a Gender Quota Committee, comprising of executive members of the women's committee and representatives of the Administrative Council, was established to investigate strategies for increasing the representation of women in decision-making positions. The victory of the Labour party's sponsored candidate, Mary Robinson, in the 1990 presidential election was seen as reinforcing the demands being made by the women's group and the Gender Quota Committee for the adoption of gender-based affirmative action measures. Agreement was reached between the central leadership of the party and the members of the Gender Quota Committee on the details of a positive action strategy which became part of the overall modernization process undertaken by the organization. The measures, which include a gender quota of 20 per cent operating at all levels of the party and in electoral politics, were not accompanied by any form of enforcement procedures.

The pattern of women's representation in the former Workers party, and the demand for an increase in women's opportunities for political office-holding, was broadly similar to that articulated by activists within the Labour party. There appears to have been less elite resistance to these demands within the smaller left-wing party, possibly because the Workers party strategists, aware of the need to develop and consolidate a political identity which was recognizably distinct from that of Labour, recognized this as a point on which they could be differentiated from their larger rival. As with the Labour party, pressures for women's inclusion in senior political structures came from the Women's Committee, which, similar to Fianna Fail's Women's Group, was a sub-committee of the national executive. Affirmative action strategies, which included a commitment to 40 per cent gender representation on the national executive, were adopted in 1991 as part of an overall reform and modernization of the party structures.

However, the reform process held within it the seeds of the destruction of the Workers Party: a split occurred in 1992, those siding with the modernization strategy leaving to form the Democratic Left. The early indications are that the new party recognizes the inclusion of women and gender as an integral dimension of its politics. On its first electoral outing in 1992, seven of the twenty-one Democratic Left candidates were women.

The small Green party retains the characteristics of a political movement rather than a political organization, with decentralized decision-making and non-hierarchical representative structures. Its electoral response to the salience of gender came in the 1991 local elections with the selection of the highest proportion of women candidates of all the parties. However, although it has incorporated and implemented a gender quota mechanism varying from 33 per cent to 40 per cent to ensure a gender balance in senior decision-making positions, the debate on favouring women as a group is one of contention within the party. This debate is being conducted on broadly ideological lines, with feminism being seen as a challenge by a particular group to the tenets of the green political philosophy.

Conclusions

Two features stand out in this discussion of the relationship between gender and party politics in Ireland. One is the continued importance of family connections in determining the opportunities for selection as candidates and the electoral success of women. The second is the extent to which electoral considerations determine party policies in relation to women's representation and influence the demand within the parties for a recognition of gender in terms of representation and policy. The response of each party to the demands of gender inclusion and representation is shaped by the dominant political ideology espoused by the individual parties and the exigencies of electoral politics.

Kinship continues to be an important factor in women's selection and election, with over twice as many women parliamentarians as men having family connections with politics. However, the situation is changing as more high-profile women from non-political backgrounds, occasionally with experience of women's movement and pressure group politics, and women from urban areas, seek selection. The likelihood of their overcoming the hurdle of the selection process depends on the party of their allegiance, the commitment of the leadership to ensure the selection of a respectable number of women candidates and the existence of effective affirmative action policies governing the selection process. Thus, Fine Gael, in the early 1980s, and more recently Labour and the Progressive Democrats have provided electoral opportunities for women with non-traditional political backgrounds. Labour, the new Democratic Left party and the Workers party have placed a priority on the prospective women candidates having a background in local politics or community activism, while in Fianna Fail, the daughter or widow of a member of parliament is highly favoured.

The second hurdle, that of being elected, reinforces the significance of kinship. Women with family connections appear more likely to gain and retain Dail seats than other candidates, although the security of incumbency is less favourable for women than men. There are also indications that women candidates may be more susceptible to a negative electoral performance by their chosen parties, but that this is greater for women from non-traditional political backgrounds than for women from political families. Many of these conclusions go to reinforce the intensely personalized and localized nature of Irish candidate selection and electoral politics.

The second strand of significance in this study is the effect of advancing an electoral strategy which incorporated gender representation and gender issues. In terms of the political system, this has resulted in a modest institutionalization of gender within the parliamentary arena. For the parties, it has involved a recognition, to a greater or lesser degree, of the need for a greater incorporation of women into party office-holding. Parties have dealt with this issue within the context of the ideology of the organization, with Fianna Fail appearing reluctant to change its allegiance to traditional gender role models while the parties of the left are prepared to adopt interventionist mechanisms to facilitate women's participation in power. In between, the liberalism of Fine Gael and the Progressive Democrats encourages a complacency based on its past record in the former and a gender-blindness in the latter. Fianna Fail and Labour have had similar records on levels of gender representation in the Dail, both amounting to less than 5 per cent women deputies since 1973. Fine Gael, at an average of 8 per cent of women deputies over the same period, was more successful in achieving modest progress in this respect. The key to the advancement of women and the successful political management of gender-based policy issues in the future lies, however, with Fianna Fail. Given the dominance of Fianna Fail in electoral politics, it is likely that there will be no significant change in the levels of women's political representation and in public policies affecting the status of women until this party begins to pay serious attention to the issue of gender in Irish politics.

8

A 'Partitocrazia' Without Women: the Case of the Italian Party System

Marila Guadagnini

The problem of gender and political parties in Italy does not lend itself easily to analysis today. The Italian multi-party system, which maintained its dominance with a high degree of continuity since the fall of Fascism, has been rocked to its foundation in the span of little more than a year and its immediate future is very difficult to predict. Political commentators are speaking of a 'revolution'. In fact, the situation seems to present many of the classic features of a revolution including: the delegitimation of the existing political elite and a widespread call for its replacement; the collapse of the existing political party identities and organizations; the rapid emergence of new political forces; and an ongoing process of modification of the rules of the game. Many factors have contributed to this crisis, but a determining factor has been the 'Mani pulite' or 'Clean hands' investigation launched by the judiciary first in Milan and later in other major cities, which brought to light a widespread pattern of corruption involving the highest levels of the political elite and the ruling class of the country. The investigations revealed that while the political class had successfully presented the Italian party system as highly fragmented and polarized on ideological grounds, it was in fact highly cohesive when involved in the task of draining the public purse into the pockets of the various party leaders. As of July 1993, no less than one-third of the members of parliament are under investigation by the judiciary for corruption, violation of party financing laws and so on (including some involvement with the Mafia), while important business leaders from both the private and public sectors, along with leading academic figures are under investigation awaiting trial. To date, the investigations have involved more than 2,600 persons.

At the same time the rules of the game have been changed radically. In April 1993 a referendum modified the electoral system for the Senate. In addition a similar modification for the lower house is close to adoption by parliament and other significant reform measures are under discussion. The law governing local elections has been changed too.[1] The transition from an electoral system based on proportional representation to one based on majority representation is expected to have further cataclysmic effects on the existing party system. The first signs of these changes can be observed already in the results of local-administration elections held in June 1993 in a number of municipalities, which clearly show the collapse of some traditional parties and the triumph of new political forces.

In the light of this new political landscape, the whole question of gender and political parties can be reconsidered. While until recently one might have complained about the marginalization of women within the political elite (for example only 8.7 per cent of the parliamentarians elected in 1993 were women), today this 'outsider status' could be seen as a point of honour.

The pages which follow were written in 1992 and represent a description of the Italian party system before the 'revolution' of 1993. Yet they can be useful to aid our understanding of the types of mechanism that limit the political participation of women and restrict their entry into the national decision-making arena. This may permit us to add some important elements for the construction of a comparative study of the models that aid or obstruct an equal participation of women in the political system.

This chapter will analyse the causes for the under-representation of women in elected offices at all levels, examining the mechanism of political recruitment – including selection, nomination and election of political personnel – and thus focusing on the political parties as the key actors in this process. Until 1992 entrance into Italian parliament has required not only party affiliation, but also – in most cases – a long apprenticeship in a succession of political offices. These were offices held within the party organization and/ or in local elective bodies. This pattern of pre-parliamentary career was shared more or less by all the parties, even if its features varied according to the internal organization of the various parties (Cotta, 1979; Guadagnini, 1983).

Parties and the party system prior to 1993

Until 1992, in the Italian party system, between seven and nine parties had been represented since the war and a further group of fringe parties had appeared and disappeared from the elective bodies. As a result of a high level of political competition favoured by an electoral law based on proportional representation, the

Italian multi-party system covered most of the imaginable political spectrum. The Christian Democrats (DCs) and the Communist party (PCI) have been by far the largest parties. From 1968 to 1987, these two parties consistently maintained electoral support at more than 30 per cent and 25 per cent respectively. The Socialist party's vote oscillated between 10 and 14 per cent, while the Italian Social Movement–National Right party (heir to the dissolved Fascist party) won approximately 6 per cent of the votes cast. A host of smaller parties brought in 2–3 per cent of votes each. As Tables 8.1a and 8.1b show, there was little significant change in terms of percentage in electoral behaviour before the beginning of the 1990s.

In 1991, however, with the dissolution of the Communist party, the second largest party in Italy, and the ensuing birth of two new parties, the Democratic Left and the Communist Refoundation, the system changed significantly. This break-up occurred after a period of great turmoil beginning at the end of 1988 when the Secretary of the PCI, Ochetto, proposed that the party undertake a process of transformation aimed at the creation of a new reformist party.[2] This new party would differ greatly from the Marxist–Leninist working-class party of the previous forty or so years. It would accept the logic of free market economy accompanied by the creation of a structure of guarantees to assure equal opportunity to all individuals. At the 1991 Party Congress at Rimini, Ochetto's proposal was accepted by a majority of the delegates (64.1 per cent) and a new party was formed with a new name (Democratic Left party – PDS) and a new symbol. The dissident minority gave birth to a second party, the Communist Refoundation, which claimed to be the true heir to the old PCI, signalling this by maintaining the old party symbol. This period of internal turmoil and eventual schism, coupled with the difficulty in establishing a clearly recognizable identity for the new PDS and combined with the impact of the damaged image of Communism following the fall of the eastern European regimes, led to a decline in electoral support in the 1992 elections to the National Chamber. The PDS received 26.1 per cent of the votes while Communist Refoundation gained 5.6 per cent (see Table 8.1a).

Overall, the 1992 election registered the most significant change in electoral behaviour since the war. For the first time the Christian Democratic party slipped below 30 per cent of the vote. Electoral volatility caused an even more extensive fragmentation of the party system (in 1992 twelve parties won parliamentary seats) (Tables 8.1a, 8.1b). This fragmentation was the result of the electoral success of 'new' parties, especially the regional Leagues, which gained a total 9.4 per cent of the vote.

Another factor that influenced many leaders of the old PCI radically to change their party was their desire to refashion a political party able to participate in governing coalitions. In the past the PCI was consistently excluded on the grounds of its presumed anti-system attitudes and its close ties with the Soviet Union. The long-lasting exclusion of the PCI contributed to a considerable continuity in successive governing coalitions. The Christian Democratic party has consistently been in power since the war, either alone or in coalition with other parties, notably the Liberals (PLI), the Republicans (PRI), the Socialists (PSI) and the Social Democrats (PSDI). The remaining coalitions have been either the centre and centre–left (Centro Sinistra – in the 1960s) or the five party (Pentapartito) and four party (Quadripartito) formulas. At the local level (regions, provinces and town councils),[3] the coalitions have been more diversified and in some cases included the Communist party, which, in this way, was able to play an important role.

'Partitocrazia'

An important feature of the Italian political system has been that the party system has held a position between society and government institutions, a position that was more important than that occupied by the parties in the other liberal democracies. The term *partitocrazia* (parties' power) is used to refer to the abnormal, disproportionate presence of the parties in interest articulation on the one hand and decision-making on the other (the literature refers to a 'dispossession' of institutions by the parties). Experts on Italian political parties believe that they have maintained control over both the articulation and mediation of interest and claims. Although mass movements have been successful in voicing and aggregating demands from various interest groups, they have not succeeded in reaching decision-making levels through bypassing party and institutional structures. Party regulation of interests was well established and survived rapid socio-economic development, the explosion of 1968, the ensuing crisis and the resulting social diversification and fragmentation (Ergas, 1986; Pasquino, 1987). Moreover, the parties have maintained their monopoly over political recruitment. It was parties that decided who would occupy public or semi-public decision-making posts. In addition, thanks to the expansion of the public economic sectors[4] and thus the consolidation of an 'entrepreneurial state', Italian parties came to acquire a role of 'employment givers'. This applied not only to

Table 8.1a   Political elections: Chamber of deputies (1972–1987), percentage values and number of seats[1]

	1972 %	1972 N	1976 %	1976 N	1979 %	1979 N	1983 %	1983 N	1987 %	1987 N	1992 %	1992 N
Votes	93.2		93.4		90.6		89.0		88.9		87.5	
Abstentions	6.8		6.6		9.4		11.0		11.1		12.5	
Valid votes	96.8		97.3		95.9		94.2		95.1		95.5	
Non-valid votes	3.2		2.7		4.1		5.8		4.9		4.5	
of which blank	1.7		1.6		2.2		2.4		1.9		1.5	
of which null	1.5		1.2		1.9		3.4		3.0		3.0	
DC[2]	38.7	266	38.7	263	38.3	262	32.9	225	34.3	234	29.5	206
PCI-PDS	27.1	179	34.4	227	30.4	201	29.9	198	26.6	177	16.1	107
Communist Refound.											5.6	35
PSI	9.6	61	9.6	57	9.8	62	11.4	73	14.3	94	13.6	92
PSDI	5.1	29	3.4	15	3.8	20	4.1	23	2.9	17	2.7	16
PRI	2.9	15	3.1	14	3.0	16	5.1	29	3.7	21	4.4	27
PLI	3.9	20	1.3	5	1.9	9	2.9	16	2.1	11	2.9	17
MSI-DN	8.7	56	6.1	35	5.3	30	6.8	42	5.9	35	5.3	34
Mixed group	0.6	4	0.5	3	0.6	5	0.6	4	0.6	4		
PSIUP	1.9											
PR			1.1	4	3.5	18	2.2	11	2.6	13		
Pannella list											1.2	7
PDUP					1.4	6						
DP			1.5	6			1.5	7	1.7	8		
Greens									2.5	13	3.0	16
RETE											1.9	12
League											9.4	55
Others	1.5		0.3	1	2	1	2.6	2	2.8	3	6.0	6
Total	100	630	100	630	100	630	100	630	100	630	100	630

[1] Percentage on valid votes.
[2] For abbreviations see Notes.
Sources: Up to 1987: Caciagli and Spreafico, 1990; 1992: *Stampa Sera*, 7 April 1992: 2

Table 8.1b Political elections: Senate (1972–1987), percentage values and seats attributed[1]

	1972 %	1972 N	1976 %	1976 N	1979 %	1979 N	1983 %	1983 N	1987 %	1987 N	1992 %	1992 N
Votes	92.7		93.3		90.4		88.6		88.4		86.8	
Abstentions	7.8		7.2		10.6		12.9		13.2		13.2	
Valid votes	95.7		96.6		95.3		93.4		94.2		93.2	
Non-valid votes	4.3		3.4		4.7		6.6		5.8		6.8	
of which blank	2.8		2.2		2.7		3.1		2.8		3.2	
of which null	1.5		1.2		1.9		3.5		3.0		3.6	
DC[2]	38.1	135	38.9	135	38.3	138	32.4	120	33.6	125	27.3	108
PCI–PDS	28.1	94	33.8	116	31.5	109	30.8	107	28.3	101	17.0	69
Communist Refound.											6.5	18
PSI	10.7	33	10.2	29	10.4	32	11.4	38	10.9	36	13.6	37
PSDI	5.4	11	3.1	6	4.2	9	3.8	8	2.4	5	2.6	3
PRI	3.0	5	2.7	6	3.4	6	4.7	10	3.9	8	4.7	14
PLI	4.4	8	1.4	2	2.2	2	2.7	6	2.2	3	2.8	6
MSI–DN	9.1	26	6.6	15	5.7	13	7.3	18	6.5	16	6.5	25
Mixed group	0.4	3	0.6	2	0.6	3	0.6	3	0.6	3		
PSIUP												
PR			0.8		1.3	2	1.8	1	1.8	3		
PSI–PSDI–PR									3.1	10		
DP							1.1		1.5	1		
Greens											3.3	3
League									2.0	1	8.2	26
Others	0.8		1.8	4	2.4	1	3.4	4	3.2	3	6.1	6
Total	100	315	100	315	100	315	100	315	100	315	100	315

[1] Percentage on valid votes.
[2] For abbreviations see Notes.

Source: Up to 1987: Caciagli and Spreafico, 1990

posts in the rapidly increasing public management sector, but also to a large number of politically appointed posts within public and semi-public bodies (see note 4). This phenomenon is known as 'civil society occupation' or *sottogoverno*.

Recruitment into both administrative and political offices has been substantially in the parties' hands. The staff of elected decision-making bodies had, in almost all cases, a party background. Italian political decision-making takes place in the parliament, particularly in the relationship between the executive and the legislative branches. The legislature consists of two chambers, the Chamber of Deputies and the Senate, which have similar tasks but which are independent of each other as to their legislative activity.[5]

The cabinet consists of the prime minister (*Presidente del Consiglio*) and a number of ministers, with or without portfolio. It is appointed by the President of the Republic and must have the confidence of the parliament. In practice, the President of the Republic merely followed the parties' proposals as to the choice of the prime minister and the latter's decisions, as to the choice of the ministers. The members of the cabinet were usually chosen from within the parliament. Outsiders were appointed only rarely (Pasquino, 1987: 61).

Prior to 1993, the cabinet was largely made up of persons with a party background (Cotta, 1979). Only a few 'experts' were able to bypass this apprenticeship. Also, the parties have been the gatekeepers in decision-making processes. Surveys have shown that decision-making processes, in Italy, have taken place in the framework of bargaining among the secretariats (political boards and departments) of the executive and the various committees of the legislature.

In short, most decision-making in Italy culminates in the promulgation of laws (Di Palma, 1977), hence the decision-making arenas are essentially limited to cabinet and parliament (see note 5), both of which have been dominated by office-holders with a party background. The system is also characterized by a rather weak parliamentary government. Governments were normally made up of unstable heterogeneous coalitions, which were not challenged by an alternative coalition. Parliament was inefficient – its two chambers had equal powers and functions – and it tended to operate slowly and confusedly.

The lack of efficiency of the political system has caused the electorate to feel a growing intolerance and uneasiness towards the political parties. Warning signals of this attitude were: the increasing abstentionism (Tables 8.1a, 8.1b); more and more frequent resort to the instrument of referendum; the mushrooming of 'new' lists and parties, widening in the course of the 1980s, to result in the access of new political formations to both local government and parliament (see Tables 8.1a, 8.1b). Ever-increasing calls for institutional reforms accompanied criticism of the party system, remedial measures, which, on the one hand, could break up the continuity and the inactivity deriving from well-rooted equilibriums, and, on the other hand, could allow for the turnover of an entrenched political class that has been keener on creating mechanisms and opportunities to reproduce itself than on working out reform plans. Such a political elite became less and less suitable to cope with such challenges as internal economic and social difficulties and the resulting overload that is so characteristic of modern government.

Finally, Italian parties in the 1980s showed those patterns of change described by Kirchheimer (1966), including: a decreasing emphasis on ideology for developing consensus and achieving party cohesion, a broadening of the party appeal which is no longer based upon a specific social class or confessional group, a diminishing role played by rank and file party activists, an increasing focus on the function of recruiting and selecting politicians and the consequent professionalization of the political elites. Beset by such transformations, Italian parties seem to have lost their traditional function of integrating the masses within the state and have come more and more to resemble a 'business' enterprise devoted to maximizing its appeal on the electoral market thus increasing its power and its ability to provide positions for its loyal cadres. The Italian parties reacted to the failure of their ideological appeal by aiming, on the one hand, to mobilize an issue-orientated consensus, but, on the other hand, to strengthen mobilization based on clientelistic appeal, which caused an exponential increase in corruption.

Gender and Italian party politics: an overview

Given this scenario, what possibilities were there for women's political representation within the parties and in the institutional decision-making bodies? Clearly, working with the parties was necessary in order to acquire both power and influence. In a context in which the electorate was less sensitive (though not completely insensitive) to the appeal of 'old' ideologies, women's optimum strategy to expand their presence in decision-making bodies was to offer challenging new platforms, capable of mobilizing a large consensus, or at least to draw up projects that would mobilize an issue-orientated electorate. They could not avoid taking into account well-rooted practices, reinforced by the structure of the Italian parties, which favoured 'clientelistic' allocations of benefits and resources. The dilemma women faced was that of how or indeed whether to work within such structures, whose organization they have not contributed to, but which were the main pathways to power and influence, so as to modify them from within.

This dilemma has divided women's attitudes for many years. The Feminist Movement has, for the most part, chosen to maintain an autonomous position rather than create centres of power within the parties. Over time, other women's associations have chosen to provide support to the parties from outside. For example, UDI (Italian Women's Union), the most influential feminist organization, was for many years an important support organization for the Communist party and a significant training ground for PCI women politicians (Guadagnini, 1980): nevertheless, it decided, in 1982, to sever its links with the PCI. A similar role was played by CIF, the most important women's Catholic organization, towards the Christian Democrat party.

The younger generation of feminists has opted for a greater involvement in the established party structures. There they have directed their efforts not only at getting support for policies to bring about change in women's working conditions but also to bring feminist values and perspectives into party politics. Italian political parties differ widely in their attitude to women's representation and these differences have become even greater over time. In the following pages we will outline the characteristic features of women's presence within the parties and political institutions both at a local and national level, taking into consideration the role of the Italian parties as 'gatekeepers' to elective bodies prior to 1992.

The PCI and the PDS

The PCI was the most accessible to women in every sense. For example, in 1986 the party established a minimum 25 per cent threshold for women's representation in the party's Executive Boards. A few years later, following a strong campaign aiming at balancing men's and women's representation in parliament, and thanks, perhaps above all, to its greater control over preference voting, the communists managed almost to double their number of women members in both the Chamber of Deputies and the Senate (see Tables 8.5a, 8.5b). At its 1989 Rome Congress the PCI explicitly adopted the principle of equal representation of men and

Table 8.2 *Number of women members of the National Council
(Consiglio Nazionale) and Executive Board (Direzione) of DC,
PCI, PDS and PSI*[1]

	DC	PCI	PDS	PSI
National Council				
%	1.8	35	37.7	20
N	3	189	190	100
Executive Board				
%	2.5	33	32.2	19.2
N	1	38	38	10

[1] For abbreviations see Notes.

Source: The political parties

women in its internal institutional bodies, Executive Boards and
congress delegations. It introduced the double-list criterion – one
of women candidates and one of men candidates – for the election
of party's bodies, reserving a minimum 33 per cent quota to the
minority sex. Women were active in the tumultuous phase leading
to the transformation of the party. Women made up 34 per cent of
the total at the Twentieth Congress in Rimini in 1991 where the
break-up of the old PCI was agreed. The majority of women
delegates voted for the creation of the new PDS and their activity
during this process strengthened their position within the successor
party in two significant ways. First, they succeeded in including in
the new party statute that 'the PDS is a party of women and men'.
Secondly, they inserted a clause stating that men's and women's
representation at leadership and executive levels, in congress
delegations, in candidates lists, as well as in offices at all levels, was
to be approximately equal. In no case can representation be lower
than 40 per cent. This is a PDS extension of practices that were
inherited from the PCI. In the 'old' PCI, the number of women
present in decision-making bodies at national level was quite large:
women comprised 35 per cent (189) of the members of the
National Council and 33 per cent (38) of the members of the
Executive Board (Table 8.2). In the 'new' PDS the percentage of
women in the party's central bodies remained substantially
unchanged (Table 8.2).

The policy of promotion of women within the party
organization was carried out during a period of crisis for the
PCI. The crisis involved not only the very identity of the party,
but also the diminishing dimensions of its membership and

electoral support: in 1990 the number of party members plummeted to its minimum in the past twenty years.

The promotion of women's causes can be explained partly as a response to the crisis, but also as part of the old PCI's strategy to create new links with emerging social groups and in particular as an attempt to capture women's electoral support and membership, which for many years belonged to conservative groups, principally the DC. The party partially succeeded in this attempt. In the context of an overall decrease in the number of party members (from 1,814,317 in 1967 to 1,421,230 in 1989), the percentage of women members rose from 24 per cent in 1976 to 26.9 per cent in 1989. In the new Democratic Left party, the number of women members in 1990 had dropped by 13 per cent since 1976, while the number of male members had dropped by 31.7 per cent. As a result, women now total 28 per cent of the overall membership. Women are, therefore, those who 'betrayed' the least.

The pattern of slow, but increasing women's support may be due to the activism of women within the party with a 'feminist' attitude who have been successful in formulating and forcing the implementation of various initiatives favouring women's concerns. One of these initiatives was a theoretical intervention, the introduction and development of a debate about the necessity of a gender-determined viewpoint in politics. According to this view, an increased feminine presence in decision-making bodies will serve not only to advance women's interests but also to change institutions from within. To accomplish this end party feminists have appealed to women with the slogan 'women's power from women', aiming to create a feminine solidarity to constitute the source of women's political power.

Communist women MPs have been very active in parliament as the prime movers for recent legislation on equal opportunities and affirmative action. The debate on what has been called the 'gender-determined political representation' (*rappresentanza sessuata*) began in the 1980s within the PCI and has been carried on into the new PDS. The present situation of transformation within the party is an opportunity to realize, in concrete terms, this long-debated concept. Women are now claiming the right to prepare and advance their own projects and are proposing the creation of new single gender structures and bodies within the party. They reason that such single gender bodies can form new ties to a wide variety of women's interest groups (associations, clubs, etc.) in civil society at large. Such an initiative, women argue, may serve to strengthen the links between the PDS and the real needs of society.

The PSI
The Socialist party was also a promoter of women's representation, if only in its intentions. The 1984 Verona Congress agreed to reserve 15 per cent of the executive posts within the party organization for women. The figure was subsequently raised to 20 per cent. Thanks to these measures, the PSI (20 per cent of whose members are women) increased the number of women within the Executive Board to 19 per cent and the National Council to 20 per cent (Table 8.2). Despite these achievements, the percentage of women in PSI delegations in local and national elective bodies has always been very limited (see Tables 8.5a, 8.5b, 8.8, 8.9, 8.10).

PSI feminist-orientated activists have given considerable support to women's issues, in implementing law on gender equality in the areas of civil rights and employment.

The Christian Democrats
The case of the Christian Democrats (DC) party is quite different. An associated DC Women's Movement has been in existence since 1947, its organization being both autonomous from and parallel to the main party. A set number of women elected to the National Committee of the Women's Movement participate with the right to vote on political issues in the party's boards. The Eighteenth Congress (February 1989) approved an agenda, according to which the National Council is committed to the approval of such statutory amendments as are necessary to allow for the principle of the minimum quotas of women on party bodies. There is no pre-set quota; the commitment limits itself to the pledge that women's representation on party bodies will be approximately proportional to the number of women members. Positive action is promised in support of women candidates for such posts to ensure that a suitable number of women will be elected. Nevertheless, women have continued to be seriously under-represented in the party's National Council (three of 180 members, see Table 8.2). Things have not changed in the National Executive of the party either. The one elected in February 1989 apparently took no account of the quota pledge. The only woman who sat by right on the executive was the Women's Movement delegate. The percentage of women among Christian Democrats elected to local and national office has remained low also (see Tables 8,5a, 8.5b, 8.8, 8.9, 8.10). Despite these disappointing figures, the DC attracted a high number of women voters (in 1987 women accounted for 55 per cent of the DC vote (Mannheimer and Sani, 1987), as well as quite a high proportion of women members, 40 per cent).

The reason that the party has not seriously advanced measures for equal participation of women in political life results from its conception of the role of women (strongly influenced by Catholic tradition) which recognizes an 'equality' for women that does not threaten their traditional family roles. Thus the party supported policies of gender equality in the workplace, since women must work to help support the family, but it stopped short of encouraging women's participation in such public activities as politics.

The smaller parties
None of the smaller parties had adopted a quota system by the end of 1992.[6] Some of them, however, the PLI and the PRI, were very active in the battle for civil rights (divorce, abortion etc.) and to improve women's conditions at work. Special note should be taken of the Radical party, which originally sprang from an alliance with elements from the Women's Liberation Movement and has been one of the strongest supporters of feminist issues. Over time, original gender equality in Radical party representation has declined (see Tables 8.5a, 8.5b). The PSDI and the MSI have continued to be the parties offering the least support to women's causes.

Parties and the selection of women for decision-making positions

There have been striking differences among parties in the recruitment of women into decision-making bodies. Recruitment into elective bodies can be seen as a complex mechanism through which available opportunities and resources are converted into resources permitting entry into elective bodies. Key factors in this mechanism are: the type of resources required; formal and informal rules related to the political system; and the role of the political structure (parties above all, in the case of Italy).

The type of internal organization of a party will be a crucial variable in its ability to recruit women into elected office. Two elements of party structure are worthy of mention here: (1) the degree of institutionalization of party organization and (2) the degree of centralization in the selection of candidates. Scholars define the level of institutionalization in terms of both the party's relationship to its external environment and the cohesion and homogeneity of its internal structure. Both of these are tied to the degree of bureaucratization of the party. If the party has a strong and cohesive bureaucracy, the central core has the resources to dominate local groups, thus ensuring homogeneity throughout the party organization. A strong internal bureaucracy can guarantee that the party as a whole enjoys a considerable autonomy within its environment. If, on the other hand, the degree of bureaucratization is slight, the party is more dependent upon its external environment, and lacks the resources to enforce homogeneity among its various sectors (Panebianco, 1982). In the first case, party organization is controlled by functionaries and a party career comes to resemble a bureaucratic one. An example of this type of party structure has been that of the PCI.

The Christian Democrats have been an example of the second type of party organization. The DC was dominated by a collection of 'notables', representatives of various interest groups and persons with a significant power base outside the party. Thus, political careers have been determined by the resources such persons could draw from outside the party environment. In the DCs, since the centre of the party was weak and fragmented, the various 'factions' each articulated their interests and demands and the party failed to produce a homogeneous programme.

These two models of party organization have clear implications for the manner of recruitment of the political elite. The highly institutionalized bureaucratic model with a centralized core facilitates the entrance of less 'advantaged' groups and individuals, like women, who possess fewer external resources. The second, weakly institutionalized model discourages the entrance of less advantaged groups because the high level of competition within such parties favours those who have been able to accumulate 'personal political capital', resources with a 'buying' power on the electoral market. Personal political capital is defined as all those resources based on personal status (social position, professional career etc.) and/or on strong external group support and/or on a political career through which an individual can develop an extensive electoral base. Recent investigations carried out by magistrates have shown that another element was the capacity to channel funds from the business community and other powerful interests to the party leadership.

For many years, the Christian Democratic and Socialist parties have followed the pattern of a weaker degree of institutionalization (fractionalized core) (Panebianco, 1982). Although Craxi's predominance within the PSI since the mid-1970s tended to restrict the importance of internal factions, this did not result in a higher degree of institutionalization or in the elimination of internal power centres, but rather in a 'personalization' of the party leadership. The smaller parties, due to their restricted number of political staff and to their less structured and wide-spread organization more closely resemble Panebianco's second model. In all the less institutionalized parties, factions have gained strength through competition for access to external resources such as the administration of state funds and the control of Civil Service appointments. In these parties, power was shared among functionaries, 'notables', professional politicians and politicians of a new type, men who could be called 'political entrepreneurs' (Panebianco, 1988), deriving their power from the management of public funds and the administration of huge state initiatives (not only state-controlled business but also programmes like that for the economic development of the South of Italy – *Cassa del Mezzogiorno*).

Having classified parties in terms of their organizations we may now examine in greater detail the three steps implicit in the recruitment process for entry into elective bodies. First, the selection of candidates, then their election and finally the job security provided for them on their way out of elected offices which serves as an incentive for entering and staying with a political career.

Selection of candidates

Our account is constrained by the problem that no studies are available on the selection process carried out by the major Italian parties. Although we are able to outline many of the procedures employed until 1992, we cannot offer a detailed analysis of each stage of the process. In each party, candidates lists were drawn up after discussion within the local and national party leadership and their final composition resulted from bargaining among party leaders. Empirical research on the biographies of the candidates chosen and of the proposed but excluded candidates might reveal the outlines of the criteria used for selection and the extent to which women have been penalized at this first step of recruitment. Research done on biographies of the successful candidates, that is to say the candidates elected into parliament (as we will see below) permits us to advance some hypotheses on the criteria for selection. It appears that to be considered as a candidate an individual must have had a record of work within the party. In the bureaucratic type of party, a long apprenticeship within the party organization was an important qualification. In the factionalized parties, a second key factor was the loyalty displayed towards the leader of a particular faction. Finally, a third factor was the perceived capacity of the candidate to attract votes. This is a determining factor for those who can rely upon outside resources such as a successful professional career, the support of external groups etc.

Although the various parties have developed formal rules governing the selection of candidates (who must be consulted, what meetings must be held etc.), in fact candidate selection has been a prerogative of top party leaders. Furthermore, as we will show below, mere inclusion on a party's list of candidates is not highly significant as it does not mean that an individual's candidacy has the real support of his or her party.

In the DC (less institutionalized/fragmented core) the candidate lists were prepared by the local party organizations at the provincial level (*Comitati provinciali*). The Regional Board then could approve or modify the list submitted and then submit the list to the National Executive Board, which had the last word in approving the lists. The DC Women's Movement could propose its own candidates. Unfortunately, we have no empirical research that enables us to assess the acceptance by the party leadership of such proposals. There was a small proportion of women among DC candidates (16.6 per cent in 1992).

In the PCI–PDS, the local boards (first the Federal Board (*Comitato Federale*), and then the Regional Board) prepared a candidate list which they submitted to the Executive Board which had the power to approve or disapprove individual candidates. The Executive Board decided which candidates were placed on the top of the list (that is, those who were virtually guaranteed election). The formal rules called for an equitable representation of each of the groupings which make up the party, but here again no empirical data exist to indicate whether or not this rule was followed in practice.

While in parties like the Christian Democrats, factions play an important role in the selection of candidates and the drawing up of candidate lists is a result of bargaining among the factions, in parties like the PCI, the selection of candidates at all levels is tightly controlled by the cohesive party elite. Turning to the question of centralization in the selection of candidates, we find that in both the models described above the central elite exerts almost complete control over selection of candidates at both local and national levels. The only difference is that central domination over local candidate selection is in one case exerted by a 'cohesive elite', and in the other case by a 'fragmented elite' at the conclusion of their internal bargaining process. Nevertheless, in the case of the parties with a factionalized core, local political leaders are not entirely powerless. The local leader of each faction does enjoy some upward-orientated bargaining power with the leader of his faction, and so can ensure that local interests are not ignored (Panebianco, 1988).

Which of the two models seems to facilitate the selection of women? It appears that to the extent that there is a sufficient number of women within the central apparatus, parties with a cohesive core favour women's candidacy. Data for the 1987 elections show that the PCI had the largest percentage of women in its list of candidates (29 per cent) while the DC had one of the lowest (14.2 per cent). This is due to the fact that a high level of competition within a party penalizes the selection of women: the more a party is fragmented and factionalized the more difficulties women encounter in gaining inclusion in the lists. This fact can be clearly documented by looking not only at the two contrasting cases (PCI and DC), but also examining the new PDS. After the dissolution of the old PCI and of its rigid principle of cohesiveness, in the new party different *correnti* (groupings) have emerged, which are not yet formally structured as factions. In the candidate list drawn up for the 1992 elections, the proportional representation of these informal groupings was considered to be more important than the representation of the various social groups. As a result of this change in priorities, women's presence on the candidate list dropped from 29 to 26.8 per cent.

Election of the candidates

The type of party organization not only influences women's chances of inclusion in the candidate list, but also their chances for election. Big differences exist among the parties in the percentage of elected women candidates at national and local level (see Tables 8.5a, 8.5b, 8.8, 8.9 and 8.10). To understand these data fully, we need first to explain certain aspects of the Italian electoral system, as it functioned until the reforms of 1993.

The members of town, provincial and regional councils (the three levels of local government in Italy)[7] and the 630 members of the Chambers of Deputies were elected from lists submitted by single parties, according to the proportional representation system, which allowed the use of preferential votes. In this system, each party offers the electors two possible ways of expressing their votes. They can either simply vote for the party or express a preference for up to four of the candidates offered on the party list. For the 1992 parliamentary elections, however, the system was modified to permit each voter to cast only one 'preferential' vote.

The Senate had a different electoral system which did not allow for preferential votes. Senatorial elections, therefore, were more predictable. Thus, if a Senate candidate was placed on or near the top of the list, he or she was virtually assured of being elected. The mechanism for the Chamber of Deputies and for the local elective councils was more complex but the role played by the parties was nevertheless fundamental.

The party could affect the election of a candidate in many ways: it might nominate the *capolista* (top-of-the-list) candidate, as we said before); it might reinforce the position of a candidate by 'coupling' her with one or more 'blockbusters', that is to say, by presenting voters with 'joint preference' choices (until 1990 elections); or else, it may give financial support to some candidates, but not to others. In principle the Italian electoral system might favour women's election, since the use of preferential votes allows parties' nominations to be altered. In practice however this did not occur. Over the years, women have tended to collect fewer preferential votes than men. The preferential votes may be of two types: 'opinion' votes and 'clientelist' votes. 'Opinion' votes are those made on the basis of evaluation of the qualities a candidate offers and his or her ability to carry out those programmes the elector feels respond to his or her needs and expectations. An opinion vote can be either based on rational considerations or conditioned by emotions, prejudices etc. For example, a voter may see in a candidate qualities which gain his or her trust without having any empirical evidence about the candidate's record. 'Clientelist' votes are those votes cast on the basis of a special relationship between candidate and electors based on an exchange of 'favours' or votes purchased outright. Women were disadvantaged in either case: in the first case, women candidates suffered because they still occupied a less prestigious place in Italian society and thus were less likely to excite feelings of trust even among women electors. Such a situation could have been improved by resorting to the mass media; but this tactic depends on the availability of financial resources and, therefore, on the support of either party or some other group. The 'clientelist' preferential vote is predicated on the availability of exchangeable resources, which women have lacked because of their exclusion from decision-making bodies.

In the bureaucratic/cohesive core model (PCI), party leadership can control preferential votes by indicating to the electorate which candidates they should elect, thus, as we have said above, personal, external resources are less important. Therefore, where the party is committed to the election of women, more women can be elected. In the fragmented, factionalized model, candidates compete for preferential votes on the basis of their 'personal capital'. This includes as we have already noted the ability and possibility to exchange both legal and illegal favours, the support of the party, and the ability to mobilize either party or personal funding. The greater the intra-party competition, the more important is the role of 'personal political capital'. Apparently, this second model penalizes women's candidacy. While the PCI not only has the largest percentage of women candidates in its lists (29 per cent, in 1987) it also, from 1972 to 1987, had an increase of the ratio of women elected to women candidates (see Table 8.3). The DC has a much smaller presence of women among its candidates (14.2 per cent in 1987) and shows a decline over time of the ratio between women elected and women candidates (Table 8.3). In the Christian Democratic party, the increase in the number of women candidates in electoral lists in the 1980s (Table 8.3) seems to be more symbolic than real and points, in any case, to a limited tendency of the Christian Democratic electorate to vote for women candidates.[8] These two contrasting cases show that the mere inclusion of women in the lists was not enough to secure their election: the type of party organization and the importance of 'personal political capital' including the real support of the party were crucial.

As noted above, in the 1992 elections the number of preferential votes permitted was reduced to one: the percentage of women elected to the Chamber of Deputies declined from 12.9 per cent to 8.0 per cent (see Table 8.4a). There are at least four reasons for this decline. First, allowing only one preferential vote served to augment competition among the candidates within each party, thus increasing the amount of 'personal political capital' necessary for election. Secondly, the change nullified a mechanism that formally favoured women. In the past party leaders 'packaged' groups of candidates, usually three in number and presented these packaged groups to the electors. When a woman candidate was 'packaged' with one or two strong male candidates, she had a good chance of being elected. Thirdly, there was increased intensity of competition among the parties. This phenomenon can be explained by two factors: the first is the dissolution of PCI and the disappearance of the frightening spectre of communism. The moderate or centrist electorate no longer feels obliged to support Christian Democracy as a bulwark against communism, but can diffuse its support among the various smaller centrists parties. The second factor has been the emergence of new parties like the Leagues and the Greens. The overall increase in inter-party competition has forced all the parties to concentrate their support behind the 'strongest' of their candidates. Unfortunately, women

Table 8.3 *Elections for the Chamber of Deputies – women elected/candidates and ratio*[1]

	DC			PCI			PSI		
	Elected	Candidates	%	Elected	Candidates	%	Elected	Candidates	%
1972	7	25	28.0	14	71	19.7	1	22	4.5
1976	9	43	20.9	41	120	34.1	1	77	1.2
1979	9	45	20.0	35	119	29.4	1	86	1.1
1983	6	47	12.7	32	97	32.9	2	63	3.1
1987	11	77	14.2	53	183	28.9	5	70	7.1
					PDS				
1992	10	103	9.7	22	167	13.2	4	123	3.2

[1] For abbreviations see Notes.

Sources: Up to 1990: Cattaneo and D'Amato, 1990: 50; 1992: Ministry of Interior

are rarely perceived to be strong candidates by the party bosses. Finally, the two successor parties to the old PCI which in the past elected many women members suffered heavy losses in the election. Given the various difficulties mentioned above, the decrease in the number of women MPs elected in 1992 should not be viewed in a wholly negative light. The fact that women gained seats in the Senate (see Table 8.4b), a house to which election of candidates proposed is more predictable, indicates the importance many parties have given to women as 'vote-getters' for the parties. In the Chamber of Deputies certain women have gained more of the preferential votes than their male colleagues, thus indicating a shift in the opinion of the electorate on the viability of women politicians.[9] The only exception to this trend was in the Christian Democratic party, whose proportion of women MPs actually decreased (see Tables 8.5a, 8.5b). In all the other parties, including new players like the Leagues, this shift towards a recognition of the viability of women candidates can be observed.

Political career patterns

What alternatives were there to party recruitment channels to political careers for Italian women? The sensible answer to this question is almost none. Outsiders rarely were nominated, lateral entry was exceptional.[10] The role of the political parties in the making of political careers has been crucial. The parties have controlled entry, exit and re-entry. Entering parliament was the culmination of a relatively long and structured career path which demanded an apprenticeship of a succession of political offices. These were offices held within the party's organization and/or in local elective bodies. There is evidence that increasing numbers of Italian women parliamentarians have followed such a career pattern. This pattern of a pre-parliamentary career has been common to all the parties, varying only in detail determined by the internal organization of each party (Cotta, 1979; Guadagnini, 1983).

In the PCI, for example, fully 60 per cent of women elected to parliament in 1987 had held offices within the party at national or local levels and more than 60 per cent had previous experience in local elective bodies (Tables 8.6, 8.7). In most cases, the women, like their male colleagues, had held both party and local elective office, either simultaneously or consecutively.

A standard pre-parliamentary career pattern for DC women MPs included experience within the elective offices and/or the party's structure (see Tables 8.6, 8.7). In common with PCI

Table 8.4a *Women in the Chamber of Deputies by legislature (%)*

	I 1948	II 1953	III 1958	IV 1963	V 1968	VI 1972	VII 1976	VIII 1979	IX 1983	X 1987	XI 1992
F	7.8	5.7	4.1	4.6	2.8	4.1	8.5	8.2	7.9	12.9	8.0
M + F	574	590	596	630	630	630	630	630	630	630	630

Sources: Up to 1987: Guadagnini, 1988: 219; 1992: Ministry of the Interior

Table 8.4b *Women in the Senate by legislature (%)*

	I 1948	II 1953	III 1958	IV 1963	V 1968	VI 1972	VII 1976	VIII 1979	IX 1983	X 1987	XI 1992
F	0.9	0.4	0.8	1.9	3.4	1.8	3.4	3.4	4.9	6.5	9.5
M + F	242	243	249	321	322	322	322	322	322	322	322

Sources: Up to 1987: Guadagnini, 1988: 219; 1992: Ministry of the Interior

Table 8.5a   *Women MPs by party affiliation and by legislature*[1]

	I 1948		II 1953		III 1958		IV 1963		V 1968		VI 1972		VII 1976		VIII 1979		IX 1983		X 1987		XI 1992	
	F	M+F	F	M+F	F	M+F	F	M+F	F	M+F	F	M+F	F	M+F	F	M+F	F	M+F	F	M+F	F	M+F
DC	18	306	12	262	11	273	11	260	8	265	8	265	9	262	9	262	6	225	11	234	10	206
PCI–PDS	21	131	16	143	11	141	15	166	9	171	17	175	39	222	25	193	35	172	44	157	22	107
Communist Refound.																					5	35
Independent Left																						
PSI	3	52	3	75	3	88	1	62	1	91	1	61	1	57	1	61	3	73	8	94	4	92
PSDI			1	19			1	32									2	20	5	20		
PLI																						
PDIUM (PNM)	1	13	2	39																		
PSIUP																						
PRI	1	10											1	14	1	16					1	27
Socialist Unity	1	33																				
MSI–DN							1	27					1	34			2	42	1	35	2	34
Mixed group															1	17						
DP													1	6					2	8		
PR													2	4	5	17	1	11	3	12		
PDUP															1	6	1	6				
Greens																			6	13		
Pannella list																					1	7
League																					5	55
RETE																					1	3

[1] For abbreviations see Notes.

Sources: Up to 1987: Guadagnini, 1988: 220; 1992: Ministry of the Interior

Table 8.5b   Women members of the Senate by parliamentary group and by legislature[1]

	I 1948 F	I 1948 M+F	II 1953 F	II 1953 M+F	III 1958 F	III 1958 M+F	IV 1963 F	IV 1963 M+F	V 1968 F	V 1968 M+F	VI 1972 F	VI 1972 M+F	VII 1976 F	VII 1976 M+F	VIII 1979 F	VIII 1979 M+F	IX 1983 F	IX 1983 M+F	X 1987 F	X 1987 M+F	XI 1992 F	XI 1992 M+F
DC	2	67					1	134	2	137	2	136	2	136	3	139	6	121	4	127	3	107
PCI–PDS					1	57	2	83	7	77	3	82	8	99	7	94	6	90	11	85	16	64
Communist Refound.																					2	20
Independent Left											1	11	1	18	1	16						
PSI	2	41	1	28	2	36	1	32	1	12							1	19	1	17	4	49
PSDI									1	46							1	38	2	45	1	3
PLI							1	19											1	7		
PRI																	1	12	1	9		
MSI–DN																	1	18	1	16	1	16
Greens																					3	4
League																					1	25
Mixed group							1	10														

[1] For abbreviations see Notes.

Sources: Up to 1987: Guadagnini, 1988: 221; 1992: Ministry of the Interior

Table 8.6　*Percentage of women MPs who held elective offices in local administration*[1]

	I 1948	IV 1963	VI 1972	VIII 1979	IX 1983	X 1987
PCI	47	30	43.7	52.7	60	52.7
DC	5.5	10	42.8	44.4	33.3	26.6

[1] For abbreviations see Notes.

Source: Guadagnini, 1987: 156

Table 8.7　*Percentage of women MPs who held party offices*[1]

	I 1948	IV 1963	VI 1972	VIII 1979	IX 1983	X 1987
PCI	64.7	70	62.5	66.6	80	60
DC	16.6	30	28.5	22.2	66.6	50

[1] For abbreviations see Notes.

Source: Guadagnini, 1987: 157

women MPs, pre-parliamentary experience, in a large number of cases, included a particular commitment to women's issues.

The restricted number of women MPs from the smaller parties does not permit such generalization. In the PSI nearly all the women parliamentarians have held offices within the party organization and half of them have had a seat in local elective bodies before their parliamentary election.

Women in elective offices

Our arguments are well illustrated by the data on the presence of women in local government. The Communist party has had a far higher percentage of women office-holders than the other parties. Between the PCI and the others there is a three to one difference as regards the percentage of women among elected persons at all levels, regional, provincial and town councils (Tables 8.8, 8.9 and 8.10: data refer to 1990 local administration elections).

As noted above, a woman's relative lack of personal resources obstructed her career potential within less institutionalized parties at the very outset of her political activity. As approximately 70 per cent of the Italian parliamentarians had served in local government (Cotta, 1979: 171), we can see that the difficulty of women's access at this level had clear implications for their ongoing exclusion on the national level. In the Italian case, an

Table 8.8 *Percentage of women holding offices in regional councils, 1991*[1]

	President (Presidente)			Chair of local board (Assessore)			Councillor (Consigliere)			Total		
	M+F	F N	F %	M+F	F N	F %	M+F	F N	F %	M+F	F N	F %
DC	14	—	—	117	3	2.5	230	7	3.1	361	10	2.7
PCI	2	—	—	36	6	16.6	169	27	15.9	207	35	16.9
PSI	2	—	—	69	3	4.3	76	1	1.3	147	4	2.7
PSDI	—	—	—	15	—	—	13	—	—	28	—	—
PRI	—	—	—	16	1	14.2	10	—	—	26	1	—
PLI	—	—	—	7	—	—	8	—	—	15	—	—
MSI-DN	—	—	—	5	—	—	31	—	—	36	—	—
Independents	—	—	—	—	—	—	3	—	—	3	—	—
Others	—	—	—	19	2	10.5	80	8	10	99	10	10.3
Total	18	—	—	290	15	5.2	672	52	7.7	980	67	6.8

[1] For abbreviations see Notes.

Source: Ministry of the Interior, Electoral Services Division

Table 8.9 *Percentage of women holding offices in provincial councils, 1991*[1]

	President (Presidente)			Chair of local board (Assessore)			Councillor (Consigliere)			Total		
	M+F	F N	F %	M+F	F N	F %	M+F	F N	F %	M+F	F N	F %
DC	36	—	—	239	9	3.7	750	29	3.8	1025	38	3.7
PCI	16	1	6.2	86	13	15.1	627	115	18.3	729	129	17.7
PSI	35	1	2.8	171	3	1.7	271	7	2.6	477	11	2.3
PSDI	2	—	—	44	—	—	55	1	1.8	99	1	1.0
PRI	—	—	—	48	1	2.0	72	5	6.9	122	6	4.9
PLI	—	—	—	15	—	—	39	—	—	54	—	—
MSI–DN	—	—	—	1	—	—	129	3	2.3	130	3	2.3
Independents	—	—	—	—	—	—	23	5	21.7	23	5	21.7
Others	2	—	—	31	3	9.7	276	24	8.7	308	27	8.7
Total	91	2	2.2	634	29	4.6	2242	189	8.4	2967	220	7.4

[1] For abbreviations see Notes.

Source: Ministry of the Interior, Electoral Services Division

Table 8.10 *Percentage of women among town councillors, 1972–1991*[1]

	1972	1982	1987	1991
DC	2.17	4.76	5.67	6.9
PCI	3.63	8.73	10.05	13.1
PSI	0.74	3.37	3.76	5.4
PSDI	0.88	2.66	2.95	3.9
PRI	1.18	3.14	4.04	8.4
MSI–DN	1.10	2.75	3.72	3.9
PLI	1.77	3.67	5.71	6.1
Others	1.34	4.94	6.23	8.1
Independents	1.76	7.10	9.09	13.1
Total	2.08	5.45	6.45	8.5

[1] For abbreviations see Notes.

Sources: Up to 1987: Bettin and Magnier, 1989: 68; 1991: Ministry of the Interior

elective post on a local level has been important not only for the duties involved, but also as a step towards a national political career. While local political office has been important for parliamentary aspirants from both of the types of party described above, this period of local government has different implications for the two models. The local office-holder belonging to the fragmented core, less institutionalized type of party will begin to cultivate local interest in order to secure a personal local power base which will serve her throughout her career. In the case of the cohesive core, highly institutionalized type of party, however, the experience in local government serves simply as a step in a career of party service.

So far, we have emphasized various factors within the party structure which have obstructed women's access to political power. However, the data show a pattern of a modest increase in the number of women elected at all levels and by all parties until 1990, although women in local government are still a restricted minority. Altogether, in 1972 the number of women in town councils came to 2,985 (2.08 per cent of those elected), by 1982 it had risen to 8,038 (5.45 per cent of those elected). The figure rose to 12,721 in the 1990 elections, that is to say, to 8.6 per cent of the total number of those elected (see Table 8.10). This increase, present in all parties, shows that women's growing pressure for political representation could sometimes overcome the rigidity of the parties.

One indication that women have not been comfortable with the party pattern is the significant presence of women in the independent lists (see Table 8.10). It may be that where party is not a factor, women are more likely to be elected. Women elected as independent candidates may not need those qualities parties habitually require. This syndrome is indicative, perhaps, of the uneasiness felt by women towards the party, a discomfort with a political culture which demands conformity within pre-set hierarchies.

Another factor that is worth mentioning is the deep dissimilarity between the various parts of Italy (Table 8.11). These are caused by regional differences, not only among the dominant local cultural attitudes, but also in the position women have gained in the workplace and society at large. In the north-west of the country, with their more secularized cultural attitudes and their higher proportion of women employed outside the home, the percentage of women elected is greater than the national average (Table 8.11). In the southern areas, where cultural attitudes are more traditional and fewer women choose a job outside the home, the percentage of women elected is approximately half of the national average.

Dissimilarities in the level of women's representation also depend on the size of the municipality in which the political activity is exercised (Table 8.12). However, we are far from being able to work out a correlation between women's political participation and urbanization (Bettin and Magnier, 1989). Indeed, if women's representation differs according to the various sizes of the municipalities, between larger and smaller towns, no close association can be said to exist between urbanization and women's presence on local councils. In the small towns (of between 5,000 and 30,000 inhabitants), the presence of women elected in 1990 is substantial (see Table 8.12).

As is the case in other European countries (Haavio-Mannila et al., 1985), the number of women elected into local councils drops at the executive level. Only 3.4 per cent of mayors and 7.9 per cent of the chairs of local boards are women, while they represent only 9.4 per cent of the councillors (see Table 8.11). The Communist party is again foremost among the major parties, with the highest percentage of women among its representatives who have attained a position on local government bodies at all levels (see Tables 8.8 and 8.9).

Recruitment and incentives

The type of party organization strongly influences the oppor-tunities offered to candidates who are not re-elected. The guarantees of employment or other forms of security that the party can offer are significant perks (or else disincentives) for those who

Table 8.11 *Number of women holding offices in town councils, 1991*

	Mayor (Sindaco)			Chair of local board (Assessore)			Councillor (Consigliere)		
	M+F	F N	F %	M+F	F N	F %	M+F	F N	F %
North West	3,027	136	4.5	13,962	1,316	9.4	35,840	4,095	11.4
North East	1,028	30	3.0	4,989	378	7.6	13,850	1,453	10.5
Centre	1,299	53	4.1	6,790	749	11.1	18,577	2,227	11.9
South	2,294	43	1.9	11,487	493	4.3	33,491	1,748	5.2
Total	7,648	262	3.4	37,228	2,936	7.9	101,758	9,523	9.4

North West: Piemonte, Valle d'Aosta, Lombardia, Liguria.
North East: Trentino Alto Adige, Veneto, Friuli Venezia Giulia.
Centre: Emilia Romagna, Toscana, Umbria, Lazio.
South: all the others.

Source: Ministry of the Interior

Table 8.12   Percentage of women holding offices in town councils according to political parties and size of municipality[1]

	Under 5,000		5,000–30,000		30,000–100,000		Over 100,000	
	M+F	F %	M+F	F %	M+F	F %	M+F	F %
DC	40,693	7.8	17,789	5.4	3,300	4.1	823	6.0
PCI	12,993	10.4	9,899	15.3	1,812	15.9	580	21.5
PSI	12,273	5.9	8,086	4.8	1,701	3.7	469	6.8
PSDI	1,772	4.8	1,219	3.3	317	0.9	87	3.4
PRI	808	7.7	1,094	4.9	373	3.7	135	7.4
PLI	447	7.8	379	4.2	144	4.8	63	7.9
MSI–DN	431	4.2	652	3.8	236	4.2	110	3.6
Independents	15,459	12.7	1,557	14.6	134	20.1	94	25.5
Others	10,026	8.8	2,386	10.1	422	14.7	222	14.9
Total	94,901	8.8	43,061	8.1	8,439	7.2	2,583	11.1

[1] For abbreviations see Notes.

Source: Ministry of the Interior

are willing to choose politics as a career, since this career is highly uncertain. Moreover, a political career and, in particular, a seat in parliament, is highly time-consuming and often causes other activities to be neglected. Thus the problem of securing a job in case of non-re-election is an important one.

The Communist party was able to give its politicians the opportunity to stay on and work within the party organization or to be elected to local office. This helped avoid gender discrimination. Thanks to its control over preference votes, it was able to assure a less uncertain political career. The other parties were different. As shown by a number of surveys, candidates who were not re-elected tended to remain within a political party circuit, not only holding posts in local decision-making bodies, but also in public and semi-public structures. This mechanism has been, at least so far, to women's disadvantage. Unfortunately, data on this syndrome are not available at the national level: however, research carried out at local level clearly demonstrates this mechanism. A study of politically appointed posts (those associated with municipal concerns, cooperative associations etc.) suggests that these have been wholly taken up by a staff with a political career background, and women have been almost completely absent (Rovero, 1990).

Final considerations

This examination of the Italian case permits us to draw several conclusions. First, as we have seen, the internal organization and culture of each party are crucial factors in facilitating or impeding women's access to elective office. A highly institutionalized bureaucratic party favours the election of women to decision-making bodies in several ways. Such a model can guarantee training and preparation within the party organization which compensates for women's initial lack of 'personal political capital'. Provided the party avoids a pattern of formal competition and bargaining among internal factions, a quota system will be effective (because the party is not obliged to secure representation for the various factions). On the other hand, the factionalized party of the 'notable' model is less favourable to the election of women because the higher level of internal competition places a premium on 'personal capital', thus eliminating the impact of any quota system designed to advance women.

Today, these two models of political recruitment are under discussion within the two parties, the PDS and the DC. The former has abandoned the principle of *centralismo democratico* (democratic centralism) with the highly institutionalized structure that was typical of the old PCI, while the DC is attempting a major restructuring of its internal organization including the change of its name to Partito Popolare (Popular Party).

Will these changes weaken the parties' role as gatekeepers for access to parliament? It is too early to say. While the traditional dominant parties are changing their names, fragmenting into smaller nuclei, or aggregating in new constellations, we cannot say that they can avoid some form of internal reorganization. In fact, among the newly formed parties, which have had the greatest success are those which have a strong organization. The Northern League, for example, seems to resemble the classic model of 'the mass mobilization party'. In a span of few years, it has developed a highly centralized, hierarchical, yet widespread internal organization. Power tends to be concentrated in the hands of its charismatic leader, Umberto Bossi and his closest lieutenants. Below them, there is a widespread network of party militants, motivated by a strong loyalty to their chief, and characterized by an intense feeling of identification with their party. While the party's leader, Bossi, has a strongly macho symbolic and linguistic style, suggesting a party culture that favours traditional gender roles, surveys show not only an increasing number of women supporting the League, voting for it and joining the party as activists, but also of women offering themselves as candidates.

As for Italy's party system as a whole, it is too soon to predict its future and definitive configuration. Apart from the League and the PDS, all the traditional parties are in a state of violent flux and transformation. Thus it is difficult to forecast future models of selection and recruitment of candidates. One qualification that would seem to be a *condicio sine qua non*, is that of being uncompromised by the scandals of the old regime. In this respect, women may be advantaged, in that very few of them appear to have been involved in the widespread corruption of the political class, a fact which also indicates how far they were from the real centres of power! In addition, the reforms intended to limit expenditure on electoral campaigns along with stricter measures to limit corruption should benefit those individuals, such as women, who have been previously excluded.

The vacuum created by the collapse of the post-war regime may offer opportunities for women not only as individuals untainted by scandal, but also as a force for political change through the moral regeneration of public life and the construction of a party apparatus that is more responsive to the needs and desires of the electorate.

In the context of the redefinition of the parties' identities, women must choose which battles to fight to prevent a regression in the progress of their political emancipation. The present economic crisis has already cost women some of the ground gained earlier in equal opportunities in the workplace.

In late July 1993, as I am adding these conclusions to this chapter (written in 1992), the crisis of the Italian political system appears to be worsening and deepening day by day. Terrorism has returned to spill blood in our cities, with a barbarity aimed at targets, in Florence and in Rome, that represent the values of civilization and humanity for which Italy has been known throughout the world. The nation's deficit remains alarming. Each day the 'Clean hands' investigations reveal an ever-expanding picture of corruption, both in terms of the number of persons implicated and of the enormity of the sums involved.

This context demands, with a greater urgency than ever before, the political involvement and commitment of women in the battle for equal opportunity for all members of society, a battle now to be defined in a far broader sense. This will entail reforms in public life, an elimination of patronage and pay-off and the adoption of a new political style in which politics are not merely an expression of personal power but a means for securing the welfare of the nation. The challenge facing women today is that of reforming the art of governance in Italy, so that it comes to be animated by intelligence, professional capacity and honesty, and by balance and wisdom.

Notes

Abbreviations

DC	Christian Democratic party
DP	Proletarian Democracy
Independent Left	It is a parliamentary group whose members are elected within the PCI list
Independents	Persons elected in the 'Independent lists'
Mixed group	Includes: PPST–SVO, UV, Sardinia Action party
MSI–DN	Italian Social Movement–National Right (Neo-fascist)
PCI	Italian Communist party
PDIUM–PNM	National Monarchic party
PDS	Democratic Left party
PDUP	Proletarian Unity party
PLI	Italian Liberal Party
PPST–SVP	South Tirol party
PR	Radical Party
PRI	Italian Radical Party

PSDI	Italian Social Democratic party
PSI	Italian Socialist party
PSIUP	Italian Socialist party of Proletarian Unity
UV	Valle d'Aosta Union

1 The new electoral reforms call for a majority system. On the national level, a recent referendum (18 April 1993) called for three-quarters of the Senate to be elected by the first-past-the-post system and a similar proposal is under discussion for the Chamber of Deputies. The remaining 25 per cent would be elected by the proportional system.

On the local level, the reform calls for different electoral systems according to the size of municipalities. For communities of under 15,000 inhabitants, the mayor will be elected through a majority system. In larger communities, the majority system applies as long as the mayoral candidate wins by more than 50 per cent of the vote. If no candidate reaches this threshold, the two leading candidates participate in a run-off contest. The party or coalition that supported the successful mayoral candidate has the right to 60 per cent of the seats of the town council. A further important innovation in electoral law at the local level is the adoption of a gender quota system for council seats: each of the two sexes must be present, within the candidate list, for no less than 40 per cent of the seats.

2 In Ochetto's view, this new party should not only be based upon the social, moral and cultural forces of the existing PCI, but should also mobilize and incorporate all those varying reformist and progressive forces of the left which aim at introducing radical reforms of political institutions and of the political system as a whole (Catholics, feminists, ecologists etc.). Ochetto's proposal was presented to the party membership in a series of meetings at the local level, and the results of these discussions were presented at the party's National Congress in 1990 in Bologna. The Congress decided to initiate a transitional phase which led ultimately to the dissolution of the PCI in February of 1991. In the course of the momentous debate within the party, certain minority positions emerged which were violently opposed to Ochetto's plan. Certain dissenters opposed the proposal to change the name and the symbol of the party, simply because of the failure and collapse of the communist regimes in eastern Europe. In their view, the failure of certain particular regimes did not imply the invalidity of the communist ideal.

3 From the administrative point of view, Italy is divided into twenty regions, ninety-five provinces and approximately 8,000 municipalities. Their governments are directly elected and their administrative tasks are autonomous or delegated to them by higher bodies. The main tasks of the regions are those of planning, drawing up guidelines and coordinating and they delegate the relevant executive tasks to provinces and municipalities.

From the organizational point of view, local administration structures present, at their top, collective bodies (an Executive Board – *Giunta* – with a president for both province and region and a mayor for municipalities), whose work is carried out by the *assessorati* (local boards), which are delegated there by either the president of the Executive Board or by the mayor.

One further characteristic of the Italian local system is to be stressed: local bodies have been an important source of recruitment for the political elite. An appointment at the local political level has represented a decisive step in one's career to the top of national politics. Over the past few years, local elites have acquired more and more relevant resources and power, which have been utilized, at the individual level, to found future political careers. According to some studies, municipalities are a big 'employer': the amount of resources they manage is equivalent to 4.6 per cent of the GNP and their investments in the facilities sector represent 25 per cent of all public investment (Caciagli, 1991: 211).

4 The scope of activity of the public sector in Italy is quite large: from army arsenals to the post office and the railways (dating back to the first public intervention in the economy), to the broadcasting network, electricity, gas, credit institutions, air transportation etc. Not only are the members of its boards of directors appointed by the parties, but, in some cases, also its managers. Owing to their nature, one would expect such public sector bodies to be managed by trained and skilled staff, according to efficiency criteria; on the contrary, these have been replaced by other, less pertinent criteria, such as links to political parties. Likewise, the parties have assumed a particularly weighty role in the administrative system's bodies.

There exist a number of semi-autonomous bodies at both national and local level; at national level, such bodies have specific functions and operate in the fields of industry, trade and social services. A large number of them are commonly grouped together and referred to as '*Parastato*'. Despite a variety of tasks and organization, these bodies share some characteristics. The staff are recruited according to a different set of regulations from the ones ruling the civil service; at the top of these structures there is a non-elected board of directors, whose appointment is affected by political choices, or else whose members are representatives of the various sectors. The activities of such bodies are wholly or partially state-financed (Minelli, 1990: 193).

The formula of the semi-public body has been adopted also at local levels to provide services and/or to deal with specific issues. Almost all town councils provide for municipalized concerns (*Aziende Municipalizzate*) and/or acquire interests in consortia (333 municipalized concerns and 4,024 consortia) (Minelli, 1990: 194). The regions, too, have set up this type of institution, whenever they have deemed it suitable to resort to more flexible structures.

5 The two chambers of the legislature separately discuss and adopt bills and bills of law, government's decrees and call on the cabinet to answer questions. Parliament's work is carried out by single chamber and two chamber committees composed of members of all the parties represented in parliament. They have investigative, advisory and, unlike other countries, deliberative faculties. This means that a law may be adopted without the need for a further discussion at Assembly level, provided it is approved by four-fifths of the committee's members.

The importance of the committees in law-making should be emphasized. On the one hand, it produces a vast array of laws, whose scope, though, is rather limited and sectorial (the literature has labelled them '*leggine*' – 'little laws'); on the other hand, it has enabled the opposition both to take part in extended alliances on specific issues and to obtain approval for its own policies. The two chambers elect the President of the Republic.

6 Social Democratic women members have requested and obtained a 10 per cent women's participation in the party's boards. Unfortunately, the proposal was accepted on a one-time only basis, instead of being regarded as an ever-acquired right. Indeed, a study of the party boards selected by the 1987 National Conference shows that women were excluded to a large extent. This was due to a reduction in the number of members of these boards and the need to award seats to individuals representing the various factions within the party.

The Statute of the Republican Party originally provided for a Women's Movement, which should be made up of 'women's groups, autonomous as to their organization'. This Women's Movement grants representation in the party leadership at all levels, even if this representation entails only the right to an advisory vote. In the MSI (Social Movement–National Right), women's presence, statutorily granted at all levels, depends, however, on men's choices, through both nomination or cooperation.

7 With the exceptions of the Communes of under 5,000 inhabitants. The councils of these Communes are elected through a majority system.

8 It is significant to notice, for instance, the fact that in the South of Italy, where the Christian Democratic party mobilized 62.3 per cent of the vote (data refer to 1983; Caciagli, 1990) the lists contained very few women (twenty-one out of seventy-seven) and only one woman was elected!

9 These data and considerations are drawn from N. Tarantini and R. Tatfiore (1992) 'Parliamento: un passo indietro', *Noi Donne*, **47** (5): 25–34.

10 A small group of women (journalists, academics, writers etc.) elected in the PCI electoral list, have taken part in the parliamentary group called 'Independent Left' (see Tables 8.5a, 8.5b).

9

A Battle for Power: Selecting Candidates in the Netherlands

Monique Leijenaar

In the Netherlands women gained the right to vote and to be elected for representative bodies more than seventy years ago. Within the political parties, the doubling of the electorate raised many questions. Would women use their right to vote as often as men did? Which parties would gain by the women's vote? Would women vote 'en masse' for women candidates? Would the number of women in the representative bodies increase? Would an increase in the number of women politicians have an impact on political outcomes? In other words, would politics be 'feminized'?

In the final decade of this century the debate about the role of women in politics continues. Compared with seventy years ago, however, the general attitude towards the political integration of women is much more positive. Practically no party currently holds the view that women should not participate in politics. The current debate focuses primarily on the question of how to increase the political involvement of women.

An important feature of the Dutch political system is that the political party has a monopoly on the recruitment of cabinet officers as well as the recruitment and selection of candidates for the legislature and local authorities. Since parties are free to organize the selection of candidates, they are responsible for the final number of women in these representative bodies. This chapter discusses the parties' attitude towards the political participation of women. The following topics will be dealt with: the parties' opinion towards women's suffrage; the actual participation of women within the party; and women's representation in government, parliament, local and provincial bodies, followed by a description of the selection process and the impact of these procedures on the selection of women, including parties' strategies to increase the number of women candidates. Currently not only the parties but also the government are concerned with the slow progress in political representation of women. In the concluding section it is argued that since we are talking about a redivision of power, without a change in the selection procedures, equal political participation of men and women in the near future is inconceivable.

The party system

The Netherlands is a constitutional monarchy, with a monarch as the formal head of state and a prime minister as head of government. The executive is responsible to a bicameral parliament, the Staten Generaal. Elections for the second chamber, the national representative body, are held at least every four years. After every election the leader of the largest party is asked to form a cabinet together with other parties to reach a majority within the parliament. The parliament controls the activities and decisions of the cabinet. The seventy-five representatives of the first chamber are elected indirectly by the members of the provincial councils. The 150 members of the second chamber are directly elected every four years, as are the members of the provincial and local councils. All the other political offices, such as the mayors or state governors, are appointive offices.

Given the great distance which separates any one party from an independent parliamentary majority, government formation requires complex coalition-making. A new cabinet must be formed after each parliamentary election, and also whenever a cabinet resigns during the term of a parliament and it proves impossible to produce a reconciliation among parties. All parties enter elections in the certainty that not one party will gain an independent electoral mandate. At all times, office depends on post-election coalition bargaining.

The electoral system in the Netherlands is relatively simple. All citizens of eighteen years and older are eligible to vote. Voters do not have to register as the Netherlands provides for a universal registration system. The voter casts a single preferential vote for any candidate on one of the lists presented by parties. For all practical purposes the country as a whole forms one constituency. For administrative reasons only, the country is divided into nineteen electoral sub-districts in which the parties, if they want, can put forward different candidate lists. Since compulsory attendance at the polls was abolished in 1970, the average turnout for parliamentary elections has been around 83 per cent.

The ballot paper contains the names of all candidates competing for seats, grouped by party. Although citizens may vote for any candidate on the ballot, depending on the election, between 75 and

85 per cent cast their vote for the first person on a party list. This means that most people effectively vote for a party rather than for a specific candidate.

The Dutch system is characterized by extreme proportional representation with no qualifying threshold. The number of seats a party acquires is proportional to its share of the total valid vote. It is the party which determines the order of their list and thereby decides the persons to be elected. For example, if a party is entitled to twenty seats in the second chamber usually the first twenty candidates on the party list will take those seats. Although preferential voting is possible, preference votes are unlikely to affect the outcome, since a candidate needs a very large number of preference votes to get elected ahead of persons placed higher on the list. It has happened only three times since 1945 that a candidate placed at a low position on the list was elected to the second chamber because of preference votes.

The low 'threshold of representation' means that there has always been a relatively large number of parties winning seats in parliament. The main dimensions of the Dutch party system are rooted in social cleavages (pillarization), which dominated Dutch politics during the last quarter of the nineteenth century and the first half of the twentieth: religion and class. There are still three parties whose origins are to be found in these social cleavages. After the parliamentary election of 1989, the largest party was the CDA, Christian Democratic Appeal (fifty-four seats). In 1980 three parties based upon religious persuasion – the Catholic party (KVP), the Anti-Revolutionaries (ARP) and the Christian Historical Union (CHU) – formally merged into a single Christian Democratic party, the CDA. The second largest party with forty-nine seats is the PvdA, the Labour (socialist) party, which is the only mass-based left-wing party in the Netherlands. The third party, with twenty-two seats, is the VVD, the Liberal party. Even though the VVD is self-described as liberal, it contains strong conservative overtones reminiscent in certain policy areas of the British Conservative party. Arranged on an ideological left–right continuum, the Labour party can be considered as left and the Liberal party as right of the Christian Democrats, who are right of the centre. Owing to their size these parties have dominated parliamentary politics and coalition formation in the entire post-war period, with the Christian Democrats as the pivot of Dutch parliamentary politics. In addition a large number of 'minor' parties have been represented in parliament. Some of these have occupied seats since long before the war, and some of them have sprung up since the late 1950s. An example is D66, founded in

1966 on a platform of constitutional reform and claiming not to fit in the traditional cleavages. Since then the party developed into a leftist-liberal party, placed between the PvdA and CDA. In the parliamentary election of 1989 it won twelve seats, but, according to recent opinion polls, it is gaining much more electoral support, to the disadvantage of the PvdA. In the cabinet period 1989–94, there are besides these four main parties five other parties represented in parliament. To the left side of the ideological continuum there is Groen Links (Green Left), a merger of the Communist, the Pacifist Socialist and the Radical Party, which has six seats. On the right side we find three small right-wing religious fundamentalist parties (with six seats): the SGP, the GPV and the RPF, all based on – different – Calvinist denominations. The fifth party is the CP, an ultra-right-wing party with one seat: its main issue is the unwanted presence of immigrants. The current cabinet (1989–94) is a coalition of CDA and PvdA, with seven cabinet ministers each.

Women's suffrage

In 1917 the qualification 'male' was erased from the Dutch Election Law. Two years later in 1919 women were able to cast their votes at elections. The struggle for women's suffrage had taken about twenty-five years. The opposition against the enfranchisement of women had been mainly based on the conception that women and politics did not belong together, that women's proper role was in the family. Arguments against women's suffrage were:

- The man represents his family, including his wife.
- Women are too emotional and not capable of judging objectively.
- Women dealing with politics – '*cette sale besogne*' – will lose their femininity.
- Women already influence decision-making indirectly. There is no need to give them direct influence (Schokking, 1958: 29, 30).[1]

In general, the socialist and liberal parties supported the demand for women's suffrage. The introduction of general suffrage for men was more important for the socialist parties than universal suffrage for men *and* women (Outshoorn, 1973: 45). In 1919 all socialist and liberal MPs voted in favour of the bill – put forward by Marchant, a liberal MP – introducing women's general suffrage.

Traditionally the religious parties criticized women's participation in the public sphere more than the other large parties. The fact that all Catholic members and a majority of the Protestant parliamentarians voted *in favour* of the Marchant bill was not so much because of a change in attitude, but more the outcome of a deal between the confessionals on the one hand, and the socialists and liberals on the other. The dominant issues at the end of the nineteenth century, reflecting religious and class cleavages in Dutch society, centred around government funding for private (religiously orientated) schools and the introduction of universal suffrage. These two issues were resolved in 1917 in a major compromise between the political parties which had been formed by that time. The socialist and liberal parties accepted equal public funding for private and public schools and the confessional parties approved the extension of suffrage. With this so-called 'pacification' of 1917, when universal suffrage for men and the right for women to be elected was established, the door to universal suffrage for women had been opened (Oud and Bosmans, 1982: 221).

Another reason to grant women the vote was the fear of a possible revolution of the left wing as had occurred in 1918 in Germany. Since women were thought to be more conservative in their voting behaviour, the participation of women in politics would be a stabilizing factor. A third reason for the religious parties to support the change in the constitution was the conviction that women were more likely to vote for the religious parties than for the liberal or socialist parties.

Integration in party politics

In 1917 when women gained the right to be elected, the electoral system was changed from a majority system with several districts into a system of proportional representation with party lists. The extension of the electorate in 1919, and the transformation of the electoral system, meant a strengthening of the role of political parties. The parties dominated the selection process and with their party platforms they formed a bridge between the representatives and the electorate. From that time the political representation of women became entirely dependent on the parties' attitude towards political involvement of women.

The women's organizations of the parties played an important role in shaping this attitude. From the founding onwards, neither the liberal nor the socialist parties had formal barriers to women's participation. In the socialist party women were organized separately after 1905, when the Sociaal-Democratische Vrouwen-propagandaclub (socialist women's organization) was established. The organization continued its activities, when the PvdA, the

Labour party, was founded in 1946. In the early period the main activities were mobilization and socialization of lower class women. In the 1970s the organization changed in character and became more action- and feminist-orientated. In 1975 the name of the women's organization was changed to Rooie Vrouwen (Red Women). Liberal women joined forces for the first time in 1921. When the VVD was installed in 1948, the women's organization, Vrouwen in de VVD, became part of the party structure.

In the religious parties separate organizations for women were formed somewhat later. In the Catholic party there has never been a formal separate women's organization. However, there were strong ties between several Catholic women's organizations and the Catholic party, because the leading women in those organizations were also important members of the party. For example, the first women minister and the first woman junior minister, both from the Catholic party, were respectively founder and chair of the Katholiek Vrouwen Dispuut, a large women's organization for Catholic women. The Protestant parties differed in their attitude towards women's integration in the parties. In the CHU a separate women's wing was established in 1935, but in the ARP it took until 1955 before the party officially recognized a women's organization. This party prohibited its women members from being nominated for election until 1953. With the merger of the confessional parties, in 1980 into the CDA, the women's organization CDA-vrouwenberaad was also established.

D66 never had a separate women's wing, neither did the smaller right-wing parties and the former communist party. The motives, however, vary among the parties. The SGP, GPV and RPF are openly against women participating in the public sphere and as a consequence very much against government supported equality policies. D66 favours gender equality, but is against separatism. The Communist party did not have a separate women's wing because of very strong ties with the Nederlandse Vrouwenbeweging, an organization of communist women. In the 1980s the Communist party went through a process of feminization. The party accepted in 1984 a resolution that both Marxism *and* feminism should be regarded as the party ideology. In 1982 the Communist party installed a quota system for women of 50 per cent (Koeneman et al. 1985: 28). Also gender equality and feminism played an important role in the other two left-wing parties. Both parties had separate women's wings, and in both parties a quota system was operating in the 1980s.

In general the women's organizations have been, and still are, an important factor in the process of getting more women involved in party politics. In the early days their main aims were to educate women politically and to mobilize them into becoming party members. Now the women's wings are much more concerned with party policies on gender equality. Generally they assume a much more radical stance on issues regarding women than the parties themselves, which on some occasions brought the women's organizations into conflict with other party bodies. Currently the most important goal is to increase the number of women party delegates. Its women delegates put pressure on the party executive by putting forward resolutions on quotas. Thanks to this continuing pressure of the women's wings, the party executives of the main parties are now in favour of more women party officials and representatives (van de Velde and Leijenaar, 1991: 2–16). The women's wings do not include all women party members. At present about 10 per cent of the female CDA party members are united in its women's organization and in the VVD 12 per cent of women members belong to the women's organization. The women's organization within the PvdA does not have a formal membership, instead they consider every female member a 'Red Woman'. No exact figures are available from the other parties.

Party membership

Not many people in the Netherlands are members of a political party. By 1992 only 3.2 per cent of the electorate belonged to a party. There has been a sharp decline since 1946, when membership was still about 15 per cent (Koole and Voerman, 1986: 148). Moreover, it appears that not even 10 per cent of these party members can be considered as activists, by which we mean those who go to party meetings, discuss party matters, become a member of a local party board or participate in the selection of candidates. This implies that only 0.5 per cent of the electorate participate in candidate selection.

The conditions for becoming a member of a political party are outlined in the party constitution: you have to pay your dues, be of a certain minimum age and possess Dutch citizenship or reside in the Netherlands. Some parties insist on specific conditions, such as membership of a denomination (GPV), no membership of other parties (PvdA), or a preference for the male sex (SGP). There are no formal restrictions for women. Although the small orthodox Calvinist SGP does not encourage women to become members, the party constitution does not exclude women formally. Very recently the local party organization in the City of The Hague allowed

Table 9.1   *Party membership*

Party	Total membership	Women N	Women %
CDA	122,738	28,546	23
PvdA	91,539	35,702	40
VVD	55,640	18,716	34
D66[1]	12,536	3,378	40
Groen Links[1]	14,340	6,000	40
SGP	23,060	<10	0
GPV	14,276	—[2]	—
RPF	8,568	—[3]	—

[1] These figures are an estimation, provided by the party secretary.
[2] The GPV does not register its members by sex.
[3] The RPF does not register its members by sex, but estimates the percentage of women to be about 14.

women to join the party. In the past most parties have not counted their members according to sex. On request they provided not very reliable estimations. According to these, in 1971 the PvdA had 30 per cent women members, the VVD 30 per cent and the Catholic KVP also 30 per cent. The more recent figures shown in Table 9.1 are more accurate.

Among the four main parties, the female membership of the Christian Democrats is rather low: 23.9 per cent compared with 40 per cent in the PvdA and D66 and 34 per cent in the VVD. The explanation is, according to a recent party report, that in most families only one person – that is the husband – subscribes (CDA, 1989: 130). The smaller parties vary in the number of women members. Groen Links estimates that about 40 per cent of the membership are women, while the percentages in the three smaller parties vary from 0 in the SGP to 14 per cent in the RPF.

Within a party female and male members do not differ much in background characteristics. The differences occur between the parties. The average age of both men and women is about forty-five years old; members of the VVD and D66 are mostly from upper-middle-class backgrounds, while most members of the PvdA come from a lower class and of the CDA from middle-class backgrounds.

In a survey held in 1986 among members of the four main parties,[2] the respondents were asked to indicate the significance of the following factors in their decision to become a member of a political party:

Table 9.2 *Significance of party membership, 1986*

Factor	Men	Women
Working together	41	47
Political influence	76	68
Meeting people	26	24
Career perspective	8	5
Citizen's duty	76	73
Experience	34	35
Sympathy	85	91
Friends/family	6	6
Religion	77	75
Total	2,718	624

Q: Can you please state for each of the following reasons how important it was for your own decision to become a party member? (Answers [very] important are presented.)

Source: Niemöller, 1991: 32

- Because I like to work with other party members.
- Because it enables me to influence decision-making.
- Because I meet interesting people in the party.
- Because it is important for my professional career.
- Because I see it as my duty as a citizen to participate in party politics.
- To gain experience.
- To show my sympathy for this party.
- Because all my acquaintances/family are members.
- To express my religious persuasion at a political level.

Numbers who answered that a factor was (very) important are presented in Table 9.2.

Gender differences in motives are rather small. More women than men become members because they like to work together with other people or to show the party their sympathy. More men than women become members because of the influence they have, because it may help their career, and because it is viewed as an act of citizenship.

Members can participate in the internal decision-making process of the parties. Decision-making takes place at different levels. In most parties there is a central body, the national executive and there are regional and local branches. No recent information is available about the participation of women in the regional and local branches. A 1983 survey among 248 local party branches in seventy-six Dutch communities reports an average of 9.7 per cent women chairs, 40.3 per cent women secretaries and 27.5 per cent

Table 9.3   *Participation of women in the national executive*

Party	Daily board		Party executive	
	N	% W	*N*	% W
CDA	9	44	68	16
PvdA	7	43	25	32
VVD	—[1]	—	15	40
D66	10	40	21	32
GL	5	40	15	40
SGP	5	0	15	0
GPV	9	11	32	9
RPF	5	0	13	8

[1] In the VVD there is no daily board.

women board members. Relatively more women can be found in the PvdA, D66 and the smaller left-wing parties (Leijenaar et al., 1983: 45). The representation of women in the national executive and daily boards of the parties is shown in Table 9.3.

It appears that the share of women in the executive is lower than their share in membership. While the female membership of D66 is 40 per cent, only 22.7 per cent of the executive is female. This is also true for the PvdA and the VVD. Only in the CDA and Groen Links is the percentage of women in the executive higher. No women can be found in the party boards of the SGP and RPF, but in the – much larger – executive of the GPV there are 9 per cent women. When we compare these figures with earlier data, it seems that the number of women party executives has somewhat increased. In 1971 for example, 22.7 per cent women were in the party executive of the PvdA and 14.3 per cent in that of the VVD.

Women in the parliamentary party

The first woman who entered parliament was a representative from the socialist party. She joined her male colleagues in 1918 and thereby was the only woman elected by male voters only. Suze Groeneweg was followed by six other socialist women in the period 1918–56. Two predecessors of the CDA followed swiftly: in 1922 the first Catholic woman gained a seat in the second chamber, as well as the first Protestant woman, representing the CHU. In the same year the liberal parties delegated three women. In 1956, before the second chamber expanded from 100 to 150 seats, nine out of 100 seats were taken by women: two for the Catholic party, one for the Protestant party CHU. four for the Socialist party and two for the Liberal party.

Until the 1970s the proportion of women parliamentarians in the second chamber remained less than 10 per cent. This percentage increased gradually after the Second World War, until women accounted for 25 per cent of seats after the 1989 elections. The representation by party is presented in Table 9.4.

The predecessors of the CDA had, with a few exceptions, about 6–8 per cent women members of parliament. After the merger this percentage increased gradually. In the second half of the 1980s women's share went up to 20 per cent and after the last elections, to 22 per cent. The breakthrough by the socialist women came in 1989 when fifteen out of forty-nine parliamentarians were women. Prior to that the figure was less than 20 per cent. The elections of 1981 were very successful for the VVD. The party went from twenty-six seats to thirty-six seats. With it the percentage of women in the parliamentary party increased to 19.4 per cent. With the last election, when the VVD lost again, the percentage of women declined to eighteen. In 1982 three of the six parliamentarians of D66 were women. This percentage dropped to 11 per cent in 1986 and jumped to 33 per cent in 1989. The smaller parties on the left always had a relatively large share of women in their parliamentary party. There was always one woman in the parliamentary party and once – in 1986 in the PSP – the only parliamentary representative was a woman. Of the current six MPs three, including the parliamentary leader, are women. After the 1991 indirect election the percentage of women representatives in the First Chamber was 28 per cent.

The same trends can be found in the party representation at the local and provincial level. The overall percentage after the 1990 and 1991 elections are 22 per cent in the local councils (1990) and 29.6 per cent in the provincial councils (1991).

Parties do not only select the candidates for the representative bodies, they also nominate candidates for offices such as mayor and state governor. These are appointive positions by the monarch and/or the cabinet. In 1992 there are 9 per cent of women mayors and no women state governors. So contrary to the literature stating that women's rates of participation are higher when political positions are filled by appointment of a candidate, in the Netherlands we find much lower percentages of women in appointive positions.[3] One of the reasons is the prevailing gender bias of the appointers, who favour male candidates, particularly those who are also serving as mayors in other cities.

Table 9.5 shows latest figures in representation of women for each party and suggests:

Table 9.4   *Percentage of women deputies in parliament by party, 1956–1989*

Party[1]	1956	1959	1963	1967	1971	1972	1977	1981	1982	1986	1989
KVP	5	8	8	7	6	7	—	—	—	—	—
CHU	8	8	8	17	10	0	—	—	—	—	—
ARP	0	0	8	7	8	7	—	—	—	—	—
CDA	—	—	—	—	—	—	10	15	13	20	22
PvdA	12	10	11	8	10	14	15	23	17	19	31
VVD	23	21	25	12	13	14	18	12	19	22	18
CPN	14	0	0	0	0	0	0	33	67	—	—
D66	—	—	—	14	9	17	25	24	50	11	33
PPR	—	—	—	—	0	0	33	33	50	50	—
PSP	—	0	0	0	0	0	0	33	33	100	—
DS70	—	—	—	—	13	17	—	—	33	—	—
EVP	—	—	—	—	—	—	—	—	100	—	—
GL	—	—	—	—	—	—	—	—	—	—	50

Percentages are based on the total number of deputies from the party in that year.
[1] SGP, GPV and RPF are not shown as they have not had any women representatives in the second chamber.

Source: Leijenaar, 1989: 105

Table 9.5 *Percentage[1] of women politicians and members by party, latest figures (1992)*

	CDA	PvdA	VVD	D66	Groen Links	GPV	SGP	RPF
Cabinet minister	14	29	—	—	—	—	—	—
Junior minister	40	20	—	—	—	—	—	—
MP	24	29	27	33	50	0	0	0
Senator	19	35	8	42	50	0	0	0
Mayor	5	14	14	28	0	0	0	0
State Commissioner	0	0	0	0	—	—	—	—
Local alderman	13	23	21	31	20	0	0	0
Local councillor	20	29	31	29	37	2	0	2
Provincial alderman	14	29	13	57	0	0	0	0
Provincial councillor	28	37	25	37	36	6	0	0
Party official	16	32	40	32	40	9	0	8
Party member	23	40	34	40	40	—[2]	< 10	—[2]

[1] Percentages are based on the total of officers for that party.
[2] The GPV and RPF do not register their members according to sex.

- The small orthodox parties are faithful to their belief that the proper place of a woman is at home and not in politics.
- For most political offices the percentages of women representatives for the CDA and VVD are somewhat lower than for the parties on the left side of the ideological continuum, D66, PvdA and Groen Links.
- D66 and Groen Links, both relatively new parties compared to the others, have the highest representation of women.
- With the exception of the office of mayor, the PvdA has reached its quotum of 25 per cent women in the political bodies.
- At the local and regional level the under-representation of women is higher than at the national level and within the parties. Especially in the position of mayor, state governor, local alderman and provincial alderman not many women can be found.

Recruitment and selection of candidates

The criteria for who is eligible to become a parliamentary candidate are stated in the Dutch Constitution: citizenship, minimum age of 18 years and a person not excluded from the right to vote. The next step, recruitment in Figure 9.1, narrows down the number of potential candidates. **Recruitment** is the process by which people get involved in political and party activities, leading

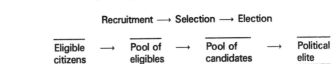

Figure 9.1   *Processes of incorporation into decision-making*

eventually to actual candidacy. The process of **selection** determines which citizens, from the pool of those who are active in politics, are eventually seen as qualified for a representative position. In the Netherlands, with selection, the major part of the pathway to power has been completed. The **election** provides the final decision as to which candidates will become members of the representative body.

Recruitment

An important question in the process of recruitment is the extent to which individual characteristics favour or hinder the attainment of a representative position. Many scholars see the persistence of women's lack of political power as a predictable outcome of the ways in which advantages, such as education and occupation, are distributed in society. A high educational level and occupational status appear to be necessary conditions to become involved in party political activities. The analysis of the background characteristics of all female (145) and male (1,208) members of parliament in the period 1918–86 confirm these findings. Half the members, regardless of sex, are university graduates. In contrast to the female adult population, the majority of women members actively pursued a profession before becoming politicians (Leijenaar, 1989: 145, 146).

Secondly, situational factors, such as being married and having children, negatively influence the chances of being recruited. The data shows that the role of married women and mothers in politics appears to have changed over time. During the first period of analysis, 1918–46, only half of the women in parliament were married and most were without children. In the final period of analysis, 1977–86, on the other hand, nearly 75 per cent of women members were married, and some 40 per cent had children, although the children were usually grown up by the time their mothers reached political prominence (Leijenaar, 1989: 147). The facts that until the 1980s the educational level of women generally was lower than men's, that women have less occupational experience than men, and that the upbringing of children is almost the exclusive task of women, all reduce the chances of women being recruited and selected for political office.

However, there have been some developments in Dutch society, which impact on the barriers to women's candidacy. By 1992 there were no gender differences in educational level. Compared with ten years previously, far more women were in paid employment (about 46 per cent of all adult women) and it was widely accepted that women may occupy political positions. At the same time developments such as the greater availability of childcare have increased the possibilities for women to emerge from their private domains. But such developments do not automatically lead to a comparable increase of women in decision-making positions. There are still the barriers within the process of selection to be overcome.

Selection
In the Netherlands political parties are free to organize the selection of candidates as they consider appropriate. The selection procedures of the parties therefore differ. The basic similarities in the selection of the parliamentary candidates are that in all parties local, regional and national party bodies are involved, and the whole process takes about a year. Otherwise, each party follows its own procedures.

Christian Democratic Appeal Local party branches are invited by the party executive to suggest not more than five names of candidates. Persons suggested by at least five local branches are put on an alphabetical roster together with the names of the members of the parliamentary party and the names of CDA ministers and junior ministers. The persons on this list are then asked whether they are willing to be nominated. Others can also apply to be nominated. A review committee decides upon these applications. In a meeting of the party executive the list is discussed and account is taken of the desired composition of the parliamentary party. A special committee consisting of the party executive and delegates of the regional party organizations draws up the advisory list. They may add new names to the list. This list is then voted upon by local branches. The executive then computes the final order of the candidates from the branch votes. Finally, the first on the list is decided by the party congress (delegates from the local party organizations).

The Labour party (PvdA) Every selection process starts with the drawing of a profile of the new parliamentary party by the party board. Qualifications to be met by the candidates-to-be are set.

The most favourable composition of the parliamentary party is defined in terms of occupational experience, age and sex. This profile is then made known to the party members, who are asked to suggest names of candidates who meet these criteria. Members of parliament and – when applicable – members of government are also asked to suggest names. A selection committee consisting of fifteen members including the chairman of the party is installed by the party board. The task of this committee is to scout and recruit potential candidates. All persons suggested by the selection committee, party members and members of parliament and government are then asked whether they are willing to be nominated as a candidate for the coming election. After that the selection committee advise the party board on the order of the list. Having heard this advice, the party board draws up an advisory list of candidates as well as a list of people who agree to be nominated but were left off the advisory list. Both lists are discussed at a special party congress (consisting of delegates of the local party branches). Prior to this congress the lists are also discussed by the local branches in order to instruct their delegates to the party congress how to vote. It is the party congress that decides upon the final order of the list of candidates.

For the election of the Second Chamber only, the regional party branches (nineteen in total equal to the nineteen electoral sub-districts) can nominate their 'own' regional candidate. This person will take the second place on the list for that specific region.

The People's Party for Freedom and Democracy The local branches initiate the process of candidate selection by suggesting names of candidates. On the basis of these suggestions the national executive, advised by a special committee consisting of members and the party secretary, then drafts an advisory list. This advisory list is published and local branches, as well as the national executive, can suggest changes in the order of names on the list. The *partijraad*, consisting of delegates of the regional organizations, advises the national executive on these changes. The final order is determined by the party congress of delegates from the local branches.

Democrats 66 D66 uses a different system. Party members can apply to become a candidate. A list in alphabetical order is sent to all party members requesting them to arrange the first twenty – or so – names. In 1986 and 1989 the party executive installed a committee to advise the members about how to vote. They do not present a straightforward alphabetical list, but instead choose ten names (in alphabetical order) for the first ten places, five names for places ten to fifteen etc. The advisory committee does not offer a justification for its preferences, stating only that these persons have the highest qualities. The outcome of the vote by members is final.

Other parties In Groen Links the local branches, the women's wing and the youth organization can suggest names of candidates. Besides this, any party member may apply for candidacy. The party congress appoints a selection committee and formulates the criteria for selection and for the parliamentary party. The selection committee, which may add more names, will interview the aspirant candidates and makes a proposal for the list of candidates. The national executive recommends a list order for the first ten to fifteen candidates to the party congress. The regions can decide themselves about the other candidates. The party congress of delegates from all local branches determines the final order of the list. The head of the list is elected by means of a referendum among all the party members. The outcome is binding when more than 50 per cent of the members have participated in the referendum.

The selection procedures in the three religious fundamentalist parties are very much alike. The local branches suggest names. Then the party executive, after some consultative rounds, draws up a proposal, which is sent back to the local branches. They decide upon a certain order and the final order is again determined by the national executive.

Formal processes are only part of the story. A lot of informal wheeling and dealing takes place during the selection of candidates. Examples are the agreements between regional party organizations to support each others' delegates when the election committee determines the final order, or visits to the regional branches by the party leader looking for support for incumbent deputies (Koole and Leijenaar, 1988: 201).

Parties' selection processes differ in the degree of centralization and participation by the members. As a result of the democratization of the 1960s, the internal party organizations had to take the wishes of their rank and file more seriously. The left-wing and central parties were more affected by these developments than the right-wing parties. In most parties, however, the strong influence of regional lobbies was clearly present, and more and more criticized. Regional lobbies sometimes neglect incumbents who concentrate too much on parliamentary affairs and overlook their own party region. Instead, the regional organizations select provincial party cadres who are in general very interested in becoming deputies.

Selection processes are highly influenced by the promotion by the party leadership of certain abilities and qualities. An example is the profile drafted by the party board of the PvdA. Dependent on the background of the incumbents, the profile can mention the need for (more) economists, lawyers, farmers, environmental experts or trade unionists. Besides, the profile can stress the importance of a balanced composition of the parliamentary party in terms of sex.

How do selection processes relate to women's candidacy

The likelihood that women will be selected is the result of the interplay of three factors:

- Who makes the selection.
- The selection criteria used.
- Whether there are any special policies to strengthen the position of women candidates.

Who makes the selection: degree of centralization

In general a decentralized selection process has tended to be disadvantageous for the selection of women. This appears to be both because decentralized procedures induce tougher competition, resulting in fewer chances for women to obtain a safe place, and regional party leaders put forward their own regional candidates, who are often males. Moreover national party leaders are more concerned about female–male balance than are the local or regional branches.

The available survey evidence supports these observations. In 1986 a representative sample of party members of the four main parties was interviewed about the desirability of a gender-balanced party list. The respondents were asked whether they thought that women and several other groups were under-represented on the party list for the parliamentary elections of 1986. In Table 9.6 their answers are categorized according to party, sex and party status.

It appears that the higher his or her party status, the more a respondent was likely to view the party list of 1986 as unbalanced in terms of sex: 64 per cent of the candidates held this opinion against 49 per cent of the members and 57 per cent of the local party officers. In all categories more women than men observe an under-representation of women candidates. Gender differences are larger among candidates and national executives than among

Table 9.6 *Opinion regarding the number of women candidates on the party list for the parliamentary elections of 1986*

	Members		Local party officers		National executives		Candidates	
All respondents	49		57		60		64	
	M	W	M	W	M	W	M	W
CDA	39	73	50	79	53	100	48	93
PvdA	56	84	63	80	66	88	67	88
VVD	31	33	32	52	32	60	39	92
D66	51	68	—	—	—	—	55	100
N	872	346	1,110	482	399	83	439	113

Q: Do you regard the number of women candidates on the list as too many, not enough or sufficient? (Percentages of respondents who answered 'not enough'.)

members and local party leaders. Among men, the PvdA respondents perceive an under-representation of women, while the VVD respondents are less concerned with this issue; among women the opinions differ within a party.

The influence of the regional party organizations on the selection of candidates causes increasing concern. The national executives are concerned about the quality of their parliamentary party. Because of the changing political climate, caused by depillarization, deconfessionalism and individualism, the personality of the parliamentary deputy is much more important than it used to be.

In 1992 the PvdA was discussing changing the selection procedures, stressing the necessity to spend more time, energy and money in the recruitment and selection of well-qualified candidates for representative office. In a recent report by a special committee, the influence of the regional organizations on candidate selection was strongly criticized: 'internal qualifications such as party experience are more valued than external qualifications like professional experience and debating skills'; 'the electorate does not vote for a regional candidate' (PvdA, 1991: 6, 7). The recent changes in the selection process (see pp. 219–20) were meant to reduce the influence of the regional branches on the selection of candidates. Although it was not intended, this more centralized procedure can have a positive effect on the selection of women.

Selection criteria
Parties also differ in their selection criteria. Candidates with higher educational and occupational status are preferred, but to be well known within the party is also valued. A long party career brings

the necessary reputation, as well as indicating that the candidate will be a trustworthy party representative. The most common route to obtain a high-level decision-making position is through previous political positions. All parties view political experience as the most crucial requirement for a potential candidate. Such selection criteria affect women's chances to be selected negatively. An empirical study of the length of membership and the number of activities carried out by women within the parties showed that they had less experience than men, which will hinder their chances of being selected (Leijenaar, 1989: 150).

An illustrative example can be found in the selection of mayors. A committee is formed consisting of the leaders of the parties represented in the council of the community in question. The main selection criterion put forward by these committees is political experience of the candidate. This is then translated into 'serving as mayor in another local community' or 'at least four years' experience as a local alderman'. Such criteria lessen women's chances, since only 9 per cent of mayors in the Netherlands are women, and 17 per cent of the aldermen. The question is to determine the qualities of a mayoral candidate. What makes a good mayor? Why is twenty years' experience as chair of a large voluntary organization not regarded as the right qualification?

Party gender strategies
Special policies to improve the position of women in the selection process have served to ensure at least some selection of women. For example, quotas are increasingly seen as essential in order to accelerate women's advancement in politics. First, quota setting may have an eye-opening effect, making selectors more aware than before of women as possible representatives. Secondly, it may encourage women to enter politics.

Dutch parties have been very reluctant to introduce quotas for women for internal bodies as well as for the party's lists for public elections. Only the PvdA resolved in 1987 that women should comprise at least 25 per cent of the internal and representative bodies. At the party congress in December 1992 the party increased this quota to 33 per cent. This reluctance by parties reflects the general opinion regarding quotas among party members. In the survey of party members held in 1986 respondents were asked about the desirability of quota setting in their party. One third of the men and more than half (54 per cent) of the women who responded were in favour of quota setting. These gender differences appear in every party (Table 9.7). In all parties, far more women than men approved of affirmative action.

Table 9.7 *Opinion about quota setting for women, 1986*

	Members		Local party officers		National executives		Candidates	
All respondents	31		37		35		31	
	M	W	M	W	M	W	M	W
CDA	22	36	22	45	21	78	22	77
PvdA	41	71	58	79	58	79	70	88
VVD	15	29	12	16	4	30	13	46
D66	24	44	—	—	—	—	26	67
N	872	346	1,110	482	399	83	439	113

Q: Do you regard quota setting for the number of women representatives in the party favourably? (Percentages of respondents who answered 'yes'.)

Differences also emerged between the parties. Respondents of the PvdA are more positive than members of the VVD, CDA and D66, possibly explained by the fact that within the PvdA the discussion to introduce quotas started in the late 1970s, so by the mid-1980s people were more used to this instrument of affirmative action. Compared with the other parties, members of the VVD are not so much in favour of quotas. Although in favour of political equality for men and women, part of the liberal ideology is not to interfere: political equality should be accomplished 'naturally'. Differences between the four categories of party members occur mainly among women. Respondents who favour introducing quotas were asked to say what quotas they preferred. Table 9.8 sets out the mean (percentage) scores of these suggestions.

Here there are only small differences between the parties; women score somewhat higher than the male respondents, but all mean scores are within the range of 30–40 per cent. Those who favour quotas agree that between 30 and 40 per cent is about right. This, except in the CDA, is approximately the proportion of female membership in these parties.

Policies to increase women's political representation

During the 1990s attitudes shifted in favour of a greater political involvement of Dutch women. Practically all political parties are engaged in one way or another in affirmative action policy-making. Even the last male bastion, the SGP, is giving in to the demands of women SGP-adherents, by permitting women membership and the right to become a delegate to party conference. At the party congress in 1992, for the first time women (three) were present as delegates. The other two orthodox Calvinistic parties, the GPV and

Table 9.8   *Mean suggested quotas, 1986*

	CDA		PvdA		VVD		D66	
All respondents	M	W	M	W	M	W	M	W
%	29	35	35	40	32	35	39	40
N	197	105	500	299	84	70	74	47

Only those respondents who were in favour of quota setting (Table 9.7) were asked to give a mean quota.

RPF, not only allow women members but also encourage women to become more involved in party matters, by organizing special seminars on gender equality. The only party without explicit gender strategies is D66. Like the VVD, they hold the opinion that positive discrimination does not belong in their progressive-liberal ideology. For D66, however, it is more easy to say so, since D66 always had relatively more women participating in party boards and elective offices than the other parties. The attraction of D66 for women can be partly explained by the time of emergence, 1966, and its appeal to young, well-educated and progressive people.

In 1989 and 1990 each of the other parties represented in parliament published a 'Positive Action Plan' of strategies to increase the participation of women. An important stimulus in this process has been the financial support of the government. It subsidized parties to organize activities to increase the number of women in the electoral bodies. All parties with the exception of the SGP accepted the money. Most parties used the money to hire someone for three years in charge of formulating affirmative action strategies. The GPV and RPF, who do not subscribe to the government's policies on gender equality, used the money for training. The new positive action plans carry many facts and figures about the present participation of women in the party. Using these figures the party executive tries to convince its members of the necessity of affirmative action. Many concrete recommendations are also mentioned in the plans. For example, a so-called 'Human Resource Data Base' of names, background characteristics and career intentions of women party members has been created, so that selectors cannot claim that 'there are no women available'. Especially within the CDA this human resource project can be evaluated positively. Another example is the introduction of cadre-training courses for women. In the three large parties special training courses are organized for women members to enhance their chances of being selected for the council of parliament. Most parties also provide funds for childcare support for those (women) members who want to participate in party activities. A last example is the introduction of 'shadow-council members'. This instrument is used in the PvdA and in Groen Links. The idea is that women who are still hesitant to be nominated for the council assist the elected council members in order to gain experience and confidence. In the plans of the PvdA and Groen Links the wish to change the party culture into a more 'woman-friendly' culture is also mentioned. Interestingly, in the policy plans of CDA, VVD and the PvdA is the intention of the national executive to set up contracts with the local and regional party boards about the percentage of women participating. These agreements consist of percentages to be reached in the near future. It is a kind of flexible quota system, i.e. the percentages are related to the percentage of women party members in that local or regional branch. This points to one of the major problems with the affirmative action plans of the parties. It is the party executive, stimulated by the financial aid of the government, that formulates the positive action plans, but the local and regional branches have to carry it out. Because of the relative autonomy of the party branches, there is no guarantee of implementation. Besides these more general recommendations, at the time of the 1990 municipal elections the parties designed specific activities directed to increase the number of women party representatives in the local councils. For example, the PvdA, VVD and CDA organized seminars to mobilize and educate women potential candidates, and their national executives informed the local and regional branches about the importance of selecting more women candidates. Until now no systematic research has been carried out to evaluate the effectiveness of these instruments. However, all this can be viewed as a sign that the parties do take the problem of under-representation of women seriously.

It is important that the national executive takes the responsibility for the formulation and implementation of these positive action strategies. In 1991 the financial grant of the government to hire an 'equality officer' ended. However, most parties continued the activities by installing committees for the implementation of the recommendations published in the positive action plans. The official goal of the VVD committee is to ensure that one-third of all party positions are taken by women; the PvdA wants to reach a 50-50 representation in 1994, and the CDA national executive expressed its wish for more balanced party boards and elective offices in the near future.

So far we have discussed only the participation of women in the internal party boards and elected legislatures. Parties also play a very important role in the selection of candidates for the appointed office of mayor or state governor and members for the external advisory boards. For these offices the under-representation of women is worse: 9 per cent of mayors are women, there are no women state governors and women account for 11 per cent of the members of advisory boards. The affirmative action programmes of the parties do not include recommendations to increase the number of women in such positions. Recently there has been an incentive for parties to encourage women to come forward as candidates for the office of mayor. The reason is that the current Minister of Internal Affairs, who appoints the mayors, is in favour of appointing women. This means that parties have a better chance to get their party candidate appointed when they put forward a female candidate.

Getting more women selected into appointive positions also demands changes in the selection procedures. Implementation of these changes is easier, in a way, since it is the government and not the parties that appoints. In September 1991 an advisory report to the cabinet made recommendations for the government to increase the number of women mayors and members of advisory boards (Emancipatieraad, 1991). The report suggested that the government should make the criteria for becoming a mayor more explicit, so that any hidden gender bias could be deleted. A further recommendation was that the government should follow the example of the Norwegian Equal Status Act, and introduce legislation to ensure gender-balanced advisory boards by designating a 40 per cent minimum membership of each sex. On the basis of this study the Dutch cabinet issued a report in 1992 with its policy intentions. For the time period 1992–5 the cabinet announced its intentions to have women comprising 30 per cent of the elected bodies after the next elections. Besides this it announced that there will be 100 women mayors (out of 620) at the end of 1995 and in every new external advisory board 50 per cent of the members *have* to be women (Kabinetsstandpunt Vrouwen in Politiek en Openbaar Bestuur, 1992). So in general, one can say that the Dutch government promotes the participation of women in positions of power.

Conclusions

Eventually more women will gain access to the political arena. Currently, the main parties are willing to select more women for political posts. However, since it means a redistribution of political power, it will be a very slow process. As Schattshneider expressed it in 1960: 'whoever decides what the game is about, decides also who can get into the game' (1960: 105). As they stand, the recruitment and selection procedures are still biased in ways that promote the continued tenure of groups and individuals, predominantly men, who are in positions of power. Incumbents are very difficult to defeat and open seats for high-level political offices are very rare. The characteristics that are most valued in political leaders are those which are mainly associated with men. Similarly, the standards by which qualifications for public office are evaluated are defined by men's experiences. Increasing the diversity of characteristics that selectors look for in political leaders would help to bring more women into public office.

But, since we are talking about redistribution of power, it cannot be expected that men will give up their seats voluntarily and promptly. Without changing the selection procedures, by setting quotas or by centralization of the selection procedures, equal political participation remains a utopia.

Notes

1 Translation by the author.

2 There are not many studies available about the background and opinions of members and officers of the Dutch political parties. The most recent study was carried out in 1986 by the Department of Political Science of the University of Leiden. The three main parties, CDA, PvdA and VVD, were the object of research. To be able to measure differences in participation and influence between the separate party branches, members, local party officers, members of the national executive and parliamentary candidates were interviewed separately. Of D66 only the members and candidates have been interviewed. The members were selected by an a-select sample from the members' directory. The total response was:

	M	F
CDA members	212	53
PvdA members	181	111
VVD members	216	84
D66 members	263	98
CDA local officers	427	104
PvdA local officers	409	188
VVD local officers	274	190
CDA national executive	97	20
PvdA national executive	95	43
VVD national executive	107	20
CDA candidates	116	31
PvdA candidates	199	64
VVD candidates	80	13
D66 candidates	44	5

3 Two reasons are presented why women are more likely to be selected for political positions by appointment than when the system calls for direct election. One reason is the fact that the authorities who make the appointments are accountable for these appointments. Therefore they are more concerned to satisfy all different social groups, including women. The second reason is that in many cases there are regulations about the appointments, e.g. with regard to rotation and succession (Darcy et al., 1987: 111; Mossuz-Lavau and Sineau, 1984: 50).

10
Ending the Male Political Hegemony: the Norwegian Experience

Hege Skjeie

The demand for political integration

The beginning of the 1970s marked a new era in party political life in Norway. A first signal of women's coming integration into party politics was provided through the municipality election of 1971, which produced a sensational *majority* of women councillors in three local councils – among them the capital, Oslo. Orchestrated by different women's groups, voting procedures were followed here which granted a small number of voters – acting in unison – the power to change the parties' own candidate nominations. 'The Women's Coup' of 1971 was highly demonstrative of the new challenge which faced the established structure of party politics: the demand that male hegemony over political life should now be brought to an end.

Twenty years later, the proved adaptability of parties to this by no means modest demand has become a prime symbol of the 'passion for equality' (Graubard, 1986), held to be characteristic of Nordic political life. It has even been suggested that this profile of equality be used as a trademark in campaigns to promote Norway abroad. And current images of public life in Norway are indeed unique. When TV broadcasts an important parliamentary debate, or reports on a crisis meeting of the cabinet, it is not a standard line of crewcuts in grey suits that appears on the screen. Instead, the hairstyles and dresses of the Prime Minister, the Minister of Justice, the Undersecretary of State or the leader of the main opposition party provide viewers with ample opportunity for comment. No Norwegian cabinet since May 1986 has included less than 40 per cent women. By May 1991, half the major political parties had elected a woman as leader. And a male journalist about to organize a debate on recent developments in the negotiations on European economic cooperation might well discover that, if he wants to include the most important political actors, he himself would be the only man on the panel.

Yet this revolution in public image was never a prime motivating force behind the participation demands of the 1970s and 1980s. Neither was the issue of individual women's equal right to pursue a political career among the most important concerns of the new women's movement that grew in strength from the late 1960s. The movement was primarily concerned with women's empowerment as a group. Contrary to dominant trends in several other western countries, many Norwegian feminists advocated integration into the existing party structure as a viable strategy for empowering women. This integrationist approach made cooperation possible between movement women and party women, which regularly took the form of non-partisan campaigns to put pressure on all the political parties to include women.[1] More separatist efforts to enter the established power arenas received less support and largely failed; as was the case with the effort to revitalize a Norwegian Women's Party in the early 1970s (Fosshaug, 1989).

The women's movement wanted women politicians to act as women's own representatives, to promote the political interests of women in general. 'Women representing women' was a slogan increasingly used also by party women. The challenge to political parties thus became explicitly formulated not only – or mainly – as a demand to make room for new individuals, but also to make room for the new causes and new political concerns which these individuals would promote. The political rhetoric of 'difference'[2] implied that women politicians would broaden the scope of decision-making. The expectation was that gender differences in attitudes would link to action; that women's common interests and common experiences would also prevail through processes of decision-making. Women would add new values and new issues to the political agendas; they might even bring about a completely different set of political priorities. There is little reason to doubt that this women's challenge was perceived by party leaders as a serious one indeed. Some thought it might form a threat to the party system as such. When the most prominent Norwegian politician of the post-war period, the Labour party leader Einar Gerhardsen, was asked formally to head the first election campaign to increase women's representation he expressed clear doubts that he ought to do this. He feared that the newly elected women could not be trusted to comply with the norms of party loyalty; that they might start voting across party lines; that women's political participation eventually might contribute to the breakdown of the established parties (Wiik, 1986).

The rhetoric of difference created an image of women's unity, sketching the possibility for new gender-structured political alliances. Few have, however, materialized. Recently, two different studies of Norwegian political elites have reinforced growing doubts that such alliances will become regular features of Norwegian politics. A 1989 interview series with the members of the Norwegian parliament (the Storting) shows that collective action on a cross-party basis by women politicians is still the exception rather than the rule. The impact of party continues to be an everyday observation; the preservation of party unity is more apparent the higher the level of political decision-making. Women politicians occasionally engage in cross-party cooperation to influence particular decisions. But, particularly on elite levels of politics, such strategic alliances remain a rarity (Skjeie, 1991a). A 1985 survey among Norwegian national party leaderships concludes that 'party' clearly remains a better indicator than 'gender' on attitudes to different political issues. In this sense the parties seem to have shaped their women politicians more than the women have shaped their parties (Heidar, forthcoming: 23).

No women's bloc has appeared – the party bloc remains the dominant feature of Norwegian politics. But to interpret a lack of divergence between men and women party members at one point in time as evidence that women, over time, have not influenced party viewpoints might be a misconception. In both the party leadership survey and the interview series with the Norwegian members of parliament, overwhelming majorities maintained that women's participation *had* made a difference to party politics. Thus the party elite survey also offered the suggestion that even as party demarcation lines prevail, women's participation may still have contributed towards changing the attitudes of male party members.

Such a suggestion implies that further analyses of the political impact of women ought to concentrate on the organizational level rather than on the level of individuals – on *processes of change* more than *individual agents of change*. Accordingly this chapter considers how Norwegian parties over the course of the past two decades have met the challenge of incorporating the new political causes associated with women's political mobilization. The focus is on changes in the profiles of the different parties; changes which also are reported by party members themselves as particularly influenced by women. What changes have occurred? What is the exact content of these changes? And how have changes in party profiles contributed towards confirming or disrupting traditional party demarcation lines?

This examination builds on two main data sources. The point of departure is the interview series with the Norwegian members of parliament carried out during the spring of 1989. These interviews addressed the question of women's political impact using evaluations made by the parliamentarians themselves. The parliamentary delegations interviewed were as follows:

- Socialist Left party (six MPs; three women).
- Labour party (seventy-one MPs; thirty women).
- Centre party (twelve MPs; two women).
- Christian People's party (sixteen MPs; four women).
- Conservative party (fifty MPs; fifteen women).
- Progress party (two MPs; no women).

Of a total of 157 members of parliament, 146 participated in this interview series.

Results from the parliamentary interviews are then compared with the results of the second data source, an analysis of issues included in five of the six major parties' programmes of action from 1973 to 1989, programmes which are drawn up before the national elections every fourth year. The programme analysis concentrates on those issues which members of parliament reported as particularly influenced by women politicians. In this analysis, changes in party profiles refer not only to the inclusion of new political issues, but also to new interpretations or a higher priority given to older political issues. In addition to the programme statements, references are made to policy statements through different parliamentary and governmental decisions over the same period. The sources here are mainly governmental proposals and reports to parliament. The one major party excluded from the party programme analysis is the right-wing Progress party. Generally this party has very few women in leadership positions. On most of the topics discussed in this chapter, the principal viewpoint expressed through the Progress party's programme is that these topics do not belong to the field of party politics.[3]

The Norwegian electoral system is one of proportional elections in multi-member districts; the multi-party electoral field has for the past fifteen years contained the following main competitors: on the left, a major social democratic party, the Labour party, and the smaller Socialist Left party; on the right, a major conservative party and the smaller Progress party; between the two poles, the Centre party and the Christian People's party. Cross-nationally,

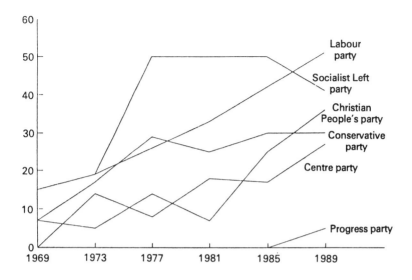

Figure 10.1 *Women members of parliament, 1969–1989, by party (percentages)*

proportional elections in multi-member districts are held to lend themselves to the election of women more readily than do majority elections in single-member districts. Cross-nationally, parties of the left are also considered as more willing to include women representatives than parties of the right. In the Norwegian case we might, however, choose to underscore the similarities in patterns of integration.

The breakthrough for women's representation came during the 1970s, their representation rates moving from below a 10 per cent limit to figures of between 20 and 25 per cent in both local and national political assemblies towards the end of the decade. By the end of the 1980s the general representation rates had increased by another 10 per cent. Over time, few parties have resisted the inclusion of women representatives. Even if the exact ratios differ between parties, the common trend across parties is one of increasing integration – the only notable exception is the Progress party (Figure 10.1).

Party membership shows a similar tendency towards decreasing differences in men's and women's membership ratios from the 1970s into the 1980s (Hellevik and Bjørklund, 1987), as do women's representation rates within different party elective bodies

(Heidar, 1988). By the beginning of the 1990s several parties had also adopted formal quota regulations which specify the composition of party-controlled political posts. Minimum quotas specifying a 40/60 percentage balance were first introduced on the left by the Socialist Left party in 1975, then adopted also by the Labour party in 1981/3. In 1989 the Centre party followed suit. The Christian People's party has 'postponed' a decision on quotas. The Conservative party has, however, so far rejected such regulations.

From this brief outline of changes in women's political representation, I move on to the main question of changes in parties' political profiles. As indicated through the sketched patterns of integration, such changes should become increasingly apparent as we move from the 1970s and through the 1980s.

'Money of one's own': a framework for analysing changes in party politics

Norwegian political elites largely share the conviction that gender differences can be stated in political terms. A clear majority of Norwegian parliamentarians perceive of policy areas where men and women party members hold different viewpoints. They similarly identify a series of political issues where women's inclusion has contributed towards changing party viewpoints. Discussing changes in party politics during the past two decades I will not, however, be equally concerned with *any difference* that might have occurred. In fact I will not even be equally concerned with all those changes which politicians themselves perceive to be caused by women. Primarily, I will be concerned with those political issues which can be stated in terms of their possible effects on gender relationships – that is, with policies that might contribute towards improving the position of individual women in society.

What are these policies? A useful point of departure for a further specification is provided through a standard model describing women's traditional relationship to the major institutions of family, labour market and social welfare (Hernes, 1987); their maintenance sources of marriage, wages and social security (Stang Dahl, 1987). In this model, the focus is thus on a *triangle of support sources*, which depicts either a situation of personal economic dependence, or a situation of personal economic independence for individual citizens (Figure 10.2).

Stang Dahl has described the gender differences in reliance on support sources in the following manner:

Figure 10.2

During most of their lives the majority of men are subjected to the wage contract, most of them using their wages to maintain not only themselves but their wife and children as well. A close personal link with the wage contract automatically entails a close link with social security, which represents a collective insurance against a failure of income, and an accumulated capital to maintain old age's spent labour power . . . men tend to be more stable wage earners, whereas women go back and forth between marriage and paid work, either simultaneously or during stages of their life-cycles. And, of course, men's work is better paid. Men's strong position in the labour market therefore means that their position is also stronger than that of women where social security is concerned. Paid work is men's chief source of support, with social security counting as a subsidiary source. Marriage practically never provides a source of maintenance for men. Marriage is a sex-related source of income, and it is predominantly used by women. (Stang Dahl, 1987: 117–18)

It is often argued that the care of small children forms the basis for the sexual division of labour, where men more often work for wages while women more often rely on economic support through the marriage contract. As long as care work goes unpaid, the child's situation of dependency is extended to include the child's caretaker. The collective choice of men not to take part in childcare helps them to uphold dominance over women (Connell, 1987). While the periods of childbirth and childcare are limited periods in a total lifespan, and more limited for new generations of women, they contribute towards fortifying more lasting divisions. Still, the triangle of support sources also suggests two roads whereby women can travel from a situation of personal economic dependence, relying on family support to a situation of more personal economic independence. In this, they might be assisted by public policies. One road is from reliance on family support to reliance on paid work, the other is from reliance on family support to reliance on social security. Both roads open access to more 'money of one's own', that is, to means of sustenance received independently of the idiosyncrasies of a personal provider.

Entering the labour market

Politically there are three basic strategies by which women's economic independence through labour market participation may be furthered. A *granting of access rights* is made, for instance, through legal rules which establish the principle of equal formal treatment with regard to education and job-hiring. Such guarantees might be provided in either gender-specific or gender-neutral form; legal regulations might either specifically prohibit the discrimination of women or in neutral terms prohibit discrimination on grounds of sex.

Legal guarantees might not be sufficient to provide access, however. For instance there is little use in having the formal right to apply for an education if your life situation makes such an application impossible. Yet resources might be provided which contribute towards equalizing the opportunity of individuals in making use of formal rights. Not only the provision of childcare facilities, but also the location of neighbourhood workplaces are examples of means of *facilitating access* to wages. While such policies might well be advocated in gender-neutral terms as being of benefit to respectively 'parents', 'children' or 'families', in practice they primarily help mothers to establish and maintain labour force attachment.

Given that new opportunities are provided, the individual still has to decide for herself whether she indeed wants to make use of the possibilities offered. And the competition among individuals will decide who in fact gets what. But then again, this element of competition might be questioned. The basis for such a questioning would be a dislike of the expected outcome: those who have much are likely to get even more, while those who have little will get even less. On this basis, a *distribution control* might be considered necessary. Quotas are examples of such means to control the final distribution of positions. Through quotas individual women may gain access to new positions. But, again, regulations can be formulated in either gender-specific or gender-neutral terms. If or when the latter option is chosen, the actual gender composition of the area where regulations are applied determines whether women in practice will benefit.

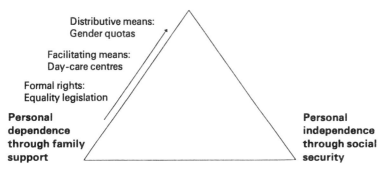

Figure 10.3

These three different policy options:

1 to create rules which grant formal access;
2 to allocate resources in ways which facilitate access;
3 to make distribution decisions which guarantee access;

can also be seen as markers on the same continuum of policies that promotes women's access to wages (Figure 10.3).

On the inside
The 'gut issue' (Friedan, 1981) of equal pay for work of equal value challenges the established pattern of actual wage distributions within different segments of the labour market. In terms of political decisions the equal pay issue can be treated principally and universally through legal regulations. It can also be treated practically, but then partially, through wage negotiations.[4] In its 'pure' version the equal pay issue is based on a comparison of the wages paid to women and men performing identical work for the same employer, and opposes a discriminatory practice where women are paid less for doing the same work as men. While the claim of equal pay necessitates a new wage distribution, and possibly also implies a wage redistribution, it is principally a claim of formal equal treatment; of women receiving the wages that in fact correspond to the positions they hold – the wages that would have been paid if the positions had been held by men.

The equal pay claim is also extended to include 'equal pay for work of equal value'. Here the wages paid within different work

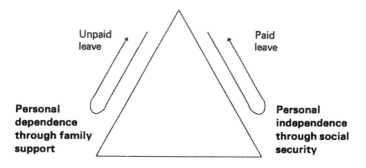

Figure 10.4

categories become a yardstick for the 'one-down' positions occupied by women. The core of the 'equal value', or 'comparable worth', claim is that work performed (mostly) by women is less valued in wage terms than comparable work performed (mostly) by men. This ranking of positions in terms of wages reflects a continuing discrimination against women not only or foremost by individual employers, but within the labour market as such. Again the equal pay claim implies that action that contributes to a levelling of the comparable positions should be taken, now preferably without regard to whether workers work for the same employer.

Retreats and re-entries
The challenge of improving women's access to the labour market is not restricted to the opening of new positions. It is also one of securing positions already obtained. Rules on the right to maternity leave – or gender-neutrally formulated as parental leave – imply a political decision which grants workers the right to return to positions formerly held, instead of having to quit their jobs. As paid leave, financed through social security, these rules provide for a continued personal economic independence. They may be seen as offering a loop of retreat – re-entry from labour market participation to reliance on social security and back to further labour market participation. As unpaid leave, the loop offered is one from labour market participation to reliance on family support and back to labour market participation (Figure 10.4).

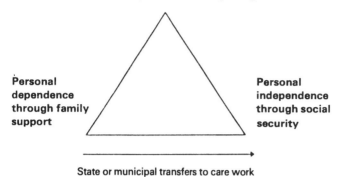

Figure 10.5

Staying home
The road by which women might travel directly from a personal economic dependence to a personal economic independence granted through social security is universally accessible to those aged 67 years or more. It is also available on an individual basis to those permanently disabled from labour market participation. All mothers – and single fathers taking care of children – receive child benefit. Single parents who stay at home to take care of small children may benefit additionally from social security. Political means which further contribute towards levelling positions of paid and unpaid work would include economic transfers to women who stay at home to take care of family members who are too young, too old or too sick to take care of themselves.[5] Formally, such transfers would be granted on the basis of the work performed – regardless of the gender or marital status of its performer. In practice, such transfers would imply a recognition that the family-based care work actually performed by women belongs to the area of state responsibility. The now familiar way of illustrating such means would be as shown in Figure 10.5.

Perceptions of change in party politics

During the past two decades many of those political means which may improve women's access to 'money of their own' have either been adopted as new public policies or expanded in terms of priority and scope. According to the Norwegian members of parliament, women's inclusion into party politics has indeed been instrumental in changing party viewpoints towards such policies. Asked to specify the issues where women's increased participation had contributed towards change in party viewpoints, MPs answered in such a way that a detailed and extensive women's political agenda was drawn up. These answers covered a total of nine identified policy areas. There were broad references made to 'disarmament politics', 'environmental politics', 'social and welfare politics' and 'family politics'. But a series of issues was also specified which mainly concerned representational politics, labour market politics, body politics or care politics. 'Representational politics' includes references to the issue of women's political participation both generally and in the members' own party. It includes references to quota regulations as well as training and preparation. Both equality legislation and equal pay issues were mentioned as examples within the category of 'labour market politics'. 'Care-and-career politics' includes the specific issues of both childcare centres and parental leave reforms. 'Family-based care politics' contains issues of care wages as well as of pension rights for caregivers. In the reported Agenda of Change (see Figure 10.6), the areas of 'labour market politics' and of 'care-and-career politics' thus in combination contain the political measures whereby women's labour market participation might be promoted. The area of 'family-based care' contains the measures which might increase the economic independence of women who stay at home to perform care work.[6]

In the politicians' own reports, one policy area clearly dominated the aggregate Agenda of Change.[7] Issues of 'care-and-career politics' alone account for 35 per cent of all reports given. The major single issue of 'care-and-career politics' is childcare centres: in all the political parties, day care was the most frequently mentioned issue of change. The area of 'labour market politics' on the other hand constitutes a clearly marginal area on the Agenda of Change reported by members of parliament. From the previous discussion on issues of relevance to gender relationships this marginal status is somewhat surprising. However, it might possibly reflect a perception among the members of parliament that more recent policies in this area remain largely unchanged from those policies which during the 1970s were proposed and adopted by assemblies still clearly dominated by men. While the official equal status policies of the 1970s portrayed women in what was then at least partly a new role, that is, in search of paid employment, they largely ignored women's tasks as caregivers. But as increasing numbers of mothers with small

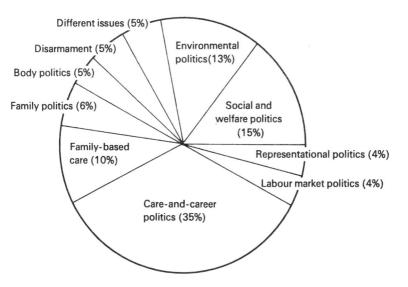

Figure 10.6   *'Agenda of Change': Norwegian parliamentarians'*
report of areas where women's increased participation has
contributed towards changing party viewpoints. Percentage basis
is total number of responses = 284

children entered the labour market, the continuing shortage of
care facilities became ever more apparent. Thus the perceptions
now stated by the parliamentarians that 'care-and-career politics'
represents a particularly important contribution from women
politicians may also reflect how the favoured political solutions of
the 1970s in fact created political problems for the decade of the
1980s.

'Care-and-career politics' is pictured as an area of change within
all parties other than the Progress party. 'Family-based care',
however, is pictured as an area of change primarily within the
three so-called 'non-socialist' parties of the Conservatives, the
Christian People's party and the Centre party. These two different
aspects of care politics have long been associated with a basic left–
right ideological controversy: while the market-based 'woman
worker' ideal has largely been associated with left parties, the
family-bonded 'caring mother' has traditionally been associated
with parties more to the right.[8] The interviews with the Norwegian
parliamentarians indicate an increased cross-party agreement on
'care-and-career politics'.

No similar agreement is apparent on 'family-based care politics'. The interviews, furthermore, reveal that when care-and-career issues come to confront issues of family-based care – when political preferences are stated in terms of priorities – the final choices of party members still follow the traditional party cleavages. Members of the parties of the left, the Labour party and the Socialist Left party, then come out in almost unanimous support of policies that contribute towards strengthening the position of the 'woman worker'. Within the parties more to the right, the Conservatives, the Christian People's party and the Centre party, members clearly prefer policies more supportive of the 'caring mother'.[9]

This particular controversy illustrates why 'changes in party viewpoints' must be discussed either as they occur and are developed within the traditional framework of party cleavages or contribute towards weakening old cleavages. Such a discussion is presented below. Taking the interview series as the departure point, I here examine in more detail the changes in party programmes on issues of labour market and care politics over the course of the past two decades.

Labour market politics: a new left–right controversy

The area of 'labour market politics' includes references made by members of parliament to the adoption of the Equal Status Act, measures to promote non-traditional educational and job choices, state loans for educational purposes and also the equal pay issue. The responses thus include examples of both regulatory, facilitatory and distributive means whereby women's labour market participation may be furthered.

Among the members of parliament it was primarily representatives of the Conservative party who reported this as an area particularly influenced by women politicians. The party programme analysis, however, reveals that such politics have been an area of concern primarily to the two parties of the left, the Labour party and the Socialist Left party. It has also been an area of steadily increasing concern, as witnessed through an increasing number of suggestions in party programmes between 1973 and 1989. The greatest increase was during the 1980s, however. Suggested measures have then concentrated on policies that would contribute to weaken the sexual division of work that characterizes the labour market.[10]

From the beginning of the 1980s these suggestions included the posting of women's counsellors in labour agencies, special grants to employers who recruit women (or men) for non-traditional jobs, state subsidies or loans to be tied to the recruitment of women employees, state subsidies to women entrepreneurs and plans to promote the recruitment of women to leadership positions in the public sector. They also introduced large-scale quota measures aimed to guarantee women's access to both higher education and public sector employment.

By contrast, Conservative party programmes have concentrated on educational politics. From 1977 onwards the party programmes included suggestions that equal opportunity and non-traditional educational choices should be actively supported through educational counselling, through non-discriminatory textbooks, and through teachers' courses on equality issues. Such proposals were later also included in the programmes of the left parties. They also began to appear in the party programmes of the Christian People's party and the Centre party between the late 1970s and the early 1980s.

Between 1973 and 1989 the Conservative party's programmes included only a handful of suggestions on employment politics. Until recently, employment politics was of little concern within the two centrist parties as well. Until the mid-1980s their programmes mainly focused on opportunities for part-time work, and also included statements that family-based care work should be given seniority credits with regard to both employment and student enrolment; policies which have also been supported by the Conservative party. In addition, the Centre party programmes have included gender-specific statements regarding their one primary reference group, the farmers. But between the mid- and late 1980s the programmes of the two centrist parties became more supportive of both the educational and employment politics promoted by the left parties.

This sketch of the development of party profiles shows how a new policy becomes subjected to an established left–right division. Traditionally, neither the Christian People's party nor the Centre party shared the conviction that the means whereby women might achieve economic independence through labour market participation was an area of state responsibility. Recently, however, this viewpoint gained strength within both parties; thus we witness a radical change in party politics. The party that changed the least, both in terms of inclusion of new issues and in terms of new interpretations, was the Conservative party. In the 1970s the Conservative party was more supportive of labour market equality politics than the two centrist parties; but by the mid-1980s this pattern changed. From the early and mid-1980s divergencies are particularly acute between the Conservative party and the two left parties.

The Equal Status Act heritage

Left–right divergencies are reflected not only in party programme statements but also in parliamentary policy proposals. Furthermore, the stated disagreements, especially those between Labour and the Conservatives, can be viewed largely as a heritage of the early parliamentary debates over the Equal Status Act. In particular, the quota controversies of the early 1980s closely followed the pattern of the left–right controversy established in the mid-1970s. The Equal Status Act, which is a pillar of official Norwegian equal status policies, was adopted by parliament in 1978. Its principal aim is to grant women equal access to education and employment through legal rules establishing the principle of equal formal treatment.[11] Following its adoption, a government Action Plan for Equality was presented to parliament by a Labour government in 1981 (Proposition to the Storting no. 122 [1980–1]). That plan sought to implement a series of educational and employment measures, many of which were also suggested in party programme statements. It introduced quota measures to regulate student enrolment in certain educational sectors. Parallel to the parliamentary proposal the Labour government tried to negotiate a recruitment plan for hiring within the state sector which also relied on the use of quotas. The Conservatives strongly opposed Labour over these proposals.

The quota controversy   It is possible to distinguish between two kinds of quota proposals. One model, now used by some of the political parties, simply requires that specified groups of party representatives shall include at least 40 per cent of each sex. This kind of ruling is facilitated, first, because party appointments often are filled 'group-wise' – several positions are vacant at the same time – and, secondly, because there is no fixed or specified qualification/merit standard which potential candidates must meet. But fixed qualification requirements are a regular feature of both group-wise student enrolments and individual, serial, job-hirings. Therefore the quota model for student enrolment and job-hiring commonly specifies conditions for the use of preferential treatment. The conditions can be either 'moderate' or 'radical'; it can, for instance, be decided that female applicants with qualifications equal or close to equal to those of male applicants shall have priority (moderate), or that female applications shall have priority if they satisfy the minimum requirements for the available position, even though male applicants may have better qualifications (radical). Preferential treatment may then be practised to fill a specified quota, most commonly a 40–60 distribution, at one (or more) group-wise admission, or be practised serially at individual hirings in order to fulfil a long-term distribution goal, again most commonly stated as a 40–60 distribution (Skjeie, 1985). For both models, quota rules are commonly formulated in gender-neutral rather than gender-specific terms, that is by stating that 'each sex' should comprise at least 40 per cent of those who are nominated, hired or admitted. They mainly operate where women are in the minority, however.

The preferential treatment measures proposed by the Labour government in 1981 were mostly of the radical variety. The suggestions, also supported by the Socialist Left party, were consistently presented as practical measures to follow up the general preferential treatment regulations in the Equal Status Act. These regulations state that while discrimination between women and men is forbidden (para. 3.1):

> Different treatment which in conformity with the purpose of the Act promotes equal status between the sexes, does not represent a contravention of the first paragraph. The same applies to women's special rights based on the existing difference in the situation of women and men. (Equal Status Act, para. 3.3)

In the 1970s both the Christian People's party and the Centre party rejected the whole idea of equal status legislation. The Conservative party, however, specifically opposed the preferential treatment regulations of the act: these regulations provided one of the stated reasons why the Conservative party chose not to support the first bill proposed (Proposition to the Odelsting no. 33 [1974–5]) which was debated by parliament in 1975. In the parliamentary debate in 1981 the Conservative party again opposed new measures; the party now argued that the Equal Status Act did not permit such radical measures as those now suggested. The Conservatives here primarily relied on references to the paragraph on education, which states that

> In respect of admission to courses, schools and studies, and other efforts designed to promote recruitment to a particular trade or profession, when circumstances otherwise are approximately equal, it shall be possible to give priority to one sex if it is the case that this will help in the long term to regulate any imbalance between the sexes in the trade or profession in question. (Equal Status Act, para. 6)[12]

In the 1981 parliamentary debate, the left–right quota controversy thus came to focus on the possible meanings inherent in the phrasing 'approximately equal'. When after the 1981 parliamentary election governmental control passed from the Labour party to the Conservative party, the new government immediately modified the proposed regulations about student enrolment and public sector hiring so that they came more in line with this party's understanding of 'approximately equal' (Skjeie, 1985).

Yet in the interview series with the Norwegian parliamentarians, it was primarily Conservative members of parliament who mentioned the Equal Status Act as one issue particularly influenced by women politicians. Actually, the act was first introduced as one of the ten major election promises in the Labour party's election programme for the 1973 election. It was not adopted by parliament until 1978, and then only with the assistance of the Conservative parliamentary delegation. As a minority government, the Labour party had originally relied on support from the Socialist Left party to pass the act. Although this party found the proposed act far too moderate, the first parliamentary debate in 1975 showed that it was still non-negotiable. Parliament thus chose to return the first bill proposal to the cabinet for further consideration. The Labour–Conservative compromise achieved a couple of years later momentarily broke with the left–right cleavage on equality politics. As demonstrated above, however, this consensus lasted for only a short while.

Equal pay   Yet another heritage of the Equal Status Act is revealed through the analysis of party programmes from 1973 to 1989. In the early stages of this law-making process the main controversy had been between the Labour cabinet on the one hand and the party's traditional ally – the Confederation of Trade Unions – on the other, concerning Labour's attempt to regulate wage negotiations through legal statements on equal pay. The first ministerial drafting of the act was supervised by an informal 'party committee', which also included trade union representatives. The trade unions first protested against a suggested pay regulation which aimed to reduce 'unreasonable' wage differences between work mainly performed by women and work mainly performed by men. According to union representatives, a regulation limited to 'equal pay for equal work' was not merely sufficient, but the only acceptable, legal regulation. At the public hearings of the law proposal most of the participants disagreed with this, referring to the phrasing 'Equal Pay for Work of Equal Value' of the ILO convention on equal pay. In its own public statement on the proposal the trade union organization conceded this point. No further concessions were granted, however. Trade Union resistance was the main reason why the bill proposal debated in parliament in 1975 was non-negotiable. Neither did the later compromise between Labour and Conservatives imply any new negotiations over the equal pay regulation. In the Labour cabinet's Action Plan for Equality, presented in 1981, equal pay issues were notably absent. While for more than fifteen years most parties' programmes have also included references to the wage issue, the one exception is the programmes of the Labour party.[13]

The heritage of the Equal Status Act is thus twofold. On the one hand it prepared the ground for a new agenda of labour market equality politics, and on the other hand, the law-making process itself seems to have contributed to the narrowing of this new political agenda. The wage solution adopted through the Equal Status Act – a solution of 'equal pay for work of equal value' – remained the official approach to the wage problem for nearly a decade. Until recently, the Labour party's experience of controversy with the trade unions thus seems to have kept the broader issue of women's wages a non-issue. Only when pressure also mounted within the trade union movement did the Labour party once again address the problem that work mainly performed by women is traditionally low paid work, and stated that the party:

> in cooperation with organized labour will work to secure that wage negotiations in particular aim to increase the lowest salaries. (1990–3 programme: 86)

'Labour market politics' is otherwise shown as an area of steadily increasing political concern during the past two decades. But new initiatives have primarily been suggested by the parties of the left. The implementation process also confirms that such politics creates a new area for left–right controversies, and thus contributes towards strengthening rather than weakening traditional cleavages between parties. Left–right divergencies are reflected in attitudes to public spending, where the Conservative party mainly advocates measures of low financial cost. But it is also reflected in attitudes to regulative and redistributive measures, where the Conservative party has consistently chosen minimal solutions. The Conservative party has not actively opposed new labour market equality politics, but neither has it actively initiated such policies. When party viewpoints change, the changes are mainly adaptive.

This general pattern is also apparent when the two main proposals on official equal status policies of the 1980s are compared; the Labour cabinet's Action Plan from 1981 and the non-socialist cabinet's continuation plan from 1985 (Report to the Storting no. 69 [1984–5]). The latter plan leans heavily on the former; the most original suggestion in the latter was that all ministries should develop their own action plans for their respective spheres of responsibility. Yet an important requirement was that new initiatives should seek not to increase the ministry's total budget (Skjeie et al., 1989).

More generally, the measures of labour market equality politics often require low public expenditure. Distributive measures have been implemented with low effectiveness. While the quota model used for political appointments for instance has been highly successful, the model practised at job-hirings seems to have had very limited effect. Different examples of 'moderate' preferential treatment regulations have clearly shown that the understanding of the requirement 'moderate' itself often prevents the regulation from being applied, because a situation where two or more applicants are judged to have equal qualifications hardly ever arises (Skjeie, 1985). In turn, the constraints of such politics may have contributed towards an increasing focus of attention on policies that might prove to be more effective means to promote women's labour market participation, but at the same time, may prove far more costly in terms of public expenditure.

Care-and-career politics: a new cross-party agreement

The major political issues of 'care-and-career politics' reported by the Norwegian members of parliament are childcare centres, parental leave and daily working hours. All these issues of care politics are formally gender-neutral; they are to the benefit of the parents of small children. In practice, however, they mainly help mothers establish and maintain labour force attachment. Childcare centres are a part of participation infrastructures; they facilitate labour market participation. Parental leave provides a temporary retreat from the market place – but, most importantly, a retreat with a guarantee of re-entry – while reduced daily working hours also reduce more permanent combination pressures.

A strengthened focus on the responsibility of the state in matters of care, particularly on means by which the state can take an active part in the organizing and financing of the care of children, is reflected through a steadily increasing number of party programme suggestions from the early 1970s to the late 1980s. In addition to the issues of childcare centres, parental leave and work hours, the issues of extending the school day for smaller school children on the one hand, and lowering the compulsory school starting age (which in Norway is at seven years) on the other, have become central issues, particularly in the 1980s. While the first of these has been of most concern to the Labour party, the second has primarily been addressed by the Conservative party.

The party programme analysis also reveals differences between parties which are not apparent in the parliamentary interviews. In all parties the issue of childcare centres was mentioned as the one major issue over which party viewpoints changed. It is not an equally *new* issue to all parties, however. The programmes of the two left parties, as well as the Conservative party, have included statements on day care since the early 1970s. In this respect, actual change is again more visible within the two centrist parties, which traditionally have been the parties least inclined to favour publicly financed day care. Only from the mid-1980s have childcare centres been given clear support in the programme statements of these two parties.

During the 1970s, childcare centres were argued for predominantly on the basis of their benefit to children (Leira, 1989). In the parliamentary debate over the Day Care Act of 1975 (Proposition to the Odelsting no. 23 [1974–5]), it was mainly members of the Socialist Left party who advocated state-sponsored childcare as a means of facilitating women's access to labour markets. Members of the non-socialist parties argued for 'the freedom of parents to choose whether to work outside the home'; a particular phrasing used to signal defence of the traditional one-wage-earner family. But in the course of the 1980s the general trend has clearly been towards a convergence of arguments. Childcare facilities are then seen as either a means for 'both parents to be participants in the workforce' or a means whereby 'parents can share work' both outside and within the home. This convergence thus signals a growing general acceptance of care-and-career dilemmas.

Five out of the six major political parties now promote childcare centres. The one exception is the Progress party, which instead prefers to *reduce public* involvement in the promotion of day care. Over the past decade, however, parties have disagreed on *how* such centres should be promoted. The publicly run Norwegian childcare centres have a high proportion of public funding; as well as state subsidies there are also municipal subsidies. In privately run day care, state subsidies are the same but municipality subsidies vary. Here the parents often pay a higher proportion of the cost. State responsibility for the provision of childcare facilities has thus been debated within the framework of the following four cost-related questions:

- What should the level of state subsidies to childcare facilities be?
- What should constitute the intermediate and long-term goals of coverage?
- Should private/public mixes be advocated?
  Should there be an obligation for local authorities to provide day care?[14]

The party programme analysis shows that on these four different dimensions there has in fact been almost no change in party profile as it is outlined in the Conservative party programmes throughout the period from 1973 to 1989. The party has consistently supported minimum solutions. All programmes have been silent on the issue of the level of subsidies. They have never suggested mandatory provision. They have never specified what the suggested 'increase in the number of places' should be and they have, since 1977, consistently advocated a private/public mix of provisions. Within the Christian People's party it is the 1989 programme which represents a major change in the party's day care policy. This programme declared a goal of 'full coverage'. It also proposed that a mandatory provision by local authorities will be considered, and for the first time the programme explicitly maintained that state subsidies should increase. A goal of 'full coverage' was also advocated by the Centre party from 1981 onwards. The Centre party otherwise shares with both the Conservative and Christian People's party a continuing preference for private/public mixes, but has remained silent on the issues of both state subsidies and mandatory provision.

The Labour party seems to have suffered continuous turbulence on day care, most notably on the issue of coverage. The party exchanged an ambitious promise to reach 50,000 places by 1977 for an even more ambitious promise of reaching 100,000 places by 1981. The next programme (1981–5) chose the potentially less compromising solution of proposing an unspecified 'increase'. The programme then moved on to state the goal of 'full coverage' (1985–9), a goal not repeated in 1989, however. Only in the mid-1980s did the party suggest mandatory provision; only by 1989 did it actively support private/public mixes. That same year the Socialist Left party finally dropped its programmatic insistence that the provision of childcare centres is solely a public enterprise. But this is the only major change in the Socialist Left party's day care politics since the early 1970s.

Still, the general trend on day care politics in terms of both new inclusions and new interpretations particularly during the latter part of the 1980s is clearly one of increasing similarity across parties. This new agreement is clear also from the parliamentary debate in 1988 on a national plan for the further development of childcare centres (Report to the Storting no. 8 [1987–8]), and the subsequent debates on follow-up measures (for example, Proposition to the Odelsting no. 40 [1988–9]). By 1988 about 30 per cent of Norwegian preschool children were offered publicly subsidized day care. The national plan aims at full coverage by the year 2000, to be realized primarily through increased state subsidies to childcare centres. Furthermore, the plan suggests granting more responsibility for centre approvals to the municipalities.

All the significant measures presented by the Labour government through the national plan in 1988 were supported by the Conservative party, the Christian People's party and the Centre party. But the Christian People's party simultaneously presented a suggestion that increased state subsidies to day care for children under three years of age should be paid directly to all parents with children in these age groups, rather than be channelled through the childcare centres to fewer parents. No other party delegation supported this suggestion. The Socialist Left party, however, disagreed with the whole plan package and proposed a plan of its own. The Socialist Left party's objection was twofold: while the measures proposed by Labour were generally adjudged too vague to increase rapidly the number of centre places, they were still considered to be effective enough to contribute to a rapid lowering of the standard of existing centres.

Since the beginning of the 1990s, day care policies thus depict a new consensus which at the national level only excludes the two parties at the extreme – on the left the Socialists, on the right the Progress party. Yet it is only within the Christian People's party and the Centre party that day care represents a recent addition to the political agendas expressed through the party programmes. Within the Labour party, changes have mainly occurred in terms of interpretations and priorities. Only within these three parties have changes been as clear as was indicated through the Agenda of Change reported by MPs.

The general tendency among parliamentarians somewhat to overestimate the actual changes in their own party's attitudes on day care may, however, signal a 'public attention effect'. Compared with other Scandinavian countries, Norwegian publicly subsidized day care has long had a low coverage rate. The actual number of childcare centres has nevertheless increased dramatically over the past twenty years, as has public expenditure in this area. But the growth was most notable in the five years from 1975 to 1980, when the number of places in childcare centres increased by almost 50,000. It has taken the whole of the 1980s to provide the same number of new places. Still the efforts made by women within the different parties to push the issue of day care may well have been more noticed by party members the more a lack of such facilities has been publicly protested.

The possibility that this is an 'attention effect' is strengthened when we consider the changes in party profiles on parental leave reforms, the other main issue within the area of 'care-and-career politics'. During the latter part of the 1980s, in four annual budget decisions, parliament increased the paid parental leave period which is covered through national social security. These extensions were initiated by both Labour and non-socialist coalition cabinets. By the beginning of the 1990s Norwegian regulations had thus finally approached the standards set by other Scandinavian countries. By 1991, parental leave regulations provided for thirty weeks of fully compensated leave, with an additional two weeks to be taken before the birth of the child. There is no disagreement among parties about the adopted reforms. All parties in fact aim higher. Since 1975 the Socialist Left party's programmes have insisted on one year's paid leave of absence. In 1977 the Labour government realized a proportion of its promise from the 1973 programme, when parental leave was extended from twelve to eighteen weeks. This extension also paved the way for fathers' leave of absence. But from 1977 until the election year of 1985 only the Socialist Left party presented specific suggestions on the issue of parental leave. Then in 1985 all the other parties also proposed to increase the paid parental leave period. The Labour party promised an extension to thirty-two weeks during the four year period to come. All the non-socialist parties included a similar proposal of six months. By 1989 all parties increased their proposals once again, promising either a full year (the Labour party), nine months (Christian People's party and Centre party) or somewhere in between six and nine months (the Conservative party). Parental leave debates now increasingly focus on possibilities to obtain reduced working hours within the total paid leave period, as well as on the fathers' use of leave. Within the left parties this includes a discussion on whether further reforms should make fathers' leave obligatory.

In contrast to the issue of childcare centres, the party programme analysis thus shows parental leave to be an issue that developed mainly in the 1980s. Earlier party programmes largely dealt with this kind of care problem with solutions which were either free of or had very limited state costs. For example, they advocated flexible hours and part-time work opportunities, or leave of absence in the case of children's illness. While parties still vary in their parental leave reform goals – the more conservative goals predictably being stated by more conservative parties – the issue nevertheless is of little controversy between parties.

Relatively few members of parliament reported parental leave as an issue where women's participation has changed party profiles. Thus once again we are faced with a partial inconsistency between actual changes in party programmes and reported changes in party profiles. On this issue the tendency among the parliamentarians is to under-report actual changes. But parental leave has not become publicly debated to the same extent that the issue of childcare centres has. On this basis, the possibility that we are dealing with an 'attention effect' in the Agenda of Change reported by the parliamentarians seems even more likely.

Family-based care politics: the reconstruction of an old concern

The main issues belonging to the area of 'family-based care politics' are the calculation of social security benefits during periods of unpaid care work, care wages and also child benefits to families. While all these issues are formally gender-neutral, in practice they imply a new recognition that the unpaid care work performed by women is an area of state responsibility. They could thus be argued to manifest a first break with a long tradition of societal undervaluation of reproductive tasks. In the interviews with the Norwegian members of Parliament, family-based care was reported high on the Agenda of Change only within the non-socialist parties. The party programme analysis confirms that actual changes with regard to this area primarily have occurred within these parties. The concern for the traditional mother/housewife role is an old – and often stated – one within the non-socialist parties. Change is thus mainly witnessed through the inclusion of new issues which imply new public funding for care work performed within the home. Such proposals are mainly the product of the late 1970s and the decade of the 1980s.

However, change is also manifested in a (partial) redefinition of established arrangements. During the 1980s all three non-socialist parties regularly proposed increases in the monthly child benefits to mothers. This transfer has been regulated by law since 1946. The more recent proposals about increases have been initiated by the Christian People's party. The 1989 programme of this party also repeated the proposal from the parliamentary debate on the plan to promote childcare centres, that is, that an additional cash amount should be available to all parents with children under three years of age. But while child benefits traditionally have been advocated as representing state support to the family maintenance, the recent suggestion about an additional cash amount has been advocated primarily as a means of financing care for the smallest children (Bay, 1988).

From 1977 onwards both the Centre party and the Christian People's party have supported arrangements which would imply transfers also to those who care for sick or elderly relatives. Since 1977 all three non-socialist parties have supported a general proposal that the calculation of old-age benefits should also take into account the years spent performing family-based care work. These benefits are otherwise determined on the basis of labour market attachment and of wage taxations. Minimal contributors to the national pension fund also receive minimum contributions from this fund.

Suggestions on new family-based care politics are now partly incorporated also as public policies. Through a parliamentary decision in 1986 a legal obligation to present an offer of wages and assistance to family members who take care of disabled children or elderly relatives was imposed on the Norwegian municipalities. This obligation was suggested by the Centre party. It was backed by all the other major parties (Recommendation to the Odelsting no. 56 [1985–6]), but with the provision that the obligation in itself did not imply any legal right to care wages. In 1989 a ministerial report on the future financing of the national social security system (Report to the Storting no. 12 [1988–9]) suggested that calculations of old age benefits should be changed to the effect of also including periods of unpaid care work for children. This proposal was in turn adopted by parliament, again through the support of all the major parties.

This last issue, however, is the only one where the Labour party programmes show any consistent support for new family-based care politics. The party agreed to such a proposal in the programmes of both 1981 and 1989. Within this area of care politics the programme analysis reveals differences between the two left parties, too. Throughout the period 1975 to 1989 the Socialist Left party included different programme proposals all of which would strengthen the economic situation of caregivers within families. The party programme analysis largely confirms the impression first created through the interview series that family-based care represents an area of change primarily within the non-socialist parties. It shows, however, that the measures are also supported by the Socialist Left party. Furthermore, within this area, 'change' refers primarily to the inclusion of new proposals.

Yet, parliamentary decisions, particularly during the latter part of the 1980s, indicate that there might be an increasing consensus not only on 'care-and-career politics' but also on issues of family-based care. Such a twofold consensus would imply a weakening of old tensions between parties; it could possibly be regarded as a clear break with old ideologies. A twofold consensus on care politics is a vulnerable one, however. As indicated through the parliamentary interview series, it might erode if and when issues within the two different areas of such politics come to be stated opposingly, that is, in terms of either/or choices.

One such either/or choice is suggested through the new proposal from the Christian People's party that state subsidies to care for the smallest children be paid directly to the parents. In the negotiations prior to the formation of a non-socialist coalition cabinet in 1989 the Christian People's party further demonstrated how central this proposal has become to party politics on care. As part of the coalition negotiations the party pushed a proposal for NOK 1.6 billion being allocated to increased cash transfers to families with children under three years of age. Such transfers would be about as large as the total state subsidies to childcare centres. There were, however, also plans to finance the subsidies partly from reductions in the grants to centre-based day care for children under three years. The arrangement was opposed by the Labour party and the Socialist Left party. When a Labour government took over in the autumn of 1990, it immediately withdrew the proposal in favour of a new proposal of increased state subsidies to childcare centres. But support from parties to the right of Labour was needed and a final compromise was negotiated, through which both state subsidies to childcare centres *and* the monthly child benefit amount to children in the youngest age groups were raised.

Another either/or choice presents itself if or when state transfers through the paid parental leave period are compared with state transfers paid as cash amounts to mothers outside the workforce. The party programme analysis shows that in all the non-socialist parties the new proposals on paid parental leave have consistently been accompanied by a new insistence that the cash amount provided to mothers outside the workforce in connection with giving birth should also increase. Parliamentary decisions on these issues over the past two decades further demonstrate how choice situations might be constructed. In 1971 a Labour government proposed to extend the paid maternity leave from twelve to eighteen weeks, a proposal which in turn was rejected by a non-socialist majority on the grounds that women working outside the home ought not to be granted better arrangements than women working at home.

Next time around, however, in 1977, parliament chose to adopt both reform options. Women working outside the home were granted an increase in the paid maternity leave period, while other women were granted a cash transfer in connection with giving birth. Both reforms were financed over the national social security system (Sørsgård, 1990: 194). Yet in 1989, a new either/or situation was evoked. This time a non-socialist government decided to finance an increase in the cash amount for mothers outside the workforce partly through heavier taxation of the amount paid as part of maternity leave.

How party demarcation lines are maintained

Within political life women now take an active part in creating those definitions of reality on which efforts to effect changes rest. They participate in the processes of policy-making where 'problems' are continuously perceived of and given priority – and 'solutions' either selected or set aside. Parallel to women's integration into party politics new political agendas have been established. Women's inclusion is perceived as having caused changes in party attitudes on a wide range of political issues. Issues of care politics clearly dominate the Agenda of Change reported by Norwegian parliamentarians; in all parties the inclusion of care and care work concerns is thus pictured as the most influential contribution of women politicians at this point in time. Still, an analysis of changes in party profiles over the past two decades shows how old political cleavage structures might be maintained even as parties come to embrace new political agendas.

At the beginning of the 1990s it would seem that most Norwegian parties accept responsibility for helping secure women's economic independence through labour market participation. But at the same time, a traditional left–right divergence, primarily expressed as a controversy between the left parties and the Conservatives, has been maintained over new educational and employment measures. This is a divergence reflected in both the favoured level of spending and the preferred scope of regulatory and distributive measures.

From the mid-1980s onwards, a new cross-party consensus has

developed on care-and-career politics. This is most clearly expressed through the series of new parental leave reforms, but also on the recently adopted national policies to promote childcare centres. As of the present, however, both parties at the extremes – the Progress party and the Socialist Left party – have chosen not to be part of the new consensus on day care policies. At the same time, the traditional model of the family-bonded 'caring mother' clearly remains a relevant model within the non-socialist parties. There is within these parties also a new recognition that it is a matter of public concern to strengthen the economic independence of caregivers. In such acceptance of new state responsibilities the parties of the left might also join. But when political choices are constructed in such ways that different groups of women are seen to benefit from different forms of state involvement in matters of care, the traditionally divergent role models of the 'woman worker' and the 'mother housewife' still come to guide final party priorities.

The one Norwegian party that has remained clearly male-dominated, the right wing Progress party, is also the only party that continues to express through party programmes a principal viewpoint that policies to secure more economic independence for women do not belong to the field of party politics. By contrast, the parties that have the longest tradition of integration politics – on the one hand the two left parties, and on the other the Conservatives – also have the longest tradition of including means to promote women's labour market participation. The integration of women in the two centrist parties is, particularly on elite levels, most notable from the mid-1980s. At this point in time, the party programmes have similarly come to embrace policies that may promote women's labour market participation. This new support is not, however, unconditional – it still hinges on the construction of choices through political bargaining and negotiation processes.

Notes

This chapter reports from a research project on women's political impact, financed by the Norwegian Research Council for Applied Social Science, NORAS, through a three-year grant from 1988 to 1991. Marit Lorentzen and Mari Teigen have been attached to the project as research assistants; they conducted the interviews with the Norwegian parliamentarians reported in this chapter. The party programme analysis also reported has been prepared by Kåre Skollerud on a special grant from UNESCO in 1989.

1 The integrationist approach is largely a feature shared by the Nordic countries, as is apparent, for example, from the work of Haavio-Mannila et al. (1985). The organizing of specific election campaigns is, however, a peculiarly Norwegian

tradition. The first election campaign was organized in 1967. Since then campaigns have been a regular feature of Norwegian elections. Here women's organizations outside the parties have cooperated with the women's factions within the parties. Gradually the initiative has more or less been taken over by state agencies which now provide both funding and administrative resources. Lately the participation from the women's party factions has also increased at the cost of participation from the women's movement. These campaigns are otherwise extensively described in Dahlerup (1989).

2 The content of this rhetoric is further elaborated in Skjeie (1991a).

3 As the Progress party is excluded from the party programme analysis, there is correspondingly no reference to this party in the party-specific analyses of the parliamentary interviews leading up to programme analyses. In the case of the Socialist Left party the programme analysis starts with the programme of 1975, when the party was constituted.

4 Political guidelines for wage negotiations are regularly provided when Cabinet chooses involvement in 'incomes policy' cooperation, which in the Norwegian context refers to cooperation between the main labour market parties and the state. In the state sector, party political preferences may also come to guide wage negotiations through the Ministry for Labour and Administration's formal negotiator role. In the municipalities, the negotiator role on the employer side has, however, been delegated to the umbrella Association of Local Authorities and is largely left to bureaucratic control.

5 Scandinavian welfare states are otherwise seen traditionally to embed 'individualism' rather than 'familism' – in this they already 'maximize capacity for individual independence', as Borchorst (1991: 12) judges it.

6 General references to 'environmental politics', 'social and welfare politics', and 'family politics', which were presented as areas of change in all the parties, clearly remain too broad to allow for discussions in terms of favoured political means. The same goes for 'disarmament politics', which in the interview series was seen as an area of change only in the parties to the left. Furthermore, the direct relevance of, for example, 'disarmament or 'environmental protection' to gender relationships is far from obvious. The discussion carried out in the subsequent paragraphs concentrates on issues of labour market politics, on the one hand, and on issues within the two different areas of care politics on the other. The dominant issue of the area of 'body politics' is the abortion issue. This clearly is one of relevance to gender relationships, and was reported as an issue of change in most parties. It is, however, a normatively based conviction of mine that this issue should not be discussed as a political means to increase women's economic independence. As an issue of political controversy it belongs primarily to the decade of the 1970s. The abortion issue did prevent the Christian People's party from joining a conservative cabinet in 1981. In 1983, however, the party had changed its viewpoint, and together with the Centre party joined a broader non-socialist cabinet. Only within the Christian People's party does the abortion issue constitute a part of the current political agenda.

7 The question in the interview series was phrased: 'Do you find that your own party's viewpoints on political issues have changed due to women's increased participation? Which issues are these?' The question was open-ended. Specifications thus depended solely on the respondents' own perceptions. Up to three specifications by each respondent were registered. On the basis of responses, issues were submitted to a total of nine categories:

Body politics which contains both the abortion issue and support of shelters for battered women and incest victims.

Labour market politics which contains general references to this area, the Equal Status Act, references to educational and employment policies and the equal pay issue.

Care-and-career politics which contains general references to this area, childcare centres, parental leave and daily working hours.

Family-based care politics which contains general references to this area, state subsidies to families with small children, care wages and the issue of supplementary pension rights for caregivers.

Representational politics which contains general references to this area and specific issues of political representation.

Social politics which contains general reference to this area, single parent policies and general references to policies for children, youth and the elderly.

Environmental politics which also includes references to collective transportation.

Disarmament politics.

Family politics which includes general references to this area only.

A residual category includes four areas: general references to developmental aid, criminal law, regional politics and consumer politics.

8 See again Borchorst (1991), who argues that as individualism is a key characteristic of Scandinavian welfare state policies, legislation is also largely formulated on the presumption that women work. This characteristic is next explicitly tied to dominant political ideologies. With reference to recent works by Gøsta Esping-Andersen, Scandinavian individualism is seen as representing 'a peculiar fusion of liberalism and socialism', whereas familism is much more embedded in conservative ideology.

9 The parliamentary interviews evoked situations of choice; members were, for example, asked to state their own prevailing preference among the following alternatives of increased state subsidies to child care:

A A substantial increase in state subsidies to childcare centres with the aim of providing full coverage.

B A substantial increase in cash transfers directly to families with preschool children, which the parents may decide how to use.

The answers indicated that the priorities of women parliamentarians differed only marginally from those of their male party colleagues, while left–right party priorities remained basically different. These interview results are further discussed in Skjeie (1991a).

10 The Norwegian labour market has been portrayed as divided by gender to such a degree that women and men rarely compete for the same jobs. Office work, teaching and caregiving of various kinds in the public sector have been the main areas of increased employment opportunities for women (Skard and Haavio-Mannila, 1986). Fifty-three per cent of working women are currently employed in occupations that are 90–100 per cent dominated by women, 32 per cent work in occupations that are 60–90 per cent dominated by women.

11 This law-making process is extensively examined in my dissertation to the Institute of Political Science at the University of Oslo in 1982, see Skjeie (1982) and also Skjeie (1991b).

12 It should also be noted that this paragraph was originally suggested by the Conservative party, and accepted by Labour as part of the 1978 compromise between the two parties on the Equal Status Act.

13 The wage issue was one other specific issue mentioned by Conservative parliamentarians as an issue where women's participation had contributed towards changing party viewpoints. When a non-socialist government evaluated the plan of action in 1985 and also suggested a continuation plan (Report to the Storting no. 69 [1984-5]), this also included a discussion of the wage issue.

14 This concentration on cost-related factors admittedly implies that one of the major controversies from the mid-1970s to the early 1980s between the left parties and the non-socialist parties, namely the issue of whether day care centres were to have a mandatory Christian (Protestant–Lutheran) stated objective is neglected. See, for instance, the parliamentary debates on the Propositions to the Odelsting no. 23 [1974–5] or no. 75 [1981–2].

11
The Politics of Increased Women's Representation: the Swedish Case

Diane Sainsbury

In an international context, the advances of women in securing elected office in Sweden and the other Scandinavian countries during the past two decades stand out. At the beginning of the 1970s the percentage of Swedish women elected to public office at the local, regional and national levels was around 14–15 per cent. At the end of the 1980s the percentage had more than doubled, and the proportion of women in regional and national elected office was in the neighbourhood of 40 per cent.

In attempting to understand the process behind these gains, this chapter initially describes contextual factors, devoting major attention to the party system and the electoral system. It then moves on to an examination of the political mobilization of women and the dynamics between women's efforts to increase their representation and party reponses. A major argument of the chapter is that women's actions to improve their political recruitment have been as important as contextual or systemic factors in this process. In particular, the strategies women utilize and how women formulate their claims have been decisive in the politics of increasing female representation.

The context of success

Comparative research has sought to identify the crucial contextual or systemic factors which promote or hinder women's political recruitment. Among the major explanations offered by this research is the political complexion of parties. As key actors in the recruitment process, the type of political party is seen as a major determinant. Leftist parties espousing equal rights and equality are more likely to put forward female candidates, whereas centrist and rightist parties are less likely to do so (Duverger, 1955; Norris, 1987: 122–3). More recently, attention has gravitated towards changes in the party system and their implications for women. It is held that the rise of new parties can provide political opportunities for previously unrepresented or under-represented groups, resulting in a circulation of elites. Similarly, a surge in the polling strength of a particular party and electoral volatility are hypothesized to aid new entrants (Darcy and Beckwith, 1991). Lastly, the modernization of parties and their responses to electoral decline or stagnation may open fresh opportunities.

The party system
Until the late 1980s the Swedish party system seemed a model of stability, and it was frequently described as a 'frozen' party system. Since the first election with universal and equal suffrage in 1921, Sweden had basically a five-party system, consisting of the Conservatives, the Liberals, the Centre party (formerly the Agrarians), the Social Democrats and the Communists (since 1990, the Left party). Apart from minor deviations, this five-party syndrome prevailed; and no new party succeeded in being elected into parliament, the Riksdag, until the 1988 election. From the mid-1980s the system came under pressure from 'new' parties whose success in gaining office is markedly different from previous decades.

A second feature has been the importance of the socialist–non-socialist cleavage, and it is still a factor of major significance. The strength of this cleavage and the left–right axis has led observers to characterize Sweden as a close approximation of a uni-dimensional party system (Berglund and Lindström, 1980; Holmberg, 1974). The issues comprising this dimension include state intervention versus a private enterprise economy, greater equality, economic democracy, social reforms, taxation, the size and nature of the public sector, and defence. Although electoral volatility has grown over the years, the socialist–non-socialist cleavage persisted in a hesitancy among voters to switch from a socialist to a non-socialist party or vice versa. The proportion of voters switching between the two, and thus determining the political composition of the executive, ranged between 2 per cent and 6 per cent in the elections of the 1970s and 1980s (Gilljam and Holmberg, 1990: 106). Furthermore, party competition has been intense because of the narrow margin of votes between the socialist and non-socialist blocs.

A third characteristic of the Swedish party system has been the dominance of the Social Democratic party. It is the only party which has the possibility of winning a parliamentary majority, and from the 1932 to 1988 elections the Social Democrats' share of the vote varied between roughly 42 per cent and 50 per cent.

Table 11.1   *Parliamentary election results, 1970–1990 (%)*

	1970	1973	1976	1979	1982	1985	1988	1991
Left	4.8	5.3	4.8	5.6	5.6	5.4	5.8	4.5
Social Democrats	45.3	43.6	42.7	43.2	45.6	44.7	43.2	37.6
Centre	19.9	25.1	24.1	18.1	15.5	12.4	11.3	8.5
Liberals	16.2	9.4	11.1	10.6	5.9	14.2	12.2	9.1
Conservatives	11.5	14.3	15.6	20.3	23.6	21.3	18.3	21.9
Christian Democrats	1.8	1.8	1.4	1.4	1.9		2.9	7.1
Greens					1.7	1.5	5.5	3.4
New Democrats								6.7
Others	0.4	0.6	0.4	0.8	0.3	0.5	0.7	1.2
N	350	350	349	349	349	349	349	349
Turnout	88.3	90.8	91.8	90.7	91.4	89.9	86.0	86.7

Source: Från riksdag och departement, 1991, No. 29, p. 4

On only a few occasions, however, have the Social Democrats managed to win an absolute majority. Instead the Social Democrats have won a plurality of the vote, and together with the Communists, they have often held a majority of the seats in the Riksdag. The fragmentation of the non-socialist opposition into three parties and their disunity have contributed to Social Democratic dominance. Electoral competition between the non-socialist parties has been a major source of electoral volatility, and the electoral fortunes of the three parties fluctuated much more than in the case of the socialist parties in the 1970s and 1980s (Table 11.1). The Social Democrats dwarf the Communist party.

An initial sign of pressure on the five-party system was the success of new parties in local politics from the early 1970s onwards. In the 1980s and 1990s three parties have posed a challenge to the established parties at the national level. An ecology party, the Greens, founded in 1981 was the first party to enter the Riksdag in seven decades. Secondly, the increasing secularization of Swedish society was a catalyst in the formation of a religious party as early as 1964. Although successful at the local level, the Christian Democrats failed to secure parliamentary representation on their own until the 1991 election. Thirdly, a populist right-wing party, New Democracy, emerged in 1990 and succeeded in its first bid to be elected to parliament. The entry of the Greens and the Christian Democrats into parliament indicates the significance of new dimensions in party politics. None the less, the 1991 election, with the swift demise of the Greens who lost parliamentary representation, and the dramatic electoral shift to the right (Sainsbury, 1992) is best interpreted as a confirmation of the importance of the left–right axis.

Thus the major characteristics of the party system do not seem to provide an overly promising context for women's political entry. The strength of the socialist–non-socialist cleavage in party politics has generally inhibited the formation of a women's coalition on political issues across parties. The stability of the party system, as reflected in the five-party syndrome and stable voting patterns for the left parties, runs counter to the literature assigning importance to new parties and electoral volatility in providing openings for women and enhancing their electability. Only on one score does the Swedish party system fit the literature's description of positive contextual factors: the domination of left parties. Yet as we shall see, the left parties have not always had the largest proportion of women in elected office – especially in the 1970s and 1980s. On the other hand, the rightward shift in voting in the 1991 election resulted in the first major setback in women's representation in parliament since 1928.

The electoral system
The Swedish electoral system incorporates three features considered to encourage women's representation: proportional representation, large multi-member constituencies and party lists. A fourth feature which is commonly assumed to be a negative influence is that the nomination process is decentralized to the constituency organizations.

The Swedish parliament is comparatively large in relation to the size of the electorate. The Riksdag is composed of 349 MPs who represent an electorate of approximately six and a half million voters. The constituencies are also large, roughly corresponding to the provinces. As a result, the constituencies have generally had several members, offering the parties the possibility of winning more than one seat. Parliamentary reform in 1970 converted the two chamber legislature into a unicameral body. The total number of members was reduced from 384 to 350 (349 from 1976), but the number of seats per constituency increased. The introduction of deputy MPs to replace cabinet members who are also members of parliament, however, offset the impact of reducing the membership of the Riksdag. The 1970 reform also introduced a 4 per cent threshold for representation in parliament, along with a system of supplementary seats to increase proportionality. At present eleven fixed seats is the average per constituency but supplementary seats may expand the number. There is considerable variation in the size of constituencies, however. The number of fixed seats varies from two (Gotland) to thirty-two (Stockholm County).

The size of the election district has been important because of the tendency to place a man at the top of the party list. In the past the only way a woman could be elected was if the party received more than one seat in the relevant constituency. The probability of returning a woman candidate increases with the size of the constituency. The first women elected to the Riksdag were in constituency party delegations of at least two MPs, and this has been the case for the vast majority of female MPs.[1] It was not until the 1980s that women candidates started to top the party lists on a regular basis.

A party list system also facilitated women's entry through its procedures of replacing MPs who retire or die during their period in office. Rather than relying on by-elections, the next candidate on the party list replaces the MP, and frequently replacements have been women. For example, at the end of the 1960s nearly 60 per cent of all the Conservative female MPs serving since 1922 had entered parliament as replacements (Carlshamre, 1969: 190). Moreover, the number of women in the Riksdag has usually been higher at the end of a term of office compared with its beginning. The system of replacing MPs who are cabinet members boosted women's parliamentary representation by two to four seats during the Social Democratic governments of the 1980s but decreased it during the terms of the non-socialist governments formed in 1976 and 1979.

Candidate selection is exclusively controlled by the parties. Contrary to the common assumption that party list systems necessarily entail substantial centralized placement powers, the role of the Swedish national party organizations is limited to recommendations and requests. It is activists and people of influence in the constituency organizations who put together the party list. The selection procedures have been more or less the same during the years under review here. So the increase in recruitment of women as party candidates may not be explained by reform of the nomination rules.

To summarize, the main features of the electoral system are largely conducive to women's representation. None the less, the electoral system as an explanatory factor cannot account for the change in women's representation over time. Paradoxically, the process of bringing women into elected office during the 1970s and 1980s resulted in dramatic increases but in a context where the party system, candidate selection procedures and the electoral system did not undergo fundamental change.

Changing attitudes and patterns of participation among women in the 1970s and 1980s

To explain the changes in women's representation we must look to other factors – especially those related to agency and women's efforts to be elected, such as their forms of organization, claims and strategies. The gains made in the 1970s and 1980s must be seen against the backdrop of a larger mobilization of women.

In all respects, women's participation in politics increased during the past two decades. Consequently, gender imbalances in participation diminished or disappeared; and in some instances women out-participated men. Furthermore, in several cases where the imbalance persisted for the adult population as a whole, differences were negligible in the younger generations (aged forty-four and under) but prevailed in the older generations. Finally, a trend of particular interest is that in the youngest age group (sixteen to twenty-four) women out-participated men in a variety of ways – and especially in political parties.

Women's interest in politics has successively grown since 1960, while it has scarcely changed among men (Holmberg and Gilljam, 1987: 55–6). Other measures of political involvement, such as discussing politics, display a similar trend (SCB, 1988: 223). Patterns of media consumption involving political, economic and trade union news also revealed a narrowing gap between women and men, and a larger proportion of women than men report watching TV programmes dealing with social issues (see SCB, 1981: 58; SM, 1986: 96).

The growing interest in politics among women was accompanied by the emergence of differences in political opinion between the sexes, and gradually the differences came to encompass a broader range of issues. Since the 1970s women have more generally disapproved of nuclear energy and have been more pro-environment compared with men. Women have also favoured prohibition of pornography and higher prices to reduce alcohol consumption. Additional differences have centred on support of the public sector, foreign aid, assistance to immigrants, social reforms and legislation to increase women's representation. The magnitude of differences between women and men's views on energy and the European Community has remained fairly constant (Holmberg, 1991: 89; Lindahl and Nordlöf, 1989: 168), whereas the differences on several issues widened over the years (Holmberg and Gilljam., 1987: 260–76). Finally, differences in political views among young women and men have been more pronounced than in older generations (Oskarson, 1985).

Table 11.2 *Percentage differences in electoral choice of women and men, 1970–1988*

	1970	1973	1976	1979	1982	1985	1988
Left	−2	−2	0	+2	+2	+1	+1
Social Democrats	−1	+1	−2	+2	+2	+5	+3
Centre	0	0	+2	+4	0	−1	−1
Liberals	+3	+1	0	0	+2	+3	0
Conservatives	0	−1	−1	−4	−4	−7	−5
Christian Democrats	0	0	+1	+1	+1	+1	+2
Greens	—	—	—	—	+1	0	0

Percentage differences where + indicates that more women compared with men support the party.

Source: Adapted from Oskarson, 1990: 241

Women's electoral participation inched ahead of men's in the mid-1970s, and subsequently women's voting participation rate has been slightly higher than men's. As in the case of political views, the difference in voting participation between women and men has been wider among younger voters. Parallel with increased voting, new patterns of electoral choice among women emerged during the 1970s and 1980s. With the politicization of the energy issue in the mid-1970s women voted increasingly for the Centre party which opposed nuclear energy, but as seen in Table 11.2 these gains were reversed in the 1980s. Two enduring trends are, however, discernible: first, since the mid-1970s women have been less likely than men to vote for the Conservatives and, secondly, left voting (the combined support for the Social Democrats and the Left party) increased among women and declined among men in the 1980s.

Women also out-participated men in demonstrations and protest activities during the 1980s (Petersson et al., 1989: SM, 1986: 72). Similarly women have been more prone to sign petitions. These actions have frequently been taken to influence local political decisions, and by the mid-1980s earlier differences between the sexes in seeking to remedy faults and problems in the local community had nearly vanished. Differences disappeared with respect to writing letters to the editor and newspaper articles to alter local conditions (see SCB, 1981: 43, 45; SM, 1986: 68, 72).

There was also an upswing in women's membership and participation in organizations. The most impressive changes occurred in trade union membership during the two decades. In the early 1970s only around one-third of all women were union members compared with two-thirds of all men. By the mid-1980s there was no difference between the sexes in trade union membership: 85 per cent of female and male employees were union members. From the late 1970s to the mid-1980s union membership increased, but activities among members generally declined with the exception of women aged 45–64 (SCB, 1988: 221–2). During the same period membership and participation in the activities of other organizations – such as housing associations, community groups, immigrant organizations, parents' associations and pensioners' organizations – rose. Women accounted for the bulk of the increase in members in the trade unions and other organizations during the 1970s and 1980s.

Women's active engagement in the political parties

A mobilization of women also occurred in the political parties. Traditionally, women were less likely than men to join a political party, and aggregate women's party membership continued to trail behind men's in the 1970s and the 1980s. But the *proportion* of women among all party members has substantially increased since 1960. During the 1970s the *number* of women members of political parties grew, to peak between 1980 and 1985. In terms of sheer numbers the increase was most dramatic within the Social Democratic party where female membership nearly doubled from 240,000 in the 1970s to 430,000 in 1985 (Karlsson, 1990: 25); however, much of this gain was through collective affiliation rather than individual membership.

The growing numbers of women in the individual parties have different political implications, depending upon membership trends. In the 1970s, all parties increased their enrolment, but in the 1980s decline set in. The five established parties suffered a loss of members but with dissimilar outcomes in terms of female–male ratios (Table 11.3). In the Centre party, the Liberals and the Left party men have exited in larger numbers compared with women, expanding the proportion of women. For the Social Democrats and the Conservatives the period of membership growth peaked in the mid-1980s; and women seem to have deserted the two parties more than men, especially the Conservative party. Thus at the end of the decade women formed an absolute majority of the members of the Centre party, and women's membership approached parity with men's in the Liberal party. In the case of the Social Democrats, the overall female–male ratio conceals interesting constituency variations. The number of constituency or district organizations where women outnumbered men or reached near parity increased during the 1980s as did the number of district

Table 11.3 *Women as a percentage of party members and members of the party boards*

	1960		1970		1980		1989	
	Members	Board	Members	Board	Members	Board	Members	Board
Left	n.a.	n.a.	25*	11	37	29	41	49
Social Democrats	27	4	27	3	34	32	33	43
Centre	23	6	29	22	30	29	54	37
Liberals	n.a.	15	40*	15	45*	50	47	57
Conservatives	30	27	44	26	40	33	29	42

Percentages are based on full members of boards and do not include deputy members.
Percentages marked with * indicate an estimate by party.

Source: Annual Reports of the Parties

organizations where women's membership rose and men's decreased.[2]

Equally important as the changing ratio of women to men is the growing level of activity among women in the parties. A larger percentage of female members in all age groups reported active party participation during the 1970s and 1980s; and similar proportions of women and men held party office. Furthermore, in the mid-1980s young women out-participated men in the sixteen to twenty-four years age group in terms of membership, speaking at meetings, active participation and holding party office. These types of activities in the parties are extremely important since one of the main criteria in the candidate selection process is party merits – party office and active engagement in the party.

Women's activation did eventually translate into leadership positions beyond the local level but the process was slow and gains were more modest in the highest echelons. With respect to delegates at party conferences and members of the national party boards the trend has been from drastic under-representation, especially in the Social Democratic and Centre parties, towards a proportion of women corresponding to or surpassing their party membership (Table 11.3).

Women's access to top party offices – the party leadership and national executive committees – has not been as impressive. So far only two women have held the position of party leader, Karin Söder, of the Centre party briefly in the mid-1980s and Gudrun Schyman of the Left party assumed the post in 1993. Leadership positions in the Green party have been shared equally between the sexes, and accordingly a woman has been one of the two spokespersons for the party and one of the two convenors for the parliamentary party (Gaiter, 1991: ch. 3).[3] In the case of party vice-presidents (an office in the Conservative, Liberal, Centre and Left parties), women have been more successful. Since the 1970s women have been one of the vice-presidents of the Liberal (from 1967), Centre and Left parties, and since the mid-1980s this is also true for the Conservatives. Young women assumed top leadership positions in three of the party youth organizations – the Liberals, the Social Democrats and the Conservatives – when they were elected president in the 1980s.[4]

Women's membership of the national executive committee of the Social Democratic party has increased slowly. Since 1948 the president of the women's auxiliary organization has had the right to attend executive committee meetings, including the right to speak and make proposals but not the right to vote. Individual women were also deputy members, but the first time a woman was elected as a full member of the committee was at the 1975 party congress. During the 1980s two women were full members and two women were deputy members; thus women accounted for slightly less than 30 per cent of the membership of the executive committee. In the other parties, women's election as vice-president of the party has ensured their membership of the national executive committees.

Women's representation in elected office

Besides advancing their positions inside the parties, women sought to improve their share of elected office. This process has four main characteristics. The first is its 'successive' nature; the percentage of women in parliament rose steadily with the exception of the 1928 and 1991 elections. Gains were marginal from the mid-1950s to the late 1960s, bordering on stagnation, but this was followed by spectacular increases during the 1970s and 1980s.

Secondly, the overall trend has been one of parallel gains at all levels of elected office. Women's representation increased in local government as well as at regional and national levels. Equally significant, women's representation in the cabinet has lagged only slightly, and after the 1991 election it was higher than in local government and the parliament (Figure 11.1). It is also worth noting that this pattern does not conform to the 'law of increasing

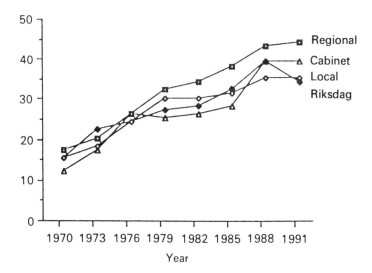

Figure 11.1 *Women in elected office, 1970–1991 (percentage)*

disproportion' which is often said to apply to women's representation. The law holds that political elites are disproportionately
drawn from high status groups but local elites mirror more closely
the social composition of the population compared with regional
and national elites. In other words, as one moves up the political
ladder, the disproportionality of high status groups increases and
the social representativeness of decision-makers diminishes
(Putnam, 1976).

Thirdly, the proportion of women MPs increased in all parties,
modifying the expected pattern of exclusion of much lower
recruitment of women in rightist and traditionalist parties (see
Eduards, 1981: 214–18). The most striking deviation is apparent in
the Centre party, formerly the Agrarians. Until 1968 the party had
only one or two women in parliament, but in the 1970s it took the
lead, surpassing the percentage of the Social Democrats. Even with
the downturn in its electoral fortunes from the late 1970s onward,
the Centre party's proportion of women MPs continued to
increase, but it was no longer the highest among the parties at the
end of the 1980s (Table 11.4). Although the Conservatives have
frequently lagged behind the other parties, their female
representation is currently about 25 per cent in parliament, 30
per cent in local councils, and 40 per cent in regional councils. As
can be observed in Table 11.4, with the exception of the Greens,
women's representation in new parties has generally been below
the average for the established parties at all levels of government.
Hence, in the Swedish setting, new parties have often offered fewer
opportunities for women to advance politically than the
established parties.

Nor has the political complexion of the government affected the
proportion of female members of the cabinet. Women's advances
have not been reversed by changes of government. The 1976 non-
socialist government increased the number of women in the
cabinet from three to five, and when the Social Democrats
returned to power in 1982 five women were included in the
cabinet. Similarly the 1991 non-socialist government appointed
eight women to the cabinet, the same number as its Social
Democratic predecessor. Women gained three of the most
prestigious posts in the cabinet – minister of foreign affairs,
minister of finance and minister of justice – along with positions as
ministers of culture and civil affairs and ministers without
portfolio in justice, education and environment.

Finally, the unprecedented increase in women's recruitment to
the Riksdag coincided with the rise of the 'new' women's movement and the mobilization of women in the 1970s and the 1980s.

Table 11.4a *Percentage of women MPs by party, 1970–1991*

	1971	1974	1977	1980	1983	1986	1989	1991
Left	17.6	21.1	23.5	25.0	20.0	15.8	38.1	31.3
Social Democrats	17.2	22.4	21.7	27.3	30.1	34.0	38.5	40.6
Centre	12.7	24.4	26.7	31.2	32.1	32.6	38.1	41.9
Liberals	8.6	14.7	20.5	23.7	14.3	39.2	43.2	33.3
Conservatives	9.8	15.7	12.7	21.9	24.4	22.4	28.8	26.3
Christian Democrats	—	—	—	—	—	—	—	30.8
Greens	—	—	—	—	—	—	45.0	—
New Democrats	—	—	—	—	—	—	—	12.0
All parties	14.0	21.1	22.9	26.4	27.2	31.0	37.5	33.0
N	49	74	80	92	95	108	131	115

Percentages for the individual parties include MPs replacing cabinet members.

Source: Allmänna valen, 1991, Del. 1

Table 11.4b *Percentage of women members of county councils, 1970–1991*

	1970	1973	1976	1979	1982	1985	1988	1991
Left	6.1	19.0	28.1	33.3	35.9	42.8	41.5	38.2
Social Democrats	15.4	18.8	24.9	31.5	34.5	37.4	42.4	42.7
Centre	17.2	23.2	28.9	35.8	33.0	37.7	44.7	43.6
Liberals	15.5	14.9	22.9	28.8	24.5	37.6	42.7	47.6
Conservatives	12.3	13.5	15.9	26.5	30.6	34.9	36.5	40.5
Christian Democrats	—	—	—	—	23.8	27.8	32.5	40.2
Greens	—	—	—	—	—	—	48.1	50.0
New Democrats	—	—	—	—	—	—	—	—
All parties	15.3	19.0	24.4	31.1	32.7	37.2	41.8	42.6

Sources: Eduards, 1981: 217; Swedish County Councils, 1989, p. 3; Federation of County Councils Press Release, 12 November 1991

Table 11.4c *Percentage of women members of local councils by party, 1970–1991*

	1971	1974	1977	1980	1983	1985	1989	1991
Left	9.3	14.2	21.9	32.2	33.2	34.6	35.2	38.3
Social Democrats	14.4	17.3	23.6	30.7	31.5	31.8	35.4	37.0
Centre	15.6	18.3	23.2	26.0	26.1	25.8	30.4	31.5
Liberals	13.8	15.7	22.6	28.2	28.6	32.8	35.9	36.4
Conservatives	12.3	17.5	23.0	28.7	28.6	29.1	30.5	31.4
Christian Democrats	8.7	7.2	9.3	12.3	15.3	16.8	19.4	29.9
Greens	—	—	—	—	38.9	41.2	46.2	41.1
New Democrats	—	—	—	—	—	—	—	20.6
Others	7.0	14.0	17.8	22.8	21.1	22.2	24.7	25.3
All parties	14.0	17.1	22.9	28.7	29.2	30.3	33.6	34.1

Sources: Eduards, 1981: 218; Kommunalt förtroendevalda, parti och kön 1980, p. 86, 1983, p. 94; National Bureau of Statistics, 1986, p. 175; Statistiska meddelanden Be 31 SM9201: 20

One of the most important effects of the new women's movement was to revitalize existing women's organizations, such as the Fredrika Bremer Association and the auxiliary organizations of the political parties. It also led to an intensification of women's activity in the party organizations themselves.

Thus, contrary to several other countries where the new women's movement initially did not seek influence in male-dominated organizations, large numbers of Swedish women activists chose to work within the parties. There were several reasons for this development. Among the most important was that specific issues closely associated with the new women's movement and important for mobilization purposes – women's equality and abortion on demand – emerged relatively early in the 1960s and were incorporated into the policy agendas of the political parties. Such responses lent credibility to perceptions that working through party channels could pay off.

Furthermore, historically, the women's party organizations both fought unrelentingly for increased political representation, and they have offered a power base for women. In a cross-national perspective, these organizations appear to have more political clout than their counterparts in other countries (for example, Dahlerup and Gulli, 1985: 21; Sainsbury, 1991). Evidence of the importance as a power base is found in the pattern of women's political careers. Women from these organizations have been recruited to high-level party positions, cabinet posts and inquiry commissions. During the first forty years or more of women's representation in parliament, active membership in the Social Democratic Women's Federation (SSKF) was a vital credential for party women's election. Currently almost all women MPs for the Centre party have entered parliament via the women's organization. Equally important, the women's organizations play a crucial role in the nomination process by virtue of their inclusion in the selectorate.

The candidate selection process

Before examining women's strategies for increasing their representation in elected office, the nomination process needs to be described in more detail since it has been a major target of women's actions. The end product of the nomination process is the party list, which often includes as many candidates as constituency seats. The party list is a 'balanced' ticket which represents the various groupings among the party's members and voters. Moreover, the major groupings are included in the selectorate. As a result, the party list mirrors the selectorate, and in fact nominees are largely drawn from the selectorate.

In the 1970s and 1980s candidate selection proceeded in three stages:

1 Putting forward of names of potential candidates.
2 The screening and ranking of nominees to produce a draft party list.
3 The adoption of the party list.

The first phase is important but the drafting of the party list is the decisive stage. The procedures for ranking candidates vary between the parties. The non-socialist parties often rely on 'party primaries' (*provval*), in which voting is limited to members as a consultative ranking device at both the local and constituency level. In the socialist parties local nomination committees and the constituency executive are the dominant influence in the ranking process (Pierre, 1986: 120–5). The five parties adopt the party lists at selection conferences which may make some modifications. For the most part, however, the conference approves the proposed list.

That the candidate selection process puts a major premium on the *political* qualifications of potential nominees may be observed in the typical route to the Swedish parliament. The standard pathway to the Riksdag is via local elected office. In the early 1980s over 80 per cent of Swedish MPs had previous office-holding experience in local and regional government. In addition, the vast majority of MPs – again around 80 per cent – held party office prior to their election. A very common pathway is a combination of a post (or posts) in local government and local party office. Furthermore, most of the MPs without local government experience entered the Riksdag as holders either of constituency or high-ranking party office.

The uniformity of the importance of political qualifications in the pathway to parliament is striking. This uniformity is reflected in the absence of major variations in the routes to the Riksdag of members of different parties even where other qualifications are present. Several Conservative MPs rank as social and professional notables, thus one might expect to find the qualification of prior office-holding in local government and the party to be of much less significance. Contrary to this expectation, the career paths of Conservatives did not deviate from the average.

Similarities rather than differences also characterized the 'apprenticeships' of female and male MPs. In comparing the pathways of women and men, we discover virtually identical

Table 11.5 *Apprenticeship positions of Swedish MPs by sex, 1982–1985*[1]

		Women		Men	
		%	N	%	N
Local office		81	87	81	216
Party activist					
Party only	31%	}			
Party and women's organization	36%	} 80	86	81	216
Women's organization only	13%	}			
Organizational activist		32	35	32	86
Organizational activist only		5	5	3	7
N			108		267

[1] Includes replacements.

Source: Riksdagen 1982–5, Biografiska uppgifter om ledamöterna

proportions of local office-holders, party activists and organizational activists (Table 11.5). One difference, of course, is that the
women's auxiliary organizations provide an additional channel of
advancement of female party activists. The extent to which this
channel has figured in the career paths of women MPs can be
observed in Table 11.5. Although relatively few were active solely
in the women's organization of the party, around half of the
women MPs had held offices in these organizations.

In conclusion, a picture of uniformity and emphasis on political
credentials evolves with respect to both party and sex. This
uniformity suggests that criteria of suitability are all-important in
the candidate selection process, and that criteria of acceptability
have been marginalized. As distinguished by Joni Lovenduski and
Pippa Norris, criteria of suitability are of a formal, technical and
objective nature, whereas criteria of acceptability tend to be
informal, ascriptive and contain a subjective element (Lovenduski
and Norris, 1991). The formalization of recruitment criteria
appears to benefit women by reducing the scope for prejudices.
The emphasis on political credentials also works to women's
advantage. Other qualifications, such as impressive academic
credentials and professional standing, put women at a disadvantage because they lack parity with men in terms of
prestigious educational and occupational backgrounds. The nature
of the selectorate also reinforces the emphasis on political
credentials.

Women's strategies: separatism and integration

In their efforts to increase female representation, women's participation in the parties has been a key vehicle for advancing their claims. A distinctive feature of women's strategy has been its dual nature – utilizing both women-based and male-dominated organizations. They have largely pursued an insider strategy, but they have been aided by outside organizations and mobilization. In particular, the Fredrika Bremer Association has acted as an external pressure group, putting forward innovative proposals and staging party hearings.

Several variants of the dual strategy are discernible. Centre party women have relied almost exclusively upon the auxiliary organization as their point of entry into politics and their springboard to positions in the main party and to elective office. Conservative women have also utilized the women's sections of the party as a base, while Liberal women have often coupled a party career with active membership in other women's organizations, such as the Fredrika Bremer Association or professional organizations. The strategy of Social Democratic women was basically the same as the Centre party women's until the 1960s when women became more active in the main party. In this way, they combined aspects of a separatist and integrative strategy. Through the auxiliary organization women could formulate independent programmes and policies and act as a pressure group to promote their demands. By working in the party they enlarged their claims to positions of influence.[5]

Women's claims: transforming women's issues into party issues

Perhaps most fundamental to bringing women into elected office in large numbers has been a major revision of women's claims. Traditionally, women's representation entailed the inclusion of women candidates on the party list but on the basis of being a 'special interest' within the party. Consequently, women tended to be included as token candidates – a single winnable place on the list for a particular constituency – and/or symbolic candidates too far down the list to be elected. Gradually women came to argue that their number in parliament should correspond to their proportion of the electorate, and that their under-representation was a contradiction of democratic principles and equal rights. Intertwined with this transformation of claims for representation was an effort to redefine women's issues as party issues. The prevailing conception that women represented an important but minority interest within the parties meant that women's issues were perceived either as a specialized but limited set of party demands or as outside the mainstream of party demands.

The process of converting women's issues into party issues is so crucial that it merits more detailed discussion. Such a documentation also furnishes insights into the workings of the dual strategy of utilizing the women's auxiliary organization and the party as adopted by Social Democratic women.

During the 1960s new patterns of women's involvement emerged in the Social Democratic party, and the Women's Federation (SSKF) experienced a weakening of its position. Nevertheless, the SSKF's actions concerning women's equality during the 1960s were indirectly crucial for the advances in women's representation in parliament. In 1960 the SSKF asked for the establishment of a working committee on women's issues within the party. Eventually a very high-powered committee was appointed with the Prime Minister as honorary chair and Inga Thorsson, president of the SSKF, as working chair. The committee completed its work in 1964 with the publication of *Women's Equality (Kvinnans jämlikhet)*, and for the first time in the party's history it adopted a women's programme. However, perhaps because it was at the initiative of the SSKF and identified with the organization, the programme received a lukewarm response within the party and had a limited impact (Karlsson, 1990: 108–9, 113–14). By contrast, the next step in the process had enormous effects; it was an all-party document, drafted by a committee headed by a woman, Alva Myrdal. The 1969 *Towards Equality* report placed equality and equality measures at the top of the political agenda, and in a more forceful way than any previous official party statement, it defined equality between the sexes as an integral part of the party's aspirations to achieve equality.

This process of making women's issues into party issues in the name of equality had two significant consequences. The integration of women's issues produced changes in the gendering of party issues. First and foremost in this context, however, it strengthened women's demands for political entry. Ironically, neither the 1964 nor the 1969 programme mentioned the issue of women's political representation. Yet once women's equality was a stated goal of the party, it could be pressed into service in efforts to improve women's representation. The other political parties also generally joined in subscribing to the goal of equality in the late 1960s and the early 1970s so that all party women could use it as leverage in their claims for representation.

Influencing nominations

In the nomination process the women's organizations of the parties have been involved in the three phases of the process in varying degrees. They have been active in the initial phase of putting forward names of potential candidates, and three factors made this task easier in the 1970s and 1980s. The general activation of women in the parties increased the pool of female eligibles. Party merits (membership, active participation and party office), as emphasized above, were the key attributes of eligibility for candidacy to local and national elective office (for their importance at the local level, see Barkfeldt et al., 1971: 119–24; Wallin et al., 1981: 79–80). In turn, the increasing proportion of women serving in local and regional government expanded the ranks of women qualified for parliamentary nomination. A second factor making the task easier was a shift in attitudes. Compared with the mid-1960s local party activists assigned higher priority to the nomination of women in the late 1970s (Jonasson, 1985: 59–60). The third factor was official party responses. As illustrations, the Liberals in 1972 adopted the recommendation that each sex should have at least 40 per cent of the seats on district or constituency boards (Eduards, 1981: 213). The same year at the Social Democratic party congress, Olof Palme emphasized equality between the sexes, and that the elimination of women's under-representation was 'a common task for the entire labour movement' (Karlsson, 1990: 158).

Besides proposing the names of candidates, women's organizations conducted frequent campaigns promoting women candidates. An additional recurring tactic to increase women's representation has been to chart deficiencies through careful investigations. A noteworthy example was a report entitled *Women in the Labour Movement (Kvinnor i arbetarrörelsen)* issued by the SSKF in 1978. It examined in detail women's recruitment in 174 local branches of the party, and concluded that most branches were passive, leaving women's recruitment and nomination up to the local branches of the SSKF. To rectify this situation, the SSKF recommended that 'if women could not be recruited and nominated through regular party channels, guarantees must be created in the form of quotas' (Karlsson, 1990: 182).

The diversification of channels of women's recruitment in the Social Democratic party is vital because a strategy based solely on the SSKF would experience severe difficulties in increasing women's representation to 40–50 per cent due to the nature of the candidate selection procedures and the composition of the labour movement. As noted earlier, the selectorate replicates itself in the nomination process, and the party list is a 'balanced ticket' representing the various components of the labour movement – the party, the unions, the youth organization, the women's organization, and in certain constituencies the Christian Social Democrats. Given the complexities of putting together a party list to accommodate all these groups, women's representation via the SSKF would be doomed to a minority position. For women to advance their positions, other channels must be used, and this has occurred since the 1968 election.

During the past two decades, the number of female candidates rose markedly in all the parties (Table 11.6). What are striking in Table 11.6 are the similarities between the percentages for 1952 and 1970 and the profound differences between those for 1970 and the 1980s when the percentage of candidates in three of the five parties corresponded to the official notion of equality between women and men: each sex should have at least 40 per cent of all positions.

Getting women on the ballot is not enough, however. It is the position of women candidates on the party list which counts – not their number or percentage. Party women and women's auxiliary organizations have therefore pushed to get more women in winning positions on the party list. One device to assure that women are nominated to winning positions on equitable terms with men has been the recommendation that every other place on the list should be allotted to the opposite sex. Only a few constituency organizations have strictly followed this procedure in recent elections. None the less, the recommendation does put pressure on the selectorate. Also essential in this process is women's increased penetration of the selectorate.

Finally, watchdog activities are important to safeguard existing gains, and the women's organizations have protested when women's representation has experienced reverses or has flagged, especially in relation to the other parties. A recent illustration followed in the wake of the 1991 election when the proportion of women in the Centre party's parliamentary delegation fell. Centre women objected, and through substitute MPs for cabinet members, women's representation increased from 32 to 42 per cent. This example is just one among many.

The next step: appointed administrative positions.

As distinct from their advances in winning elected office, women were far less successful in gaining important appointed administrative positions during the 1970s and the first half of the 1980s. A pattern of pronounced under-representation of women

Table 11.6 *Percentage of women candidates and elected women MPs by party, selected years*

	1952		1970		1982		1988	
	Candidates	MPs	Candidates	MPs	Candidates	MPs	Candidates	MPs
Left	15	20	18	18	40	20	47	38
Social Democrats	15	14	22	17	38	30	43	38
Centre	17	0	24	13	36	32	40	38
Liberals	17	14	19	9	40	14	45	43
Conservatives	18	13	22	10	33	24	35	29
Greens	—	—	—	—	44	—	48	45
All parties	17	12	21	14	36	28	41	38

Sources: Brändström, 1971: 54, 79, 108, 163; Sköld, 1958: 301, 303, 305, 307, 309; Statistiska meddelanden Be 35 SM8501, Be 34 SM8901

Table 11.7   *Percentage of women in appointed positions, selected years*

	1965	1975	1986	1991
Boards of national administrative agencies				
Director			6	10
Members	3	6	18	30
Regional boards				
Members			15	26
County boards (*länsstyrelser*)				
Members		3	13	19
Inquiry commissions				
Chair			4	13
Members, staff, experts	6	11	17	27

Source: Eduards, 1980; Ds A, 1986: 4, 34, 48; Prop. (Government bill) 1991/92: 100, Bil. (appendices) 12, 205, 209; Kommitteberättelse, 1992, 223

has existed for members of the boards of national administrative agencies and regional administrative boards as well as inquiry commissions. Recruitment to these positions is via nominations from the parties, interest organizations and the state bureaucracy. Thus, in Sweden it seems to have been easier to be elected than to be appointed to office which contrasts with the experiences of several other countries. For example, where the upper house of the national legislature is by appointment rather than election, the percentage of women is often higher than in the lower house.

In the mid-1980s, only 18 per cent of the regular board members of the national administrative agencies were women. The corresponding percentage for regional administrative boards was 15 per cent, and for inquiry commissions 17 per cent. The proportion of women further diminishes in the case of positions as the head of national agencies (6 per cent), regional boards (12 per cent) and inquiry commissions (4 per cent) (Ds A, 1986: 4; Eduards, 1980; SCB, 1986). None the less, the above percentages represent increases compared with ten years earlier (Table 11.7).

Because of the low figures, the slow rate of progress and the discrepancy between women's representation in elected and appointed positions, an inquiry commission was established in 1985 to consider the problem. The first phase of its work was the production of a detailed inventory of women and men in appointed positions and the channels of recruitment in an effort to identify the obstacles to women's appointment. The study revealed substantial variations in nominating women. The parties accounted for the highest percentages, whereas the state bureaucracy and interest organizations lagged behind. In particular, the Confederation of Trade Unions (LO) and the Employers' Association (SAF), were much less likely to put forward female nominees. In identifying the obstacles to women's recruitment, the commission focused on the number of women in the nominating bodies and among the potential nominees, along with the criteria for appointment (Ds A, 1986: 4; SOU, 1987: 19).

The final report of the commission, *Every Other Seat for a Woman*, formulated specific goals for the future. The report recommended that women's representation should reach 30 per cent by 1 July 1992 and 40 per cent by 1995 culminating in full parity at the end of ten years. To monitor changes, the commission proposed that annual reports on women's representation in these positions be presented to parliament. The tactics behind the annual reports was to make the recruitment process more visible. To alter recruitment, the commission recommended earmarking grants for projects to increase women's representation (cf. Eduards, 1991).

The commission also advocated an open discussion and evaluation of the criteria for appointment. Using Lovenduski and Norris's terminology, a chief complaint of the commission was that appointments were currently based on criteria of acceptability, which should be replaced by a clearer specification of the criteria of suitability. Although competence was cited as the main criterion for appointment, interviewed officials noted the importance of informal criteria, such as seniority or long service, belonging to a particular vested interest or faction, and high status. At the same time, the commission argued that competence was defined unclearly, in too narrow terms, or variously.

The most radical proposal of the commission called for the legislation of quotas if its goals were not met. On the basis of the positive experiences of quotas in the other Nordic countries, the commission argued that legislated quotas were the only sure way to achieve results. In Norway and Denmark, the percentage of women in appointed positions was around 30 per cent, which was nearly double the Swedish percentage. Both the commission and the minister presenting the government bill noted the existence of solid opposition to legislated quotas and assurances that women's nominations would increase with time. Because of the assurances of improvement, the minister declared, she and the commission had decided to rely on the word of the nominating bodies and postpone the introduction of quotas. In effect, this put the onus on the parties and organizations to increase women's nominations voluntarily. The final report did, however, outline a proposal for the legislation of quotas.

An equally important result of the commission were changes in the government's routines for appointments to administrative boards. The first change was a stricter application of a rule adopted in 1981 that the nominating bodies propose two candidates – one of each sex. The relevant ministry was made responsible for requiring an explanation of any deviations from the rule. A second change was to give priority to the under-represented sex when making appointments. Thirdly, joint consideration of appointments by the relevant ministry, the ministry of labour (responsible for equality between the sexes) and the ministry of civil affairs (in charge of personnel policy in the state administration) was introduced.

The annual statements to parliament allow us to trace developments since the commission report and the government bill. As can be observed in Table 11.7, women's representation on the boards of the national administrative agencies in 1991 had already reached the 1992 goal, and for the regional boards and inquiry commissions it was three or four percentage points from the goal. One of the most notable changes was that the percentage of female nominations for regional administrative positions by union organizations increased dramatically, outstripping that of the parties in 1991. The record of the various parties in this case was mixed. Compared with the mid-1980s the proportion of women nominated by the Conservatives and the Centre party actually declined slightly, while it increased for the other parties.

In summary, it needs to be stressed that these advances are an example of women using acquired positions of power to further the goal of equality between the sexes. In other words, this policy is the result of the political recruitment of women. The minister appointing the commission and drafting the government bill, along with the staff of the commission, were all women. Furthermore, we see a reassertion of certain features of women's strategies to gain elected office: first, a detailed investigation charting women's under-representation and focusing on the routes of recruitment, and secondly, the threat of formal quotas. What distinguished women's strategy in this instance was the formulation of explicit goals and a time-table for their achievement.

Conclusions

Two broad sets of conclusions can be drawn from this study. The

Swedish case enables us to question a number of assumptions in the literature on women's political recruitment. Secondly, it raises issues of practical importance to advocates of gender equality in party politics and political representation.

The Swedish case challenges several assumptions as to what factors and conditions determine women's political representation. Electoral volatility and dramatic shifts in the political fortunes of parties are assumed to enhance women's chances of election. Yet from a cross-national perspective the Swedish party system has been an example of stability, especially in the 1970s, when women's representation doubled. Corollary assumptions hold that women are favoured as parties expand and conversely disadvantaged as parties decline. Although supporting instances can be found, the broad trends tend to contradict these assumptions. Centre party women did profit from intensifying their demands for political entry at a time when the party was expanding, but women's representation retained its high level even as the party experienced electoral decline (Table 11.4). The Conservatives' expansion has resulted in rather modest gains for women; their female parliamentary representation has frequently lagged behind the other established parties, and it has been consistently below the average for all parties despite increasing polling strength. Finally, with the exception of a single major victory in 1982, the electoral support of the Social Democrats has generally waned since 1968, but women's representation in the Riksdag has increased from 17 per cent of party deputies in 1970 to 41 per cent in 1991. For four of the established parties it makes more sense to interpret their efforts to incorporate women as attempts to modernize and as responses to electoral stagnation and decline.

The rise of new parties, with the exception of the Greens, has not especially promoted women's electability. In fact, the ascendancy of New Democracy in the 1991 election has been to the detriment of women's representation in parliament. Only 12 per cent of the party's MPs were women. Furthermore, the fragmentation of the party system may work against women's representation to the extent that men continue to top the party lists. An increasing number of parties heightens the likelihood of parties winning only one seat per constituency.

The type of party has had only marginal importance for women's representation during the 1970s and 1980s – the period of major advances. Only in the 1970 election did female parliamentary representation conform to the hypothesis of left parties favouring women's election, and the subsequent tendency is towards convergence. Perhaps what is important is not the type of individual party for electing women but the dominance of left parties. The hegemonic position of the Social Democratic party, especially at the end of the 1960s, led to adaptations by the other parties and efforts to outbid the Social Democrats as the champions of equality. The dynamics of party competition also strengthened the trend towards convergence. During the 1970s competition between the two blocs increased, resulting in a razor-thin difference between them. In the 1973 election the difference was an infinitesimal 0.1 per cent and in 1979 a mere 0.2 per cent (Holmberg, 1981: 26). In this situation the parties could not afford to offend any major segment of the electorate. Keen competition also made it possible to exploit the gains made by women in other parties, holding them up for comparison in their own party.

Many descriptions of party list systems assume nominations are centralized, and that such a centralization favours women. This is not the case in Sweden where women's gains can only be explained by a mobilization from below at the local and constituency levels. Constituency variations in electing women to parliament make it clear that national party recommendations do go unheeded. Constituency variations also suggest that the nomination process is central to women's success or failure. Differences among constituencies in the pools of female eligibles cannot account for the variations.

A central theme of this chapter has been the importance of introducing agency and strategies into the analysis of women's increased political representation. In addressing the practical issues of bringing women into elected office, four features of women's strategies seem decisive and deserve comment.

First, the logic of women's strategy has been primarily to seek change inside the parties. Within each party, women have worked to secure elected office, but largely independent of women in other parties and frequently in competition. At times, however, party women have joined forces to press for women's representation, and this is one of the few issues where cooperation across party lines has been possible.

Secondly women have utilized both separate organizations and male-dominated arenas for advancing their claims. This dual strategy combines the advantages of both separatism and integration. An integrative strategy entails seeking to gain positions of influence within the party and government to shape official policy. Its main advantage is the greater potential for political influence; the cost, however, may be a dilution of women's demands. A separatist strategy via women-based organizations provides the possibility of acting as a pressure group, formulating independent policy positions and applying a feminist critique to party policies. A dual strategy is imperative to the achievement of women's representation because a separatist strategy can easily lead to minority representation.

Thirdly, one of the crucial aspects of the process was converting women's issues into party issues. Feminist critics have emphasized the 'damned if you do, damned if don't' syndrome which disadvantages women irrespective of whether they operate in male-dominated arenas or separate organizations. These critics point out that 'universal' interests are often defined in exclusively or primarily male terms, whereas women's interests are specified as special, thus setting them apart and divesting them of the legitimacy of things universal. This distinction leads to a vicious circle because if women work for 'universal' interests they may deny their own interests as women, but if they work for women's interests they are demoted in status. By making women's issues into party issues, it may be possible to break the circle.

Lastly, it is worth noting that the increases in women's representation have been achieved without imposing formal quotas. Instead women have relied on recommendations and argumentation, recurring analyses of the current situation to determine progress or lack of progress, and threats to work for quotas if their representation failed to improve. The main recommendation adopted or acknowledged by the parties has been the goal that each sex should have representation amounting to at least 40 per cent. This goal has served as a recommended guideline for all levels of party and elected office, and the parties have made substantial headway in reaching this goal during the past two decades.

Notes

I would like to thank Maud Eduards for her critical and helpful comments.

1 However, the first exception to this rule occurred as early as 1944. Of the candidates elected in 1982 fifteen were women who headed the party list, and in the 1991 election the number had risen to forty-four.

2 For example in Stockholm County women members are more numerous than men, and in the largest district organization in southern Sweden women's membership increased and men's declined.

3 The Greens' losses in the 1991 elections have led to a major reconsideration concerning the organization of the party's leadership, which may result in changes along the lines of the organizational structure of the established parties.

4 The Liberals' youth organization has a stronger tradition of electing women to key positions. In the mid-1940s the first woman headed the organization, and the second was elected in the 1970s.

5 Women in the Left party, lacking a separate organization, have operated mainly within the party. For a more detailed discussion of the Social Democratic and Centre party women's strategies, see Sainsbury, 1991.

12

Party Decline, Party Transformation and Gender Politics: the USA

Barbara C. Burrell

Political parties in the United States of America are distinctive organizations compared with party organizations in other western democracies. Two factors in particular drive this distinctiveness and are important in considering the relationship between party politics and gender, namely the candidate nomination process and the federal nature of party organizations.

American political parties are comparatively weak organizational institutions. They have no mechanism for formally controlling who their nominees for public office will be. The system of primary elections has removed the candidate selection process from the party organization and made it a governmental function. Registered voters not just formal party members (except in a few caucus systems in a few states) elect party nominees. In some states with no party registration whatsoever and a completely open primary system, anonymous individuals can even vote for a candidate of one party to be the nominee for one office and choose from candidates of another party to be a nominee for another office in the privacy of the voting booth. This is the case in the state of Wisconsin. In other states, such as Louisiana, there is more-or-less no such thing as major party nominees to the national legislature. Candidates run in a non-partisan primary election with a runoff election of the top two candidates if no candidate gets 50 per cent of the vote. Thus in the 'general election' it is possible for two Democrats or two Republicans to be the opponents.

In the comparative parties' literature the term 'selectorate' refers to 'party members involved at some stage in the nomination, shortlisting and selection of prospective candidates'. Norris et al. (1989) describe party selectorates in Australia, Britain and Canada as functioning as gatekeepers to legislative elites through their choices of prospective party candidates. No such gatekeepers exist in the United States. Here the talk is of self-nomination and candidate-centred campaigns. A 'party selectorate' here is a virtually meaningless term. Primary elections mean that parties do not control their own nominations, and in contemporary politics, candidates often recruit themselves or are encouraged to run by other groups.

Secondly, American parties' texts describe the local, state and national parties as three separate organizational entities within a federal system of government. The organizational strength of the parties also varies from state to state and the cultures of the parties differ regionally as well as internally (Freeman, 1986). Traditionally the national parties were characterized as 'committees without power'. Power, if it resided anywhere in the parties, lay within largely autonomous local party organizations. A few state organizations, too, were known for being strong units, such as in Connecticut under the tutelage of John Bailey. In recent years, the national offices have acquired more resources while the local units seem to have atrophied. Thus, we cannot talk about one party structure affecting women as organizational members or as candidates for public office when we attempt to characterize the role of US parties in gender politics.

Rule and Norris (1992) describe the difference between the situation in the United States and that in countries with the parliamentary system of government.

> Responding to women's groups, several parties in the parliamentary countries have adopted effective plans to nominate and support more women for winnable parliamentary seats. In contrast, America's division of government among the president, the congress, and the states has resulted in fragmented political recruitment groups, organized around particular offices. Consequently there are no unified national party organizations in the US to require and support local parties' recruitment of women to Congress.

As we describe and seek to understand the relationship between party politics and gender in the United States we have to account for the lack of a selectorate in a traditional comparative literature sense, and for the diversity of party organizational presence and strength at different levels of the party structure and in different areas of the country. In addition, we must consider the implications of the changing nature of party life in the contemporary era.

Contemporary US parties' literature affirms the declining status of parties in the political life of the United States. The electorate has come to rely less on party affiliation for cues in voting. They have become more independent in their political attitudes and increasingly vote-split tickets, choosing candidates from different parties for different offices. Local organizations have atrophied with the lessening of patronage politics and candidates relying more on the media to communicate with the voters. But some scholars argue that the case for party organizational atrophy, even at the local level, has been overstated. Eldersveld argued that local party organizations are active, combative, adaptive and linked to electoral success (1982: 17–18). The work of Cotter and associates (1984) has shown increasingly organizationally secure state party committees, and Joseph Schlesinger (1991) believes that greater independence on the part of the electorate has been an opportunity for party organizational growth and competition nationally.

This chapter reflects on the implications of party decline and party transformation for the candidacies of women for public office. Its focus is on the role of political party organizations in effecting women's quests for national office. In this study women as voters and women within the party organizations serve as independent factors influencing party action regarding the recruitment of women to candidacy and participation in their campaigns. The connection between the themes of party decline and party change and women's candidacies for public office is the thread that runs through this investigation. The account is necessarily more qualitative than quantitative because of the inability to capture the parties as a singular structure controlling the nomination and campaign process.

Party opposition to women's candidacies

A priority of the contemporary women's movement in the United States has been to elect more women to public office. Women's rights activists have viewed party organizations as obstacles to the achievement of that goal. They have been considered bastions of male domination closed to women. At the end of the 1986 elections, a Women's Campaign Fund spokesperson complained that women in state-wide races were unable to enlist the full support of the party to the extent enjoyed by male candidates of equal calibre, and that 'the old boys couldn't stand these women getting so close to the nominations for governorships'.

Examples of local party opposition to women's candidacies for top elective positions still exist. This is evidenced by the experiences of Harriet Woods in 1982, when she announced her candidacy for the US Senate from Missouri, and of Betty Tamposi in 1988, who sought the Republican nomination for US Congress in New Hampshire's second district. Woods has remarked that when she entered the Missouri Democratic primary, the state Democratic leaders rejected her because she 'was too liberal, too urban, and even worse, a woman' (Abzug, 1984). Tamposi was publicly scolded by her state's US Senator Gordon Humphrey to stay home with her children. According to Senator Humphrey, 'there is no way a mother of a two-year-old child can serve her constituents' (Kiernan, 1988). Betty Tamposi lost that primary, even though Senator Humphrey was forced to apologize.

The negative influence of party organizational activities on women's candidacies has been a theme in much of the women and politics literature, too. (See, for example, Tolchin and Tolchin, 1976.) The parties have even been viewed as more of an obstacle to women's achieving elective office than the opposition of voters. In 1976, Darcy and Schramm examined voter response to women candidates in elections for the US House of Representatives for 1970 through 1974. They found the electorate indifferent to the sex of congressional candidates at the general election stage – that is, female candidates did as well as male candidates in similar situations. They concluded that the reason why so few women were serving in Congress was due to the recruitment and nomination process; it was noted that 'the districts in which the nomination process manages to draw women are still the few, atypical, largely Democratic urban districts'. This conclusion was, however, only an assertion, not the result of an empirical analysis of the nomination process.

It has long been argued that women receive a party's nomination primarily in situations where the party has little hope of winning the contest. Former Connecticut state party and Democratic National Committee chair John Bailey is noted for his comment that 'the only time to run a woman is when things look so bad that your only chance is to do something dramatic'. Gertzog and Simard (1981) tested the idea that women candidates receive party backing disproportionately for congressional seats in districts dominated by the opposition party. Analysing the nomination patterns for the US House of Representatives between 1916 and 1978, they concluded that 'women have been nominated for hopeless contests more often than men'. But they also speculated that with increasing numbers of women running for public office the numbers in the hopeless category should decline. However, such a trend has run up against a shrinking opportunity structure for newcomers seeking a seat in the House. Incumbents have become increasingly advantaged, making more and more election contests hopeless for challengers, both male and female. For example, 'hopelessness' marked the candidacies of an incredible 91 per cent of non-incumbent women nominated for the US House in 1984. But 86 per cent of the male non-incumbent candidates also faced incumbents. Few political opportunities existed in that election for newcomers of either sex (Burrell, 1988). The situation did not change in elections through 1990. Further, if parties no longer control the nomination process, they can hardly be responsible for failing to stand women for national office; although informal practices in some locales may still hinder women's opportunities. Women did better in 1992 when redistricting created more districts without an incumbent, and many more incumbents retired than in the recent past.[1]

Party decline: a positive or negative factor for women candidates?

If parties have declined, then they should no longer serve as barriers to women's candidacies. Male and female candidates would organize their own campaigns and depend upon their own resources to win elections. Thus, it would be fairly meaningless to talk about party organizations as negative gatekeepers blocking women's rise to power in the contemporary era. If party organizations traditionally tended to pose an obstacle to women's recruitment, their lessened influence should have favourable consequences for women candidates. But a number of authors have suggested that the decline of parties has adversely affected women's political opportunities. From a cross-national perspective, Matthews (1984) found that weak political parties, the entrepreneurial style of primary nominations, and candidate-orientated election campaigns seemed 'to discriminate against women politicians . . . In countries with stronger parties, nominations controlled by established party leaders and proportional representation elections, women have a somewhat easier time of it.'

Raisa Deber (1982) made a similar point in her study of female congressional candidates in Pennsylvania. The few women who 'won office were those who did receive organizational backing from a major party organization or from another strong faction'. She concluded 'to the extent that party loyalty can elect candidates who are "different", "reform" can act to remove the one force that has elevated outsiders'. Bledsoe and Herring, too, argued that strengthened political parties would increase political opportunities for women (1990: 221).

Robert Bernstein (1986) found a decline in the percentage of women who won open seat races for the US House of Representatives in the 1970s compared with the 1960s. He believed that the breakdown in party control accounted at least in part for this decline. The demise of party organizations made it increasingly possible for ambitious candidates to compete for congressional nominations. Contests for open-seat nominations pitted 'young men in a hurry' against women without that kind of drive. Consequently, Bernstein hypothesized that women have become less competitive in open seat primaries and presented data to support this idea. Commenting on Bernstein's work, Darcy et al. (1987) suggested that primaries 'may actually work· against behind-the-scenes party efforts to recruit women congressional candidates for desirable races'.

My own research, however, refutes Bernstein's thesis that open seat primaries explain the low presence of women in the US House of Representatives. Women's success rate in open seat primaries may indeed have declined in the 1970s relative to an earlier era. But the number of women candidates greatly expanded during this time, and women candidates' success compared favourably with that of male candidates, especially if we carry the analysis through the elections of the 1980s. Also, female open seat primary election contenders have *not* been substantially older than their male counterparts (Burrell, 1992). It is possible, however, that a stronger party organizational system in the contemporary era would have facilitated women's candidacies. The major problem was the dearth of women candidates, not the performance of those who ran.

Party transformation and women's candidacies

National party organizations responded much more favourably to women's candidacies in the 1980s than in previous years. A number of factors account for this transformation: changes in party leadership personnel, political response to the 'gender gap' in voting behaviour, and women organizing on behalf of women within the parties.

Women as party activists
A useful place to begin a reflection on the relationship between party change and gender in the United States political system is with the presidential nomination of 1972. The importance of that year lies in the Democratic party's adoption of the reforms recommended by the McGovern–Fraser Commission for the 1972 presidential nomination. The Commission's Guidelines A-1 and A-2 required each state's delegation to the national convention to include representation of minority groups, women and young

persons 'in reasonable relationship to their presence in the population of the state' (Ranney, 1976). Its significance for women's role in party politics cannot be understated. As Jennings has shown, 'beginning in 1972 and continuing for the next four conventions, women far exceeded their earlier presence' as national convention delegates (1990: 224). The average percentage of female delegates between 1948 and 1968 was 15 per cent and 13 per cent respectively for Republicans and Democrats. In 1972, the percentage of female Democratic delegates jumped to 40 per cent, and women comprised 30 per cent of the Republican delegates. In 1978, the Democratic party wrote equal representation of women and men as national convention delegates into its rules.

The party rules were not adopted without a great deal of acrimony, however, and they have been blamed for the inability of the Democratic party to mount successful presidential campaigns in the years since then. Also, significant numbers of women who have managed to enter the ranks of party elites still view men within their party as negative gatekeepers. The University of Michigan's Center for Political Studies in a series of surveys asked delegates to the Republican and Democratic national conventions from 1972 through 1984 to respond to the statement 'most men in the party organization try to keep women out of leadership roles'. Women were far more likely than men to agree that men do try to exclude women. Moreover, the gap was fully as large among Democrats in 1984 as it was in 1972 and was still substantial even among the 1984 Republicans. But over time, the trends were in the direction of more positive perceptions (Jennings, 1990: 240).

Writing in 1984, Mary Lou Kendrigan described the most common role of women in the political party organizations as 'that of the volunteer who pours coffee, rings door bells, licks envelopes, "mans" booths, and takes care of many of the other petty details that need to be done . . . As within the traditional family, women are quite visible and very unequal' (p. 27). But this description ignored the fact that women won the convention delegate battle in the Democratic party (Crotty, 1983; Shafer, 1983), and it did not consider the effect of party transformation on women's roles inside the parties. It accepted the traditional stereotype.

Party change has included a change in the status of women within the party organizations. Women have become both 'insiders' and leaders. Of course, they may have become leaders of organizations with little life or influence in the electoral process, *or* they may have been catalysts in the revival of the parties. The role of gender has not been explored in the transformational process of

the parties. It may be that the 'good old boys' are being replaced
by women who are often feminists. Baer has recently suggested
that 'an entire area of political science *central* to the political
influence of women – political parties – has been both ignored and
misunderstood' (1990). She also argues that the growth in women's
presence and an increase in women's influence has 'coincided with
an increase in power of the national parties'.

Observers have described a 'backstage revolution' in the parties
and in campaigning in general in which 'a new breed of women
political professionals' have developed an expertise in the practical
day-to-day details of politics (Glenney, 1982; Romney and
Harrison, 1988). Republican women and Democratic women have
taken different routes to power. Men at the Republican National
Committee have been credited with bringing women in and
nurturing them to become campaign professionals. Within the
Democratic party, Romney and Harrison describe a process where
women have achieved influence by taking advantage of the interest
group- or constituency-based nature of the Democratic party.
There, women gained expertise through their involvement in
women's and feminist organizations and then moved into
campaign positions within the party (1988: 206).

Feminists obtained positions of leadership in the national party
organizations at the same time that national party organizations
expanded their resources and role in federal and state level
campaigning. Ann Lewis, political director of the Democratic
party in the early 1980s, is a major example. Mary Louise Smith,
who served as chair of the Republican National Committee during
the Ford administration, had been a founding member of the Iowa
Women's Political Caucus. These individuals in party leadership
were positioned to use the allocation of party resources to recruit
women candidates and to assist in their campaigns.

By 1982, according to *Campaigns and Elections*, a woman was
directing the Republican National Committee's field division with
three female political directors working under her and two female
regional finance directors. The Democrats had two women in top
executive slots – Lynn Cutler and Polly Baca Barragan – while
Ann Lewis, noted above, headed the political staff. Women were
the directors of campaign services, polling and finance and a
woman served as counsel to the DNC. Women were also in top
positions in the congressional campaign committees. Especially
notable was Nancy Sinnott the youngest and first female executive
director of the National Republican Congressional Committee. By
1986, women were managing sixteen of the US senatorial
campaigns. In 1988, Susan Estrich became the first woman to

manage a presidential campaign, although not in the most positive of circumstances. These activists hardly confirm the image of women in the parties as the lickers, the stickers and the pourers of coffee.

Women also emerged as leaders at state and local levels. In 1991, five of the Democratic and seven of the Republican state party chairs were women.[2] Women were executive directors of the Democratic party in seventeen states, and the Republicans had eight female executive directors. Massachusetts provides an example of the difference female presence can make at the state party leadership level. The Massachusetts Democratic party's female executive director played an instrumental role in the establishment of the Women's Impact Network (WIN) in 1988. Realizing that the party organization could not favour female candidates, especially in primary contests (of crucial importance in that one-party dominated state at that time), she developed a network dedicated to raising money for progressive Democratic women candidates outside the formal party structure. Also noteworthy was the response of Betsy Toole, New York state's Democratic party vice-chairwoman, when Barber Conable announced his retirement in 1984 as US representative from the 30th Congressional district. She said, 'Women – that's what went through my mind when I first heard Conable's seat was vacant. The right woman could win in this district, you know' (Fowler and McClure, 1989). Indeed, a woman won the seat in 1986.

Whereas no woman had by mid-1992 made it to the top levels of the party or committee system in the US Congress, nor to the ranks of the inner cabinet in the White House, let alone been elected to the presidency or vice-presidency, at least an occasional woman has cracked the 'glass ceiling' within the party structures. Women have directed congressional campaign committees and both parties have had a woman as the head of their national committee (albeit only for short periods) in the 1970s. Women have served as spokespersons for their party.

But what about the strategic top levels of the parties and their presidential campaign committees? Does the presence of women continue to be the exception rather than the rule? Although it has been cracked, does a 'glass ceiling' generally still describe the situation for women within the parties? In 1987, Ann Lewis described 'presidential campaigns [as] still the last locker room in American politics'. *The Boston Globe* characterized women's role in the upcoming 1988 presidential campaign as being 'so thin, and their influence so spotty, that they will have almost no power to shape issues or call the shots in campaigns' (Alters, 1987). Yet one year later, Ellen Goodman tagged women at the 1988 Democratic convention as '"the new insiders" . . . Women are no longer a special interest group in Atlanta. Nor are they outsiders agitating for a place at the table. They are simply players . . . in the inner circles of campaigns and conventions' (Goodman, 1988).

Thus, the issue of the influence and presence of women at the top remains unsettled. In 1992, Anna Quindlen in a *New York Times* editorial, criticized both President Bush and Governor Clinton for not having women in their inner circles. She described Clinton's closest advisers as the 'standard issue white guys'. While this is true, women were prominently placed in the Clinton campaign, including his former chief of staff Betsy Wright, and his political director and his press secretary. Women were very visible in the top levels of the Republican National Committee, although invisible among the Bush team with the exception of campaign director Mary Matalin.

The gender gap

Although present in earlier elections, the gender gap became a political phenomenon in the aftermath of the 1980 election. The term refers to differences in men's and women's voting patterns, and to sex differences in political attitudes. In that election men favoured Ronald Reagan by a large margin (20 points), while women were more evenly divided between Reagan and Jimmy Carter. Nine per cent fewer women than men voted for Ronald Reagan. The 1980 election was also the first time that women voted at higher rates than men (59.4 vs 59.1 per cent) (Kenski, 1988). Even in the landslide of 1984, exit polls showed that while 62–64 per cent of men voted for President Reagan, only 54–56 per cent of women did. By the early stages of the 1988 election, women were perceived by the media as commanding the balance of power (Matlack, 1987), and having 'power at the ballot box' (Alters, 1987).

Sex differences in voting in the 1980s were not restricted to presidential elections, either. Heiderpriem and Lake (1987) report that 'in 1982, [the] presidential phenomenon spread to congressional races. In apparent reaction to the Reagan recession, the pro-Democratic [gender] gap was particularly pronounced in open and in incumbent Republican seats'. In 1984 and 1986, exit poll data showed twenty-eight states where women voted differently than men in top state-wide election contests and fourteen states in which women's votes were the margin of victory (Women's Agenda Conference, 1988: 5).

In a phenomenon described as 'the feminization of the

Democratic party', the *National Journal* showed a trend which led by 1982 to a 26 point gap between Democratic and Republican party affiliation of women, but only a 13 point male differential (Kirschten, 1984: 1083). The gap between young men and women in party affiliation was especially notable in the 1984 campaign. Young men in that year were much more Republican than young women (Keeter, 1985: 104). The gap continues. Asked in November of 1991 which party would be best able to handle the problem they considered to be most important facing the nation, 38 per cent of the men but only 25 per cent of the women cited the Republican party. But in 1988, Dukakis squandered an early advantage he had among women, and the inability of the Democratic party to be effective in presidential elections resulted in campaigners turning attention from the advantage the Democratic party seemingly had developed among women to a focus on the problem the party has with men.

The significance of the gender gap in voting behaviour for our purposes is its effect on the activities of the parties. Just as they responded to the threat of a women's voting bloc and the creation of a women's party after the passage of the 19th Amendment granting women the franchise in 1920, the parties reacted between 1980 and 1984 to the gender gap. In 1983, for example, both parties held women leadership conferences. The leaders of both parties agreed the gender gap stimulated these meetings (Klemesrud, 1983). The response was especially noticeable in the Republican party which had been hurt by the gender gap. In anticipation of the 1984 election the Reagan–Bush campaign committee, according to the *National Journal*, acted vigorously to involve women in party affairs. Margaret Tutwiler was named the liaison between the White House and the various Republican political arms and campaign committees. 'In that capacity, Tutwiler . . . crashed the top-level strategy meetings of the Reagan White House' (Kirschten, 1984: 1084). Sonia Landau was made chair of 'Women for Reagan–Bush'. Women became respectively national co-chair, campaign treasurer, director of voter registration and a regional director. Jo Freeman describes the attention paid to women by the Republican party convention apparatus in 1984.

Republican women were cajoled into running for delegate spots and men discouraged by top party leaders, including the President. . . . party leaders had to exert steady pressure to persuade men originally selected as delegates to step aside for the 'envelope stuffers and precinct walkers'. One-third of the major speakers were women, and for the first time the Republican convention had a large booth in the press area solely to provide information on women. The Republican Women

Information Services also set up interviews and sponsored or advertised receptions, luncheons, and breakfasts aimed at women. (1987: 232)

And, as we will see in the next section, the Republican party found it to their advantage to promote women's candidacies. They began in 1983 to search for female Senate candidates in part to counter Democratic stress on the 'gender gap' (Muscatine, 1984).

Party activities on behalf of women candidates
As early as 1974, the Democratic party had sponsored a Campaign Conference for Democratic Women aimed at stimulating the election of more women to political office (Scott, 1974). Similar conferences did not occur within the Republican party until a decade later. This is not to say, however, that the Republican party has necessarily been less receptive to female candidacies. Indeed, Eleanor Smeal, former chair of the National Organization for Women has credited the Republican party with acting more affirmatively than the Democrats in supporting women's candidacies (Freeman, 1989). Women in the Republican party have tended to credit men for bringing them into the organization (Romney and Harrison, 1988). But the Democratic party has appeared to be the place where the action was early on, primarily because of its different culture (Freeman, 1987).

Feminists have become an accepted organized group within the Democratic party and therefore been able to impose themselves on the leadership, in addition to having a sympathetic ear within the liberal wing of the party. The fact that nearly all of the female members of the US House of Representatives in the 1970s were Democrats reflects this organizational basis of representation within the party. A number of these women won their seats not because they were championed within their local party organizations, but because they challenged the local party structure and beat it.

Moreover, research has found differences between the two major parties in their receptivity to women's candidacies. However, this pattern is not consistent over time and across office levels. Rule's 1974 study singled out Democratic party dominance as a barrier to women's recruitment to state legislative office even while controlling for southern states. In the same period, however, almost all of the women in Congress were Democrats (Rule, 1981). Both patterns have changed in the past decade and a half. Nechemias reported that 'by 1984 . . . outside of the South the Democratic party no longer operates as a constraint on women's access to state houses' (1987).

The number of female major party nominees for the US House of Representatives doubled between 1972 and 1984 (from 32 to 65). Since then it has levelled off (see Table 12.1). The increases in the number of female Republican nominees principally accounts for this rise. Female Republican nominees (and law-makers) were scarce at the beginning of this period, but over the course of these elections, Republicans gained parity with the Democrats, not only in the number of their female nominees, but in the number of those elected to the House. Given the much smaller overall Republican representation in the House, women are now a larger proportion of their membership than of the Democrats. However, Republican women's fortunes reversed in 1990 as a result of three incumbents leaving the House to run unsuccessful campaigns for the US Senate. At the same time, the Democrats elected five new women to the House (including the non-voting delegate from the District of Columbia).

The cohort of women elected to the US House of Representatives in the 1986–90 period have come from more liberal, and wealthier districts in urbanized areas compared with those districts not electing women to the national legislature. (Table 12.2).

In the 1980s it became politically expedient to be out in front in the promotion of women candidates. The Republican party even publicly acknowledged this fact. Republican Senatorial Campaign Committee (RSCC) Senator Richard Lugar issued a press statement in 1983 declaring 'a concerted drive by the Republican party to stamp itself as the party of the woman elected official would serve our nation as well as it served our own political interests . . . The full political participation of women is a moral imperative for our society, and intelligent political goal for the Republican party.' Thus, he pledged to 'commit the RSCC to the maximum legal funding and support for any Republican woman who is nominated next year, regardless of how Democratic the state or apparently formidable the Democratic candidate. I am prepared to consider direct assistance to women candidates even prior to their nomination, a sharp departure from our usual policy' (Lugar, 1983).

This pledge, however, did not result in even the close election of any new Republican women to the US Senate in 1984. However, the party did break precedent by giving female senatorial candidates $15,000 each to use in their *primaries* against other Republican contenders (Muscatine, 1984). It is relatively easy for a party with a flush treasury, as the Republican party had in 1983, to make a big public relations splash by advocating women's

Table 12.1 *Major party female nominees and winners,*
1968–1990

Year	Female nominees	Winners		Non-incumbents	Non-incumbent winners	
		%	N		%	N
1968						
Democrats	12	50	6	7	14	1
Republicans	7	71	5	2	—	0
Total	19	58	11	9	11	1
1970						
Democrats	15	53	8	9	33	3
Republicans	10	40	4	6	—	0
Total	25	48	12	15	20	3
1972						
Democrats	24	50	12	15	27	4
Republicans	8	25	2	7	14	1
Total	32	43	14	22	23	5
1974						
Democrats	30	47	14	20	20	4
Republicans	15	27	4	13	15	2
Total	45	40	18	33	18	6
1976						
Democrats	34	38	13	22	5	1
Republicans	20	25	5	16	6	1
Total	54	33	18	38	5	2
1978						
Democrats	26	42	11	14	7	1
Republicans	18	28	5	15	13	2
Total	44	36	16	29	10	3
1980						
Democrats	28	36	10	19	5	1
Republicans	25	36	9	20	20	4
Total	53	36	19	39	13	5
1982						
Democrats	28	39	11	18	5	1
Republicans	27	33	9	19	11	2
Total	55	36	20	37	8	3
1984						
Democrats	30	37	11	19	—	0
Republicans	35	31	11	26	8	2
Total	65	34	22	45	4	2
1986						
Democrats	29	41	12	19	11	2
Republicans	35	31	11	26	8	2
Total	64	36	23	45	9	4
1988						
Democrats	33	42	14	21	10	2
Republicans	26	42	11	15	—	0
Total	59	42	25	36	5	2
1990						
Democrats	39	49	19	24	17	4
Republicans	30	30	9	21	—	0
Total	69	41	28	45	9	4

Table 12.2 *Characteristics of House districts of women members, 1986–1990*

District characteristics	Women members	No women members	Difference of means	T
Percentage of population Black	14.5	11.2	3.3	−0.97
Percentage in urban areas	84.7	72.4	12.8[1]	−3.80
Median family income	$21,469	$19,915	$1,554[2]	−1.86
Percentage of vote for Dukakis[3]	51.5	46.0	5.5[2]	−1.63

[1] Significant at the 0.01 level, one-tailed *T*-test.
[2] Significant at the 0.05 level, one-tailed *T*-test.
[3] Democrat presidential candidate, 1988, with Geraldine Ferraro as his vice-presidential running mate.

candidacies in seemingly hopeless situations. The real test comes when the office is perceived as being winnable. Women need early support in open seat primaries. Neither party is likely to contribute to such campaigns because of the potential backlash from other candidates. But in 1990 the Republicans made a major effort on behalf of three women senatorial candidates with much greater chance of victory. All three were US members of the House of Representatives, but two faced incumbents and the third, Pat Saiki, in Hawaii, lost in a close race in a state that traditionally has overwhelmingly favoured the Democratic party.

The Democrats have also adopted special strategies for women candidates for federal office. For example, former US Representative Tony Coelho, in his tenure as chair of the Democratic Congressional Campaign Committee, established the Women's Congressional Council (WCC) to raise money for female House candidates. According to Mr Coelho, 'Not only have we not done enough, but what the women candidates legitimately have said is that we don't give them enough help up front . . . it is important to "invest" in women running for the House by aiding them early in their electoral efforts' (*New York Times*, 28 May 1986). The WCC raised $100,000 in 1984 and had a goal of $200,000 for women running for the House of Representatives in 1986. The Council solicited memberships, with a subscription fee of $500. Members received invitations to luncheons with members of Congress and to the annual Geraldine Ferraro Women Making History Award Reception, and received legislative updates on issues of concern to women. This project was in existence during

Table 12.3 *Average amount of party contributions to male and female congressional nominees, 1980–1988*

| | Democrats | | Republicans | |
	Men	Women	Men	Women
1980	$2,717	$2,056	$8,822	$10,369
1982	$2,820	$2,609	$12,140	$13,788
1984	$3,414	$3,474	$10,754	$11,651
1986	$2,660	$1,953	$6,685	$7,804
1988	$2,984	$5,033	$6,766	$6,766

Coelho's tenure as chair of the Democratic Congressional Campaign Committee.

Senator Lugar's and Representative Coelho's activities are characteristic of the efforts by the parties on behalf of women during the 1980s. These efforts have been very much dependent on the interest and creativity of individuals in positions to make them happen. They were not institutionalized as part of the party structures.

Research on the financing of election campaigns for the US House of Representatives fails to show discrimination in party contributions to women nominees in recent elections (Table 12.3). Women have tended to receive as much, if not more, aid than their male counterparts.

In 1983, both parties sponsored national conferences for female party activists to (a) inform them of party policies, (b) urge them to run for office and (c) provide training workshops in campaigning (Williams, 1984). The national parties have also established units to aid women candidates. In 1982, the Democratic party created the Eleanor Roosevelt Fund, which provided support to women running for state and local office. This Fund was active through 1986. It contributed more than $300,000 nationwide. In 1986, six candidates for state-wide office received financial support from the fund. The fund also provided services, such as direct mailings, training sessions and networking with political action committees. In keeping with the 1984 Democratic party platform, it also assisted progressive women candidates who are pro-choice on abortion. In addition, the fund developed a women's recruitment project in four states to encourage the general involvement of women in party politics. Through 1990, the Democratic party also held special sessions for women as part of its regional training workshops for new candidates.

For female Republican candidates, the National Federation of

Republican Women is an autonomous, financially independent affiliate of the Republican National Committee. This grassroots organization, which lists 160,000 paying members, runs regional candidate seminars and campaign management schools for women activists. The NFRW expanded the focus of its programme as women's political interest evolved from volunteerism to campaign management and in the late 1980s into the recruitment and training of women candidates. In 1989, the NFRW sponsored five regional weekend campaign management schools for members, a programme begun in 1979 (Baer, 1990). In 1990, the Federation established Project '90, a candidate recruitment programme aimed at finding and training Republican women club members to run for state and local office. Within the context of Project '90, the Federation conducted a women's candidates' seminar in Washington. As Baer states, the NFRW 'advances[s] the cause of women in the party' (1990).

In 1988, for the first time both national party platforms included statements endorsing 'full and equal access of women and minorities to elective office and party endorsement' (Democrats) and 'strong support for the efforts of women in seeking an equal role in government and [commitment] to the vigorous recruitment, training and campaign support for women candidates at all levels' (Republicans). These are symbolic statements, not substantive mandates to implement specific action. Their significance lies in the recognition by the parties of the problems of women candidates, and the influence of women within the parties to make that recognition explicit and public.

Conclusions

Traditionally the operative message from party leaders was 'no woman need apply' as far as the idea of women seeking a party nomination was concerned. In the 1980s, while female candidacies were still more the exception than the rule, women's campaigns came to be highlighted by the parties (where a 'woman could win this'), although not always and certainly not everywhere. In the 1990s, women's candidacies were 'mainstreamed' in the parties, in that generally they were treated like any other candidates. The Democrats, for example, developed a 'coordinated campaign' where national party staff work with candidates at all levels. There are no special programmes for women candidates. But at the same time the Democratic women members of Congress have pledged to adopt the campaigns of female non-incumbent nominees. Women candidates in the 1990s have the advantage of being perceived by the public as 'outsiders' – at a time when that is viewed as a plus in the scandal-ridden era – while simultaneously having access to the resources of the establishment.

This transformation in the relation between political parties in the United States and women candidacies is accounted for by the changing status of women within the party organizations and the importance of women's votes in the politics of the 1980s. Party organizations are no longer negative 'gatekeepers' for women candidates. But neither do they control the nomination process which could facilitate the nomination of more women candidates.[3] Women who seek office have to compete in an entrepreneurial world of independent candidacies. They have to operate in a weak party system. Ironically one can see that as both a plus and a minus for women candidates. But overall, stronger parties should advantage women candidates. Stronger parties should help the US overcome its lowly position among democracies in the percentage of national legislators who are women. The lack of substantial numbers of women in elective office in the United States reduces the country's ability to serve as a democratic model for other nations.

Notes

1 In addition to this structural change, 1992 was a year in which incumbents are not psychologically advantaged given the numerous scandals that have plagued the national legislature.

2 The Democratic National Committee's list of state chairs in 1988 listed ten women in those positions.

3 The two most celebrated nomination victories in 1992 for women candidates were cases where women have successfully challenged the established candidates. Carol Moseley Braun in Illinois, who defeated US Senator Alan Dixon (D-Il.) for re-nomination to the US Senate, and Lynn Yeakel, who crushed the Lieutenant Governor of the state to gain the right to oppose US Senator Arlen Specter (R-Pa.) in the general election. Both candidacies were conceived in anger at the Anita Hill/ Clarence Thomas US Supreme Court controversy.

13
Conclusions: Comparing Legislative Recruitment

Pippa Norris

Political parties serve vital functions as one of the main linkages between citizens and government: structuring electoral choice, recruiting legislative candidates, providing a legislative agenda in government. Parties provide a range of opportunities for women to participate in political life from the polling booth to local meetings, the conference platform, legislature and cabinet. Evidence in this book indicates gender differences in grassroots participation within parties have tended to diminish over the years in France, Germany and Sweden, where women are now playing a more equal role as members, activists and local party officers.[1] Yet in many countries, as shown in Table 13.1, women continue to be under-represented at the apex of the party power structure, as elected members of national parliaments.

Among the countries compared in this book, the number of women members of parliament has increased most significantly in Sweden, Norway, the Netherlands and Germany. In these countries change has been a fairly recent phenomenon, dating from the mid-1970s, but it has been substantial and, it can be argued, probably irreversible. There have been moderate improvements in recent years in Canada, Ireland, Italy, the United States and Britain, while consistent progress has eluded both Australia and France.

Except for the United States, which uses state-controlled voter primaries, parties are the crucial gatekeepers to elected office.[2] With some exceptions, most citizens in a country are legally eligible to stand as independent candidates.[3] But, in most countries, independents are rarely elected. There may be other gatekeepers to nominations and election – affiliated factions like organized labour, the church, financial contributors, interest groups, or local 'notables' – but party members, officers and leaders are normally the key players. Therefore what is the role of parties in changing or perpetuating the pattern of female under-representation?

Table 13.1 *Women's representation in the Lower House*

	Year	Candidates %	MPs %
Sweden	1988	41.0	38.1
Norway	1989	41.0	35.8
Netherlands	1989		21.3
Germany	1990		20.4
Canada	1988	19.2	13.2
Italy	1987	16.1	12.8
USA	1992	12.4	10.8
Britain	1992	18.3	9.2
Ireland	1989	14.3	7.8
Australia	1990	17.8	6.7
France	1988	11.9	5.7
All		21.3	16.5

Source: Inter-Parliamentary Union, 1991

The purpose of this chapter is not to replicate the particular, complex story of party developments within each country presented by each author. Nor to cover the strategies women have followed to change the policy agenda and party organizations, and the demands women have made on political parties, analysed in the introduction by Joni Lovenduski. Rather the aim is to focus on women's representation in national legislatures – the most symbolic indicator of political equality – to draw together some of the common threads across countries, to integrate some of the themes which emerge from this book, drawing on evidence presented in each chapter.

Women's representation and the political system

The study of comparative candidate recruitment has tended to focus on variations between countries, the main factors determining recruitment within any country, and whether different candidate selection practices have different consequences (see Czudnowski, 1975: 219–29; Duverger, 1955: 353–64; Epstein, 1980: 201–32; Gallagher and Marsh, 1988; Loewenberg and Patterson, 1979; Loewenberg et al., 1985; Mezey, 1979; Norris et al., 1990; Ranney, 1981). Unfortunately too many generalizations have been based on a limited range of countries, often Britain and the USA, and there has been little attempt to integrate this literature with the particular factors affecting women's representation. Accordingly we can build on this work by developing a systems model (see Figure 13.1) to

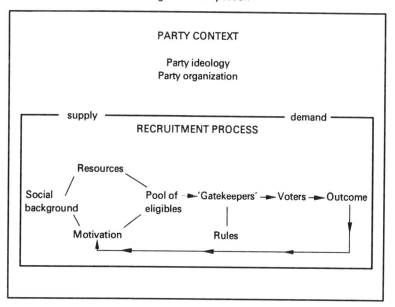

POLITICAL SYSTEM

Political culture
Electoral system
Party system
Legislative competition

PARTY CONTEXT

Party ideology
Party organization

supply ——————————————— demand
RECRUITMENT PROCESS

Resources

Social background

Pool of eligibles → 'Gatekeepers' → Voters → Outcome

Motivation

Rules

Figure 13.1 *Model of the recruitment process*

compare the common features of the recruitment process across countries. This model seeks to structure our understanding of the process, to identify factors influencing recruitment in different systems, and thereby to stimulate avenues for further research.

The model distinguishes between three levels of analysis. First there are factors which set the broad context within any country – the electoral system, political culture, party system and legislative competition. Secondly, there are factors which set the context within any particular political party – notably the party ideology and organization. Lastly, there are factors which most directly influence the recruitment of individual candidates within the selection process – notably the resources and motivation of candidates, and the attitudes of gatekeepers. This model therefore proceeds from the general political system, through party organizations, down to the specific factors influencing particular decisions to run for office.

The context of the political system

The systemic variables are most distant from decisions made within the recruitment process. Unless there is a significant change, such as a reform of the electoral system, these factors are often overlooked by studies focusing on party developments within countries. But it can be argued the systemic context is critical since it sets the general 'rules of the game'. Among the most important of these factors are the electoral system, the party system, the political culture and legislative competition. The significance of these rules becomes apparent from a comparative perspective. Once made explicit – once we shift the level of analysis – these rules may become part of the political debate which 'out-groups' seek to change. How do these variables influence women's representation?

Political culture

By 'political culture' we mean the dominant values and attitudes towards the role of women in society and in political life. Where traditional attitudes prevail it might be expected that women would be hesitant to pursue a political career, selectors would be reluctant to choose them as candidates, and parties would be unwilling to introduce effective gender equality policies. In contrast, in egalitarian cultures we would expect the goal of gender equality to be widely shared by all parties across the political spectrum. It is difficult to compare cultural attitudes towards gender relations on a systematic basis within this brief review (see, however, Bystydzienski, 1992; Klein, 1987; Wilcox, 1991). But the evidence presented in this book underlines a clear contrast in levels of women's representation between the egalitarian Scandinavian countries and otherwise similar democratic systems (Table 13.1).

Electoral system

One of the most widely accepted factors which explains cross-cultural differences in the representation of women is the electoral system (see Norris, 1985a; Rule, 1981, 1987; Rule and Zimmerman, 1992). Electoral systems vary substantially in different countries, but the main alternatives are: simple plurality (first past the post, FFTP); alternative vote (AV); the second ballot; single transferable vote (STV); additional member (AMS); and party list (for a review see Bogdanor and Butler, 1983).

What difference would these systems make for women? Comparative studies suggest three factors in electoral systems affect women's representation, namely, in order of priority; the ballot structure (whether party list or single candidate); district magnitude (the number of seats per district); and the degree of proportionality (the allocation of votes to seats) (see Norris, 1985a; Rule, 1981, 1987; Rule and Zimmerman, 1992). All other things being equal, women tend to do best under multi-member constituencies with a high number of seats per district. It follows that national party list systems tend to be the most favourable for women. The system of single transferable vote falls somewhere in the middle, depending upon the number of representatives per district. In contrast plurality and majoritarian systems – first past the post, second ballot and alternative vote – are least favourable to the representation of women. What evidence is there for this?

Australia uses the alternative majoritarian vote in single-member electoral divisions for the House of Representatives, and multi-member state-level districts using proportional quotas for the Senate. In the 1990 general election women MPs were 7 per cent of the House but 25 per cent of the Senate. The classic case used to confirm this argument is Germany, where in federal elections to the Bundestag half the seats are allocated by majoritarian single-member districts and the rest by proportional Land (regional) party lists. In 1990 80 per cent of women who were elected to the Bundestag entered through the Land list route. Therefore in the same country, in simultaneous elections, women do far better under party list systems.

There is also evidence from countries which changed their electoral system over time, such as France. Between 1945 and 1956, and again in 1986, the French used proportional representation with *département* party lists without preference voting in the National Assembly. Although proportional, the system used in France in 1986 employed few seats per *département*. In contrast, in the national elections from 1958 to 1981, and again in 1988, the system was changed so that candidates were elected by a single-member first ballot majority system, with a second runoff plurality ballot. As a result more women were elected each term to the National Assembly by proportional representation than to any Assembly using the majoritarian system, with the exception of elections in 1981 and 1988.

Lastly we can compare the countries in this book, in Table 13.2. All the countries where women comprise more than 20 per cent of MPs use regional or national party lists, with the variation of the additional member system in Germany. In contrast, the countries at the bottom of the list use majoritarian or plurality systems, with the exception of Ireland which uses the single transferable vote in

Table 13.2   *Women's representation and electoral systems*

	Year	MPs %	Electoral system
Sweden	1988	38.1	Party list
Norway	1989	35.8	Party list
Netherlands	1989	21.3	Party list
Germany	1990	20.4	Additional member
Canada	1988	13.2	FPTP
Italy	1987	12.8	Party list
USA	1992	10.8	FPTP
Britain	1992	9.2	FPTP
Ireland	1989	7.8	STV
Australia	1990	6.7	AV
France	1988	5.7	2nd ballot
All		16.5	

FPTP, first past the post.
STV, single transferable vote.
AV, alternative vote.

Source: Inter-Parliamentary Union, 1991

small multi-member constituencies. In the middle strata the pattern is not wholly uniform, for example Canada with a first-past-the-post system has about the same proportion of women MPs as Italy, with party lists.

We can conclude that electoral systems with a high number of seats in multi-member constituencies facilitate the entry of women, but it would be misleading to see this factor in isolation from its cultural and political mileux. Arguably a party list system is a necessary but not sufficient condition for high levels of female representation. As Sainsbury suggests, in Sweden the electoral system is conducive to women's representation but, by itself, it cannot account for change over time. We need to understand the interaction of factors within the political system in a comprehensive model, rather than relying upon simple, deterministic and monocausal explanations.

Why would party list systems facilitate women's entry? There are three main reasons. In single member constituencies local parties pick one standard bearer. Therefore selection committees may hesitate to choose a woman candidate, if women are considered an electoral risk. In contrast, there is a different 'logic of choice' under proportional systems where voters are presented with a list of candidates for each party. Here parties have a rational incentive to present a 'balanced ticket'. With a list of names it is unlikely that any votes will be lost by the presence of women candidates on the list. And their absence may cause offence, by advertising party prejudice, thereby narrowing the party's appeal. Secondly, there is the strategic argument. If parties want to help women by affirmative action programmes, selection quotas, positive training mechanisms, or financial assistance, this is easiest where there are national or regional lists of candidates. Lastly, there is the argument that greater proportionality increases the number of seats which change hands and party competition. This improves access for any group currently under-represented in parliament, including women.

Legislative competition

By 'legislative competition' we mean the number of contestants for nomination and election. Competition for seats is affected by a range of costs and benefits: the status, power and rewards of legislative office compared with other political positions; the number of elected offices which are available; the function of the parliament; the geographic location of the capital; the full or part-time demands of the legislature; the ability to combine a legislative career with outside occupations; the salary, fringe benefits, and powers of patronage associated with the post; the number of competitive parties; the risks of standing; and, in particular, the turnover of incumbents (for a discussion see Matthews, 1985).

There is limited systematic evidence comparing legislative competition between countries, and that which exists, on basic salaries and incumbency rates, suggests considerable variation between countries (see Loewenberg and Patterson, 1979: 106–8; Mezey, 1979: 224–35). The common assumption is that where legislative competition is weak, 'out-groups' seeking entry stand a better chance of getting elected. Where competition for seats is strong, 'out-groups' face more difficulties challenging the status quo. On this basis we can suggest that legislative competition may play an important role in explaining cross-cultural differences in recruitment, but this hypothesis awaits further empirical evidence for confirmation.

Many of the contributors to this book mention low levels of incumbency turnover, measured by the percentage of new members every election, as a significant barrier to change. In the US House of Representatives and the British House of Commons, over 90 per cent of incumbents who choose to run again are normally returned (Norris et al., 1992). Voluntary retirements, and by-elections caused by illness and death, swell the total vacancies.

Since much of the work on legislative turnover has been confined to the United States, we lack recent comparative data (for a review see Matthews, 1985: 38–42). Nevertheless one study suggests that from the 1950s to the mid-1970s turnover rates in the US, Italy and Britain were fairly similar, in the 17–19 per cent range, while there were slightly higher rates in Ireland, France and West Germany (Ragsdale, 1985). Incumbency represents a bottleneck to change where the number of women with political experience at local and state level is increasing faster than the opportunities for good parliamentary seats.

The constitutional context may influence recruitment. In unitary states like Britain there is a narrow career track for political life: a seat in parliament is an essential prerequisite for ministerial office, and the centralization of power at Westminster means there are few other channels for elected politicians with ambition. Parliamentary office is not particularly rewarding for backbenchers – the hours are long, the working conditions inadequate, the pay ungenerous, the opportunities for independent legislative initiatives limited, and backbench members enjoy only moderate status and influence – nevertheless in British politics it is the only route to government. In federal states like Germany and Australia, powerful state governments provide another avenue into political office, although a career in the national parliament remains critical for government office.

In contrast, in the United States the separation of powers, federalism and the nature of public service means politicians frequently have multiple career paths. Politicians may move from Congress to Gubernatorial office, from the House to the Senate, from the legislature to the executive, from academia to state departments, from appointed office to lobbyist, or from public life to the judiciary. Career paths are not unidimensional: members have to resign from Congress to enter the administration, but there are therefore multiple openings to enter political life. In practice the overwhelming strength of incumbency, plus residency requirements, places effective restrictions on opportunities to run for congressional office. In France traditionally politicians simultaneously held multiple offices, recently this has been restricted to two, often a seat in the National Assembly combined with a local mayoral base.

Where seat competition is less we would assume, all other things being equal, women might tend to do better. In Canada, for example, Lynda Erickson notes that when a woman's name was officially placed in nomination she tended to be very successful: a female candidate was selected almost three-quarters of the time.

The reason was that candidacies were frequently awarded by acclamation as there were no competitors. In contrast, in Britain good Conservative open seats may sometimes attract 200–300 applicants, and even hopeless seats draw many who want campaign experience. We should not draw any hard and fast conclusions based on the limited evidence which is currently available, but it seems likely that the effects of legislative competition on opportunities for women's participation are worth exploring further.

Party competition

Opportunities for candidates to run are further influenced by the 'party system', meaning the structure of party competition which occurs in the legislature. The number of parties competing for votes, combined with the size of the legislature, determines the total number of opportunities to become a candidate. But it is party competition in the legislature which determines opportunities to become an elected representative. Party politics are in constant flux but the party system includes the relatively enduring features which persist across a series of elections. Party competition has two principle dimensions: the strength of parties, conventionally measured by seats in the legislature, and the position of parties across the ideological spectrum. These alternatives can be conceptualized as ideal types in Figure 13.2.

In party systems such as in Ireland, the USA and Canada there

	Few parties	**Many parties**
'Catch-all' centrist	Ireland USA Canada	
Ideologically polarized	Britain Australia	Sweden Italy Netherlands France Norway Germany

Figure 13.2 *Party competition*

are few major parties represented in the national legislature and these tend to be 'catch-all', appealing widely across the ideological and social spectrum. In Canada, Erickson notes, the Progressive Conservatives, Liberals and New Democratic (NDP) dominate the lower house, but face electoral competition in two provinces from the Bloc Québecois and the Reform party. For most of their post-war history the main parties appealed on leadership and competence, rather than a distinct policy stance, although ideological polarization has increased in the past decade. In Ireland, the central electoral fight is between Fianna Fail and Fine Gael, both centre–right parties, although, Gallagher indicates, competition has increased in the 1980s with Labour and the Worker's parties on the left, and the Progressive Democrats on the right. In the United States, party competition is largely confined to the loosely organized and ideologically diverse Democrats and Republicans, although occasional third party candidates like John Anderson and Ross Perot have periodically challenged the system.

In contrast, in Australia and Britain the legislatures are dominated by two major parties of left and right, with minor parties holding few seats. In the electorate the British system is a more fragmented, multi-party system, with substantial if uneven support for the Liberal Democrats, Scottish Nationalists and Plaid Cymru on the mainland, along with the separate parties of Northern Ireland. But in Parliament, despite these developments, over 90 per cent of all seats are held by Labour and the Conservatives, and post-war governments have been majoritarian, with the single exception of the mid-1970s Lib–Lab pact. The Australian system is dominated by Labor and Liberals, along with the National party and Australian Democrats.

Lastly Italy, Norway, the Netherlands and France have fragmented party systems, with multiple parties represented in the legislature and considerable divisions across the ideological spectrum. Post-unification Germany also falls into this category, although it remains difficult to classify in the light of recent developments. From 1958 to the early 1980s Germany used to be seen as a classic 'two-and-a-half party system, with catch-all, middle-of-the-road parties. From 1983 to 1990 the growth of the Greens produced a four-party system. Since unification, support for the PDS (the reformed Communist party) in eastern Germany, coupled with the resurgence of far right parties (the Republicans and German People's Union, DVU List-D), with sporadic success in some Lander elections, suggests Germany is becoming a more fragmented and ideologically polarized multi-party system (von Beyme, 1991; Irving and Paterson, 1991; Pulzer, 1991; Roberts, 1992).

Opportunities for women candidates may also be influenced by the growth of new parties in the system, although this depends in part upon their ideological persuasion. Many countries have seen new parties develop in recent years, including the Greens in most European countries, the far right in France, Belgium and Germany, and new or revived regional parties like the Bloc Québecois in Canada, the Scottish Nationalists, and the Lombard League in Italy, leading to more fragmented systems. Until 1988 Sweden could be characterized as a 'dominant one-party' system, with the Social Democrats governing since 1932, and five parties in the Riksdag. In more recent elections, however, the party system has become more multi-dimensional with challenges from new parties including the Greens, the Christian Democrats and New Democracy, and seven parties represented in parliament. Until recently Italy could be seen as a multi-party system, with seven to nine parties in parliament, or alternatively as a 'dominant one-party system', with a succession of coalition governments led by the Christian Democrats. The decline of support for the Christian Democrats in the 1992 general election, challenged by the Lombard League in the north, has contributed to a crisis of governability and further fragmentation.

Accordingly, does the nature of the party competition influence women's representation? It seems plausible to hypothesize, as Sainsbury suggests, that increased competition, combined with the growth of new parties, would provide more opportunities for women candidates (see Chapter 11). Yet once more the evidence is mixed, there is limited systematic research, and we need to take care to observe the complex interactions of political culture, the party system and the electoral system. It does appear that multi-party systems, where there are more opportunities for candidates to run in a range of parties, tend to have a higher number of women in office than systems with few parties, whether catch-all or ideologically polarized along the left–right dimension. Yet the pattern is not clear-cut: France is classically seen as a fragmented multi-party system yet it has the fewest women in office out of all the countries under comparison. We can conclude that this would be a fruitful area for further research, to establish a systematic case, but we need to go beyond simple classifications of party competition, to see how party ideology and party organization also play a role.

The party context

From systemic factors which influence all parties we need to turn to factors which affect the promotion of women by particular political parties. In the introduction Joni Lovenduski noted that parties have implemented three types of policies to increase women's representation in elected office. Rhetorical strategies aim at changing the party ethos by affirming the need for more women in leadership speeches, official statements and party platforms. Positive action programmes aim to encourage women to run by providing training sessions, advisory gender targets, special conferences, financial assistance and gender monitoring. Positive discrimination sets mandatory gender quotas, at a specific level – whether 20, 40 or 50 per cent – applied to internal party bodies, shortlists of applicants, or lists of candidates. The distinction between advisory targets and mandatory quotas is often blurred in practice, particularly if quota rules are not implemented. The term 'quotas' is often employed quite loosely, and may have different cross-cultural connotations. But this does not invalidate the basic distinction between formal regulation and informal guidelines.

Party ideology

A key question is why some parties have favoured one strategy over others. One answer to emerge from this book is the role of party ideology: social democratic and Green parties are far more likely to believe intervention in the recruitment process is necessary and appropriate, hence positive discrimination is justified to bring about short-term change. Parties of the right and centre are more likely to rely upon rhetorical strategies, and possibly affirmative action, in the belief that women should be encouraged to stand, and party members should be encouraged to select them, but the recruitment process has to involve 'fair' and open competition. This pattern of greater intervention in the recruitment process in left-wing parties, via different mechanisms, is evident in the use of positive discrimination by the Socialists in France (20 per cent quotas), Labour in Britain (for shortlisting only), the Socialist Left and Labour in Norway (40 per cent quotas), Labour (PvdA) in the Netherlands (25 per cent quotas), and the Social Democrats in Germany (40 per cent quotas). Just as parties of the right tend to favour a minimal role for government in the free market economy, so they lean towards non-intervention or regulation of the candidate recruitment process.

This generalization needs one major qualification: once positive discrimination is successfully implemented by left-wing and Green parties, others within the political system may follow suit. Where this has occurred, the parties of the left and the Greens have usually set the pace of change. As Sainsbury suggests, in Sweden the Social Democrats were the first to favour women's elections in the late 1960, setting advisory guidelines where each sex should have representation of at least 40 per cent, and their dominant position led the other parties to compete, and even outbid, the Social Democrats as champions of equality. The result has been a convergence of trends across Swedish parties. In Norway, however, Skjeie notes the Conservatives and Christian People's parties have not, so far, followed the gender quotas adopted by the left and centre.

Party organization

Whether parties use rhetorical strategies, positive action or positive discrimination depends on political ideology and also their type of organization. Here we need to introduce a simple classification which distinguishes between four main types of recruitment process based on the degree of centralization and institutionalization (see Figure 13.3).

These are ideal types, nevertheless they allow us to focus on the major contrasts between parties. In this classification the first criterion is the institutionalization of the process. In formal systems the application process is defined by internal party rules which are detailed, explicit, standardized, implemented by party

	Centralized	Localized
Informal	Italy DC, PSI French UDF	US Democrats Canadian Liberals
Formal	Netherlands VVD French PC Italian PCI NZ Labour Austrian Socialists SPÖ	British Lab, Cons German SDP, CDU/CSU Swedish SDP, Cons

Figure 13.3 *Exemplar party organizations and the recruitment process*

officials and authorized in party documents. The steps in the application process, the decision-making process, voting procedures, and the relative importance of different party bodies in selecting candidates, are relatively clear to outside observers. Where applicants wish to challenge breaches of the rules there are formal procedures of appeal. The significance of the rules for the distribution of internal party power means proposed changes may produce heated conflict.

In contrast, in informal systems the nomination procedure is relatively closed, the steps in the application process are familiar to participants but rarely made explicit and open, and procedure may vary from one selection to another. If there are published guidelines in official party regulations or constitutions these tend to have *de jure* rather than *de facto* power. Since formal rules are rarely implemented, there are few effective courts of appeal. The process is less bureaucratic and more open to personal patronage by 'party notables'.

The second dimension of this typology concerns the centralization of the decision-making process. In centralized systems the key players are central authorities within the party. This category can be defined as including national executives, elected or appointed party and faction leaders at the national and regional/state levels. In localized systems, on the other hand, the key players are at constituency level, including within this category local leaders, constituency executives, local factions, grassroots members and voters in constituency (that is, district, riding or branch) meetings, conferences or conventions. The question of how we define the key players is complex, because power over the selection process can be exercised by many bodies which interact with each other. Systems can vary on a continuum from highly centralized to highly localized, rather than discrete categories. The selection process will be influenced by those who set, implement and adjudicate over the rules of the game, as well as those who participate at different stages in directly nominating individual candidates. Nevertheless the chapters in this volume suggest that we can identify whether the key players within each party tend to be predominantly centralized or localized (see also Gallagher and Marsh, 1988: 12–15, 236–65).

Informal-centralized recruitment

The differences between these systems can be illustrated by describing how the process operates examples of each type. In informal-centralized recruitment systems, such as the Christian Democrat (DC) and the Socialist Party (PS) in Italy, a central elite exerts considerable control over the selection of candidates. In these fragmented parties selection is decided by a process of bargaining between central leaders of competing internal party factions. Local leaders try to ensure their interests are heard in the process, but faction elites play the major role in recruitment.

In France the UDF is characterized as a 'caucus–cadre' organization, a loose network of like-minded followers coalesced around local and national notables. In such parties the key party gatekeepers tend to be the national party leaders or regional notables who can 'place' their favoured candidate in good positions, after taking account of proposals from departmental organizations. With no tradition of internal party democracy, party members play almost no role in the process (Thiébault, 1988: 73). The French Socialist Party (PS), which developed a more organized mass base, provides a weaker example of this type. PS candidate selection, in principle, is decentralized, with local constituencies choosing their own candidates by secret ballots of members, yet in practice the national party organization has very significant powers of supervision which it has used to intervene and change nominations during the final stage of candidate ratification. The party has adopted quota requirements for candidate selection since the mid-1970s, but Appleton and Mazur stress these have not been implemented in recruitment, except to the European Parliament. The quota rules adopted by the Socialist party have proved largely rhetorical gestures rather than effective regulations. In practice the proportion of women as party members, leaders, candidates and elected officials in the Socialist party is little different from the position in the Rally pour la Republique (RPR), without such rules.

In informal-centralized systems of recruitment, if party leaders are sympathetic to the need to promote gender equality, for example if they wish to appeal to women voters, then they have considerable power to do so. Through patronage party leaders can improve the position of women in party lists or place them in good constituencies. As a result under this system of 'benevolent autocracy' women can be promoted relatively quickly, although without institutional safeguards the gains can be quickly reversed. One further danger of this system is that if the leadership does not wish to disturb the status quo, the 'old boy network', they can block opportunities. Under this system positive discrimination strategies will probably prove ineffective, since any regulations or guidelines will not necessarily be implemented. Since the process is not rule-governed, changing the rules will not alter the outcome.

Informal-localized recruitment

In informal-localized systems it is difficult for the central party leadership to play a major role – whether positive or negative – in the recruitment process. The most extreme example of this type is the United States. Traditionally, American party organizations were relatively weak 'caucus–cadre' rather than 'mass–branch' organizations. The decline of the power of party bosses to choose their candidates in the proverbial smoke-filled rooms, due to the growth of primary elections, produced the rise of entrepreneurial candidates with their own independent funding, organization and campaign. In the countries under comparison, American parties are the only ones which leave the selection of their nominees to voters. Very few parties elsewhere have made use of direct voter primaries (for exceptions see Gallagher and Marsh, 1988: 238–9). In the United States the process is regulated by state law rather than internal party rules. Any candidate who wishes to run in a primary can do so, once they fulfil the minimal legal requirements. This has led many observers to stress that 'self-recruitment' is the norm.

This is true for candidates who refuse Political Action Committee (PAC) money. But this overlooks the way party selectors have been replaced for all but self-financed candidates by other powerful 'gatekeepers', notably PACs, who carefully evaluate candidates before they are prepared to offer funding. Candidates may be interviewed by PACs in a formal process, and may need to provide documentation to support their application. Other actors who play a gatekeeping role, albeit one which is fairly diverse, competitive and open, include the local media, individual financial contributors, campaign professionals and local volunteers. Unless individuals are seen as strong and credible candidates by these gatekeepers they may be unable to run an effective campaign. Accordingly, as Burrell concludes, in the United States party organizations can no longer block women's candidacies, which can be seen as a positive step. But neither can they do much to facilitate the nomination of women.

A different example of the informal-localized process is Canada, where local party members in Liberal and Conservative constituency associations determine most of their own rules and practices for choosing their nominee. As a result some constituency parties open the selection process to the whole membership, while others give a greater role to elected party officers. Constituency associations make their final selection with minimal supervision from the wider party establishment. National leaders have formal veto power over the final choice of names, but in the past two decades this has only been used twice by the major parties. The leaders of the major parties have encouraged women to run, assisted ridings searching for prospective candidates, and provided some training conferences, but Erickson concludes their hands have been tied by the localized nature of the process.

Accordingly we can conclude under 'informal-localized' systems that opportunities for women candidates are not restricted by the central party leadership. At the same time it is difficult to see what steps, beyond rhetorical encouragement or possibly positive action, these parties can take to increase the representation of women. If the final decision rests in the hands of each local constituency party, and there are no standardized party rules concerning the nomination process, or reviews of the overall party slate, this seems to exclude the possibility of positive action guidelines for candidates, or shortlisting targets for applicants.

Formal-localized recruitment
The most common system in Western European parties is probably 'formal-localized' recruitment, where explicit bureaucratic rules are established and implemented to standardize the selection process throughout the party organization at national or state level. Within this framework decisions about which individuals get chosen are taken largely at constituency level, although regional bodies may play a part.

The major parties in Britain, Sweden, Ireland and Germany exemplify this type. In the British Labour and Conservative parties the main decisions about nominations, shortlisting and selection take place among different bodies at constituency level. National party leaders have the power to veto candidates. Conservative Central Office establishes the 'model rules' and vets potential applicants at the start of the process, before accepting names on the Approved List. The Labour National Executive sets the detailed rules, monitors the process and formally approves nominations at the last stage. But more active interference in the selection of individual candidates is rare, unless guidance is sought by local parties, and carries the dangers of party disunity.

In the Swedish Social Democrats, Conservatives and Liberals there are three stages: putting forward names, ranking nominees and adopting the list. The middle stage is the most critical. Here the non-socialist parties often rely on meetings of activist members at the local and constituency level. In the Social Democrats the local nominating committees and the constituency executives play a decisive role. The party lists are based on large multi-member constituencies. In ranking candidates on the party list the party aims to produce a balanced ticket. To ensure that women are nominated, and placed in winnable positions, the Social Democrats recommend that at least 40 per cent of candidates should be women, and every other place on the party list should be allocated to the opposite sex. While not always implemented to the letter, this sets the normal expectation for the local selectorate.

In Ireland candidates for Fianna Fail and Fine Gael are chosen at constituency level by selection conferences or conventions of party members. These meetings are selecting a party ticket with three to five candidates in multi-member constituencies. While the main decisions are taken at local level, party leaders may impose additional candidates. This power is not widely exercised but is used occasionally through adding a further candidate to balance the party ticket in terms of locality, age, electoral appeal and gender.

Lastly, Germany provides a weaker instance of this type; it has a formal party system based on 'mass–branch' organizations. The process of candidate selection in constituencies is established by electoral law. Either a meeting is held in a constituency where all party members may vote, or party members elect delegates who in turn vote on candidates. The local parties play a major role in recruitment for parliamentary elections but regional party organizations influence the process, particularly in the nomination of candidates on the Länder lists. Kolinsky notes that the regional and national party leaders have played a significant role in persuading local constituencies to accept more women. The names of nominees for constituencies and regional lists are compiled by the constituency and the regional executive, then passed to local parties for confirmation by party members. Gender quotas in the Social Democrats and Greens regulate the composition of party lists, while in other parties certain positions near the top of the list are earmarked for women.

Formal-centralized recruitment

The decline of what Duverger termed 'caucus–cadre' and 'militant-cell' party organizations mean that today few parties in the countries under comparison in this book use a formal-centralized recruitment process. In formal-centralized systems national party leaders, national executives or national faction leaders have the constitutional authority to decide which candidates are placed on the party ticket and to impose their choice on local constituencies. In the past this system operated most clearly in traditional communist parties organized according to the principle of democratic centralism, such as the PCF in France. In Italy Guadagnini notes within the old communist party, the PCI, there was a cohesive leadership elite which selected candidates for party lists. In the Netherlands the degree of centralization varies between parties, but the national executive plays an important role in the People's Party for Freedom and Democracy and the Liberal party (VVD). Elsewhere, one comprehensive review of the evidence in other countries notes the national leadership or executive is the main selector of candidates in the Austrian Socialist Party, in many Israeli parties before 1977, in the New Zealand Labour party, in the Greek PASOK and New Democracy parties, in the Japanese Liberal Democratic party, and in several African one-party states (Gallagher and Marsh, 1988: 243–5). Nevertheless, pressures towards internal party democracy, and the importance of maintaining a link between representatives and local party organizations, mean that currently there are few clear examples of parties using formal-centralized recruitment in the countries included in this book.

What are the implications of this typology? The classification seeks to illuminate the common features of how recruitment works across a range of countries, and therefore what strategies might be effective to change the process in different systems. The typology suggests each type of party can employ rhetorical and positive action strategies, but positive discrimination operates most effectively in formal-localized systems. It makes little sense to think about using positive discrimination in the major parties in the United States or Canada. And, even if rules are passed, they are not likely to be implemented in the French UDF or the Italian Christian Democrats.

Accordingly positive discrimination quotas are taken seriously in a rule-bound and bureaucratic culture where decisions by different bodies within an organization need to be standardized. In the German Social Democrats the decision about who gets nominated are taken at local level, but they are taken within a framework of positive discrimination which has been effective in raising the proportion of women candidates, and their position on party lists. In Sweden positive action guidelines have been equally effective in most parties. Accordingly the nature of party organizations is one factor, among others, which seems worth exploring further to understand the strategies women can employ to increase their representation.

The recruitment process within parties

Lastly we can turn to the recruitment process within parties, the factors that influence most directly the nomination of individuals.

The level of analysis therefore moves from the party unit to the individual candidate. Here we can draw a basic distinction between 'supply-side' factors, which influence whether individuals come forward, and 'demand-side factors, which influence whether they get chosen. The model assumes the individual decides to run for office, just like the employee entering the workforce, by calculating the costs and benefits within a particular opportunity structure.

On the 'supply side' individuals decide to pursue a political career based on their motivation and resources. Eligibility is determined by resources: time, money, support networks, political experience and relevant skills. Most accounts in this book stress individuals need to serve a long political apprenticeship before they are seen as credible candidates for national parliaments. In different countries individuals need to demonstrate a political track record in local government, community activism, party service, possibly trade union work, professional networks or family connections, or, in factionalized systems, loyal service within factions. Candidates elected to lower levels of government, in local and state office, will have acquired experience, skills and networks for higher office.

Running for the national legislature in single-member districts is usually a time-consuming occupation, requiring commitment, often for two or three years before election day: organizing volunteers, attending community functions, canvassing door-to-door, speaking at public meetings, raising funds, holding local surgeries, cultivating the press, meeting local groups. The formal campaign is only the tip of the iceberg. Candidates may experience successive defeats before finally succeeding. In multi-member districts candidates may spend less time on local campaigning, but, as Kolinsky notes, in Germany a good place on the ticket requires a long-term investment in party-related work. The personal financial costs of electioneering vary substantially cross-nationally. The role of independent financial resources is most important in the entrepreneurial system in the United States, but even in systems where official campaign expenses are fully funded by political parties, a comfortable personal income facilitates the costs and risks of a political career.

Motivation is equally important. Candidates need ambition to seek elected office, given the uncertainties and difficulties of this goal, and a strong sense of political efficacy, the confidence they can influence political events. Motivations may be diverse and multiple: the desire for power, public service, status, sociability, group representation, material rewards, partisan loyalty, ideological goals. The incentive will vary in different types of legislature, hence local government may provide a sense of community service while national parliaments may give greater status and financial rewards. But the political drive must be strong to overcome barriers where there is tough competition for elected office.

In addition to resources and motivation, there is a 'feedback' loop in the process, since the outcome (the characteristics of successful candidates) may influence the motivation of new applicants. If successful candidates seem mainly affluent, white, male, middle-class professionals, those who do not fit this category may be discouraged from applying, on the grounds they may be unlikely to succeed. Party gatekeepers may also influence potential applicants more positively by encouraging women to consider standing. As Erickson notes, in at least one-fifth of cases candidates were 'talked into running', and party search committees may play an important role in stimulating applicants.

Gatekeepers

On the 'demand side', eligible candidates face the problem of acceptability by the 'gatekeepers'. If willing to stand, who among the pool of eligibles is seen as suitable? Here at the individual level, once we understand who decides, and under what procedural constraints, we need to take account of the attitudes of the selectors: what are they looking for in a candidate? How do they see the role of a representative? What do they count as 'relevant' experience? How do they evaluate potential applicants? What are the differences in the attitudes of rank-and-file members, officers and leaders? Survey evidence is required to explore these attitudes and understand what influences their decisions. While work on this has started, in most countries such evidence is unavailable at present. Research has tended to focus on the outcome, and actors, rather than the internal decision-making process.

Therefore we can conclude that the recruitment process can be seen as complex and multi-layered. Individual decisions by candidates and selectors operate within a particular party context. In turn, the ideology and organization of any party operates within a broader political system. While we can focus our attention on the political system, the party context, or the individual-level candidate and selector, any comprehensive explanation needs to take account of all three levels, and their complex interaction.

Notes

1 Unfortunately in many countries information about trends in party membership often tend to be fairly unreliable, since parties have not established accurate records of total numbers, or the gender of members.

2 It should be noted that other political systems, such as Norway, Canada and Israel, use 'primaries' but these are elections where party members are enfranchised. These will be referred to as membership primaries. In the United States party 'membership' is a much looser concept, and 'open' primaries allow any voter to participate, irrespective of party affiliation.

3 Legal eligibility requirements commonly specify requirements of citizenship and age, and may specifically exclude non-residents, members of certain groups (the civil service, the armed forces, the church) or legal status (bankrupts, criminals).

Bibliography

Abélès, Marc (1989) *Jours tranquilles en 89: ethnologie politique d'un département français*. Paris: Editions Odile Jacob.

Abzug, Bella (1984) *Gender Gap*. New York: Houghton, Mifflin.

Accornero, A. and Ilardi, M. (eds) (1982) *Il Partito Comunista Italiano. Struttura e storia dell'organizzazione: 1921–1979*. Milan: Feltrinelli.

Adamson, Nancy, Briskin, Linda and McPhail, Margaret (1988) *Feminist Organizing for Change: The Contemporary Women's Movement in Canada*. Toronto: Oxford University Press.

Aitkin, Don (1972) *The Country Party in New South Wales*. Canberra: ANU Press.

Almond, Gabriel and Verba, Sidney (1963) *The Civic Culture: Political Attitudes and Democracy in Five Nations*. Princeton, NJ: Princeton University Press.

Alters, Diane (1987) 'Women, strong at the polls, still lag in campaign leverage', *The Boston Globe*, 26 May, p.1.

Anderlini, F. and Leonardi, R. (1991) *Politica in Italia. I fatti dell'anno e le interpretazioni Edizione 1990*. Bologna: Il Mulino.

Appleton, Andrew (1992) 'Party implantation, organizational adaptation, and local power in France, 1968–88', PhD dissertation, New York University.

Atkinson, Valerie and Spear, Joanna (1992) *The Changing Labour Party*. London: Routledge.

Baer, Denise (1990) 'Political parties: the missing variable in women and politics research', paper presented at the Midwest Political Science Association annual meeting, Chicago.

Balbo, L. (1988) 'Rappresentanza e non rappresentanza', in G. Pasquino (ed.), *Rappresentanza e democrazia*. Bari: Laterza.

Ballestrero, M.V. (1979) *Dalla tutela alla parità. La legislazione italiana sul lavoro delle donne*. Bologna: Il Mulino.

Ballestrero, M.V. (1985) *Parità ed oltre. Donne, lavoro e pari opportunità*. Rome: Ediesse.

Barkfeldt, Bengt et al. (1971) *Partierna nominerar*. Stockholm: Almqvist and Wiksell.

Barry, Jim (1991) *The Women's Movement and Local Politics*. Aldershot: Avebury.

Bartolini, S. (1984) 'The French party system', *West European Politics*, 7: 4.

Bashevkin, Sylvia (1985) *Toeing the Lines: Women and Party Politics in English Canada*. Toronto: University of Toronto Press.

Bashevkin, Sylvia (1991) 'Women's participation in political parties', in Kathy Megyery (ed.), *Women in Canadian Politics: Towards Equity in Representation* (Volume 6 of the research studies of the Royal Commission on Electoral Reform and Party Financing). Ottawa and Toronto: RCERPF/Dundurn Press, pp. 61–80.

Bay A.H. (1988) *Penger eller barnehageplass? Offentlige overføringer til småbarnsfamilier*. INAS rapport 88: 7. Oslo: Institutt for sosialforskning (INAS).

Becker, Horst, Hombach, Bode et al. (1983) *Die SPD von innen. Bestandsaufnahme an der Basis der Partei*. Bonn: Neue Gesellschaft.

Beckwith, Karen (1984) 'Structural barriers to women's access to office: the cases of

France, Italy and the United States'. Paper presented at the APSA meeting, 30 August–2 September, Washington, DC.

Bengtsson, Lars et al. (1972) *Svenska partiapparater*. Stockholm: Aldus/Bonniers.

Berglund, Sten and Lindström, Ulf (1980) *The Scandinavian Party System(s)*. Lund: Studentlitteratur.

Bernstein, Robert (1986) 'Why are there so few women in the House?', *Western Political Quarterly*, 39 (March): 155–63.

Bettin, G. and Magnier, A. (1989) *Il consigliere comunale*. Padua: CEDAM.

Beyme, Klaus von (1991) 'Electoral unification: the first German elections in Dec 1990'. *Government and Opposition*, 26: 2.

Black, Naomi (1988) 'The Canadian Women's Movement: the second wave', in Sandra Burt, Lorraine Code and Lindsay Dorney (eds), *Changing Patterns: Women in Canada*. Toronto: McClelland and Stewart, pp. 80–102.

Blake, Donald E. (1991) 'Party competition and electoral volatility: Canada in comparative perspective', in Herman Bakvis (ed.), *Representation, Integration and Political Parties in Canada* (Volume 14 of the research studies of the Royal Commission on Electoral reform and Party Financing). Ottawa and Toronto: RCERPF/Dundurn Press.

Bledsoe, Timothy and Herring, Mary (1990) 'Victims of circumstances: women in pursuit of political office', *American Political Science Review*, 84 (March): 213–23.

Boccia, M.L. and Peretti, I. (eds) (1988) 'Il genere della rappresentanza', *Materiali ed Atti n.10, Democrazia e Diritto*, Supplement XXVIII(1).

Bogdanor, V. and Butler, D. (1983) *Democracy and Elections*. Cambridge: Cambridge University Press.

Borchorst, A. (1991) *The Scandinavian Welfare States – Patriarchal, Gender-neutral or Women-friendly?* Aarhus: Institute of Political Science, University of Aarhus.

Brand, Jack (1992) 'SNP members: the way of the faithful', in Pippa Norris, Ivor Crewe, David Denver and David Broughton (eds), *British Parties and Elections Yearbook*. Hemel Hempstead: Harvester Wheatsheaf.

Brändström, Dan (1971) *Nomineringsförfarande vid riksdagsval*. Umeå: Department of Political Science, Umeå University.

Bréchon, Pierre, Derville, Jacques and Lecomte, Patrick (1987a) *Les cadres RPR*. Paris: Economica.

Bréchon, Pierre, Derville, Jacques and Lecomte, Patrick (1987b) 'Plongée libre au sein du RPR', *Revue Politique et Parlementaire*, (927) January/February.

Briggs, Phillip (1977) 'The role of women as policy-makers and candidates in the National Country Party of Australia (NSW)', *Australian Quarterly*, 49: 36–41.

Brinkmann, Heinz Ulrich (1990) 'Zeigen Frauen ein besonderes Wahlverhalten?', *Frauenforschung*, 3: 55–75.

Brodie, Janine (1985) *Women and Politics in Canada*. Toronto: McGraw-Hill.

Brodie, Janine (1989) 'The gender factor and national leadership conventions in Canada', in George Perlin (ed.), *Party Democracy in Canada: The Politics of National Party Conventions*. Scarborough, Ontario: Prentice-Hall Canada, pp. 172–87.

Brodie, Janine (1991) 'Tensions from within: regionalism and party politics in Canada', in Hugh G. Thorburn (ed.), *Party Politics in Canada,* 6th edn. Scarborough, Ontario: Prentice-Hall Canada, pp. 221–33.

Browne, Vincent (ed.) (1981) *The Magill Book of Irish Politics*. Dublin: Magill Publications.

Bürklin, Wilhelm (1987) *Wählerverhalten und Wertewandel*. Opladen: Westdeutscher Verlag.

Burrell, Barbara (1988) 'The political opportunity of women candidates for the U.S. House of Representatives in 1984', *Women and Politics* (Spring).

Burrell, Barbara (1992) 'The presence and performance of women candidates in open seat primaries for the U.S. House of Representatives: 1968–1990', *Legislative Studies Quarterly* (November).

Busteed, M.A. (1990) *Voting Behaviour in the Republic of Ireland – a Geographical Perspective*. Oxford: Clarendon Press.

Bystydzienski, Jill M. (1992) *Women Transforming Politics*. Bloomington: Indiana University Press.

Caciagli, M. (1990) 'Erosioni e mutamenti nell'elettorato democristiano', in M. Caciagli and A. Spreafico (eds), *Vent' anni di elezioni in Italia, 1968–1987*. Padua: Liviana.

Caciagli, Mario (1991) 'Vita e opere di un ceto politico', *Polis*, v(2): 209–15.

Caciagli, N. and Spreafico, A. (eds) (1990) *Vent' anni di elezioni in Italia, 1968–1987*. Padua: Liviana.

Calise, M. and Mannheimer, R. (1982) *Governanti in Italia*. Bologna: Il Mulino.

Campbell, Beatrix (1987) *The Iron Ladies*. London: Virago.

Canadian Advisory Council on the Status of Women (1987) *Women in Politics: Becoming Full Partners in the Political Process*. Ottawa.

Carlshamre, Nils (1969) 'Kvinnor och den konservativa rörelsen', in Ruth Hamrin-Thorell et al. (eds), *Kvinnors röst och rätt*. Stockholm: Allmänna Förlaget.

Carrieri, M. (1987) 'Dopo la stagione dei leader una leadership negoziale? Il gruppo dirigente del PCI 1975–1986, *Democrazia e Diritto*, XVII (6): 269–314.

Carroll, Susan (1985) *Women as Candidates in American Politics*. Bloomington, Ind.: Univesity of Indiana Press.

Carty, R.K. (1980) 'Women in Irish Politics', *Canadian Journal of Irish Studies*, 6(1): 90–104.

Carty, R.K. and Erickson, Lynda (1991) 'Candidate nomination in Canada's national parties', in Herman Bakvis (ed.), *Canadian Political parties: Leaders, Candidates and Organization* (Volume 13 of the research studies of the Royal Commission on Electoral Reform and Party Financing). Ottawa and Toronto: RCERPF/Dundurn Press.

Cattaneo, A. and D'Amato, M. (1990) *La politica della differenza. Dati e analisi per uno studio del rapporto donne/partiti*. Milan: Franco Angeli.

Cayrol, Roland and Perrineau, Pascal (1991) *Le Guide du Pouvoir*. Paris: Editions Doumic.

Cazzola, F. (1985) 'Struttura e potere del partito socialista italiano', in G. Pasquino (ed.), *Il sistema politico italiano*. Bari: Laterza.

Cazzola, F. (1991) 'Le affinità elettive: partiti e potere municipale'. *Polis*, v(2): 267–97.

CDA (1989) *Vrouwen en mannen van de partij, een onderzoek in het kader van een positief actiebeleid voor vrouwen in het CDA*. The Hague: CDA-uitgeverij.

Choisir (1981) *Quel Président pour les femmes?* Paris: Gallimard.

Chubb, Basil (1986) *The Government and Politics of Ireland*, 2nd edn. London: Longman.

Collins, Hugh (1985) 'Political ideology in Australia: the distinctiveness of a Benthamite society', in S. Cranbard (ed.), *Australia: The Daedalus Symposium*. Sydney: Angus and Robertson.

Commission on the Status of Women (1972) *Report to the Minister for Finance.* Dublin: Stationery Office.

Connell, R.W. (1987) *Gender and Power.* Stanford, Ca: Stanford University Press.

Corbetta, P. et al. (1988) *Elezioni in Italia. Struttura a tipologia delle consultazione politiche.* Bologna: Il Mulino.

Cotta, M. (1979) *Classe politica e Parlamento in Italia.* Bologna: Il Mulino.

Cotter, Cornelius, Gibson, James, Bibby, John and Huskshorn, Robert (1984) *Party Organization in American Politics.* New York: Praeger.

Craig, F.W.S. (1989) *British Electoral Facts 1832–1987.* Dartmouth: Parliamentary Research Services.

Crewe, Ivor (1992) 'Why did Labour lose (yet again)?' *Politics Review*, 2(1), September.

Crewe, Ivor, Day, Neil and Fox, Anthony (1991) *The British Electorate 1963–1987.* Cambridge: Cambridge University Press.

Crewe, Ivor, Norris, Pippa and Waller, Robert (1992) 'The 1992 Election: Conservative hegemony or Labour recovery?', in Pippa Norris, Ivor Crewe, David Denver and David Broughton (eds), *British Elections and Parties Yearbook, 1992.* Hemel Hempstead: Harvester Wheatsheaf.

Crotty, William (1983) *Party Reform.* New York: Longman.

Czudnowski, Moshe M. (1975) 'Political recruitment', in Fred Greenstein and Nelson W. Polsby (eds), *Handbook of Political Science*, Vol. 2: *Micropolitical Theory.* Reading, Mass., Addison-Wesley.

Dahlerup, D. (1989) *Vi har ventet lenge nok – håndbok i kvinnerepresentasjon.* Copenhagen: Nordisk Ministerråd.

Dahlerup, Drude and Gulli, Brita (1985) 'Women's organizations in the Nordic countries: lack of force or counterforce?', in Elina Haavio-Mannila et al. (eds), *Unfinished Democracy: Women in Nordic Politics.* Oxford: Pergamon Press.

Darcy, Robert (1988) 'The election of women to Dáil Eireann: a formal analysis, *Irish Political Studies*, 3: 63–76.

Darcy, Robert and Beckwith, Karen (1991) 'Political disaster, political triumph: the election of women to national parliaments'. Paper presented at the Annual General Meeting of the American Political Science Association, 28 August–1 September, Washington, D.C.

Darcy, Robert and Schramm, Sarah Slavin (1977) 'When women run against men', *Public Opinion Quarterly*, 41: 1–12.

Darcy, R., Welch, Susan and Clark, Janet (1987) *Women, Elections, and Representation.* New York: Longman Inc.

De Vaus, David and McAllister, Ian (1989) 'The changing politics of women: gender and political alignment in 11 nations', *European Journal of Political Research*, 17.

Deber, Raisa (1982) 'The fault dear Brutus': women as congressional candidates in Pennsylvania', *Journal of Politics*, 44 (May): 463–79.

Department of the Taoiseach (1987) *First Report by Ireland on the Measures Adopted to Give Effect to the Provisions of the Convention.* Dublin: Stationery Office.

Der Spiegel 1992 'Cliquen, Kartelle, Seilschaften'. 6: 56–8.

Di Palma, G. (1977) *Surviving without Governing. The Italian Parties in Parliament.* Berkeley, Ca: University of California Press.

Dixson, Miriam (1975) *The Real Matilda.* Ringwood: Penguin.

Dogan, Mattéi and Narbonne, Jacques (1955) *Les françaises face à la politique, comportement politique et condition sociale.* Paris: Albin Colin.

Ds A (1986) *Ska även morgondagens samhälle formas enbart av män?* Stockholm: Ministry of Labour.

Duhamel, Olivier (1989) 'President and Prime Minister', in Paul Godt (ed.), *Policy Making in France,* London: Pinter Publishers.

Durant, Henry (1969) 'Voting Behaviour in Britain 1945–66', in Richard Rose (ed.), *Studies in British Politics,* 2nd edn. London: Macmillan.

Duverger, Maurice (1955) *La participation des femmes à la vie politique (The Political Role of Women).* Paris: UNESCO.

Dyck, Rand (1989) 'Relations between federal and provincial parties', in Alain G. Gangnon and A. Brian Tanguay (eds), *Canadian Parties in Transition: Discourse/Organization/Representation.* Scarborough, Ontario: Nelson Canada, pp. 186–219.

Edney, Ray (1991) 'Affirmative action given green light', *The Democrat* (June/July): 14.

Eduards, Maud (1980) 'Kvinnorepresentation och kvinnomakt', Department of Political Science, University of Stockholm.

Eduards, Maud (1981) 'Sweden', in Joni Lovenduski and Jill Hill (eds), *The Politics of the Second Electorate.* London: Routledge and Kegan Paul.

Eduards, Maud (1991) 'Toward a third way: women's politics and welfare politics in Sweden', *Social Research,* 58: 677–705.

Eggleton, Tony (1987) *Women: The Next Liberal Government's Policy.* LPA: Canberra.

Ehrmann, Henry and Schain, Martin (1992) *Politics in France,* 5th edn. New York: Harper Collins.

Eldersveld, Samuel (1982) *Political Parties in American Society.* New York: Basic Books.

Emancipatieraad (1991) *Vrouwen in politiek en openbaar bestuur.* The Hague: Emancipatieraad.

Encel, Sol, Mackenzie, Norman and Tebbutt, Margaret (1974) *Women and Society: an Australian Study.* Melbourne: Cheshire.

Epstein, Leon (1980) *Political Parties in Western Democracies.* New Brunswick, NJ: Transaction Books.

Ergas, Y. (1986) *Nelle maglie della politica. Femminismo, istituzioni e politische sociali nell'Italia degli anni '70.* Milan: Franco Angeli.

Erickson, Lynda (1991) 'Women and candidates for the House of Commons', in Kathy Megyery (ed.), *Women in Canadian Politics: Towards Equity in Representation* (Volume 6 of the research studies of the Royal Commission on Electoral Reform and Party Financing). Ottawa and Toronto: RCERPF/Dundurn Press, pp. 101–25.

Evin, Katleen (1991) 'Dieu est-il misogyne?', *Biba,* May.

Falke, Wolfgang (1982) *Die Mitglieder der CDU.* Berlin: Duncker and Humblot.

Fanello Marcucci, G. (1987) *Donne in Parlamento: i conti che non tornano.* Rome: Bagatto Libri.

Farneti, P. (1983) *Il sistema dei partiti in Italia. 1946–1979.* Bologna: Il Mulino.

Farrell, Brian (1990) 'Forming the government', in M. Gallagher and R. Sinnott (eds), *How Ireland Voted 1989.* Galway: Centre for the Study of Irish Elections.

Farrell, David M. (1992) 'Ireland', in Richard Katz and Peter Mair (eds), *Party Organizations: A Data Handbook.* London: Sage, pp. 389–457.

fdk: Pressedienst der FDP, published monthly, and edited by the FDP Bundesvorstand, Bonn.

Fianna Fail (1977) *Action Plan for National Reconstruction. Manifesto 1977 General Election.* Dublin.

Fianna Fail (1981) *Our Programme for the '80s.* Dublin.

Fianna Fail (1982) *The Way Forward.* Dublin.

Fianna Fail (1987) *The Programme for National Recovery.* Dublin.

Fianna Fail (1989) *National Recovery: The Next Phase.* Dublin.

Fianna Fail/Progressive Democrats (1989) *Programme for Government 1989–93 in the National Interest.* Dublin.

Fine Gael (1981) *A Better Future – Let the Country Win.* Dublin.

Fine Gael (1982) *Fine Gael Priorities, Election 1982, Nov.* Dublin.

Fine Gael (1987) *Breaking Out of the Vicious Circle.* Dublin.

Fine Gael (1989) *Putting the Country First.* Dublin.

Fine Gael/Labour (1981) *Coalition Document: Programme for Government 1981–86.* Dublin.

Fine Gael/Labour (1982) *Programme for Government, December 1982.* Dublin.

Fitzsimons, Yvonne (1991) 'Women's interest representation in the Republic of Ireland: the Council for the Status of Women', *Irish Political Studies*, 6: 37–51.

Fogt, Helmut (1989) 'The Greens and the new left: influences of left-extremism on the Green party organisation and policies', in Eva Kolinsky (ed.), *The Greens in West Germany: Organisation and Policy Making.* Oxford/New York: Berg, pp. 89–122.

Fosshaug, L. (1989) *Ubuden gjest i lukket selskap.* Hovedoppgave: University of Bergen.

Fowler, Linda and McClure, Robert (1989) *Political Ambition.* New Haven, Conn.: Yale University Press.

Från riksdag och departement (1991). No. 29.

Frauen in der CDU (1985) Der Beitrag der Frauen in der CDU zur Politik für eine neue Partnerschaft zwischen Mann und Frau. Eine Auswahl in Dokumenten von 1973–1985. Bonn: Ed. CDU-Frauenvereinigung.

Frauen in der SPD (1988) Dokumentation der Quotendebatte vom 30 August 1988 auf dem Bundesparteitag in Münster. *Sozialdemokratischer Informationsdienst.* Dokumente No. 28, Bonn.

Frauenbeauftragte der hessischen Landesregierung (ed.) (1985) *Quotierung – Reizwort oder Lösung?* Wiesbaden.

Frauenpolitik der CDU (1986) Bonn: Ed. CDU-Frauenvereinigung.

Freeman, Jo (1986) 'The political culture of the Democratic and Republican parties', *Political Science Quarterly*, 101: 327–56.

Freeman, J. (1987) 'Whom you know versus whom you represent: feminist influence in the Democratic and Republican parties', in Mary Katzenstein and Carol Mueller (eds), *The Women's Movement of the United States and Western Europe.* Philadelphia: Temple University Press.

Freeman, Jo (1989) 'Feminist activities at the 1988 Republican convention', *PS: Political Science and Politics*, 22: 39–46.

Frevert, Ute (1989) *Women in German History.* Oxford: Berg.

Friedan, B. (1981) *The Second Stage.* New York: Summit Books.

Fülles, Mechtild (1969) *Frauen in Partei und Parlament.* Cologne: Wiseenschaft und Politik.

Gabriel, Oscar W. (1979) *Kommunalpolitik im Wandel der Gesellschaft.* Meisenheim: Hain.

Gaiter, Philip (1991) *The Swedish Green Party: Responses to the Parliamentary Challenge 1988–1990.* Stockholm: The International Graduate.

Gallagher, M. and Marsh, M. (eds) (1988) *Candidate selection in comparative perspective.* London: Sage.

Gallagher, Michael (1980) 'Candidate selection in Ireland: the impact of localism and the electoral system', *British Journal of Political Science*, 10 (4): 489-503.

Gallagher, Michael (1984) '166 who rule – the Dail Deputies of November 1982', *Economic and Social Review*, 15 (4): 241–64.

Gallagher, Michael (1985) *Political Parties in the Republic of Ireland.* Dublin: Gill and Macmillan.

Gallagher, Michael (1988) 'Ireland: the increasing role of the centre', in M. Gallagher and M. Marsh (eds), *Candidate Selection in Comparative Perspective.* London: Sage.

Galligan, Yvonne (1992a) 'Women in Irish politics', in John Coakley and Michael Gallagher (eds), *Politics in the Republic of Ireland.* Galway: PSAI Press.

Galligan, Yvonne (1992b) 'The Legislative Process', in Alpha Connolly (ed.), *Gender, the Law and the Legal System in Ireland.* Dublin: Gill and Macmillan.

Garraud, Philippe (1989) *Profession: Homme politique – La carrière politique des maires urbains.* Paris: l'Harmattan.

Garvin, Tom (1981) *The Evolution of Irish Nationalist politics.* Dublin: Gill and Macmillan.

Gaspard, Françoise, Goldet, Cécile and Lhuiller, Edith (1978) *Déclaration de Courant Femmes au PS.* Mimeograph, June.

Geddes, Andrew, Lovenduski, Joni and Norris, Pippa (1992) 'Reforming the candidate selection process' *Contemporary Record*, 4: 19–22.

Geissler, Heiner (ed.), (1986) *Abschied von der Männergesellschaft.* Frankfurt-am-Main: Ullstein.

Gertzog, Irwin and Simard, M. Michele (1981) 'Women and "hopeless" Congressional candidacies: nomination frequency, 1916–1978', *American Politics Quarterly*, 9: 449–66.

Gilljam, Mikael and Holmberg, Sören (1990) *Rött blåt grönt.* Stockholm: Bonniers.

Gleichstellungsbericht des SPD Parteivorstandes (1991) Parteitag Bremen 28–31 May. Bonn.

Glenney, Daryl (1982) 'Women in politics: on the rise', *Campaigns and Elections*, 3 (Winter).

Goodman, Ellen (1988) 'Arrival of the new insiders', *Boston Globe*, 19 July.

Goot, Murray and Reid, Elizabeth (1984) 'Women: if not apolitical, then conservative', in Janet Siltanen and Michelle Stanworth (eds), *Women and the Public Sphere.* London: Hutchinson.

Government Report (1987) First report by Ireland on the measures adopted to give effect to the provisions of the convention (UN convention on the elimination of all forms of discrimination against women). Dublin: Stationery Office.

Graubard, S.R. (1986) *Norden – the Passion for Equality.* Oslo: Norwegian University Press/Dædalus.

Graziano, L. and Tarrow, S. (eds) (1979) *La crisi italiana.* Vol. II: *Sistema politico e istituzioni.* Turin: Einaudi.

Greven, Michael (1987) *Parteimitglieder.* Opladen: Westdeutscher Verlag.

Guadagnini, M. (1980) 'Politics without women: the Italian case'. Paper presented at the ECPR Joint Sessions of Workshops, Florence.

Guadagnini, M. (1983) 'Partiti e classe parlamentare negli anni settana', *Rivista Italiana di Scienza Politica*, XIII (2): 261–4.

Guadagnini, M. (1984) 'Il personale politico dalla 'periferia' al 'centro'. Le amministrazioni locali come area di reclutamento del personale parlamentare', *Le Regioni*, XII (4): 589–620.

Guadagnini, M. (1987) 'Una rappresentanza limitata: le donne in Parlamento dal 1948 ad oggi', *Quaderni di Sociologia*, XXXIII (8): 130-57.

Guadagnini, M. (1988) 'The representation of women in decision-making arenas'. Paper presented at the Conference 'Women, men and political power', Saalfelden.

Guadagnini, M. and Porro, G. (1989) *La normativa internazione in materia di parità donna-uomo*. Turin: Ed. Consiglio regionale del Piemonte.

Haavio-Mannila, E. et al. (eds) (1985) *Unfinished Democracy. Women in Nordic Politics*. London and New York: Pergamon Press.

Handschuh, Ekkehard et al. (1986) *Wegweiser Parlament*. Bonn: Bundeszentrale für politische Bildung.

Heidar, K. (1988) *Partidemokrati på prøve*. Oslo: Universitetsforlaget.

Heidar, K. (forthcoming) 'A new party leadership?', in K. Strøm and L. Svassand (eds), *Challenges to Political Parties*.

Heiderpriem, Nikki and Lake, Celinda (1987) 'The winning edge'. *The Polling Report*, 6 April.

Hellevik, O. and Bjørklund, T. (1987) *Barrierer mot kvinners deltakelse i lokalpolitikken*. ISF-Rapport 11/87.

Hernes, H. (1987) *Welfare States and Women Power. Essays in State Feminism.* Oslo: Norwegian University Press.

Hills, Jill (1981) 'Britain' in Joni Lovenduski and Jill Hills (eds), *The Politics of the Second Electorate*, London: Routledge and Kegan Paul.

Hoecker, Beate (1987) *Frauen in der Politik*. Opladen: Leske and Budrich.

Hofmann-Göttig, Joachim (1986) *Emanzipation mit dem Stimmzettel. 70 Jahre Frauenwahlrecht in Deutschland*. Bonn: Dietz.

Hofmann-Göttig, Joachim (1989) 'Die Frauen haben die Macht, mit dem Stimmzettel den Ausschlag zu geben', *Frauenforschung*, 3.

Holmberg, Sören (1974) *'Riksdagen representerar svenska folket': Empiriska studier i representativ demokrati*. Lund: Studentlitteratur.

Holmberg, Sören (1981) *Svenska väljare*. Stockholm: LiberFörlaget.

Holmberg, Sören (1991) 'Kärnkraft – ett seglivat stridsäpple', in Sören Holmberg and Lennart Weibull (eds), *Trendbrott?* Gothenburg: Gothenburg University.

Holmberg, Sören and Gilljam, Mikael (1987) *Väljare och val i Sverige*. Stockholm: Bonniers.

Holtmann, Everhard (1992) 'Politisierung der Kommunalpolitik und Wandlungen im lokalen Parteiensystem', *Aus Politik und Zeitgeschichte*, B 22-23: 13–22.

Hosek, Chaviva (1983) 'Women and the constitutional process', in Keith Banting and Richard Simeon (eds), *And No One Cheered: Federalism, Democracy and the Constitution Act*. Toronto: Methuen, pp. 280–300.

Hughes, Colin A. (1990) 'A target missed: women in Australian elections'. Paper presented to the American Political Science Association Meeting, San Francisco.

Hunter and Denton (1984) 'Do female candidates "lose votes"? the experience of female candidates in the 1979 and 1980 Canadian general elections', *Canadian Review of Sociology and Anthropology*, 21: 395–406.

Hutchison, Jenny (1982) 'Political Party Conferences', *Current Affairs Bulletin*, 59 (6): 4–14.

Ignazi, Piero (1992) *Dal PCI al PDS*. Bologna: Il Mulino.

INSEE (1986) *Femmes en chiffres*. Paris: Documentation Française.

INSEE (1991) *Les Femmes*. Paris: Hachette.

Inter-Parliamentary Union (1991) 'Distribution of seats between men and women in national parliaments, statistical data from 1945 to 30 June 1991', *Rapports et Documents*, 18.

Irish Political Studies (1988) volume 3. Irish Political Studies Association: Dublin.

Irish Political Studies (1990) volume 5. Irish Political Studies Association: Dublin.

Irving, Ronnie and Paterson, W.E. (1991) 'The 1990 German Election' *Parliamentary Affairs*, 44(3): 353–72.

Jaensch, Dean (1988) *The Australian Party System*. Sydney: Allen and Unwin.

Jennings, M. Kent (1990) 'Women in party politics', in Louise Tilly and Patricia Gurin (eds), *Women, Politics and Change*, New York: Russell Sage Foundation.

Jesse, Eckhard (1990) *Elections, The Federal Republic in Comparison*. Oxford: Berg.

Jonasson, Birgit (1985) 'Åsikter i tre jämställdhetsfrågor', *Kvinnovetenskaplig tidskrift*, pp. 54–62.

Kaack, Heino and Roth, Reinhold (eds), (1980) *Handbuch des deutschen Parteiensystems*, vol. 1. Opladen: Leske and Budrich.

Kabinetsstandpunt Vrouwen in Politiek en Openbaar Bestuur (1992).

Karlsson, Gunnel (1990) *Manssamhället till behag?* Stockholm: Tiden.

Katz, Richard (1981) 'But how many candidates should we have in Donegal? Numbers of nominees and electoral efficiency in Ireland', *British Journal of Political Science*, 11 (1): 117–23.

Katzenstein, Mary and Mueller, Carol (eds) (1987) *The Women's Movement of the United States and Western Europe*. Philadelphia: Temple University Press.

Keeter, Scott (1985) 'Public opinion in 1984', in Gerald Pomper (ed.) *The Election of 1984*. Chatham, NJ: Chatham House Publishers.

Kendrigan, Mary Lou (1984) *Political Equality in a Democratic Society: Women in the United States*. Westport, Conn.: Greenwood Publishers.

Kenski, Henry (1988) 'The gender factor in a changing electorate', in Carol Mueller (ed.), *The Politics of the Gender Gap: The Social Construction of Political Influence*. Beverly Hills, Ca: Sage.

Kiernan, Laura (1988) 'Humphrey: Motherhood remarks "Just plain stupid"', *Boston Globe*, 9 September: 1.

Kirchheimer, O. (1966) 'The transformation of the West European party system', in J. LaPalombara and U. Weiner (eds) *Political Parties and Political Development*. Princeton: Princeton University Press.

Kirschten, Dick (1984) 'The Reagan reelection campaign hopes 1984 will be the year of the women', *National Journal* (2 June): 1082–5.

Klein, E. (1987) 'The diffusion of consciousness in the United States and Western Europe', in M.F. Katzenstein and C.M. Mueller (eds), *The Women's Movements of the United States and Western Europe*. Philadelphia: Temple University Press.

Klemesrud, Judy (1983) 'Women study art of politics', *New York Times*, 28 November.

Koeneman, L., Lucardie, P. and Noomen, I. (1985) 'Het partijgebeuren: kroniek van de partijpolitieke gebeurtenissen van het jaar 1984', in R.A. Koole (ed.), *Jaarboek van het Documentatiecentrum Nederlandse Politieke Partijen, 1984*. Groningen: Rijksuniversiteit Groningen.

Kolinsky, Eva (1984) *Parties, Opposition and Society in West Germany*. London: Croom Helm.

Kolinsky, Eva (1988) 'The West German Greens – A Women's Party?', *Parliamentary Affairs*, 41.

Kolinsky, Eva (1989a) 'Women in the Green Party', in Eva Kolinsky (ed.), *The Greens in West Germany*. Oxford: Berg.

Kolinsky, Eva (1989b) *Women in West Germany*. Oxford: Berg.

Kolinsky, Eva (1991a) 'Women's quotas in West Germany', *West European Politics*, 14 (1).

Kolinsky, Eva (1991b) 'Political culture change and party organisation: The SPD and the Second "Fräuleinwunder"', in John Gaffney and Eva Kolinsky (eds), *Political Culture in France and Germany*. London: Routledge.

Kolinsky, Eva (1992a) *Women in Contemporary Germany* (2nd rev. edn of *Women in West Germany*) Oxford: Berg.

Kolinsky, E. (1992b) 'Parliamentary careers and the impact of women's quotas'. Unpublished report of a survey of elections held in 1990. Keele University.

Kome, Percy (1985) *Women of Influence: Canadian Women and Politics*. Toronto: Doubleday Canada.

Koole, R.A. and Leijenaar, M.H. (1988) 'The Netherlands, the predominance of regionalism', in M. Gallagher and M. Marsh (eds), *Candidate Selection in Comparative Perspective*. London: Sage, pp. 190–209.

Koole, R.A. and Voerman, G. (1986) 'Het lidmaatschap van politieke partijen na 1945', in R.A. Koole (ed.), *Jaarboek van het Documentatiecentrum Nederlandse Politieke Partijen, 1985*. Groningen: Rijksuniversiteit Groningen, pp. 115–76.

Kvinnans jämlikhet (1964) Stockholm: Tiden.

Labour Party (1981) *Labour '81 Election Programme*. Dublin.

Labour Party (1982) *Jobs, Equality and Justice in Labour*. Dublin.

Labour Party (1987) *People Matter Most: Labour Party Election '87 Manifesto*. Dublin.

Labour Party (1989) *Now more than ever! Labour's Policy Proposals*. Dublin.

Lang, Regina (1989) *Frauenquoten. Der einen Freud, des anderen Leid*. Bonn: Dietz.

Lecocq, Elisabeth and Fabre, Elisabeth (1988) *Participation des femmes à la vie publique et politique en France*. Mimeograph prepared for the Comité Promotion de la Famme aux Responsibilités Publiques.

Lederer, Gerda (1983) *Jugend und Autorität*. Opladen: Westdeutscher Verlag.

Leijenaar, M.H. (1989) *De geschade heerlijkheid. Onderzoek naar politiek gedrag van vrouwen en mannen in Nederland, 1918–1988*. The Hague: SDU-uitgeverij.

Leijenaar, M.H. and Niemöller, B. (1986) 'Vrouwen in politieke partijen', in R.A. Koole (ed.), *Jaarboek van het Documentatiecentrum Nederlandse Politieke Partijen, 1985*. Groningen: Rijksuniversiteit Groningen, pp. 177–94.

Leijenaar, M.H. et al. (1983) *De helft als minderheid, verslag van een onderzoek naar vrouwen in politieke functies*. The Hague: VNG Uitgeverij.

Leira, A. (1989) *Models of Motherhood*. Oslo: ISF-Rapport 89: 7.

Leitsätze der CDU für eine neue Partnerschaft zwischen Manan und Frau (1985) CDU Dokumentation 12, 1 April.

Leonardi, L. and Wertman, D.A. (1989) *Italian Christian Democracy. The Politics of Dominance*. London: Macmillan.

Liberal Party of Canada (1986) *Constitution*. Ottawa.

Lijphart, Arend and Irwin, Galen (1979) 'Nomination strategies in the Irish STV system: the Dail elections of 1969, 1973 and 1977', *British Journal of Political Science*, 9 (3): 362–9.

Lindahl, Rutger and Nordlöf, Tina (1989) 'EG-frågen i svensk opinion', in Sören Holmberg and Lennart Weibull (eds), *Åttiotal. Svensk opinion is empirisk belysning.* Gothenburg: Gothenburg University.

Lipset, Seymour Martin (1960) *Political Man*, Glencoe, Ill., Free Press.

Lloyd, Clem and Swan, Wayne (1987) 'National Factions and the ALP', *Politics*, 22 (1): 100–10.

Loewenberg, Gerhard and Patterson, Samuel C. (1979) *Comparing Legislatures.* Boston, Mass.: Little, Brown.

Loewenberg, Gerhard, Patterson, Samuel C. and Jewell, Malcolm (eds), (1985) *Handbook of Legislative Research.* Cambridge, Mass.: Harvard University Press.

Lohmar, Ulrich (1968) *Innerparteiliche Demokratie.* Stuttgart: Enke.

Lovenduski, J. (1986) *Women and European Politics. Contemporary Feminism and Public Policy.* Brighton: Wheatsheaf Books.

Lovenduski, Joni and Hills, Jill (1981) *The Politics of the Second Electorate.* London: Routledge and Kegan Paul.

Lovenduski, Joni and Norris, Pippa (1989) 'Selecting women candidates: obstacles to the feminisation of the House of Commons', *European Journal of Political Research*, Autumn, 17: 533–62.

Lovenduski, Joni and Norris, Pippa (1991) 'Party rules and women's representation: reforming the labour party selection process', in *British Elections and Parties Yearbook, 1991.* Hemel Hempstead: Harvester Wheatsheaf, pp. 189–206.

Lovenduski, Joni and Randall, Vicky (1993) *Contemporary Feminist Politics.* Oxford: Oxford University Press.

Lovenduski, Joni, Norris, Pippa and Levy, Catriona (1993) 'The party and women', in A. Seldon and D. Butler (eds), *The Conservative Party 1900–1990.* Oxford: Oxford University Press.

Lugar, Richard (1983) 'A plan to elect more GOP women', *Washington Post*, 21 August, C8.

Lynch, Amanda (1989) 'The coalition women in the state', *The Weekend Australian*, 21–22 July.

Macgregor, John (1989) 'Persons in the pursuit of power', *Age*, 27 July.

Machin, Howard (1991) 'Changing patterns of party competition', in Peter Hall and Jack Hayward (eds), *Development in French Politics.* New York: St. Martin's Press, pp. 33–54.

Macmillan, Sally (1989) 'A point of disorder', *Weekend Australian*, 9–10 December.

Mair, Peter (1987) *The Changing Irish Party System.* London: Pinter.

Mair, Peter (1990) 'The Irish party system into the 1990s', in M. Gallagher and R. Sinnott (eds), *How Ireland Voted 1989.* Galway: Centre for the Study of Irish Elections.

Mangin, Catherine and Martichoux, Elizabeth (1991) *Ces femmes qui nous gouvernent.* Paris: Albin Michel.

Mannheimer, R. (1990) 'Vecchi e nuovi caratteri del voto comunista', in M. Caciagli and S. Spreafico (eds), *Vent' anni di elezioni in Italia.* Padua: Liviana.

Mannheimer, R. and Sani, G. (1987) *Il mercato elettorale. Identikit dell' elettore italiano.* Bologna: Il Mulino.

Manning, Maurice (1972) *Irish Political Parties.* Dublin: Gill and Macmillan.

Manning, Maurice (1978) 'Women in Irish national and local politics 1922–77', in M. McCurtin and D. O'Corrain (eds), *Women in Irish Society: the Historical Dimension*. Dublin: Arlen House.

Manning, Maurice (1987) 'Women and the elections', in H. Penniman and B. Farrell (eds), *Ireland at the Polls 1981, 1982 and 1987*. Washington: American Enterprise Institute/Duke University Press.

Marsh, Michael (1981a) 'Electoral preferences in Irish recruitment: the 1977 election', *European Journal of Political Research*, 9 (1): 61–74.

Marsh, Michael (1981b) 'Localism, candidate selection and electoral preferences in Ireland, the General Election of 1977', *Economic and Social Review*, 12 (4): 267–86.

Marsh, Michael (1987) 'Electoral evaluations of candidates in Irish elections', *Irish Political Studies*, 2: 65–76.

Marsh, Michael (1989) 'Transformation with a small 't': candidates for the Dail, 1948–82', *Irish Political Studies*, 4: 59–82.

Marsh, Michael and Richard Sinnott (1990) 'How the voters decided', in M. Gallagher and R. Sinnott (eds), *How Ireland Voted 1989*. Galway: Centre for the Study of Irish Elections.

Massari, O. (1987) 'Leadership e strutture di partito: il caso del PSI', *Democrazia e diritto*, XXVII (6): 85–102.

Matlack, Carol (1987) 'Women at the polls', *National Journal*, 19 December: 3208–15.

Matthews, Donald (1984) 'Legislative recruitment and legislative careers', *Legislative Studies Quarterly*, November: 547–85.

Matthews, Donald R. (1985) 'Legislative recruitment and legislative careers', in Gerhard Loewenberg, Samuel C. Patterson and Malcolm E. Jewell (eds), *Handbook of Legislative Research*. Cambridge, Mass.: Harvard University Press.

Mayer, Hans-Ludwig (1991) 'Wählerverhalten bei der Bundestagswahl 1990 nach Geschlecht und Alter. Ergebnis der repräsentativen Wahlstatistik', *Wirtschaft und Statistik*, 4.

Mazur, Amy G. (1991) 'Agendas and egalité professionelle: symbolic policy at work in France', in Elizabeth Meehan and Selma Sevenhuijsen (eds), *Equality Politics and Gender*. London: Sage, pp. 122–41.

Mazur, Amy G. (1992) 'Symbolic reform in France: Egalité professionelle during the Mitterand years', *West European Politics*, October.

McCormick, Peter (1991) 'The Reform Party of Canada: new beginning or dead end?', in Hugh G. Thorburn (ed.), *Party Politics in Canada*, 6th edn. Scarborough, Ontario: Prentice-Hall Canada, pp. 342–52.

McKerrow, Shirley (1982) 'The Next Three Years'. Speech to the Australian Institute of Political Science Seminar on Women and Party Politics, Melbourne.

Mény, Yves (1987) 'Les Restrictions au cumul des mandats: Réforme symbolique ou changement en profondeur?' *Tocqueville Revue*, 8.

Metje, Matthias (1991) 'Die Beteiligung von Frauen und Männern an Bundestagswahlen', *Zeitschrift für Parlamentsfragen*, 22 (3).

Mezey, Michael L. (1979) *Comparative Legislatures*. 223–254 Durham, NC: Duke University Press.

Michels, Robert (1962[1911]) *Political Parties*. New York: Free Press.

Minelli, Anna R. (1990) *Amministrazione, politica, società*. Milan: Franco Angeli.

Mintzel, Alf (1990) 'Auf der Suche nach der Wirklichkeit der Großparteien in der Bundesrepublik Deutschland', *Passauer Papiere zur Sozialwissenschaft*, 5.

Mintzel, Alf (1989) 'Großparteien im Parteienstaat der Bundesrepublik Deutschland', *Aus Politik und Zeitgeschichte*, B11.

Mossuz-Lavau, Janine and Sineau, Mariette (1981) 'France', in Joni Lovenduski and Jill Hills (eds), *The Politics of the Second Electorate*. London: Routledge and Kegan Paul, pp. 112–33.

Mossuz-Lavau, Janine and Sineau, Mariette (1983) *Enquête sur les femmes et la politique en France*. Paris: PUF.

Mossuz-Lavau, Janine and Sineau, Mariette (1984) *Women in the Political World in Europe*. Strasbourg: Council of Europe.

Mossuz-Lavau, Janine and Sineau, Mariette (1988) 'La mutation de l'électorat féminin', *Le Monde Dossiers et Documents*, May.

Mueller, Carol (ed.) (1987) *The Politics of the Gender Gap*. Beverly Hills, Ca: Sage.

Muscatine, Alison (1984) 'Women in uphill struggles for Senate seats', *Washington Post*, 25 June.

Myers, Patricia (1989) '"Noble Effort": the National Federation of Liberal Women of Canada, 1928–1973', in Linda Kealey and Joan Sangster (eds), *Beyond the Vote: Canadian Women and Politics*. Toronto: University of Toronto Press, pp. 39-62.

National Progressive Conservative Women's Federation (1989) *Initiatives: 'Re-election Driven' – 'Revenue Driven'*. Ottawa: Women's Bureau.

National Women's Liberal Commission (1990) *Programme: Biennial Meeting*. Ottawa: Liberal Party of Canada.

Nealon, Ted (1974) *Ireland: a Parliamentary Directory*. Dublin: Platform Press.

Nealon, Ted (1977) *Guide to the 21st Dail and Seanad*. Dublin: Platform Press.

Nealon, Ted (1981) *Guide to the 22nd Dail and Seanad*. Dublin: Platform Press.

Nealon, Ted (1982) *Guide to the 23rd Dail and Seanad*. Dublin: Platform Press.

Nealon, Ted (1983) *Guide to the 24th Dail and Seanad*. Dublin: Platform Press.

Nealon, Ted (1987) *Guide to the 25th Dail and Seanad*. Dublin: Platform Press.

Nealon, Ted (1989) *Guide to the 26th Dail and Seanad*. Dublin: Platform Press.

Nechemias, Carol (1987) 'Changes in the election of women to U.S. legislative seats', *Legislative Studies Quarterly*, 12 (February): 125–42.

Network (1990) vol. 7, no. 1.

New Democratic Party (1991a) *Constitution of the New Democratic Party* (as amended by the Federal Convention, Halifax, 1991).

New Democratic Party (1991b) *Affirmative Action Policy*. November.

Niemöller, B. (1991) *Partijleden: achtergronden en houdingen*. Amsterdam: University of Amsterdam.

Norris, P. (1985a) 'Women's legislative participation on Western Europe', *West European Politics*, 8 (4): 90–101.

Norris, Pippa (1985b) 'The gender gap: America and Britain', *Parliamentary Affairs*, Spring, 38 (2): 192–201.

Norris, Pippa (1986) 'Conservative attitudes in recent British elections: an emerging gender gap?', *Political Studies*, XXXIV: 120–8.

Norris, Pippa (1987) *Politics and Sexual Equality*. Boulder, Co: Rienner.

Norris, Pippa (1991) 'Gender differences in political participation in Britain', *Government and Opposition*, 26 (1): 56–74.

Norris, Pippa (1993) 'The gender–generation gap in British elections', in D. Denver, P. Norris, C. Rallings and D. Broughton (eds), *British Elections and Parties Yearbook, 1993*. Hemel Hempstead: Harvester Wheatsheaf.

Norris, Pippa and Lovenduski, Joni (1989) 'Pathways to Parliament', *Talking Politics*, 1 (3): 90/94.

Norris, Pippa and Lovenduski, Joni (1992) Paper Presented to the American Political Science Association Annual Meeting, August.

Norris, Pippa, Carty, Ken, Erickson, Linda, Lovenduski, Joni and Simms, Marian (1989) 'Party selectorates in Australia, Britain and Canada: legal context, party procedures and outcome'. Paper presented at the IPSA/ISA First Annual Workshop on Elections and Parties, Fondation Nationale des Sciences Politiques, Paris, April.

Norris, Pippa, Carty, R.K., Erickson, Lynda, Lovenduski, Joni and Simms, Marian (1990) 'Party Selectorates in Australia, Britain and Canada: prolegomena for research in the 1990s', *The Journal of Commonwealth and Comparative Politics*, XXVIII (2): 219–45.

Norris, Pippa, Vallance, Elizabeth and Lovenduski, Joni (1992) 'Do candidates make a difference? Gender, race, ideology and incumbency', *Parliamentary Affairs*, October.

O'Brien, Alison (1982) Speech to the Australian Institute of Political Science Seminar on Women and Party Politics, Canberra.

Oberndörfer, Dieter and Schmitt, Karl (eds) (1991) *Parteien und regionale politische Traditionen in der Bundesrepublik Deutschland*. Berlin: Duncker and Humblot.

Oberreuter, Heinrich and Mintzel, Alf (eds) (1990) *Parteien in der Bundesrepublik*. Munich: Olzog.

Oskarson, Maria (1985) 'En "ny" politisk kvinna? Kvinnors politiska åsikter ur ett generationsperspektiv'. Paper presented at the Annual Meeting of the Swedish Political Science Association, Stockholm, 28–9 October.

Oskarson, Maria (1990) 'Klassröstning på reträtt', in Mikael Gilljam and Sören Holmberg (eds), *Rött Blått grönt*. Stockholm: Bonniers.

Ostrogorski, M. (1964[1903]) *Democracy and the Organisation of Political Parties*. Chicago: Quadrangle Books.

Oud, P.J. and Bosmans, J. (1982) *Honderd jaren. Een eeuw van staatkundige vormgeving in Nederland 1840–1949*. Assen: Van Gorkum.

Outshoorn, J. (1973) *Vrouwenemancipatie en socialisme. De SDAP en het vrouwenvraagstuk 1894–1919*. Nijmegen: SUN.

Panebianco, A. (1982) *Modelli di Partito*. Bologna: Il Mulino.

Panebianco, A. (1988) 'I partiti', in 'Le relazioni fra amministrazione e partiti', *Archivio ISAP*, 5:109–36.

Pasquino, G. (1980) *Crisi dei partiti e governabilità*. Bologna: Il Mulino.

Pasquino, G. (1982) *Degenerazione dei partiti e riforme istituzionali*. Bari: Laterza.

Pasquino, G. (1987) 'Regolatori sregolati: partiti a governo dei partiti', in P. Lange and M. Regini (eds), *Stato e regolazione sociale*. Bologna: Il Mulino.

Perrigo, Sarah (1991) 'The Labour Party and the promotion of women'. Paper Presented to the ECPR Joint Sessions of Workshops, Essex, April.

Petersson, Olof, Westholm, Anders and Blomberg, Göran (1989) *Medborgarnas makt*. Stockholm: Carlsson.

Philippe, Annie and Hubscher, Daniel (1991) *Enquête à l'intérieur du parti socialiste*. Paris: Albin Michel.

Phillips, Anne (1991) *Engendering Democracy*. Cambridge: Polity Press.

Piel, Edgar (1989) 'Kein Interesse für Politik Motive und Reaktionen junger Nichtwählerinnen', *Frauenforschung*, 3.

Pierre, Jon (1986) 'Riksdagsledamöterna och de regionala partiorganisationerna', *Folkets främsta företrädare.* SOU vol. 27.

Progressive Democrats (1987) *A Nation that Works. PD Blueprint for Jobs, Fair Taxation and Social Justice.* Dublin.

Progressive Democrats (1989) *Putting People First: Forcing Real Change.* Dublin.

Pulzer, Peter (1967) *Political Representation and Elections in Britain.* London, Allen and Unwin.

Pulzer, Peter (1991) 'The German Federal Election of 1990', *Electoral Studies,* 10(2): 145–54.

Putnam, Robert (1976) *The Comparative Study of Elites.* Englewood Cliffs, NJ: Prentice-Hall.

PvdA (1991) *Een partij om te kiezen.* Amsterdam, PvdA.

Quindlen, Anna (1992) 'Gender Contender', *New York Times,* 26 April.

Ragsdale, Lyn (1985) 'Legislative Elections' in Gerhard Loewenberg, Samuel C. Patterson and Malcolm Jewell (eds), *Handbook of Legislative Research.* Cambridge, Mass: Harvard University Press.

Randall, Vicky (1987) *Women and Politics,* 2nd edn. London: Macmillan.

Randall, Vicky and Smyth, Ailbhe (1987) 'Bishops and Bailiwicks: obstacles to women's political participation in Ireland', *Economic and Social Review,* 18 (3): 189–214.

Ranney, Austin (1976) *Curing the Mischiefs of Faction.* Berkeley, Ca: University of California Press.

Ranney, Austin (1981) 'Candidate selection', in D. Butler, H. Penniman and A. Ranney (eds), *Democracy at the Polls.* American Enterprise Institute: Washington, DC.

Rey, Henri and Subileau, Françoise (1991) *Les militant socialistes à l'épreuve du pouvoir.* Paris: Presses de la FNSP.

Richardsen, Elke A. and Michalik, Regina (eds) (1985) *Die Quotierte Hälfte. Frauenpolitik in den grün-alternativen Parteien.* Berlin: LitPol.

Riksdagen 1982–1985, Biografiska uppgifter om ledamöterna Stockholm: Office of the Parliament.

Roberts, Geoffrey (1992) 'The growth of the far right', *Parliamentary Affairs,* July.

Rohe, Karl (ed.) (1990) *Elections, Parties and Political Traditions. Social Foundations of German Parties and Party Systems, 1867–1987.* Oxford: Berg.

Rokkan, Stein and Lipset, Seymour (eds) (1967) *Party Systems and Voter Alignment. Cross-National Perspectives.* New York: The Free Press.

Romney, Ronna and Harrison, Beppie (1988) *Momentum: Women in American Politics Now.* New York: Crown Publishers.

Rose, Richard and McAllister, Ian (1990) *The Loyalties of Voters.* London: Sage.

Rovero, M. (1990) 'Women participation to decision-making processes at a local level: second-degree elective bodies. The Piedmont case'. Paper presented at the Council of Europe 2nd Conference on Equal Participation by Women and Men in Local and Political Life, Aarhus.

Royal Commission on the Status of Women in Canada (1970) *Report.* Ottawa: Information Canada.

Rudig, Wolfgang, Bennie, Lynn G. and Franklin, Mark (1991) *Green Party Members: A Profile.* Glasgow: Delta Publications.

Rule, Wilma (1981) 'Why women don't run: The critical contextual factors in women's legislative recruitment', *Western Political Quarterly,* 34: 60–77.

Rule, Wilma (1987) 'Electoral systems, contextual factors and women's opportunity for election to parliament in twenty-three democracies', *Western Political Quarterly*, 40: 477–86.

Rule, Wilma and Norris, Pippa (1992) 'Anglo and minority women's under-representation in the Congress: Is the electoral system the culprit?', in Joseph Zimmerman and Wilma Rule (eds), *The Impact of U.S. Electoral Systems on Minorities and Women*. Westport, Conn: Greenwood Press.

Rule, Wilma and Zimmerman, Joseph F. (eds) (1992) *U.S. Electoral Systems: Their Impact on Minorities and Women*, Westport, Conn: Greenwood Press.

Ryan, Susan (1982) *The ALP and Women Towards Equality*. Canberra: ALP National Secretariat.

Sainsbury, Diane (1991) 'Bringing women into elected office in Sweden: women's strategies, party responses and political opportunity structures'. Paper presented at the ECPR workshop on 'Party Responses to Women's Demands for Political Entry', ECPR Joint Sessions, University of Essex.

Sainsbury, Diane (1992) 'The 1991 Swedish election: protest, fragmentation and a shift to the right', *West European Politics* (15) 2.

Saint-Criq, Régine (1989) *Une autre place pour les femmes*. Study conducted for the Fédération Nationale des Elus Socialistes et Républicains (FNESR).

Sawer, Marian (1993) *A Woman's Place*. 2nd ed. Sydney: Allen and Unwin.

SCB (1981) *Politiska resurser*. Stockholm: National Bureau of Statistics.

SCB (1988) *Inequality in Sweden. Living Conditions 1975–1985*. Stockholm: National Bureau of Statistics.

Schäfers, Bernhard (1990) *Gesellschaftlicher Wandel in Deutschland*, 5th rev. edn. Stuttgart: Enke.

Schattschneider, E.E. (1960) *The Semi-Sovereign People – A Realists's View of Democracy in America*. New York: Holt, Rinehard and Winston.

Schlesinger, Joseph (1991) *Political Parties and the Winning of Office*. Ann Arbor, Mich.: The University of Michigan Press.

Schmidt, Vivien (1991) *Democratizing France*. New York: Cambridge University Press.

Schokking, J.C. (1958) *De vrouw in de Nederlands politiek*. Assen: Van Gorkum.

Schumacher, Kurt (1949) *Ruft die Frauen*. Sonderdruck Hanover: Archive of Social Democracy (Bonn no. 10051, A26871).

Scott, Austin (1974) 'Democratic women see gains in 1974', *Washington Post*, 31 March.

SEDF (1990) *Les Femmes en France*. Document prepared for the Conference on Women and Political Power, Montreal, June.

Seidenspinner, Gerlinde and Burger, Angelika (1982) *Mädchen '82*. Munich: Deutsches Jugendinstitut.

Sellier, Michèle (1983) 'La mairie dans le cursus politique', *Pouvoirs*, 24.

Seyd, Pat and Whiteley, Paul (1992) *Labour's Grassroots: The Politics of Labour Party Membership*. Oxford: Oxford University Press.

Shafer, Byron (1983) *Quiet Revolution*. New York: Russell Sage Foundation.

Shell (1985) *Jugendliche und Erwachsene, Generationen im Vergleich*, vol. 3. Ed. Jugendwerk der Deutschen Shell. Opladen: Leske und Budrich.

Sheppard, Robert (1991) 'And may the best non-man win?', *Globe and Mail*, 12 June, A15.

Sigoda, Pascal (1984) 'Les cercles extérieurs du RPR', *Pouvoirs*, 28.

Simms, Marian (1979) 'Conservative feminism in Australia: a case study of feminist ideology', *Women's Studies: International Quarterly*, 3: 305–18.

Simms, Marian (1984) 'A woman's place is in the House . . . and in the Senate: women and the 1983 Federal election', *Australian Quarterly*, 55 (4): 364–74.

Simms, Marian (1985) 'The 1984 Federal elections: find the women', *Politics*, 20 (1): 105–12.

Simms, Marian (1988) 'Women', in I. McAllister and J. Worhurst (eds), *Australian Votes*. South Melbourne: Longman Cheshire.

Simms, Marian and Stone, Diane (1990) *Women in Australian Politics: A Research Project for UNESCO*. Bangkok: UNESCO.

Sineau, Mariette (1988) *Des femmes en politique*. Paris: Economica.

Sineau, Mariette (1991) 'D'une présidence à l'autre: La politique socialiste en directions des femmes (10 Mai 1981–10 Mai 1991)', *French Politics and Society*, 9 (Summer/Fall).

Skard, T. and Haavio-Mannila, E. (1986) 'Equality between the sexes: myth or reality in Norway?', in Stephen R. Graubard (ed.), *Norway: The Passion for Equality*. Oslo: Norwegian University Press/Dædalus.

Skjeie, H. (1982) *Likestillingsloven som beslutningsprosess*. Hovedoppgave: Institutt for statsvitenskap, University of Oslo.

Skjeie, H. (1985) *Fortrinnsrett – ingen forpliktelse. Om bruk av kvotering som virkemiddel i den offentlige likestillingenspolitkken*. Oslo: ISF-Rapport 4/85.

Skjeie, H. (1991a) 'The rhetoric of difference. On women's inclusion in political elites', *Politics and Society*, no. 2.

Skjeie, H. (1991b) 'The uneven advance of Norwegian women', *New Left Review*, no. 187.

Skjeie, H., Fougner Førde, B. and Lorentzen, M. (1989) *Forvaltningsansvar: likestilling. Det sentrale likestillingsapparatets oppgaver og organisering*. Oslo: ISF-Rapport 3/89.

Sköld, Lars (1958) *Kandidatnominering vid andrakammerval*. SOU vol. 6.

SM (1985) *Statistiska meddelanden*: 'Nominerade och valda kandidater vid allmänna valen 1982', Be 35 SM 8501. Stockholm: National Bureau of Statistics.

SM (1986) *Statistiska meddelanden*: 'Politiska resuser', Be 40 SM 8601. Stockholm: National Bureau of Statistics.

SM (1989) *Statistiska meddelanden*: 'Nominerade och valda kandidater vid allmänna valen 1988', Be 34 SM 8901. Stockholm: National Bureau of Statistics.

Smith, Gordon (1986) *Democracy in Western Germany*, 3rd edn. Aldershot: Gower.

Smith, Gordon (1992) *Democracy in Germany*, new edn. Aldershot: Gower.

Smith, Gordon, Paterson, W.E., Merkl, Peter and Padgett, Stephen (eds) (1992) *Developments in German Politics*, 2nd edn. Basingstoke: Macmillan.

SOU (1987) 'Varannan damernas'. Final report of the commission on women's representation. Stockholm: Ministry of Labour.

Sørsgård, A.K. (1990) 'Fra mors plikt til fars rettighet: Om betalt fødselspermisjon i Norge og Sverige 1892–1987', in S. Kuhnle and P. Selle (eds), *Frivillig organisert velferd – et alternativ til offentlig?* Bergen: Alma Mater.

Stang Dahl, T. (1987) *Women's Law. An introduction to Feminist Jurisprudence*. Oslo: Norwegian University Press.

Stetson, Dorothy (1987) *Women's Rights in France*. New York: Greenwood Press.

Stöss, Richard (1983) *Parteien Handbuch*, 2 vols. Opladen: Westdeutscher Verlag.

Strachey, Ray (1979) *The Cause: A Short History of the Women's Movement in Great Britain*. Virago Press: London.

Summers, Anne (1975) *Damned Whores and God's Police*. Harmondsworth: Penguin.

Tansey, Jean (1985) *Women in Ireland – a Compilation of Data*. Dublin: Council for the Status of Women.

Terry, John (1984) 'The gender gap: women's political power'. Unpublished paper, Library of Parliament, Canada.

Thiébault, Jean-Louis (1988) 'France, the impact of electoral system change', in Michael Gallagher and Michael Marsh (eds), *Candidate Selection in Comparative Perspective: the Secret Garden of Politics*. London: Sage, pp 72–93.

Thönessen, Werner (1976) *The Emancipation of Women in Germany*. London: Pluto.

Thorburn, Hugh G. (1991) 'The development of political parties in Canada', in Hugh G. Thorburn (ed.), *Party Politics in Canada*, 6th edn. Scarborough, Ontario: Prentice-Hall Canada, pp. 2–10.

The Times (1992) *Guide to the House of Commons*. London: Times Books.

Towards Equality, The Alva Myrdal Report to the Swedish Social Democratic Party (1971) Stockholm: Prisma.

Tolchin, Susan and Tolchin, Martin (1976) *Clout: Womanpower and Politics*. New York: Coward, McGann and Geoghegan.

Van de Velde, H. and Leijenaar, M.H. (1991) 'Women's access to political parties'. Paper presented at the Joint Sessions of the ECPR, Essex, 23–27 March.

Walker, Nancy (1986) 'Are women more peaceminded than men?'. Unpublished paper presented at the ECPR Joint Sessions of Workshops, Gothenburg.

Wallin, Gunnar, Bäck, Henry and Tabor, Merrick (1981) *Kommunalpolitikerna: rekrytering – arbetsförhållanden – funktioner*. Stockholm: LiberFörlaget.

Ward, Ian (1992) 'Media intrusion' and the changing nature of the established parties in Australia and Canada'. Paper to the Colloquium in Parties and Federalism in Australia and Canada, The Australian National University.

Wearing, Joseph (1981) *The L Shaped Party: The Liberal Party of Canada, 1958–1980*. Toronto: McGraw-Hill Ryerson.

Wearing, Joseph (1988) *Strained Relations: Canadian Parties and Voters*. Toronto: McClelland and Stewart.

Wearing, Peter and Wearing, Joseph (1991) 'Voting and gender', in Joseph Wearing (ed.), *The Ballot and Its Message: Voting in Canada*. Toronto: Copp Clark Pitman, pp. 341–50.

Weber, M. (1977) *Il voto delle donne*. Turin: Editrice Biblioteca della Libertà.

Weber, M. (1989) 'La donne come cittadine', in M.A. Confalonieri et al. (eds), *Governo e cittadini. Come gli elettori giudicano il ruolo del governo in sei paesi democratici*. Milan: Franco Angeli.

Weidenfeld, Werner and Zimmermann, Hartmut (eds) (1989) *Deutschland Handbuch. Eine doppelte Bilanz 1949–1989*. Munich: Hanser.

Welch, Susan and Thomas, Sue (1988) 'Explaining the Gender Gap in British Public Opinion'. *Women and Policy*, 8(3/4): 25–43.

Whitehorn, Alan (1989) 'The New Democratic Party in Convention', in George Perlin (ed.), *Party Democracy in Canada: The Politics of National Party Conventions*. Scarborough, Ontario: Prentice-Hall Canada, pp. 272–301.

Wiik, B. (1986) 'Norges nye kvinneregjering', *Dagbladet*, 5 February 1986.

Wilcox, Clyde (1991) 'The causes and consequences of feminist consciousness among western European women', *Comparative Political Studies*, 23, 4 January, pp. 519–45.

Williams, Juan (1984) 'Republicans told women on slate a help', *Washington Post*, 4 June: A4.

Wilson, Frank (1982) *French Political Parties under the Fifth Republic*. New York: Praeger.

Wilson, Frank (1989) 'Evolution of the French party system', in P. Godt (ed.), *Policy Making in France*, London: Pinter, pp. 57–72.

Winkler, Gunnar (ed.) (1990) *Frauenreport '90*. Berlin: Die Wirtschaft.

Wisniewski, Roswitha, (1984) 'Die Anfänge der christlich-bürgerlichen Frauenbewegung', in Renate Hellwig (ed.), *Die Christ-demokratinnen. Unterwegs zur Partnerschaft*. Stuttgart: Seewald

Wohlfahrtssurvey (1989) In Statistisches Bundesamt (ed.) *Datenreport*. Bonn.

Women's Agenda Conference (1988) *Women and Politics Election '88*.

Workers' Party (1981) *Peace, Work, Class Politics*. Dublin.

Workers' Party (1987) *No job? Overtaxed? Welfare cut? Forced to Emigrate? Fight back with the Workers' Party*. Dublin.

Workers' Party (1989) *Workers' Party: The Socialist Alternative*. Dublin.

Worms, Jean-Pierre (1966) 'Le Préfet et ses notables', *Sociologie de Travail*, 8: 3.

Wright, Vincent (1989) *The Government and Politics of France*, 3rd edn. London: Unwin Hyman.

Young, Walter (1968) *The Anatomy of a Party: The National CCF 1932–1961*. Toronto: University of Toronto Press.

Zakuta, Leo (1964) *A Protest Movement Becalmed: A Study of Change in the CCF*. Toronto: University of Toronto Press.

Zeuner, Bodo (1969) *Innerparteiliche Demokratie*. Berlin: Colloquium.

Zincone, G. (1988) 'Women in decision-making arenas: Italy', in M. Buckley and M. Anderson (eds), *The Women Equality in Europe*. London: Macmillan.

Zincone, G. (1992) *Da sudditi a cittadini*. Bologna: Il Mulino.

Index

Page references in *italics* indicate figures and tables.